The Club

The Club

JOHNSON, BOSWELL, AND THE
FRIENDS WHO SHAPED AN AGE

Leo Damrosch

Yale UNIVERSITY PRESS

New Haven and London

Published with assistance from the Annie Burr Lewis Fund.

Published with assistance from the Louis Stern Memorial Fund.

Yale University Press books may be purchased in quantity for educational,
business, or promotional use. For information, please e-mail sales.press@yale
.edu (U.S. office) or sales@yaleup.co.uk (U.K. office).

Set in Adobe Garamond type by IDS Infotech Ltd.
Printed in the United States of America.

Library of Congress Control Number: 2018952381
ISBN 978-0-300-21790-2 (hardcover : alk. paper)

A catalogue record for this book is available from the British Library.

This paper meets the requirements of ANSI/NISO Z39.48-1992 (Permanence of
Paper).

10 9 8 7 6 5 4 3 2 1

Contents

Color Plates follow Page 232

Acknowledgments

My deepest thanks to Tina Bennett, my agent, for her invaluable counsel; to Jennifer Banks, my editor, for her shrewd and sympathetic management of the entire process; and above all to Joyce Van Dyke, who sharpened and clarified every chapter of this book, in large matters as in small.

Prologue

This is the story of a group of extraordinary individuals, a constellation of talent in eighteenth-century London that was known simply as the Club. Though not a large group, its members made brilliant contributions to our culture that are still celebrated today. But there was another, perhaps even more important, requirement for Club membership: you had to be good company—ready to talk, laugh, drink, eat, and argue until late into the night at the weekly meetings at the Turk's Head Tavern. Unlike some later clubs, it had no premises of its own, but met in an ordinary London pub.

The members included Samuel Johnson, James Boswell, Edmund Burke, Edward Gibbon, and Adam Smith—arguably the greatest British critic, biographer, political philosopher, historian, and economist of all time. Others were equally famous at the time: the painter Joshua Reynolds; the playwrights Richard Brinsley Sheridan and Oliver Goldsmith; and David Garrick, the greatest actor of the century. New members could be elected only by unanimous vote.

In most cases, these were self-made men. Some were prosperous, but others, including Johnson and Goldsmith, lived in near poverty. And although intellectual distinction was expected, fame was not. Over the years, new members were often elected at an early stage in their careers.

It would be hard to exaggerate the influence the Club's members had on the culture of their age and on later generations. Johnson created an altogether new way of combining literary criticism with deeply sympathetic biography. Boswell revolutionized biography as the art of bringing people to life in all their idiosyncrasy and depth. Burke was a spellbinding parliamentary orator, and his writings embodied political wisdom that continues to inspire liberals as well as conservatives. Gibbon developed a new way of writing history that has borne fruit, directly or indirectly, in virtually every history written since his time. And Smith, of course, did more than anyone to launch the discipline of economics as we know it.

Other members of the Club, if less influential for posterity, likewise played a central role in their own culture. Reynolds was the most popular and successful artist of the time, and as the founding president of the Royal Academy, a pioneer in formalizing artistic instruction. Garrick astounded audiences with a naturalistic acting style that had never before been seen, and was also the first to direct and rehearse his actors as a modern director would. And to give one more example, a botanist named Joseph Banks accompanied Captain James Cook during his first voyage to the South Seas, and was afterward a distinguished president of the Royal Society.

The Club is the virtual hero of this story, which will trace the intersecting lives, interests, friendships, rivalries, and careers of this extraordinary group, from its founding in 1764 to its waning twenty years later. Thanks to Boswell, who recorded many of the conversations he heard there, at times we can even get a ringside seat as they talk during evenings that took place over two hundred years ago. The ideas they tried out on each other, across a very wide range of fields and professions, did much to shape the age they lived in.

Distinguished though the Club quickly became, it was born out of a private and personal need. During the winter of 1763, Joshua Reynolds, the leading painter of his generation in England, was worried about his friend Samuel Johnson. Johnson was subject to episodes of black depression, and was sunk in one now. His wife had died a decade earlier, leaving him lonely but also guilty, since they lived apart much of the time. Eight years earlier he had completed a massive writing project, his great *Dictionary of the English Language,* but he had accomplished little since then. Especially distressing was his failure to get on with a major edition of Shakespeare's plays for which he had signed a contract back in 1756.

Lack of funds had forced Johnson to give up the comfortable house in which he compiled the *Dictionary,* and in cramped lodgings he was now presiding over a ménage of unfortunates who relied on him for support. They included a learned but irritable blind lady, an unlicensed medical practitioner who treated the poor, a woman who had been his late wife's companion, and a reformed prostitute. Though they helped to assuage Johnson's loneliness, they were hardly a congenial lot. Describing the situation to a friend, he reported, "Williams hates everybody; Levet hates Desmoulins, and does not love Williams; Desmoulins hates them both; Poll loves none of them."[1]

Reynolds knew that Johnson loved conversation and also loved taverns— Johnson once called a tavern chair "the throne of human felicity." So he proposed that they invite a few friends to join them once a week at the Turk's Head Tavern in Gerrard Street. Just off the busy Strand, it was close to where Waterloo Bridge stands today. Every Friday evening, Johnson and Reynolds and other friends engaged a private room where they dined and drank and talked until midnight.[2]

In an era when brilliance in conversation was much admired, the members met to socialize but also to argue and learn from each other. From the start they wanted to have at least one member from each of the most important professions—political, legal, medical, literary, artistic. Eventually the group became known to the public as the Literary Club, but to its members it was always simply "the Club."

Of course nobody spent more than a fraction of his time at the Turk's Head, and the perspective in this book will constantly widen to the larger world in which they made their lives. As in a Chinese landscape scroll gradually unrolling, the same individuals will keep reappearing in new contexts. Sometimes the strands of their experience diverge, and sometimes they reunite. It is fascinating to follow these figures both together and apart, and none more than Johnson and Boswell, whose lives were recorded with unparalleled richness.

THE ODD COUPLE AT THE CENTER

James Boswell had met Johnson just a few months before the Club was formed, and they had immediately established a strong friendship, but Boswell soon left for an extended tour of the Continent and wouldn't return until 1766. When he did get back he was wildly eager to join. Most of the members regarded him as an agreeable lightweight and were reluctant, but in 1773 Johnson prevailed on them to admit him. From then on Boswell proudly referred in his writings to THE CLUB in capital letters.

All his life Boswell kept an extraordinarily full journal, and in due course he drew upon it for the *Life of Johnson,* published in 1791, in which the most memorable passages are accounts of conversations, many of which took place at the Club. Carlyle wrote that even though "the mysterious river of existence rushes on," Boswell preserved much that he heard and saw as it went rushing past. His own life experience is full of interest, too, and he and Johnson are very appropriately the central figures in our story.[3]

Johnson and Boswell were an odd couple, even physically, as caricaturists were fond of noting. Johnson was six feet tall in an era when that height was exceptional, and very powerfully built. Boswell was five feet six and plump. Johnson was profoundly learned in several languages, ancient and modern, though he had to drop out of Oxford after one year for lack of funds (his honorary doctorate wasn't awarded until 1775). Boswell had studied at two Scottish universities and had qualified as a lawyer; he was intelligent and fond of reading, but always something of a dilettante. Boswell was proud of his descent from a long line of Scottish patricians that went back to the Norman Conquest; Johnson was a self-made man and proud of it, commenting that although his writings on society stressed birth and hierarchy, "I can hardly tell who was my grandfather."[4]

When they met, Johnson was in his early fifties and Boswell in his early twenties, a young Scot with a romantic attraction to Scotland's feudal past but a desperate yearning to spend his life in glamorous London. Johnson was already a celebrated writer, which is why Boswell sought him out. At first Johnson was rather put off by the pushy young man, but he always enjoyed the freshness and optimism of people much younger than himself, and everyone who knew Boswell testified that he was exceptionally good company. Burke called him "the pleasantest man he ever saw." Johnson once said, "I have heard you mentioned as *a man whom everybody likes*. I think life has little more to give."[5]

W. H. Auden observed that Boswell's devotion to Johnson was "as remarkable in its way as Dante's to Beatrice." Everyone who knew them agreed that Boswell was uniquely gifted at capturing Johnson's talk—its energy and rhythms, and also its intellectual strength. He wrote proudly in the *Life*, "When my mind was, as it were, strongly impregnated with the Johnsonian aether, I could, with much more facility and exactness, carry in my memory and commit to paper the exuberant variety of his wisdom and wit."[6]

Sometimes Johnson did lose patience with Boswell: "Sir, you have but two topics, yourself and me. I am sick of both." When Boswell quoted that in the *Life* he said it was addressed to "a gentleman," not identified as himself. Still, as the years went by, the great man was pleased to know that his young friend was accumulating materials for a major biography.[7]

Much of the time, however, Boswell was obliged to be in Scotland, pursuing his legal career. It has been calculated that, all told, he and Johnson were in each other's company just 425 days during a friendship that lasted twenty-one years, and fully a quarter of those days were during a single journey they took together. Of course we also have their correspondence, and when he was working on the *Life of Johnson* Boswell secured reminiscences from many other people who knew him, building up an extraordinarily rich portrait. In a sense he really became what George Bernard Shaw called him, "the dramatist who invented Dr. Johnson."[8]

A deep point of affinity in this friendship was a shared dread of mental illness. The dread was all the more potent since so little was then understood. The empiricist psychology made popular by John Locke described insanity as simply misconstruing sense data. Locke gave the not very helpful example of a man who was perfectly normal in every way except that he believed he was made of glass, and had to take care not to get broken. The example is hyper-rational and astoundingly lacking in empathy, with no awareness of the confusing, turbulent, and inarticulate experience of the mentally ill.

Boswell had mercurial mood swings that would almost certainly be diagnosed today as bipolar disorder. One of his grandfathers had been a victim of the same affliction, and he had a brother who had to be institutionalized. No wonder he was always alert to possible signs of danger in himself. As for Johnson, from his teenage years onward there were extended episodes of incapacitating depression. In addition, he had strange physical mannerisms: tics and gesticulations and puffings of breath that startled people who met him, and were an obstacle to any conventional career. Today he would probably be diagnosed as suffering from obsessive compulsive disorder. We now recognize these behaviors as neurological disorders, but to Johnson they were frightening symptoms of incipient madness.

Whenever their cause, the tics and compulsive behavior were only part of the problem. Whether neurosis is the best term for Johnson's deepest issues may be debatable, but his sense of life as one long battle is not. In the *Life of Johnson* Boswell came up with a brilliant analogy: "His mind resembled the vast amphitheatre, the Coliseum at Rome. In the center stood his judgement, which, like a mighty gladiator, combated those apprehensions that, like the wild beasts of the arena, were all around in cells, ready to be let out upon him. After a conflict, he drove them back into their dens; but not killing them, they were still assailing him."[9]

1. Samuel Johnson, after
   Ozias Humphry

Above all, Boswell admired Johnson for having accomplished so much in spite of his disabilities—saw him, indeed, as a moral hero. Most portraits of Johnson make him seem off-putting, elderly, bewigged, and scowling. The people who loved him, and they were many, may have perceived him more in the spirit of a nineteenth-century etching that was based on a contemporary portrait by Ozias Humphry. Its expressive Romantic style brings out deep nobility of character (figure 1).

A SHADOW CLUB

Some of Johnson's most valued early colleagues in journalism were women, and all his life he maintained strong friendships with women. Reynolds's sister Frances (he affectionately called her "Renny") said that "he set a higher value upon female friendship than, perhaps, most men." His friend and biographer Sir John Hawkins commented that "of the female mind, he conceived a higher opinion than many men; and though he was never suspected of a blamable intimacy with any individual of them, had great esteem for the sex." Boswell, very differently, prided himself on innate superiority to women, and although he made a loving marriage, blamable intimacy was a way of life for him.[10]

Two of Johnson's women friends were so close to him that they saw aspects of his personality that would never emerge at the Club. These were Hester Thrale and Frances ("Fanny") Burney. Through their journals we know what Johnson was like when he was charmingly playful. Beyond that, Hester and her husband Henry provided crucial emotional support. It was they, more than any of Johnson's other friends or the Club itself, who rescued him from depression.

Johnson lived for extended periods of time in the Thrales' house at Streatham across the river, with a bedroom of his own and an excellent library for which he helped to choose the books. This was a comfortable and loving environment such as he had never before experienced. Hester was virtually his therapist, and she understood his torments far more deeply than Boswell ever did.

The well-to-do Thrales loved to entertain, and through Johnson they made friends with many members of the Club. Some of our most memorable accounts of Reynolds, Goldsmith, and Garrick come from Streatham—and also some notably unenthusiastic impressions of Boswell. It is fair to say that the Thrales and their social circle formed a kind of shadow club, overlapping with the one at the Turk's Head while contributing perspectives that are all its own.

A BOOK WITH PICTURES

" 'What is the use of a book,' thought Alice, 'without pictures or conversations?' " Images are invaluable in making the world of the past real. The historian Asa Briggs says that they can be as important as text: "They remind us that much of social history is not abstract, and that the art of seeing is a necessary quality in the social historian."[11]

It was a real pleasure to seek out pictures that could effectively complement this text, and that often deserve extended reflection. And I would like to add that while some museums and collections charge hefty fees for permission to reproduce images, several others—notably the Yale Center for British Art, Metropolitan Museum of Art, and Houghton Library at Harvard—make all of their wonderfully rich holdings available without charge. This book would have been far poorer but for their generosity.

There will be portraits of all of the principal characters, and also many illustrations of places and events. These vary greatly in what they seek to tell us. When wealthy patrons commissioned paintings of scenery, what they wanted was glossy elegance. Gentlemen who had admired Canaletto's work in Venice encouraged him to come to England, where for nine years he turned out paintings that have been described as "imposing order, symmetry, space, and a Venetian grace upon the bustle of London's teeming wharfs, streets, and squares."[12]

Canaletto's view of the Thames from Richmond House is just such an image (color plate 1). At first glance this could almost *be* Venice, with its expanse of water and sky, a very un-English shimmer of light, scattered steeples in the hazy distance, and the great dome of St. Paul's Cathedral instead of Santa Maria della Salute. Elegant gentlemen and ladies stroll on the terrace of Richmond House in the foreground, with St. Paul's dominating the skyline beyond the river.

Inside the leafy courtyard of Richmond House at the left, a lordly visitor can be seen rapping on the door, while above him a serving man is sweeping and a housemaid is leaning over a balcony. Small skiffs, the water taxis of the day, carry passengers along the river and over to the opposite shore, and commerce is also represented, but in a highly symbolic manner. The ornate barges belong to livery companies, guilds that controlled individual trades and celebrated their eminence with pageantry on the river.

Johnson's London was not Canaletto's. For that we need to go to Charing Cross, a major intersection about which he said memorably, "I think the full tide of human existence is at Charing Cross." It was a surging and even threatening tide, as Tobias Smollett described it: "The different departments of life are jumbled together. . . . Actuated by the demons of profligacy and licentiousness, they are seen everywhere rambling, riding, rolling, rushing, justling, mixing, bouncing, cracking, and crashing, in one vile ferment of stupidity and corruption."[13]

An early nineteenth-century view of Charing Cross by Thomas Rowlandson (color plate 2) shows a scene that would have been familiar to Johnson and his contemporaries. A wealthy person's carriage is trotting along at the far left, skirting the crowd that has gathered to watch two men condemned to spend the day in the public pillory. Sometimes onlookers thought the sentence unjust and treated the victims with kindness, but not always. If they thought the crimes were vicious, their behavior could turn savage. Bricks and stones were often thrown, and quite a few people died. "Of all the punishments to strike fear into the criminal's heart," a historian says, "death in the pillory was the most terrible."[14]

A whole series of little dramas are playing themselves out around the pillory. At the far left four women hurry to join in, while at the center front another woman, dressed in green, stoops to pick something up (perhaps a stone to throw?) while a dog takes advantage of her distraction to invade her basket. Above her, others are waving and shouting, while the woman in the blue dress has her back to the excitement and is complacently accepting a man's hand on her breast. Further to the right a woman in pink is playfully flirting with a soldier, and at far right a man in spectacles peers myopically at the action while his portly friend describes it. Above them a coachman is whipping his horse to get moving, causing a jolt that has made two female passengers topple backward off its roof.

Still livelier is a close-up *London Street Scene* by John Collet (color plate 3). At the center, bestriding the cobblestone street, a well-dressed gentleman has just triumphed in a sword fight. Striking a stagey pose, he has dropped his sword and is now brandishing a knife to warn off a pair of watchmen who are about to charge at him with their staffs. One of them gestures at a street lamp that got broken in the melee. On the pavement behind him is a big basket belonging to a strawberry vendor, and his fallen opponent on the ground still has one of her smaller baskets on his sword; she is courageously attempting to disarm him. In the loser's pocket is an instruction manual entitled *Peter Parry on the Use of the Small Sword*, which he has obviously failed to profit from. Further back, a constable has handcuffed a criminal, very likely a pickpocket taking advantage of the confusion to ply his trade.[15]

The New Bagnio at the right advertises "sweating, cupping [medical bloodletting], and bathing" for two shillings and sixpence. It would indeed have been a bathhouse, as its name indicates, but a brothel as well. One of the prostitutes is leaning out of an upper window with a customer behind her; the leaflet fluttering down advertises a play by Henry Fielding, *The Virgin Unmasked, or, An Old Man Taught Wisdom*. At the door another woman is emerging from a sedan chair and dropping her payment into the hat of one of the chairmen. She is probably not a prostitute herself, but a higher-class woman who has an assignation with a lover at the bagnio.

In the background, a stagecoach known as the Bath Fly (its name is on the door) is just setting out for that destination. On the roof one man has already started drinking for the day and another is puffing a long pipe; between them sits a pet monkey dressed in a turban. A sober and disapproving older couple look on from inside, as does the lady's kerchief-wearing lapdog.

Beyond the coach, "The Original Blanket Warehouse" identifies itself for the illiterate with a sign showing a Golden Fleece, an emblem that was commonly used by woolen drapers. (Toward the end of the century hanging signs were made illegal, since all too often they fell on people below.) Around to the left another sign rather ominously advertises "Peter Probe, Surgeon."

Two women lean from an upstairs window to enjoy the commotion, and above them a chimney sweep emerges from a chimney.

This book seeks to bring to life the teeming, noisy, contradictory, and often violent world of eighteenth-century London. It will offer what the historian Ian Mortimer calls time travel, the imaginative adventure of bringing back "the sensations of being alive in a different time." Looking back, we see it as a time when Britain strove to maintain a vast empire but suffered the traumatic loss of the North American colonies. But what may seem clear in historical hindsight was anything but clear to those living through it. As G. M. Trevelyan reminds us, "the past was once as real as the present and as uncertain as the future."[16]

A historian has recently called Johnson "the greatest Londoner of the eighteenth century," and this book will constantly evoke the London life that he and his friends shared. By the time the Club was founded he was middle-aged and acknowledged as the leading writer of his time, but the story will begin when he was an obscure provincial struggling with psychological as well as material handicaps, and with no clear path to success. His resolute fight to *become* Samuel Johnson is itself a moving story.[17]

Likewise Boswell, though he started out in life with more advantages than Johnson, had issues of his own to contend with. Young though he was when they met, his journals already represented a portrait in depth of a fascinating personality. Each man brought important hopes and needs to their fateful meeting in 1763.

CHAPTER I

Johnson before Boswell

THE YEARS OF STRUGGLE

UNPROMISING BEGINNINGS

Samuel Johnson was fifty-four when Boswell met him, and had already lived a full life, fighting his way into reputation and success. He wrote with feeling, "To strive with difficulties, and to conquer them, is the highest human felicity; the next is, to strive, and deserve to conquer; but he whose life has passed without a contest, and who can boast neither success nor merit, can survey himself only as a useless filler of existence; and if he is content with his own character, must owe his satisfaction to insensibility."[1]

Johnson was born in 1709 in Lichfield in Staffordshire, a cathedral town with a population of three thousand, 120 miles northwest of London. It was surrounded by open countryside, as was Birmingham, the nearest large town, whose industrial future was still far away.

Samuel's father Michael kept a bookstore, and felt hopeful enough to have a large house built, with the shop on the ground floor. A year later Samuel, the first of two children, was born there; it is now a Johnson museum (figure 2). Michael Johnson was fifty-two at the time and his wife Sarah was forty.

To make ends meet Michael made regular appearances at market days in neighboring towns, and also maintained a tannery and parchment manufactory. He wasn't much of a businessman, however, and his wife never tired of reminding him that his employees got richer while he got poorer; Sarah was proud of coming from higher social origins than his. Temperamentally they

2. Johnson's birthplace, Lichfield

weren't especially compatible. They quarreled a lot, and there is personal feeling in a phrase Johnson later used in an essay, "the house of discord."[2]

The infant's entrance into the world was inauspicious. His mother, he was
told, "had a very difficult and dangerous labour. . . . I was born almost dead, and
could not cry for some time." It is very possible that deprivation of oxygen at
that stage may have caused neurological damage. It may also have exacerbated a
congenital disorder. Portraits show his head tilted markedly to the right. In his
time that was ascribed to "palsy," but it can now be identified more precisely:
"the association of head tilt with paralysis of the fourth cranial nerve is classic."[3]

There was still more damage to come, for Sarah was unable to nurse the
infant, and the wet nurse with whom he was placed unfortunately infected
him with scrofula, the common name for a tubercular condition that permanently damaged his eyesight. "In ten weeks," he continued, "I was taken
home a poor, diseased infant, almost blind." An aunt told him years later
"that she would not have picked such a poor creature up in the street."[4]

The scrofular infection produced disgusting swellings on the neck and
arms, which had to be tied down to keep him from scratching them open. In

addition, an oozing incision in his arm was deliberately kept open until he was six. The theory was that the swellings were due to a "peccant humour" that could be encouraged to migrate to a different part of the body.[5]

Sarah even made a daunting journey to London for the annual "touching for the King's Evil," a traditional ceremony reflecting a belief that scrofula could somehow respond to the touch of a monarch. In this instance the monarch was Queen Anne, the very last to perform that ritual. Sam was not yet three years old, but he always retained "a confused, but somehow a sort of solemn recollection of a lady in diamonds, and a long black hood." She gave him a little amulet on a chain that he wore around his neck throughout his life. As for the scrofula, it spontaneously cleared up after some years, but left ugly scars on his neck, and one eye that was all but useless.[6]

We don't know much about Johnson's earliest years, except that his mother was hard to please. He told his friend Hester Thrale, "She was always telling me that I did not *behave* myself properly; that I should endeavor to learn *behavior,* and such cant; but when I replied that she ought to tell me what to do and what to avoid, her admonitions were commonly, for that time at least, at an end." He added that his father's regular tactic to escape nagging was "to take his horse and ride away for orders [for books] when things went badly." The boy couldn't ride away, but he was capable of backtalk. Once, when she angrily called him a puppy, "I asked her if she knew what they called a puppy's mother."[7]

When Samuel was three a brother, Nathaniel, was born. They never got along, either in childhood or later. In a letter to their mother that was discovered long afterward, Nathaniel complained that Samuel "would scarcely ever use me with common civility." He had thoughts of emigrating to the American colonies, but died in Somerset in 1737 at the age of twenty-four. His body was brought back to Lichfield for burial. Johnson did finally include him in a Latin epitaph for his family, to be engraved on a stone in the church floor, which he ordered less than two weeks before his own death. A few years before that he had written to someone in Somerset to see if they had any recollection of "one Johnson" from years before—"he was my near relation." Evidently he couldn't bring himself to say "brother."[8]

Soon came a "dame school" taught by a kindly lady, who was impressed by the boy's exceptional intelligence. But he never forgot an incident when her concern for his disabilities humiliated him. He told Boswell that a servant usually brought him home from school, but one day when no one showed up he set out on his own, so nearsighted that he had to examine the gutter on his

hands and knees before he felt safe to step over it. His anxious teacher followed him at some distance, but when he noticed her, "feeling her careful
attention as an insult to his manliness, he ran back to her in a rage, and beat
her as well as his strength would permit." It's not clear whether Johnson himself described his "manliness" as having been challenged, or whether that was
Boswell's contribution to the story.[9]

At the age of seven it was time for the Lichfield Grammar School, which
happened to be first-rate, and he stayed there until he was fifteen. He excelled
at Latin, and in later life he always claimed that the beatings the boys received
were the best way to drive the language into their heads. "There is now less
flogging in our great schools than formerly, but then less is learned there; so
that what the boys get at one end, they lose at the other." Less sympathetically, Swift recalled "the terror of the rod," and Gibbon said that a school was
"the cavern of fear and sorrow: the mobility of the captive youths is chained
to a book and a desk. . . . They labour, like the soldiers of Persia, under the
scourge."[10]

There were plenty of Latin books to explore in Sam's father's shop, which
was patronized by the cathedral clergy and other professionals. In addition
the boy was deeply affected by imaginative literature in English, which undoubtedly helped to form his powerful prose style. When he was nine, he recalled, he was reading *Hamlet* in the kitchen "till coming to the ghost scene,
he suddenly hurried upstairs to the street door, that he might see people about
him." He loved fiction, too: "he was immoderately fond of reading romances
of chivalry, and he retained his fondness for them throughout life." When he
told that to Thomas Percy, editor of a classic collection of old ballads, he
claimed that "extravagant fictions" must have been responsible for "that un-
settled turn of mind which prevented his ever fixing in any profession."[11]

Hester Thrale heard that there were only three books that he wished were
even longer—*Robinson Crusoe, The Pilgrim's Progress,* and *Don Quixote.* Walter Jackson Bate comments, "These three wanderers—one a castaway, one a
pilgrim, and one on an impossible quest—were prototypes of what he felt to
be his own life."[12]

As Johnson grew into his massive body, he developed impressive strength.
He liked to relate that his father's brother had been a champion wrestler and
bare-knuckle boxer at Smithfield in London, "and was never thrown or conquered." He took lessons from his uncle and "was very conversant in the art
of attack and defense by boxing." He was also a powerful swimmer at a time
when that was most unusual; even most sailors didn't know how.[13]

A poem he wrote much later about learning to swim is very moving, re-calling his father's affection. For his most personal poems Johnson used Latin, perhaps to give some distance to his emotions. In any case someone who knew him well said that Latin "was as natural to him as English."[14]

The poem begins *Errat adhuc vitreus per prata virentia rivus:* "To this place the glassy stream wanders through green fields." John Wain, a poet and novel-ist as well as biographer of Johnson, supplies a translation:

> Clear as glass the stream still wanders through
> green fields.
> > Here, as a boy, I bathed
> my tender limbs, unskilled, frustrated, while
> with gentle voice my father from the bank
> taught me to swim.
> > The branches made
> a hiding place: the bending trees concealed
> the water in a daytime darkness.
> > > Now
> hard axes have destroyed those ancient shades:
> the pool lies naked, even to distant eyes.
> But the water, never tiring, still runs on
> in the same channel: once hidden, now exposed,
> > still flowing.[15]

Affectionate though Michael Johnson was, his fecklessness exasperated his son, and on one occasion Sam refused to go with him to sell books in the mar-ket at nearby Uttoxeter. Guilt for that willful act troubled him for the rest of his life, especially since he was only twenty-two when his father died in 1731. "A few years ago," he told a friend shortly before his own death, "I desired to atone for this fault; I went to Uttoxeter in very bad weather, and stood for a considerable time bareheaded in the rain, on the spot where my father's stall used to stand. In contrition I stood, and I hope the penance was expiatory." After Boswell's *Life* was published the story became well known, and a statue in Johnson's honor was erected in that marketplace. Nathaniel Hawthorne found it very affecting. "He stands bareheaded, a venerable figure, and a countenance ex-tremely sad and woebegone, with the wind and rain driving hard against him, and thus helping to suggest to the spectator the gloom of his inward state."[16]

Next came Oxford, which would normally have been impossibly expen-sive for the family's resources, but his mother had received a small inheritance, a family friend made a contribution, and a wealthy schoolmate who was also going to Oxford promised to help. Johnson wasn't impressed by the teaching there (neither were Gibbon and Adam Smith a generation later), and he didn't put much effort into his studies. He did, however, form a lifelong friendship with William Adams, his tutor at Pembroke College. Boswell heard from Adams that Johnson "was caressed and loved by all about him, was a gay and frolicsome fellow, and passed there the happiest part of his life." But when Boswell repeated that to Johnson, "he said, 'Ah, Sir, I was rude and violent. It was bitterness which they mistook for frolic. I was miserably poor, and I thought to fight my way by my literature and my wit; so I disregarded all power and all authority.'" (Incidentally, Boswell must have misread his own writing, or else failed to notice a printer's mistake when he proofread this passage, so for many years it wrongly appeared as "mad and violent.") In the *Life of Johnson* Boswell added an anecdote about some well-meaning person leaving a pair of new shoes at Johnson's door, having noticed his toes sticking out of the only ones he had. Humiliated at being offered charity, "he threw them away with indignation."[17]

Boswell was able to gratify Johnson by reporting another comment by Adams: "He said to me at Oxford, in 1776, 'I was his nominal tutor; but he was above my mark.' When I repeated it to Johnson his eyes flashed with grateful satisfaction, and he exclaimed, 'That was liberal and noble.'" That conversation happened fifteen years before the publication of the *Life;* Boswell was already gathering materials for it.[18]

Unfortunately the classmate who was supposed to contribute support reneged, and after little more than a year Johnson was forced to withdraw. Graduating with a degree would have required two more years; not getting one meant that the major professions were closed to him. Leaving Oxford was deeply shaming, and it would be twenty-five years before he would go there again. It struck him later, however, that if he had indeed graduated he might have remained an academic for life. His friend Thomas Warton, a well-known scholar and poet, did make a career at Oxford, and told Boswell about a visit from Johnson there. They ran into an obscure tutor, the Reverend John Meeke, and Johnson said afterward, "I used to think Meeke had excellent parts when we were boys together at the college, but alas! 'Lost in a convent's solitary gloom!' I remember at the classical lecture in the Hall I could not bear Meeke's superiority, and I tried to sit as far from him as I could, that I might not hear him construe." It was with a kind of pity that Johnson added, "About the same time of life, Meeke was left behind at Oxford to feed on a fellowship, and I went to London to get my living. Now, Sir, see the difference of our literary characters!"[19]

JOHNSON'S TROUBLED MIND

As soon as Johnson arrived home from Oxford, he plunged into a devastating depression. As he described it to Boswell, "he felt himself overwhelmed with an horrible hypochondria, with perpetual irritation, forgetfulness, and impatience; and with a dejection, gloom, and despair, which made existence misery." At times, in fact, "he was so languid and inefficient that he could not distinguish the hour upon the town clock." Exercise was no help, though he often walked from Lichfield to Birmingham and back, a round trip of nearly fifty miles that must have taken two days each time. "His expression concerning it to me," Boswell adds, "was 'I did not then know how to manage it.'" Johnson told another friend that he inherited from his father "a morbid disposition both of body and mind—a terrifying melancholy, which he was sometimes apprehensive bordered on insanity."[20]

"Melancholy" in those days didn't just mean gloom and sadness; it meant what we now call clinical depression. Likewise "hypochondria" didn't mean wrongly imagining a physical illness; it meant suffering from a very real mental disorder, which was assumed to be linked to some bodily imbalance. According to a medical theory that went back to ancient Greece and was still respected, diseases were caused by an imbalance of four bodily fluids or "humors"—blood, phlegm, yellow bile, and black bile. These disorders gave their name to temperamental differences whose names we still use, though we've forgotten about the four humors. Someone with an excess of blood was sanguine, and the others were phlegmatic, choleric, and bilious.

In humor theory, hypochondria was caused by an excess of black bile, produced by the spleen. Likewise Johnson's *Dictionary* defines "melancholy" as "a disease, supposed to proceed from a redundance of black bile; but it is better known to arise from too heavy and too viscid [i.e., viscous] blood: its cure is in evacuation, nervous medicines, and powerful stimuli." That alleged advance in medical thinking wasn't much of an advance. Letting blood was the default treatment for practically everything, and usually did more harm than good. George Washington died after he came down with a respiratory infection and his doctors, at his own request, drained something like forty ounces of blood.

Johnson's godfather, Samuel Swynfen (for whom he may have been named), was a respected Lichfield physician, and Johnson consulted him.

That was unfortunate. He wrote out a description of his case so impressive that Swynfen showed it around among his friends. Johnson was horrified at the breach of trust, and even more so at the diagnosis. "From the symptoms therein described," his friend and early biographer Sir John Hawkins said, "he could think nothing better of his disorder than that it had a tendency to insanity, and without great care might possibly terminate in the deprivation of his rational faculties." Another biographer confirmed that "an apprehension of the worst calamity that can befall human nature hung over him all the rest of his life, like the sword of the tyrant suspended over his guest."[21]

In Victorian times Johnson was often regarded as a complacent, pontificating sage, but his best readers knew how wrong that was. Thomas Carlyle said admiringly, "Nature, in return for his nobleness, had said to him, Live in an element of diseased sorrow." Carlyle also wrote eloquently about Johnson's "great greedy heart, and unspeakable chaos of thoughts." And Johnson's comment on his apparent cheerfulness at Oxford could be generalized, as Boswell did, to apply to his celebrated wit: "There is no doubt that a man may appear very gay in company who is sad at heart. His merriment is like the sound of drums and trumpets in a battle, to drown the groans of the wounded and dying."[22]

In those days psychology was only beginning to advance beyond the old humor theory, as well as beyond the empiricist assumption that a mentally ill person was simply adding up data incorrectly. The word "psychology" itself doesn't appear in Johnson's *Dictionary,* though a few writers were beginning to use it to mean the study of mind rather than of *psyche,* the soul. Still, that was barely a start. A writer in 1767 said frankly, "Psychology is the knowledge of the mind in general and of the human mind in particular, about the substance of which, notwithstanding every effort, it is still exceedingly difficult to say anything reasonable, and yet more to say anything positive."[23]

Most modern writers on Johnson's troubles have followed a Freudian line, as Bate did in his impressive biography. Another interpreter, George Irwin, highlighted what had been generally overlooked, Johnson's deeply conflicted feelings about his mother and his avoidance of her in later life. For many years he kept declaring that he was on the point of going to Lichfield to see her, but for the last nineteen years of her life he never did it even once. Irwin's conclusion seems inescapable: "Though he tried to go, he could not; though he thought he wanted to, he did not." Once Sarah Johnson was safely in her grave, he returned to Lichfield no fewer than a dozen times during the next twenty-five years, often staying for weeks on end.[24]

Pondering the same evidence, a psychiatrist suggests that Johnson's relentless self-criticism may have derived from a perceived lack of love in childhood. The logic would be: if I'm not loved as much as I need to be, it must be because I'm not lovable and don't deserve it. Still, I have to suppress my anger at those who should love me, or else they'll love me even less than they do now.[25]

One thing Johnson did learn: the way to deal with his anxieties was to distract himself from them, not wrestle with them. "To think them down," he told Boswell, "is madness." All his life he reproached himself bitterly for "indolence," by which he meant not just normal procrastination, but a general slackness that allowed his demons to emerge. His friend Arthur Murphy said acutely that for him, "indolence was the time of danger: it was then that his spirits, not employed abroad, turned with inward hostility against himself."[26]

A book Johnson greatly admired was Robert Burton's massive 1638 treatise *The Anatomy of Melancholy,* which stressed the suffering of melancholics who allow themselves to become idle: "It crucifies their souls, and seizeth on them in an instant, for whilst they are any ways employed, in action, discourse, about any business, or recreation, or in company to their liking, they are very well; but if alone, or idle, tormented instantly again." Johnson always acknowledged that his hunger for companionship was rooted in his dread of solitude.[27]

There was another aspect of Johnson's experience that he saw as just one more manifestation of the same "madness," and that Freudian interpreters used to explain as neurotic symptoms. This can be understood far differently today. It was a whole constellation of compulsive tics, gestures, and noises, which clearly afforded some kind of release but could be controlled if necessary by force of will. People who met Johnson for the first time were always startled, to put it mildly. Fanny Burney's account is typical: "His mouth is in perpetual motion, as if he was chewing—he has a strange method of frequently twirling his fingers, and twisting his hands—his body is in continual agitation, seesawing up and down; his feet are never a moment quiet; and in short, his whole person is in perpetual motion."[28] She and others noticed that he often made puffing or grunting noises under his breath.

When walking, Johnson's behavior seemed even more baffling. He would avoid stepping on cracks in the pavement, would touch every other post along the street and go back if he missed one, and would perform mysteriously repetitive movements. His close friend Reynolds recalled that when they were visiting a friend and looking at a collection of paintings, Johnson "retired to a corner of the room, stretching out his right leg as far as he could reach before him, then bringing up his left leg and stretching his right still further on." Their host courteously assured him that the floor was perfectly safe. "The Doctor started from his reverie like a person waked out of his sleep, but spoke not a word."[29]

Reynolds thought that Johnson's peculiar gestures, and also the suppressed noises, "were meant to reprobate some part of his past conduct." That could well be true and would support the psychoanalytic interpretation. But so would a diagnosis that seems all but inevitable today: Johnson suffered from what nobody then understood, obsessive compulsive disorder. If only he could have known that! A neurological affliction is still an affliction, but it would have been a relief to know it didn't mean he was losing his mind.[30]

MARRIAGE

The post-Oxford breakdown resulted in five lost years for Johnson, about which hardly anything is known except that he must have helped his mother with the bookshop and that he wrote a few poems from time to time. Eventually he decided to move to Birmingham and stay with Edmund Hector, an old school friend who was practicing as a surgeon there. Before long he got to know a cloth merchant named Harry Porter, his wife Elizabeth, and their daughter Lucy. After a year Porter died, and less than a year after that Johnson and Elizabeth were married. He was twenty-six and she was forty-six. Some people who knew them in those days thought he was initially attracted to Lucy, six years younger than himself, whose stepfather he rather incongruously became.

We have a vivid image of Johnson at this time because Boswell interviewed Lucy when he was writing his biography.

Miss Porter told me that when he was first introduced to her mother, his appearance was very forbidding: he was then lean and lank, so that his immense structure of bones was hideously striking to the eye, and the scars of the scrofula were deeply visible. He also wore his hair [i.e., not a wig], which was straight and stiff, and separated behind; and he often had, seemingly, convulsive starts and odd gesticulations, which tended to excite at once surprise and ridicule. Mrs. Porter was so much engaged by his conversation that she overlooked all these external disadvantages, and said to her daughter, "This is the most sensible man that I ever saw in my life."[31]

Johnson told a friend long afterward that "he had never sought to please till past thirty years old, considering the matter as hopeless."[32] That may have been true in general, yet he did please Elizabeth Porter, whom he always called Tetty. It's common to say that he must have been responding to a mother figure, but be that as it may, he seems to have found her sexually attractive and probably responsive. She was also highly intelligent and well-read, having grown up in a family that was comfortably off and had sent both of her brothers to Cambridge. Not much is known about the only surviving portrait of her (color plate 4), not even when it was made, but it shows a self-assured lady displaying a good deal of décolletage.

Tetty had a considerable inheritance of £600, and with that they resolved to set up a school in the village of Edial, three miles from Lichfield. Latin was the principal subject young gentlemen were taught, and that was one thing— at this stage, really the only thing—that Johnson was especially good at. Very few students showed up, not surprisingly since the grammar school in Lichfield was excellent, but one of them was David Garrick, in his early teens at the time. Long afterward it struck everyone who had known them how remarkable it was that two obscure young men from the same town should end up with memorials next to each other in Westminster Abbey.

With an irrepressible talent for mimicry, Garrick used to do a party piece imitating the newlyweds. "The young rogues," Boswell reports, "used to listen at the door of his bedchamber, and peep through the keyhole, that they might turn into ridicule his tumultuous and awkward fondness for Mrs. Johnson." Boswell also quoted Garrick's ungenerous description of Tetty "as very fat, with a bosom of more than ordinary protuberance, with swelled cheeks of a florid red, produced by thick painting, and increased by the liberal use of cordials; flaring and fantastic in her dress, and affected both in her speech and her general behaviour."[33]

To be sure, Garrick always exaggerated for effect. He also liked to imitate Johnson's lifelong Staffordshire accent. "Garrick sometimes used to take him off, squeezing a lemon into a punch bowl with uncouth gesticulations, looking round the company, and calling out 'Who's for *poonsh?*'" He would relate that when somebody had taken Johnson's seat at a play in Lichfield, "he took chair and man and all together, and threw them all at once into the pit." Hester Thrale once asked Johnson whether this really happened, and he replied, "Garrick has not spoiled it in the telling; it is very *near* true to be sure."[34]

SLAVING IN GRUB STREET

The money that had been sunk in the Edial school was gone. How to make a living now? A historian notes that eighteenth-century Englishmen found their identity in birth, social rank, property, and occupation. Only the last of these was open to Johnson. Lacking a university degree, he couldn't enter one of the professions. The attempt at school teaching had failed dismally. What he said of a friend from those years was equally true of himself: "He was therefore obliged to seek some other means of support, and having no profession, became by necessity an author."[35]

To do that meant moving to London. In 1737 Johnson set out with his former student Garrick; Tetty waited to join him until he was settled. Garrick had theatrical dreams that would be fulfilled very soon. Johnson brought with him the manuscript of a blank verse tragedy, *Irene,* but he would have no luck getting that produced, and for him success would be long in coming.

Unfortunately, writing paid badly. Publishers, who were known as "booksellers," might grow rich, but royalties did not exist, and once an author sold a manuscript for a modest sum he could expect no further income from it. The novelists whom we still read today all supported themselves in other ways: Fielding was a lawyer, Smollett a naval surgeon and afterward a journalist, Sterne a clergyman. Writers who had independent means, such as the patrician aesthete Horace Walpole, were proud of never accepting money at all. Someone who hoped to live entirely by writing, as Johnson did, had only one choice: to join the ignoble workforce known as Grub Street hacks.

There was an actual Grub Street (later politely renamed Milton Street), but it became a collective name for anonymous writers who supplied publishers with material on demand and were paid by the page. In an essay Johnson later called them "the drudges of the pen, the manufacturers of literature" who never gave a thought to posterity, "for their productions are seldom intended to remain in the world longer than a week."[36] They were known as "garreteers" because the top floor of a rooming house was the cheapest in the days before elevators. In his *Dictionary* Johnson sardonically defined "Grub Street" as "the name of a street in Moorfields in London, much inhabited by writers of small histories, dictionaries, and temporary poems; whence any mean production is called *grubstreet.*"

A pair of pictures by Thomas Rowlandson, made in the 1780s, captures the poverty and humiliation of these writers. The Grub Street poet (figure 3) has disheveled and ill-fitting clothes, with a toe sticking out of his right shoe. One hand is thrust into a probably empty pocket, and he is looking about furtively, very likely for fear of being arrested for debt. The other picture is called *Bookseller and Author* (figure 4). In his book on eighteenth-century culture John Brewer says that the "corpulent prosperity" of the sneering book-seller contrasts with "the cringing emaciated figure of the imploring author." The picture is also a reminder that booksellers, in addition to acting as pub-lishers, literally sold books. A clergyman at the left is truculently examining the wares. Johnson had good relations with his employers, and told Boswell that they were "generous liberal-minded men, the patrons of literature." But most of their piecework employees were less valuable to them than Johnson became.[37]

When he got to London, Johnson had an objective in mind. In 1731 a bookseller named Edward Cave had launched a monthly called the *Gentle-man's Magazine,* a compendium of miscellaneous material of all kinds, that by

3. A Grub Street Poet

4. Bookseller and Author

1737 was widely known. Cave actually invented the modern sense of the word "magazine." Up until then it had meant simply, as Johnson would define it in the *Dictionary*, "a storehouse, commonly an arsenal or armory, or repository of provisions." But now there was a new meaning: "Of late this word has signified a miscellaneous pamphlet, from a periodical miscellany named the *Gentleman's Magazine,* by Edward Cave."

It was published at St. John's Gate, which still stands today, as the first page of each issue proudly declared (figure 5). Cave used the pseudonym "Sylvanus Urban," and in a portrait made a year after Johnson met him, he is shown holding a letter addressed to him at "St. John's Gate, London" (figure 6). Johnson told Boswell that when he first saw it, he "beheld it with reverence."[38]

Johnson had written ahead from Lichfield to offer his services, and Cave quickly recognized his gifts. They worked well together, and after Cave's death Johnson wrote affectionately that although his reserved temperament made him hard to know, "such he was, as they who best knew him have most

5. *The Gentleman's Magazine*

6. Edward Cave

lamented." Johnson ended on a touchingly personal note: toward the end Cave "fell into a kind of lethargic insensibility, in which one of the last acts of reason which he exerted was fondly to press the hand which is now writing this little narrative."[39]

Before long Johnson became the de facto editor of the magazine, to which he contributed various little pieces of his own—no one knows how many, because in later years he cheerfully acknowledged that he had forgotten many of them. One that he didn't forget involved an extraordinary feat of sustained invention. It was illegal to publish speeches in Parliament, but accomplices in the audience could jot down notes for Johnson to develop later. His imaginative expansion of what the speakers might have said came out regularly, under pretense of reporting on the Parliament of Lilliput, with thinly disguised allusions to British names and events. Over the space of three years these added up to half a million words. Naturally they had only the vaguest resemblance to the actual speeches, and it amused Johnson years later when a classical scholar said that a speech by the elder Pitt was better than anything in Demosthenes. Johnson remarked calmly, "That speech I wrote in a garret in Exeter Street."[40]

WOMEN COLLEAGUES

At the lower levels of society there were many women in the workforce, but for middle-class women options were few. Authorship was one of them.

Elizabeth Carter, a clergyman's daughter from the town of Deal in Kent, had been given an impressive education that included the classics, Hebrew, mathematics, and natural science. She also learned several modern languages, keeping herself awake during arduous study by copious use of snuff. When she moved to London she and Johnson worked closely as Cave's principal writers, and she contributed a number of poems to the magazine. An especially interesting one, entitled simply *A Dialogue,* allegorizes what philosophers would later call the mind-body problem:

> Says Body to Mind, 'tis amazing to see
> We're so nearly related, yet never agree,
> But lead a most wrangling strange sort of life,
> As great plagues to each other as husband and wife.

Like a number of other intellectual women, she never married; loss of independence was the inevitable result for wives. She was known as "Mrs. Carter," however. As a contraction of "Mistress" the title was applied to unmarried as well as married women.[41]

Carter went on from miscellaneous journalism to publish a translation of the Stoic philosopher Epictetus that would remain standard for over a century, and that brought her the impressive sum of £1,000. In a portrait painted in 1745 when she was twenty-eight, eight years younger than Johnson (figure 7), an attendant is about to receive a laurel wreath with which to crown her. The book in her hand is presumably her Epictetus. As late as 1910 the distinguished classicist W. H. Rouse reprinted it unaltered in the Everyman's Library series, with this prefatory comment: "Mrs. Carter's own style is not the style of Epictetus, but it *is* a style, which is more than can be said of most writers at this time. At least she has represented the author's ideas faithfully and coherently."[42]

Now financially secure, Carter retired comfortably to her hometown, but came up to London from time to time, and she and Johnson remained good friends for the rest of his life. Her nephew said long afterward, "I have frequently heard her say that he never treated her but with civility, attention, and respect." Johnson admired her for combining exceptional learning with solid practicality; "My old friend, Mrs. Carter, could make a pudding, as well as translate Epictetus from the Greek."

7. Elizabeth Carter

Her mastery of Greek was in fact extraordinary. Johnson said that his good friend Bennet Langton "understood Greek better than anyone whom he had ever known—except Elizabeth Carter." On one occasion she had a friendly dispute with Bishop Thomas Secker (later Archbishop of Canterbury), who disputed her claim that in the King James Bible, a verb in First Corinthians was translated in the active voice when referring to a man and in the passive voice for a woman. To settle the argument they looked it up, and her feminist insight proved correct.[43]

Another friend and colleague of Johnson's was Charlotte Lennox, who was born in Gibraltar in 1730, grew up in New York where her father was lieutenant governor, and turned to writing after she came to London and married a feckless customs office employee named Alexander Lennox. She turned her hand to miscellaneous forms of writing, including poems, a collection of sources used by Shakespeare called *Shakespeare Illustrated,* and a translation of a three-volume French history of theater in ancient Greece, part of which was contributed by Johnson.

Lennox became best known as a novelist. When her first novel—*The Life of Harriot Stuart, Written by Herself*—came out in 1751, when she was just twenty-one, Johnson and other friends of hers organized a celebration at the Devil Tavern, which had strong literary associations. It had been a favorite long before of Ben Jonson, whose friend Drummond said that drink was "one of the elements in which he liveth."[44]

Sir John Hawkins was present and remembered that Johnson ordered up a magnificent hot apple pie "stuck with bay leaves, because, forsooth, Mrs. Lennox was an authoress, and had written verses; and further, he had prepared for her a crown of laurel, with which—but not till he had invoked the muses by some ceremonies of his own invention—he encircled her brows." By five in the morning, "Johnson's face shone with meridian splendour, though his drink had been only lemonade." The revelers began to think of going home, "but the waiters were all so overcome with sleep that it was two hours before we could get a bill, and it was not till near eight that the creaking of the street door gave the signal for our departure."[45]

A modern commentator says, "Here is a literary party on the very fringes of polite society. Making their own festivity, bestowing their own honors, bohemian and avant-garde before those categories were invented, this is a joyous celebration of independence from the world of patrons and booksellers." Hawkins's "forsooth" suggests condescension toward the female author—or authoress. Boswell harbored similar feelings, which helps to account for the relative invisibility of women in the *Life of Johnson*. He borrowed a lot of material from the early biography of Johnson by Hawkins, but left this story out.[46]

Lennox's breakthrough was her second novel, *The Female Quixote,* about a young woman who thinks extravagant romances are reliable guides to life, and regards every man she meets as either an adoring lover or a terrifying rapist. No less a judge than Henry Fielding reviewed it as "a most extraordinary and most excellent performance," promising that readers "will at once be instructed and very highly diverted." Years later Jane Austen loved it, and seems to have gotten the idea from it for *Northanger Abbey.* By then Lennox had become enough of a celebrity to have her portrait painted by Joshua Reynolds (figure 8).[47]

A FAILING MARRIAGE

Tetty had joined her husband in London a few months after he moved there in 1737. They lived for a while in Woodstock Street, Hanover Square, after that in Castle Street, Cavendish Square, and still later in Carey Street. People moved often in those days. By the time of his death Johnson had resided at no fewer than seventeen different London addresses.[48]

But by the early 1740s Johnson was living effectively as a bachelor. Tetty never went with him to visit friends, and friends were never invited to their

8. Charlotte Lennox

lodgings. She was increasingly dependent on alcohol and opium, and suppos-edly in quest of better air, went to stay in a small rented house in Hampstead. Hester Thrale heard from someone who had known her back then that "she was always drunk and reading romances in her bed, where she killed herself by taking opium." Hawkins thought that Johnson's ostentatious fondness for her "was a lesson that he had learned by rote," adding that "there was some-what crazy in the behaviour of them both: profound respect on his part, and the airs of an antiquated beauty on hers."[49]

When Johnson went out to Hampstead Tetty refused his sexual advances, saying that her poor health made it impossible. Years later he told Boswell, "Wise married women detest a mistress but don't mind a whore. My wife told me I might lie with as many women as I pleased, provided I loved her alone." Boswell intended to include this conversation in the *Life of Johnson,* but friends he showed it to were "struck with its indelicacy" and warned him that "it might hurt the book much." So he told the printer to cancel the passage, lamenting however that "it is mighty good stuff."[50]

Actually Boswell had a lot more material than that. Elizabeth Desmoulins (pronounced "Demullins"), seven years younger than Johnson, was the daughter of his godfather Samuel Swynfen and had moved in with Tetty in Hampstead as a companion. She had married a Birmingham man named Desmoulins, but he died soon afterward, and she would spend the rest of her life in Johnson's household. Toward the end of his life, Boswell and a painter named Mauritius Lowe had a remarkable conversation with Mrs. Desmoul-ins, who was then in her sixties. After writing it up Boswell labeled it "Ex-traordinary Johnsoniana—*tacenda,*" meaning "not to be spoken, kept secret."

Lowe suggested archly that Johnson's feelings toward women must always have been platonic, at which Desmoulins replied, "Ah, Sir, you are much mistaken. There never was a man who had stronger amorous inclinations than Dr. Johnson. But he conquered them." Under eager prodding by Bos-well as well as Lowe, she went on to reveal that in those years Tetty never slept with her husband, "but that was her fault; she drank shockingly and said she was not well and could not bear a bedfellow." He would then often go into Desmoulins's room and lie down beside her with his head on the pillow.

> BOSWELL. What would he do? Come now. (Lowe like to jump out of his skin.) Would he fondle you? Would he kiss you?
> MRS. DESMOULINS. Yes, Sir.

BOSWELL. And it was something different from a father's kiss?

MRS. DESMOULINS. Yes, indeed.

LOWE (approaching his hand to her bosom). But would he? eh?

MRS. DESMOULINS. Sir, he never did anything that was beyond the limits of decency.

LOWE. And could you say, Madam, upon your oath, that you were certain he was capable?

MRS. DESMOULINS. Y-yes, Sir.

BOSWELL. But he conquered his violent inclination?

MRS. DESMOULINS. Yes, Sir. He'd push me from him and cry, "Get you gone."

Boswell, who hardly ever conquered a violent inclination, may not have grasped just how poignant this story was. His only comment on it was "Strange."[51]

In 1752 Tetty died, at the age of sixty-three, and was buried in the church at Bromley just outside London. Johnson grieved for the rest of his life, and impressed friends who had not known her with his devotion. In fact the main impulse seems to have been guilt for his part in the failure of the marriage. Psychologists tell us that it is troubled and conflict-ridden marriages that leave the surviving spouse most haunted by grief.

A few months before he died twenty-four years later, Johnson told a friend a poignant story.

> "I remember that my wife, when she was near her end, poor woman, was advised to sleep out of town; and when she was carried to the lodgings that had been prepared for her, she complained that the staircase was in very bad condition, for the plaster was beaten off the walls in many places. 'Oh,' said the man of the house, 'that's nothing but by the knocks against it of the coffins of the poor souls that have died in the lodgings!'" He laughed, though not without apparent secret anguish, in telling me this.[52]

Shortly before his own death, Johnson ordered a memorial stone for Tetty's grave and composed a Latin epitaph. To his stepdaughter Lucy he sent an English translation, calling Tetty "a woman of beauty, elegance, ingenuity, and piety," and recording that "her first husband was Henry Porter; her second

Samuel Johnson, who having loved her much, and lamented her long, laid this stone upon her." A sympathetic scholar comments, "He put the concluding touch on a romance that imagination had made infinitely moving, and perhaps infinitely more satisfactory than the reality of the marriage of Tetty and Samuel Johnson could ever have been."[53]

However complicated Johnson's feelings were, the sense of loss was profound. Two years after Tetty's death he wrote to a friend, "I have ever since seemed to myself broken off from mankind, a kind of solitary wanderer in the wild of life, without any certain direction or fixed point of view. A gloomy gazer on a world to which I have little relation."[54]

At this time Johnson contemplated remarrying. The woman he had in mind was the attractive and deeply religious Hill Boothby. She was an old acquaintance from Ashbourne, not far from Lichfield, with whom he is known to have corresponded regularly, though nearly all the letters are lost. The few that survive date from December 1755, when he learned with alarm that she was seriously ill, at a time when he himself was down with bronchitis and possibly pneumonia. He addresses her as "My Sweet Angel" and "Dearest Dear," and the longest of the letters begins and ends like this:

> It is again midnight, and I am again alone. With what meditation shall I amuse this waste hour of darkness and vacuity? If I turn my thoughts upon myself, what do I perceive but a poor helpless being reduced by a blast of wind to weakness and misery. . . . You know Descartes' argument, "I think, therefore I am." It is as good a consequence, "I write, therefore I am alive." I might give another, "I am alive, therefore I love Miss Boothby," but that I hope our friendship may be of far longer duration than life.

A week later Johnson wrote, "I beg of you to endeavour to live," and one week after that she was dead. Hester Thrale heard from someone who knew him then that he was "almost distracted with his grief, and the friends about him had much to do to calm the violence of his emotion."[55]

A POEM AND A BIOGRAPHY

Johnson always wrote well. It is often possible to be confident that an anonymous piece is his from the style alone, and he was beginning to produce work with the full eloquence and moral energy we think of as "Johnsonian." One example, in 1738, was *London*, a poetic adaptation of the sixth satire of

Juvenal, with modern examples in place of the ancient ones. Composed in the rhymed couplets that Pope had been using for "imitations" of Horace, it was energetic and angry. One couplet in particular spoke from Johnson's own experience (the capital letters are in the original):

> This mournful truth is everywhere confessed,
> SLOW RISES WORTH, BY POVERTY DEPRESSED.

Johnson was deeply flattered when he heard that Pope himself admired *London* and said that the anonymous author would soon be *déterré*—unearthed. "What keeps the poem alive," T. S. Eliot wrote, "is the undercurrent of personal feeling, the bitterness of the hardships, slights, injuries, and privations, really experienced by Johnson in his youth."[56]

Johnson's first truly major work was *An Account of the Life of Mr. Richard Savage,* published in 1744. Some years later Joshua Reynolds, who was not yet acquainted with him at the time, happened upon it and began to read it while he was leaning against a mantelpiece. Reynolds told Boswell that "it seized his attention so strongly, that not being able to lay down the book till he had finished it, when he attempted to move he found his arm totally benumbed."[57]

The *Life of Savage* is a small masterpiece, but a strange one. Richard Savage was sophisticated, charming, and a poet of some talent. Twelve years older than Johnson and connected with the Pope circle, he seemed a brilliant guide to the ways of the world. He was also a conceited, manipulative, and probably delusional character who needed a royal pardon—wangled by influential friends—to escape execution for a murder he never denied committing. And he made a career out of claiming to be the illegitimate son of a noblewoman who was inexplicably persecuting him, a story the normally skeptical Johnson swallowed whole. Modern scholars are certain that Savage made it up and that the alleged mother was the one being persecuted.

Johnson's *Life of Savage* is full of special pleading, reflecting not just loyalty to a former friend, but deep identification with him as an outsider struggling to rise above the ignominy of Grub Street; Savage too wrote for money, when he wasn't cadging it from friends. Johnson recalled his way of life with grim outrage. "He lodged as much by accident as he dined, and passed the night sometimes in mean houses which are set open at night to any casual wanderers, sometimes in cellars among the riot and filth of the meanest and most profligate of the rabble, and sometimes, when he had not money to support even the expenses of these receptacles, walked about the streets till he was weary, and lay down in the summer upon a bulk, or in the winter, with his associates in poverty, among the ashes of a glasshouse." Though Johnson doesn't say so, he himself was one of the associates in poverty.[58]

The simple terms "bulk" and "glasshouse" need amplification for us, which Richard Holmes provides in his superb *Dr. Johnson and Mr. Savage.* His explanation brings to life the underworld of Hogarth and Rowlandson, as contrasted with the upper world of Canaletto and Reynolds.

> The "cellar" would be a single dark basement dossing-room of sacks and straw heaps, fouled with urine and vomit, populated by drunks, diseased and aging prostitutes, lunatics, tramps and psychopaths. The "bulk" was a low wooden stall attached to a shopfront on which fresh market produce was displayed by day and left to rot at night: old vegetables at Covent Garden, old fish at Billingsgate, old meat at Smithfield. The "glasshouse" was a small factory (like a bakery or kiln) where carriage glass, windowpanes, water jugs, wineglasses, decorative buttons, cane tops and other fancy ornaments were melted and cast in fast-burning coal fired ovens. Here even a complete down-and-out could keep warm, just as the modern tramp sleeps on a ventilation grill.

Holmes and others have pointed out that Johnson could after all have spent the night in his own lodgings. He evidently preferred life in the streets to going home.[59]

Savage eventually accepted enough money from friends to live frugally in the country, "and parted from the author of this narrative with tears in his eyes." He got as far as Bristol, ran into debt, and was consequently imprisoned. There he fell ill and died. There is pathos in Johnson's account of his last recorded words: "The last time that the [jail] keeper saw him was on July the 31st, 1743, when Savage, seeing him at his bed-side, said, with an uncommon earnestness, 'I have something to say to you, Sir;' but after a pause, moved his hand in a melancholy manner, and finding himself unable to recollect what he was going to communicate, said, ' 'Tis gone.' The keeper soon after left him; and the next morning he died, at the age of forty-six."

Johnson concludes the story with a challenge to the reader: "Those are no proper judges of his conduct who have slumbered away their time on the down of plenty, nor will a wise man easily presume to say, 'Had I been in Savage's condition, I should have lived, or written, better than Savage.'"[60]

One thing Johnson never did was romanticize poverty. In one of his first conversations with Boswell he said, "When I was running about this town a very poor fellow, I was a great arguer for the advantages of poverty; but I was, at the same time, very sorry to be poor. Sir, all the arguments which are brought to represent poverty as no evil show it to be evidently a great evil. You never find people labouring to convince you that you may live very happily upon a plentiful fortune." In an essay Johnson put it still more forcibly: "In the prospect of poverty there is nothing but gloom and melancholy. The mind and body suffer together; its miseries bring no alleviations; it is a state in which every virtue is obscured and in which no conduct can avoid reproach; a state in which cheerfulness is insensibility, and dejection sullenness, of which the hardships are without honour, and the labours without reward."[61]

CHAPTER 2

Johnson before Boswell

FAME AT LAST

DISCOVERING A VOCATION

If Johnson had died in 1748, when he was about to turn forty, only a few specialists today would recognize his name. The 1750s was when he produced a series of major works that raised him to virtually unchallenged eminence as a man of letters. Boswell's assessment is convincing: "No man of humble birth who lived entirely by literature, in short no author by profession, ever rose in this country into that personal notice which he did."[1]

After a decade of anonymous writing, in 1749 Johnson finally had two works, a poem in rhyming couplets and a play in blank verse, to publish under his own name. A generation or two earlier these would have been the genres most likely to win prestige, and he seems not to have suspected that their day was past.

The play was *Irene,* based on a story from Turkish history. Johnson never had much enthusiasm for the theater, and *Irene* was fatally untheatrical. For years he found it impossible to get it produced, until Garrick finally did it as a personal favor, and a printed edition was published. The poem was *The Vanity of Human Wishes,* like *London* an adaptation of Juvenal but more powerful, and the only major poem Johnson ever wrote. Figure 9 shows the first page of the original manuscript.

Juvenal's original is corrosively contemptuous of human folly. Johnson could never be that. He once wrote, "The only end of writing is to enable the

9. *The Vanity of Human Wishes*
manuscript

readers better to enjoy life, or better to endure it." In general he avoided satire, always reaching for a larger and more generous view of human experience,
although as Bate says, he was a "satirist *manqué*"—someone who had a satiric
gift but suppressed it. He took the title of his poem from Ecclesiastes: "Vanity
of vanities, saith the preacher, all is vanity." The first words are:

> Let observation, with extensive view,
> Survey mankind from China to Peru . . .

Johnson seems to have been aiming at an Olympian perspective, gazing at
the whole world from far enough away to see its follies as heartbreaking, not
ridiculous.[2]

The poem surveys examples of hope ending in failure in many domains—
among them political, military, ecclesiastical, and scholarly.

> Unnumbered suppliants crowd preferment's gate,
> Athirst for wealth, and burning to be great;
> Delusive Fortune hears th' incessant call,
> They mount, they shine, evaporate, and fall.

"Preferment" was advancement through the intervention of a powerful patron. Johnson himself had never received preferment of any kind.[3]

Johnson was haunted by a feeling that life is a stream in which we are irresistibly carried along.

> Must helpless man, in ignorance sedate,
> Roll darkling down the torrent of his fate?

In the draft of the poem, the second of these lines originally read "Swim darkling down the current of his fate." Now it's not "swim," but "roll"; not "current," but "torrent."

No wonder the final lines appeal to a power beyond the human:

> Celestial wisdom calms the mind,
> And makes the happiness she does not find.

The ending is meant to counter Juvenal's paganism with Christian consolation, but that consolation is what Johnson himself was never able to achieve.[4]

Johnson was determined to make a name as a writer, but the two genres that had seemed most promising were leading nowhere. He never again attempted a major poem, and his single play proved only that he would never be a playwright. In hindsight it's clear that the best path to success would have been as a novelist. But novels were just beginning to be recognized as worthy successors to the older genres, and Johnson never thought much of them. Later on he did write one brief novella called *Rasselas,* but his talent was never for fiction.

There still remained another promising form to consider, the periodical essay, which Joseph Addison and his collaborator Richard Steele had made immensely popular with the *Spectator,* forty years before. So Johnson persuaded a group of publishers to pay him two guineas each for a twice-weekly series called *The Rambler.*

Johnson later told Reynolds that he chose the name pretty much at random, under time pressure before the first number went to press. "What must be done, Sir, will be done. When I was to begin publishing that paper, I was at a loss how to name it. I sat down at night upon my bedside, and resolved that I would not go to sleep till I had fixed its title. *The Rambler* seemed the best that occurred, and I took it." It amused Boswell that when it got translated into Italian it was called *Il Vagabondo.*[5]

There was no ignoring the deadlines every Tuesday and Saturday, daunting though they were for a lifelong procrastinator. Johnson often wrote right up to the moment when copy had to be sent to the printer, and from 1750 to 1752 he turned out no fewer than 208 *Rambler* essays, with only a handful contributed by friends (Elizabeth Carter did one). In the beginning they averaged around 1,500 words but became progressively shorter, until they came in at 1,200 or so toward the end. A typical *New York Times* op-ed today is about that length.

The *Rambler* essays were issued originally as six-page pamphlets, widely reprinted in various publications, and afterward collected in book form. There were ten successive editions during Johnson's lifetime, by which time it was considered a modern classic. He was deeply touched when Tetty told him, "I thought very well of you before, but I did not imagine you could have written anything equal to this."[6]

Johnson had discovered a vocation as a moralist, as that term was then understood (and in France still is). In the *Dictionary* he defined it as "one who teaches the duties of life." The goal was not to startle readers with novelties, for as he wrote in the second *Rambler,* people "more frequently require to be reminded than informed."

A characteristic method soon emerged. Johnson would state some familiar truism at the beginning of an essay, unpack it to reveal all the ways it was inadequate, and then put it together again—turning truisms into truth. Bate says that he had the gift of "turning a thing upside down and shaking the nonsense out of it."[7]

Johnson liked to be dogmatic in conversation, to provoke people to argue, but he was seldom dogmatic in writing. Boswell quotes a historian who said that Johnson's writings contained "great thoughts which had been rolled and rolled in his mind, as in the sea."[8]

Not that Johnson ignored important issues in contemporary life. He did discuss them, and with far deeper sympathy than the worldly "Mr. Spectator" had shown. Some thirty-five essays in the *Rambler* and its sequels, the *Idler* and *Adventurer,* are cast as first-person accounts of female experience: "Sir, I am a young woman of a very large fortune"; "Mr. Idler, I am the unfortunate wife of a city wit." An imaginary male correspondent writes, "I was known to possess a fortune, and to want a wife." This might have been in the mind of Jane Austen, an admirer of Johnson's writing, when she wrote the famous opening sentence of *Pride and Prejudice:* "It is a truth universally acknowledged, that a single man in possession of a good fortune must be in want of a wife."[9]

In other essays Johnson exposed forms of cruelty that society condoned or even enforced. He was deeply concerned with the plight of prostitutes, having known many in his early days in London (just how well he knew them was a question his friends later puzzled over). His housemate Elizabeth Desmoulins described a moving incident. In Fleet Street at two in the morning "he was alarmed with the cries of a person seemingly in great distress," and found a woman in rags "perishing on a truss of straw, who had just strength enough to tell him that she was turned out by an inhuman landlord in that condition, and to beg his charitable assistance not to let her die in the street." He carried her on his back to his house, and after it became obvious that she was suffering from venereal disease, kept her there for three months while a physician succeeded in curing her. After that, ascertaining that she hated the life of prostitution, he got his friends to contribute to set her up in a milliner's shop in the country, "where she was living some years ago in very considerable repute." Hazlitt commented that this was "an act which realizes the parable of the good Samaritan."[10]

Another topic in Johnson's essays was the horrible institution of debtors' prisons, where an offender would be permanently incarcerated unless he could pay off his debts. Some might have friends who would do that for them; those who didn't were out of luck. If any creditors, Johnson says, could really be indifferent to the suffering endured by a prisoner's wife and children, "I must leave them to be awakened by some other power, for I write only to human beings."[11]

The most moving of the essays address elements of psychic experience that we now know, though Johnson's first readers didn't, to have been profoundly personal. "The vacuity of life," Hester Thrale said, "had so struck upon the mind of Mr. Johnson that it became by repeated impression his favourite hypothesis, and the general tenor of his reasonings commonly ended in that." That theme does indeed pervade his writings: a horror of the emptiness of life unless forcibly filled up—with constructive interests if possible, but with distractions of any kind if not.[12]

Pascal says something very similar in the *Pensées,* which we know Johnson greatly admired. "Ennui" is not just boredom, but a dreadful spiritual emptiness. "Ennui: nothing is so intolerable to man as to be completely at rest, without passions, without occupation, without diversion, without work. He then feels his nothingness, his abandonment, his insufficiency, his dependence, his powerlessness, his emptiness. Immediately from the depth of his heart will emerge ennui, gloom, sadness, resentment, vexation, despair."[13]

At bottom Johnson was concerned with what he called "the moral discipline of the mind," and by that he meant what he found so hard to achieve in his own life, control over unwanted thoughts and desires. Just because his inner experience was so turbulent and threatening, there may have been therapeutic value for him in generalizing it in measured formulations. The patient sought to turn himself into a teacher.[14]

Johnson was glad to find that *The Rambler* was widely respected, if not loved, but he knew that he could never please the huge audience that Addison and Steele had. When it came time to stop, he said so, with a poignant mixture of pride and disappointment. "He that is himself weary will soon weary the public. Let him therefore lay down his employment, whatever it be, who can no longer exert his former activity or attention; let him not endeavour to struggle with censure, or obstinately infest the stage till a general hiss commands him to depart."[15]

JOHNSONESE

Johnson favored a complex, ornate prose style. During his lifetime and afterward that style was often criticized, and parodied, as "Johnsonese." In particular he was fond of big words constructed from Latin roots, many of which were not familiar to ordinary readers. When George Orwell said, "Never use a long word where a short one will do," he was objecting to cynical obfuscation in politics and advertising, using long words to cover up dishonest meaning. No one could be more critical of that than Johnson. But in many cases, he would argue, a short word simply will *not* do. Besides, big words can help to highlight well-chosen short ones.[16]

Of course style is much more than words alone, whether long or short. In one of the essays Johnson describes the challenge of shaping each sentence and paragraph into a compelling whole: "It is one of the common distresses of a writer to be within a word of a happy period, to want only a single epithet to give amplification its full force, to require only a correspondent term in order to finish a paragraph with elegance, and make one of its members answer to the other; but these deficiencies cannot always be supplied; and after a long study and vexation, the passage is turned anew, and the web unwoven that was so nearly finished."[17]

Johnson refers to "a happy period" because his style is the kind that used to be known as periodic. When we use the word "period" we mean simply the punctuation mark. But in traditional rhetoric it meant the whole interconnected structure of clauses that brings us to that conclusion. "The periodic stylist," Richard Lanham says, "works with *balance, antithesis, parallelism,* and

careful patterns of *repetition*. All of these dramatize a mind which has dominated experience and reworked it to its liking." To build sentences and para-
graphs in that way is a compliment to readers, inviting them to ponder the
way ideas deepen in meaning as they are joined or opposed to each other.[18]

For Johnson the periodic style was not just an intellectual construct, but
an aesthetic and emotional experience as well, with a rhythm that might well
be called musical. In the final *Rambler* he said that he hoped he had added
something to the "elegance of construction" of the English language, "and
something to the harmony of its cadence."[19]

THE LEXICOGRAPHER

Back in 1746, a consortium of publishers had contracted with Johnson to
produce a major dictionary, and he had been laboring on it fairly steadily
since then. In 1755 it finally appeared, and was immediately recognized as a
monument; an early biographer called it "Johnson's world of words." On the
two hundredth anniversary of his death an editorialist in the *Times* declared,
"The chief glory of the English is their language; and Johnson's *Dictionary*,
the only one in any language compiled by a writer of genius, had a lot to do
with its rise to glory."[20]

That is no overstatement. Previous dictionaries of English were just word
lists. They seldom gave much attention to nuances of meaning, and none at
all to the way meanings mutate over time. Johnson had a great writer's love of
the flavor of words, awareness of nuance, and consciousness of the way a language changes as a living thing. In France the Académie Française was also
preparing a dictionary, with the intention of fixing the "correct" meaning of
every word for all time. Johnson, altogether differently, invented the mode of
defining words that was later carried forward by the *Oxford English Dictionary*. He wanted to show all the ways they had ever been used, and to include
examples from earlier writers that would illustrate their usage in specific
contexts.

There were roughly 40,000 entries in Johnson's *Dictionary of the English
Language* and three times that number of illustrative quotations, filling 2,300
double-column pages in two massive folio volumes. A folio was twelve by
eighteen inches, about the size of a modern atlas, and the result was literally
weighty, the kind of book that an earlier writer called "portable, if your horse
be not too weak." The title page identified Johnson by name with the title
of AM (today we would say MA); his Oxford friend Thomas Warton had

arranged for an honorary degree to add academic prestige. Adam Smith, who had not yet met Johnson, wrote an enthusiastic review: "When we compare this book with other dictionaries, the merit of its author appears very extraordinary."[21]

The forty-member French academy had already been laboring for years on its unfinished project, and alluding to that fact, Garrick celebrated his friend's achievement in verse:

> Johnson, well-armed like a hero of yore,
> Has beat forty French, and will beat forty more!

Soon it became common to refer to him as the Great Lexicographer.[22]

The publishers who commissioned the *Dictionary* paid Johnson the impressive sum of £1,575, but expenses were great, and by the time the book came out nine years later, he had spent more than that. To provide adequate space for the project he rented the largest house he ever had, 17 Gough Square off Fleet Street, which still exists as a Johnson museum (figure 10). A team of six paid assistants came in each day and labored in the garret to amass the raw materials. Johnson would buy or borrow standard works by authors in English, read through them, and underline words he wanted to use. The assistants would then copy out, on individual slips of paper, the sentences in which the underlined words appeared. The editors of the *Oxford English Dictionary* later adopted the same method.

When the enormous collection of slips was eventually alphabetized, Johnson would choose the examples he wanted to accompany each definition, thereby giving an overview of changing usage, and also a kind of anthology of good writing. He especially enjoyed including quotations from Shakespeare. Probably no other writer but Shakespeare ever used the word "bedpresser," but it shows up in the *Dictionary* as "a heavy lazy fellow," illustrated by Prince Hal's insult to Falstaff: "This sanguine coward, this bedpresser, this horseback-breaker, this huge hill of flesh."[23]

In his magnificent preface to the *Dictionary,* Johnson acknowledged frankly that there is no possibility of arresting change in "the boundless chaos of a living speech." Latin was stable because Latin was dead. It mutated into the modern romance languages, and they were still changing and would always change. English, without the French top-down attempt to arrest change, was still more mutable, and the range of possible meanings for even the simplest words could be immense. Johnson's definitions for "put" fill three pages, and those for "take" fill five. "These words," he said, "are hourly shifting their

10. 17 Gough Square

relations, and can no more be ascertained in a dictionary than a grove, in the agitation of a storm, can be accurately delineated from its picture [i.e., reflection] in the water."²⁴

When a couple of ladies congratulated Johnson for not including any "naughty" words, he replied teasingly, "What, my dears! then you have been looking for them?" It's true that a few of the most obscene are absent, but he had no objection to defining "bubby" as "a woman's breast." We also find "rump," "bum," and "arse" (all defined with variants of "the buttocks; the part on which we sit") and the expression "to hang an arse" ("a vulgar phrase, signifying to be tardy, sluggish, or dilatory"). In these cases correct usage was illustrated with humorous examples. For "bubby" Johnson cites Dr. Arbuthnot, the witty friend of Swift and Pope who invented the character John Bull: "Foh! say they, to see a handsome, brisk, genteel young fellow so much governed by a doting old woman; why don't you go and suck the bubby?" "Fart" ("wind from behind") is illustrated from a seventeenth-century poem by Sir John Suckling:

Love is the fart
Of every heart;
It pains a man when 'tis kept close,
And others doth offend when 'tis let loose.²⁵

The *Dictionary* defines a great many Latinate words that Johnson found in old books, but that few of his contemporaries had ever encountered. T. E. Lawrence (of Arabia) knew that an Oxford economist friend was fond of such words. When Lawrence was returning from London one day, the friend asked him, "Was it very caliginous in the metropolis?" Lawrence replied, "Somewhat caliginous, but not altogether inspissated." Both words appear in Johnson's *Dictionary.* "Caliginous" means "obscure; dim; full of darkness," and "inspissate" means "to thicken; to make thick." Johnson used it himself in a conversation about Shakespeare: "In the description of night in *Macbeth,* the beetle and the bat detract from the general idea of darkness—inspissated gloom."²⁶

At times Johnson clearly used such words for fun. Boswell relates that at one dinner party Johnson said that no one was ever "made a rogue" by the fictional highwayman in *The Beggar's Opera.* "Then collecting himself, as it were, to give a hearty stroke: 'There is in it such a *labefactation* of all principles, as may be injurious to morality.' While he pronounced this response we sat in a comical sort of restraint, smothering a laugh, which we were afraid might burst out."²⁷

There were endless delays in getting *Dictionary* copy to the printers, which had to be done in stages so that after each installment had been printed, the metal type could be redistributed for reuse. Urgent messages arrived at Gough Square to speed up the flow. Boswell heard what happened when the job was finally finished. "When the messenger who carried the last sheet to Millar returned, Johnson asked him, 'Well, what did he say?' 'Sir,' answered the messenger, 'he said, thank God I have done with him.' 'I am glad,' replied Johnson with a smile, 'that he thanks God for anything.'"²⁸

The *Dictionary* was a majestic achievement, but for Johnson it meant nearly a decade of commitment to an essentially impersonal project. Tetty had been dead for three years when it was done, and the final words of the *Preface* strike a note that is anything but impersonal. "I may surely be contented without the praise of perfection, which if I could obtain, in this gloom of solitude, what would it avail me? I have protracted my work till most of those whom I wished to please have sunk into the grave, and success and miscarriage are empty sounds. I therefore dismiss it with frigid tranquility, having little to fear or hope from censure or from praise."[29]

Philip Dormer Stanhope, fourth Earl of Chesterfield, was a literary dilettante who thought of himself as a distinguished authority. Soon after Johnson began work on the *Dictionary* he realized that the stipend from the publishers would not be enough, and it struck him that Chesterfield might take an interest. In his *Plan of a Dictionary of the English Language,* published in 1747, he appealed to Chesterfield personally as a potential patron. The *Plan* concludes, "Whatever be the extent of my endeavours, I shall not easily regret an attempt which has procured me the honor of appearing thus publicly, my Lord, your Lordship's most obedient and most humble servant, SAM. JOHNSON."[30]

Chesterfield may have been flattered, but he didn't take the bait. Eight years later, however, when publication of the *Dictionary* was imminent, he brought out a couple of essays in a periodical recommending the forthcoming work, and praising Johnson as a dictator in language. No doubt he wanted to give the impression of having made the *Dictionary* possible; his name would appear on the title page and he would expect a handsomely bound presentation copy. But he followed his praise with an insult: that Johnson should be classed among the "pedantic" rather than "polite" writers. Alluding to his lack of social graces, Chesterfield said that he thought more highly of Johnson's impartiality as a judge "than of his gallantry as a fine gentleman." As Lawrence Lipking says, "No one could doubt that a very polite fine gentleman wrote the paper."[31]

Furious, Johnson sent Chesterfield a letter that soon became widely known, though not published for many years. Chesterfield himself left it openly on a table for his visitors to see, and would remark on how well written it was. It is more than just well written.

> Seven years, my Lord, have now passed since I waited in your outward rooms or was repulsed from your door, during which time I have been pushing on my work through difficulties of which it is useless to complain, and have brought it at last to the verge of publication without one act of assistance, one word of encouragement, or one smile of favour. Such treatment I did not expect, for I never had a patron before.
>
> The shepherd in Virgil grew at last acquainted with love, and found him a native of the rocks. Is not a patron, my Lord, one who

looks with unconcern on a man struggling for life in the water, and when he has reached ground encumbers him with help? The notice which you have been pleased to take of my labours, had it been early, had been kind; but it has been delayed till I am indifferent and cannot enjoy it, till I am solitary and cannot impart it, till I am known and do not want it.

I hope it is no very cynical asperity not to confess obligation where no benefit has been received, or to be unwilling that the public should consider me as owing that to a patron, which Providence has enabled me to do for myself.

Having carried on my work thus far with so little obligation to any favourer of learning, I shall not be disappointed though I should con- clude it, if less be possible, with less; for I have been long wakened from that dream of hope, in which I once boasted myself with so much exultation, my Lord, your Lordship's most humble, most obedi- ent servant, SAMUEL JOHNSON.[32]

In a new edition of *The Vanity of Human Wishes* Johnson made a notable revision. In a description of scholars threatened by "toil, envy, want, the gar- ret, and the jail," the word "garret" was replaced by "patron."[33]

A ROYAL PENSION

In 1759, letters from Lichfield warned Johnson that his mother was close to death. Yet even then he delayed going home to see her. He claimed, and it was surely a rationalization, that the only reason he didn't hurry home was that he had to earn money for her care, and if necessary her funeral. That was supposedly why he was writing *Rasselas*.

Johnson wrote his last letter to his mother on January 20, 1759, at what turned out to be the very moment of her death. "Dear honoured Mother, neither your condition nor your character make it fit for me to say much. You have been the best mother, and I believe the best woman in the world. I thank you for your indulgence to me, and beg forgiveness of all that I have done ill, and all that I have omitted to do well. . . . I am, dear, dear Mother, your duti- ful son, Sam Johnson." Sarah Johnson was buried, while her dutiful son was still in London, on January 23. A psychiatrist suggests plausibly that "seeing her would risk the destruction of the symbolic fantasy of her that he had cre- ated in her absence: an idealized image of her as 'the best mother.' "[34]

Whether or not *Rasselas* was written for the reason Johnson alleged, he was desperately short of money throughout these years. In 1756, famous at last after publication of the *Rambler* and the *Dictionary,* he sent an urgent note to Samuel Richardson, who was a wealthy printer as well as popular novelist: "I am obliged to entreat your assistance. I am now under an arrest for five pounds eighteen shillings. Mr. Strahan, from whom I should have received the necessary help in this case, is not at home, and I am afraid of not finding Mr. Millar. If you will be so good as to send me this sum, I will very gratefully repay you, and add it to all former obligations." In the margin of the letter Richardson noted that he promptly sent six guineas (eight shillings more than requested), for which Johnson returned "sincerest thanks."[35]

In 1762 relief finally came. Unexpectedly, Johnson was awarded a royal pension of £300 a year. That was enough to live on comfortably, and from then on anything he might earn from writing was so much the better, not just necessary to keep afloat. There was one embarrassment, though. In the *Dictionary* he had defined "pension" as "an allowance made to anyone without an equivalent. In England it is generally understood to be pay given to a state hireling for treason to his country." Johnson's critics liked to dwell on his apparent hypocrisy in accepting a pension now, but he accepted the explanation that it was intended to honor his previous work, not for any quid pro quo. King George III had been on the throne for just two years, and unlike his predecessors he was a voracious reader and genuinely respected Johnson's distinction.

Still, there probably were expectations. It was a time of political controversy, with the Seven Years War not yet ended and increasing unrest in the American colonies. It's likely that the Tory government did hope to make use of Johnson's pen, even if they didn't explicitly demand it. And he would in fact go on to write polemical pamphlets on their behalf that many people considered unwise.

CHAPTER 3

Boswell before Johnson

SETTING OUT FOR THE WIDE WORLD

THE JUDGE'S SON

James Boswell's father, Alexander, was known as Lord Auchinleck. That was not a hereditary title, but an honorific given to judges at the highest level; he was a member of the Courts of Session and also of Justiciary, the highest civil and criminal courts in Scotland. Auchinleck was the name of the family estate, still held at this time by James's grandfather, sometimes pronounced "Affleck" with the accent on the second syllable. In his private capacity Alexander Boswell did have a hereditary title: he was the eighth Laird of Auchinleck. The additional word "of" indicated relationship to a specific place: a laird was the holder of a large and long-established estate.

James, the eldest of three sons, was born in Edinburgh in 1740. His father took it for granted that James would pursue a distinguished career and eventually succeed him as head of the estate. Lord Auchinleck was stern, demanding, and woundingly sarcastic. He also prided himself on deep learning, though his estate overseer said that he "went through books like a moth, without getting any instruction from them." His portrait, painted by the distinguished Allan Ramsay when James was fifteen, gives a good sense of how intimidating he was (color plate 5).[1]

The only thing James would acknowledge his father ever taught him was a habit of strict veracity, and indeed he was remarkable all his life for that, which would turn out to be a great asset in recording the conversations of

Johnson and other friends. "I do not recollect having had any other valuable principle impressed upon me by my father except a strict regard to truth, which he impressed upon my mind by a hearty beating at an early age." Boswell made that remark in his journal with regret, upset because he had uncharacteristically beaten his own four-year-old son.[2]

Johnson grew up with a weak father and a domineering mother, Boswell just the opposite. He could never manage to please his father, and even in his thirties would complain that he was treated like a little boy. His mother had a very different personality. Born Euphemia Erskine and ten years younger than her husband, she was timid, reclusive, and profoundly pious. The piety had painful consequences for her children, since she was determined to raise them in an exceptionally stern faith.

Scottish Presbyterianism was strongly Calvinist, with an emphasis on predestination and hellfire. "I shall never forget," James wrote in his early twenties, "the dismal hours of apprehension that I have endured in my youth from narrow notions of religion while my tender mind was lacerated with the infernal horror." He would have been required to memorize the *Shorter Catechism,* which declared that "all mankind by their fall lost communion with God, are under his wrath and curse, and so made liable to all miseries in this life, to death itself, and to the pains of hell forever." When he had a chance to meet Jean-Jacques Rousseau, who was also raised a Calvinist but adopted a much more generous view of religion, he told him bitterly that he had been taught to fear "the terrible being whom those about me called God."[3]

The Edinburgh of Boswell's youth was a city of 50,000 inhabitants, roughly one-fifteenth the size of London. In 1707 the Act of Union joined Scotland to England as the United Kingdom (the Union Jack flag combined the red cross of St. George for England and the white cross of Saint Andrew for Scotland). The Scots now elected members of Parliament to sit in Westminster, but political union was not matched by cultural unity. "Scotland even after the Union," a historian says, "remained largely another country, different substantially in its social thought, its legal system, its political and economic structure, its educational and religious institutions and principles." Boswell had a lifelong love affair with England and especially London, but he always cherished his national identity as a Scot.[4]

The adjective "Scotch," incidentally, began to fall out of favor during this period. David Hume used it in the first edition of his popular *History of Great Britain* in 1754, but changed it to "Scottish" in later revisions. Boswell never made the change. In the *Life of Johnson* he says that he would despise "any

Scotchman" who tried to lose his native accent completely, and English people who knew him confirmed that he never did lose his.[5]

Not only was Boswell a Scot, he very much looked forward to inheriting the estate and becoming its laird. As a boy he lived in Edinburgh but spent summers at Auchinleck. The old family house no longer exists; his father replaced it after he became the laird. An impressive granite mansion in the fashionable classical style was completed in 1762 (color plate 6).

What Boswell loved best at Auchinleck was the ruins of an old medieval castle (figure 11). His father's new mansion had three stories, with a grand staircase leading to the principal rooms on the second floor, including the master bedroom and a large library. On the top floor were five more bedrooms, one of which was James's, with a view of the castle ruins that he found romantic.[6]

Boswell once acknowledged, with considerable insight, "The honour of my family is perhaps a species of self-love." He was proud of "the French Boisville, our ancestor who came over with William the Conqueror," and prouder still of Thomas Boswell of Fife, whose charter as first Laird of

THE OLD HOUSE OF AUCHINLECK.

11. Castle ruins at Auchinleck

Auchinleck was confirmed in 1505, and who died fighting the English at Flodden Field in 1513. When James succeeded his father in 1782, he became the ninth Laird of Auchinleck. During his travels he happened to meet a gentleman who actually owned Flodden Field. Boswell wrote, "He promised me leave to erect on it a monument to my ancestor Thomas Boswell, who fell there." That never happened. He always cherished fantasies of presiding over his tenants as a much-loved country squire, but it was the status that appealed to him, not the actual life. When he did finally take possession he could barely stand to spend time there, greatly preferring Edinburgh and, when possible, London.[7]

At the age of six, young James was enrolled at a private academy in Edinburgh. In later life he enjoyed annual reunions at a tavern with his old schoolmates. "We have always a kind of curious merriment, the same jokes every time, and all are willing to be pleased." At thirteen he entered the University of Edinburgh, which was a normal age of matriculation at the time, and took classes off and on for the next six years. There he made several lasting friendships. The most important was with William Temple, an Englishman from Berwick-upon-Tweed in Northumberland, just a couple of miles south of the Scottish border. Temple would go on to become a clergyman, and throughout Boswell's life it was in letters to Temple that he revealed his feelings most frankly.[8]

One classmate neither of them thought much of was Henry Dundas, who would rise rapidly in national politics, and from whom Boswell would later seek patronage in vain. In middle age he and Temple "recollected Dundas when our companion at college, when we thought him much our inferior, and wondered at his great preferment." Boswell would never get over the idea that his native talents, rather than hard work, ought to be enough to get ahead in the world.[9]

Boswell didn't object to education, but he clearly felt that he was in this world to have fun. He learned to drink, though not yet to excess, and to spend countless social hours with friends. He could never resist showing off. "A shocking fault which I have," he wrote when still young, "is my sacrificing almost anything to a laugh, even myself." His playful humorousness was contagious, and always would be. A Scottish judge said much later, "It was impossible to look in his face without being moved by the comicality which always reigned upon it. He was one of those men whose very look is provocative of mirth." Another acquaintance said that amusing as his stories were when printed, they were even more so when he told them in company, "not only from the picturesque style of his conversational, or rather his convivial

diction, but still more from the humorous and somewhat whimsical seriousness of his face and manner."[10]

Something Boswell excelled at was mimicry, a gift that would stand him
in good stead when he was capturing the speaking style of Samuel Johnson.
He could convincingly assume the facial expressions, gestures, and vocal
idiosyncrasies of the people he was "taking off." At the age of twenty-two
he wrote after a social evening, "I was all spirit and entertained them prodigiously. I began this night to take off Mr. David Hume, which I did amaz-
ingly well. Indeed it was not an imitation but the very man. I had not only
his external address, but his sentiments and mode of expression."[11]

Still more important for Boswell's literary accomplishments, he was beginning to keep a journal and learning how to bring social encounters to life
on the page. He happened to meet a retired attorney at a dinner party, and
described him with crisp strokes: "He is precise, starched and proud. Wears a
dark brown coat, a buff vest and black breeches; has a lank iron countenance;
wears a weather-beaten scratch wig; sits erect upon his chair, and sings *Tarry
Woo* with the English accent." As it happens, this is one of the few songs that
Sir Walter Scott was willing to sing in company:

> Who'd be king, can ony tell,
> When a shepherd sings sae well?
> Sings sae well, and pays his due
> With honest heart and tarry woo.

("Tarry woo" was wool fouled with tar.) Boswell added, "We passed the evening very merrily—I was very facetious and took much." That is, he drank a lot.[12]

Boswell had a good voice and sang well. He was rightly proud of that, but
unfortunately he fancied himself a poet, and would publish doggerel poems
throughout his life. He thought his verses were extremely good; everyone else
thought they were terrible. Everyone was right. Some of them have been collected in a little volume called *Boswell's Book of Bad Verse,* which is putting it
generously.

One of these poems has an affectionate self-portrait that gives a good
sense of how Boswell liked to present himself socially:

> He talks with such ease and such grace
> That all charmed to attention we sit,
> And he sings with so comic a face
> That our sides are just ready to split.

It's characteristic that he imagines himself a member of the audience, thus joining in the applause for himself.[13]

Edinburgh had relaxed its former Calvinist prohibition of theater, and Boswell was enchanted with the imaginary world that gifted actors could create. He also identified intensely with an English performer named West Digges, who starred as the dashing highwayman hero in John Gay's *Beggar's Opera*. Going to the theater was a direct rebellion against his mother's values. The only time she entered a theater herself, she burst into tears.[14]

It came to Lord Auchinleck's attention that his son was turning into a playboy, known to be pursuing affairs with actresses, and he commanded James to leave Edinburgh and enroll in the University of Glasgow. That happened in 1759, when he was just turning nineteen.

Glasgow was a bustling commercial city, very different from the more sophisticated Edinburgh, and in the strictest Calvinist tradition theaters were not allowed. Boswell hated it there, and recalled it as "a place which I shall ever hold in contempt as being filled with a set of unmannerly, low-bred, narrow-minded wretches." Writing to a friend, his verses struck a sad note:

> Unhappy me! who in the bloom
> Of youth, must bear the heavy gloom
> Of a grief-clouded mind.[15]

The discipline at the university was rigorous, for faculty as well as students. Adam Smith taught philosophy and rhetoric (economics was not yet an academic subject) every single weekday from October to June, from 7:30 A.M. until 1:00 P.M., and spent the rest of the afternoon in tutorials with students, Boswell included. Smith was a dedicated teacher, and his students responded to him with warmth as well as respect. "His private character," Boswell wrote to a friend, "is really amiable. He has nothing of that formal stiffness and pedantry which is too often found in professors. So far from that, he is a most polite well-bred man, is extremely fond of having his students with him, and treats them with all the easiness and affability imaginable." Smith was not yet famous, though about to be; his *Theory of Moral Sentiments* was published in the same year that Boswell studied with him.[16]

After six months in Glasgow, Boswell did a daring thing. He absconded from the university and escaped to London, making the entire three-hundred-mile journey on horseback. Along the way he rode from Carlisle to London in two days and a half, an impressive feat. When he recounted this to some accomplished horsemen they cried out, "What, sir, upon the same horse?"

"No, gentlemen," he replied, "that would be no merit of mine. But I'll tell you what is better: it was upon the same bum."[17]

Once in London, Boswell toyed briefly with the idea of converting to Roman Catholicism. It appealed to him for its lavish ceremonials and its promise of forgiveness of sins. That would have been a shocking rebellion against his parents, as well as a fatal bar to professional advancement, but he soon got over it. Although he returned to the established church (paradoxically Presbyterian in Scotland, but Anglican in England), he favored relaxed religiosity not confined to any denomination. A few years later he told a Jesuit priest "that I took my faith from Jesus, that I endeavoured to adore God with fervency; that I found my devotion excited by grand worship, and that I was happy to worship in a Romish Church. I said my notions of God made me not fear him as cruel."[18]

In London, Boswell made a point of going to as many plays as he could. Audiences were demonstrative, and it may have been at this time (the date is unclear) that he was sitting in the pit at Drury Lane with a friend from Edinburgh, the clergyman Hugh Blair. "In a wild freak of youthful extravagance, I entertained the audience prodigiously by imitating the lowing of a cow." That was such a success that the audience cried out, "Encore the cow! Encore the cow!" Boswell then attempted various other animals, but with inferior effect. "My reverend friend, anxious for my fame, with an air of the utmost gravity and earnestness, addressed me thus: 'My dear Sir, I would confine myself to the cow.'"[19]

Ever the exhibitionist, Boswell couldn't resist telling this story much later in print, which inspired the caricaturist Thomas Rowlandson to illustrate it (figure 12). The spikes in the foreground were to discourage spectators from scrambling up on stage, as they were otherwise likely to do. Boswell liked to be as close to the stage as possible; on another occasion he mentions sitting "just at the spikes."[20]

It didn't take long for Lord Auchinleck to locate his renegade son, who was ordered home to Edinburgh. He didn't return to Glasgow and never took a degree (young Scottish gentlemen often didn't bother to). Instead he undertook private legal study—there were no law schools as such—with a promise that if he could pass an examination in civil law he would be allowed to return to London. After that he would be expected to pursue further studies in Holland, whose system was based on Roman law and was similar to Scottish law.

No journal by Boswell survives from this time, but there are enough scattered notes to confirm further intrigues with actresses, with an unidentified

12. Boswell mooing

lady of rank, and with a "curious young little pretty" who was probably a servant. That may have been Peggy Doig, about whom all that is known is that she bore Boswell two illegitimate children, a daughter and a son. After leaving Edinburgh he would stay in touch with Peggy and send her financial support. But as was dreadfully common in those days, both children died very young.[21]

THE HYPOCHONDRIACK

At the age of seventeen Boswell had suffered a frightening bout of depression. Another episode happened right after he returned from London, and twenty-five years later he still remembered vividly "that desperate melancholy which afflicted me in my twentieth and twenty-first years." The tendency to depression ran in his family. His grandfather suffered from it; so did his physician uncle John, whom he found much more congenial than his father; and so did a younger brother, also named John, who had to be confined for long periods in the home of a doctor.[22]

What made it worse was that Lord Auchinleck not only didn't suffer from depression himself, but had absolutely no sympathy for it. "It was irksome beyond measure," Boswell wrote after he finally got away, "to be a young laird in the house of a father much different from me, of a mind perfectly sound, and who thought that if I was not a man of business I was good for nothing." Thomas Carlyle, likewise a Scot, heard stories about Boswell's father and remarked, "Old Auchinleck had, if not the gay, tail-spreading vanity of his son, no little of the slow-stalking, contentious, hissing vanity of the gander."[23]

Melancholy and hypochondria were considered synonymous, and Boswell used both terms, sometimes referring to himself as feeling "hipped." After he got to know Johnson, he took it for granted that they must be victims of the same disorder, both of them "melancholic." But unlike Johnson, Boswell might wake up any morning in high spirits and enjoy a spell of elation that no theory yet addressed. What he suffered from was undoubtedly bipolar disorder, understood dimly if at all in those days.[24]

There is, however, a suggestive passage in the then-standard text on hypochondria, a treatise by George Cheyne called *The English Malady* (foreigners claimed that the English were peculiarly subject to it). After describing some common physical symptoms, Cheyne went on to psychological ones in terms that apply closely to Boswell's experience: "a deep and fixed melancholy, wandering and delusory images on the brain, and instability and unsettledness in all the intellectual operations, loss of memory, despondency, horror and despair. . . . sometimes unaccountable fits of laughing, apparent joy, leaping and dancing; at other times, of crying, grief, and anguish." That was indeed how the disorder manifested itself in Boswell's uncle John, of whom he was fond. Fifteen years later he wrote in his journal, "The Doctor was rather too flashy in his spirits, and showed symptoms of that unquiet temperament which is in our blood. But he and I were warmly affectionate."[25]

For the rest of his life Boswell would continue to ponder his condition, and from 1777 to 1783 he would publish a series of occasional essays, seventy in all, entitled *The Hypochondriack* (he favored a final "k," following the example of Johnson). There he described his condition insightfully:

It was once proposed to me as a difficult problem, by an elegant lady of good understanding but subject to hypochondria, how to account for that complaint, being sometimes most uneasy when one is to all appearance in the best health. My solution of this problem is that often when there are no visible symptoms of bodily disorder, the finer parts, the nerves, or the nervous fluid, or whatever is the exquisite seat of sensation and sensibility, may be hurt and fretted, of the effects of which, in variety of degrees, every person of any delicacy of feeling has had experience; or the mind may be sick, it may be "full of scorpions," or have a "pale cast of thought" altogether unconnected with the state of the body.

Macbeth says that his mind is full of scorpions, and Hamlet that his native resolution is "sicklied o'er with the pale cast of thought."[26]

It was assumed at the time that some sort of fluid must transmit impulses along the nerves, and as with the old humor theory, that mental disorders must have a physiological basis. The word "neurosis" has the same origin, and at the end of the nineteenth century it still meant any disorder of the nervous system, not necessarily manifested in mental illness. During periods of depression Boswell would often make comments such as "The nervous fluid was disordered." What seemed so baffling to him was that these episodes could happen even when his physical condition seemed excellent.[27]

FREE AT LAST

After passing the examination in civil law just before his twenty-second birthday, Boswell exultantly departed Edinburgh on November 15, 1762, following a farewell conversation with his parents. "They were very kind to me. I felt parental affection was very strong towards me, and I felt a very warm filial regard for them. The scene of being a son setting out from home for the wide world, and the idea of being my own master, pleased me much." The clichés are bland—"parental affection," "filial regard"—and Boswell probably wanted to feel those emotions more than he did feel them. But he certainly rejoiced in his role as a fairytale prince embarking on adventures. "Scene" still had a theatrical connotation, and he would always imagine his life in scenes.[28]

When the goodbyes were over he got into a chaise, a small carriage shared with one other passenger, "and away I went. As I passed the Cross [an ornamental structure with the city arms on top], the caddies and the chairmen bowed and seem to say, 'God prosper long our noble Boswell.'" That was a reminiscence of the old ballad of *Chevy Chase,* which begins "God prosper long our noble king." The caddies were porters, a word not confined to golf, and the chairmen were strong fellows who carried customers in sedan chairs. Boswell imagines them pausing in their labors to admire him going by.

Boswell asked the driver to stop so he could bow theatrically to the palace of Holyroodhouse and to Arthur's Seat, "that lofty romantic mountain on which I have so often strayed in my days of youth, indulged meditation, and felt the raptures of a soul filled with ideas of the magnificence of God and his creation." After congratulating himself on his warm imagination and his "genius for poetry," he got back in and the journey proceeded.[29]

The journey to London usually took five days or even six by coach, a mode of travel that Boswell loved. With his gregarious temperament, he enjoyed friendly conversation with strangers. Well-maintained turnpikes were just beginning to be established, however, and most roads were in appalling shape. A traveler a few years later called the ones in the north of England "detestable," and measured the ruts in one mucky road as four feet deep.[30]

Stagecoaches (figure 13), whose name comes from the practice of putting in fresh horses at each successive "stage," had no springs of any kind. Up to six passengers sat inside on a pair of benches. If more wanted to ride they could sit on top, which was unsafe as well as jolting, for half price. Boswell sometimes did.

On this occasion Boswell's traveling companion was "a jolly honest plain fellow" named Stewart, and they got on well, but the journey was not without

13. A stagecoach

incident. One of the wheels broke and forced a long delay in "a little dirty village" where there was nothing to drink but "thick muddy beer." Boswell never cared for beer. Three days after that there was a worse mishap when a runaway horse caused the vehicle to overturn. "We got a pretty severe rap. Stewart's head and my arm were somewhat hurt. However, we got up and pursued our way." No wonder that when London finally came into view, "I was all life and joy. . . . I gave three huzzas, and we went briskly in."[31]

After a few nights at an inn Boswell found lodgings with a civil servant in Downing Street, Westminster—"a genteel street, within a few steps of the Parade, near the House of Commons, and very healthful." That probably means there wasn't any sewage in the street. He didn't give a street address because there were none; those were just beginning to be assigned. One might imagine that he was a near neighbor of the prime minister, but not so. Though the official residence was indeed in Downing Street, it had fallen into disrepair and successive prime ministers preferred to live elsewhere. As for the house where Boswell stayed, it was demolished long ago.[32]

Lord Auchinleck allowed his son an allowance of £200 a year, and prudently had an agent dole it out in £25 installments every six weeks. Boswell generally ran through that pretty fast, and felt "elevated to a most extraordinary pitch" whenever he received the next payment. "Many a time did I lay the lovely shining pieces upon my table, count them over, put them in rank and file like the Guards, and place them in many different sorts of figures. In short, a boy at school could not be more childishly fond of sugar plums than I was of golden guineas." The government issued no paper money at that time, just coins. Banks issued their own notes, but metal money still felt more real than paper to most people.[33]

For £40 a year Boswell had a floor of the house to himself, with a sitting room as well as bedroom and a fireplace in each. And at this time he began keeping a remarkably detailed journal, giving vivid glimpses of what everyday life was like. On one occasion he sat up late and then accidentally put out his candle. "As my fire was long before that black and cold, I was in a great dilemma how to proceed." He tiptoed cautiously down to the kitchen and found "as little fire there as upon the icy mountains of Greenland." He knew that there must be a tinderbox somewhere ready for lighting a fire in the morning, but had no luck groping around for it. At that point he recalled that his landlord kept a pair of loaded pistols by his bed in case of disturbance, crept quietly back upstairs, and waited until he heard the night watchman outside calling "Past three o'clock." He called down to the man, who came to the door, and with his lantern got the candle re-lit. "Thus was I relieved, and continued busy till eight next day." At this time in his life it was not unusual for Boswell to stay up all night, with no apparent ill effects.[34]

Liberated from his father's authority, Boswell began to dream of a very different kind of career than the law. That was the reason he was glad to live close to the Horse Guards Parade, where they and the Foot Guards performed their drills (color plate 7). Officers, at least in certain regiments, were considered glamorous, like the cocky and flirtatious young men in Jane Austen's novels. Adam Smith wrote, "We are led by custom to annex the character of gaiety, levity, and sprightly freedom to the military profession."[35]

A satiric piece in the *Gentleman's Magazine* confirms what Boswell found so attractive:

Q. What is the duty and business of an officer?
A. In time of peace, to saunter from tavern to tavern, and from coffeehouse to coffeehouse; from court to the play, and from the play to the bagnio; from the bagnio to Vauxhall, thence to Ranelagh, and from that to Hyde Park.

Vauxhall and Ranelagh were popular pleasure gardens, convenient for picking up women. If war should come, of course, the officer would have other duties: "to stand patiently as a mark to be shot at, till he is bid to move, and then to kill as many people (whose faces he never saw before) as he possibly can."[36]

Boswell had no appetite whatever for duties like that. At dinner one evening an officer, lately returned from the Seven Years War, "talked of battles and dreadful wounds, which made us shudder. Really, these things are not to be talked of, for in cool blood they shock one prodigiously." The Foot Guards were assigned to the capital and never sent abroad to fight.[37]

The normal way to get a commission was to pay for it, but Boswell knew his father would never consider that. The alternative was to curry favor with some highly placed patron. With this in view, he began to pay court persistently to Lady Northumberland, who gave lavish entertainments in Northumberland House at Charing Cross. She liked him, but what he could never grasp was that neither she nor any other highly placed person was prepared to act against the known wishes of Lord Auchinleck.

To present himself there, Boswell outfitted himself splendidly. As he commented years later, "A man's dress is really a considerable part of him, both in his own idea and in that of others." He also said, "Dress affects my feelings as irresistibly as music." Gentlemen were peacocks. It was not until the 1790s, a historian says, that "the great male renunciation of lace, silk and color" suddenly took place. Lace was favored as a sign of affluence. Johnson, though always careless about his own dress, once commented, "Greek, Sir, is like lace; every man gets as much of it as he can."[38]

Shortly after he arrived in London, Boswell acquired "a genteel violet-coloured frock suit," which would have been made to order by a tailor. When he was preparing to pay his first call at Northumberland House he was tempted to buy "rich laced clothes," but in the end dressed relatively modestly: "I commanded my inclination, and got just a plain suit of a pink colour, with a gold button." Although on a tight budget, he always paid attention to his appearance. "I have my hair dressed every day, which gives me an idea of being well. I have an excellent hairdresser. His name is Chetwynd. He lives just opposite to me. He is a genteel chatty fellow, like the generality of his profession."[39]

As the months went by Boswell couldn't bear to give up his dream of the Guards, and began to feel resentment against Lady Northumberland for her inaction. "O these Great People! They are a sad set of beings. This woman who seemed to be so cordially my friend and promised me her good offices so strongly is, I fear, a fallacious hussy." To a friend he nevertheless wrote hopefully, "Surely I am a man of genius. I deserve to be taken notice of. O that my grandchildren might read this character of me: 'James Boswell, a most amiable man. He improved and beautified his paternal estate of Auchinleck; made a distinguished figure in parliament; had the honour to command a regiment of Foot Guards; and was one of the brightest wits in the court of George the Third.'"[40]

Fate would not be so kind. Boswell did get to improve the estate, although driving it deeply into debt, but despite lifelong attempts he never managed to get into Parliament, and joining the Foot Guards was nothing more than a pipe dream. As for being "one of the brightest wits," even when the *Life of Johnson* became a great success near the end of his life, few of his contemporaries would have ranked him like that. More accurately prophetic was what he wrote as he contemplated the prospect of a career in the law: "I considered that I would at once embark myself for all my life in a labyrinth of care, and that my mind would be harassed with vexation."[41]

Meanwhile, Boswell concentrated on enjoying himself. He reconnected with some friends from his first London visit, three of whom were Scots. The Honorable Andrew Erskine was his own age and has been described aptly as

"a poet with a minor talent (though considerably greater than Boswell's)."
One evening "Erskine and I walked down the Haymarket together, throwing
out sallies and laughing loud. 'Erskine,' said I, 'don't I make your existence
pass more cleverly than anybody?' 'Yes, you do.' 'Don't I make you say more
good things?' 'Yes. You extract more out of me, you are more chemical to me
than anybody.'"[42]

Another friend was George Dempster, thirty years old and a member of
Parliament. In England Boswell always felt uneasy about his Scottishness; he
was afraid of seeming rustic and provincial. On one occasion Erskine and
Dempster annoyed him with their "Scotch tones and rough and roaring freedom of manners." He told them solemnly that he intended to "get rid of folly
and to acquire sensible habits," to which their reaction was succinct. "They
laughed."[43]

The third Scot was the Earl of Eglinton, who had succeeded to the peerage at the age of six and was now almost forty. A bachelor playboy, he was well
connected in politics, and Boswell clearly hoped to get a boost himself
through his friend. At one point Eglinton did see a possibility of getting him
a commission in a regiment stationed abroad, but Boswell explained that that
would never do. "I assure you, my Lord, that my meaning was this: my great
plan in getting into the Guards was not so much to be a soldier as to be in the
genteel character of a gentleman." Irritated, Eglinton replied, "Indeed, Jamie,
I did not understand you so." It's notable that he always called Boswell "Jamie" and Boswell always called him "my Lord."[44]

Eglinton found Boswell an amusing companion, but not necessarily an
impressive one. When Boswell first went to see him after arriving in London,
he said that he had acquired much composure and wisdom since his first time
there. "'My Lord,' said I, 'I am now a little wiser.' 'Not so much as you think,'
said he." Later on Eglinton gave a characterization that Boswell had to admit
was accurate: "Jamie, you have a light head, but a damned heavy arse; and to
be sure, such a man will run easily downhill, but it would be severe work to
get him up." Boswell commented in his journal, "This illustration is very
fine. For I do take lively projects into my head, but as to the execution, there
I am tardy."[45]

In addition to these men about town, Boswell resumed a friendship with
someone he had known previously in Edinburgh. This was Thomas Sheridan,
in his early forties, an Irishman who had written an excellent biography of his
godfather, Jonathan Swift. Sheridan managed a theater in Dublin for a while,
and when that failed he became an actor in London (figure 14) and a teacher

of elocution, in which capacity Boswell had studied with him in Edinburgh. Nowadays the term "elocution" has a quaint flavor of nineteenth-century oratory. What Sheridan really was, a commentator says, was a combination of speech therapist, dialogue coach, theatrical director, specialist in accents, and public speaking consultant. Scots with aspirations in England were anxious to get rid of their regional accent, though it was odd to be taught to do it by someone who never lost his Irish brogue. A book of Sheridan's on public speaking was very widely read, for example by Thomas Jefferson.[46]

Sheridan had an interesting wife, Frances, whom Boswell later described as "sensible, ingenious, unassuming, yet communicative." She was best known for her novel *Memoirs of Miss Sidney Biddulph,* in which a virtuous young woman and her devoted lover are constantly thwarted by fate, impelling her after his suicide to accept the mysterious ways of divine providence. Johnson paid her a teasing compliment: "I know not, Madam, that you have a right upon moral principles to make your readers suffer so much." She would go on to have several plays produced by Garrick at Drury Lane. Their youngest son, twelve years old at the time, was a boarding student at Harrow School, and although Boswell had no reason to think much about it, he met the boy in passing. That was Richard Brinsley Sheridan, who would become a brilliant playwright himself and a member of the Club.[47]

14. Thomas Sheridan as Brutus

BOSWELL'S LONDON

As it still is today, central London was very walkable, and Boswell walked everywhere unless he needed to transport heavy belongings, in which case he would hire a hackney coach. Only the wealthy traveled in sedan chairs, borne by two men and shielded from the weather by windows and a roof. Only the extremely wealthy had horses and carriages of their own.

The map (figure 15) provides a virtual walk through Boswell's London, and it shows many sites that will figure significantly in this book. The only one of importance to him that is not shown here would be further to the east, St. Paul's Cathedral, two miles away from Downing Street. In St. Paul's Churchyard he frequented Child's coffeehouse, mainly because "Mr. Spectator" used to overhear conversations there. "It is quite a place to my mind," he wrote in his journal, "dusky, comfortable, and warm, with a society of citizens and physicians who talk politics very fully, and are very sagacious and sometimes jocular."[48]

With the popular *Spectator* essays as his model, Boswell tried his hand at recording little scraps of dialogue:

> CITIZEN. Pray, Doctor, what became of that patient of yours? Was not her skull fractured?
> PHYSICIAN. Yes. To pieces. However, I got her cured.
> CITIZEN. Good Lord.[49]

He was called a "citizen" because the financial district around St. Paul's was known (and still is) as the City with a capital C, and its coffeehouses were a major locale for business transactions. Jonathan's in Exchange Alley served as the original unofficial stock market, and Lloyd's offered shipping and insurance services, the predecessor of Lloyd's of London.

Near the top of the map is Lincoln's Inn, the most famous of the Inns of Court where lawyers received their qualification to practice, as Boswell himself would do much later when he decided to try for the English bar. He often went for a stroll in nearby Lincoln's Inn Fields, and in the 1780s would rent a house in Great Queen Street a little to the west.

Clustered below Lincoln's Inn is a whole group of sites that are significant in this story. Since 1760 Johnson had been living at the Temple, another Inn of Court that accepted nonlawyers as residents. Boswell would stay there himself after he quarreled with his landlord and left Downing Street. The Black Lion Inn—an actual inn—is where he first stayed after arriving in London. Later on he would take an actress whom he called Louisa there for a

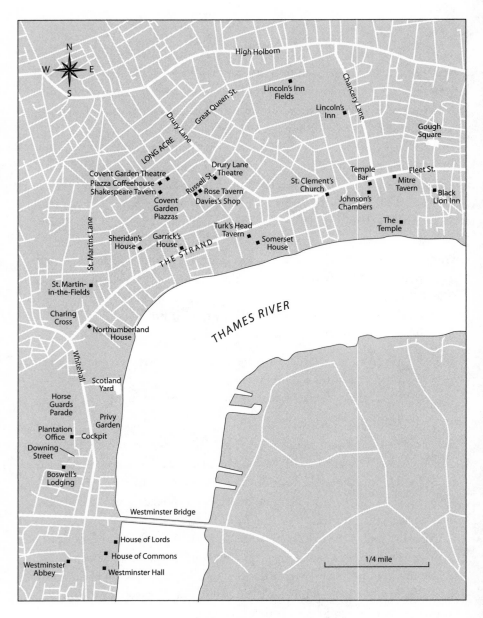

15. Boswell's London

memorable assignation. Just above it, the Mitre Tavern would become Boswell's favorite place for spending time with Johnson. And above that, on the other side of Fleet Street, is Gough Square, where Johnson had compiled his *Dictionary* a decade previously.

There were many things to see in or close to Fleet Street, and Boswell took in several of them during his London stay. One afternoon "I went and saw Mrs. Salmon's famous waxwork in Fleet Street. It is excellent in its kind, and amused me very well for a quarter of an hour" (figure 16). Among the displays were Antony and Cleopatra with their two children, King Charles I on the scaffold, Canaanite women offering their children in sacrifice to the god Moloch, and the seraglio of the Turkish sultan.[50]

Just off Fleet Street was a more disturbing site that Boswell visited one chilly December day. Reflecting that the English were proverbially beef eaters and cruel, he decided to act like "a true-born Old Englishman," starting with a hearty meal at a beefsteak house. For a shilling he got beef, bread, and beer, with a penny left over to tip the waiter. Then, to experience cruelty, he went to the Cockpit, where the birds, "armed with silver heels, are set down and fight with amazing bitterness and resolution. Some of them were quickly dispatched. One pair fought three quarters of an hour. The uproar and noise of betting is prodigious. A great deal of money made a very quick circulation

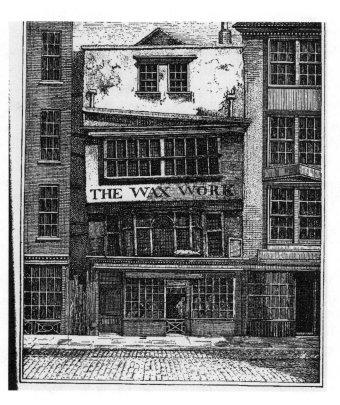

16. The Waxwork

from hand to hand." Boswell added, "I was sorry for the poor cocks. I looked round to see if any of the spectators pitied them when mangled and torn in a most cruel manner, but I could not observe the smallest relenting sign in any countenance."[51]

Proceeding westward, we come to the Turk's Head Tavern, where the Club would begin to meet the following year. Along the Strand, near the river, are the lodgings of Garrick and Sheridan, and also Somerset House where Joshua Reynolds's Royal Society would later hold its annual exhibitions.

Moving northward now, we arrive at two sites of tremendous importance to Boswell. The little bookshop of Thomas Davies is where he would at last meet Johnson in May of 1763, after trying for months to get an introduction. Just to the west of that is the celebrated Covent Garden, where he would regularly go for a good time. It became his favorite place in all of London.

Artists loved to depict Covent Garden. A placid and spacious view was painted by Balthasar Nebot around 1750, looking westward toward the classical façade of St. Paul's Church, which had been designed by Inigo Jones and completed in 1633 (color plate 8). The church is still there today, but not the column, which was taken down in 1790. At the left are market stalls filled with vegetables, brought in fresh from the countryside early every morning.

Much less tranquil is an engraving made later in the century by Thomas Rowlandson, showing the same scene during an election campaign (color plate 9). In front of the church a hustings for speeches has been erected— that's literally what a hustings was—and since naval officers often represented the Westminster constituency, sailors are carrying their candidate aloft in a boat, while people look down from the windows above. The banners are labeled with churches in the constituency that identified localities: St. Margaret's, Westminster, and St. Martin-in-the-Fields. Coal smoke is puffing from chimneys; that was how London buildings were heated, when they were heated at all.

One more scene, not jolly at all: the first of Hogarth's *Four Times of Day* series, entitled *Morning* (figure 17). A clock on the church pediment indicates that it's eight o'clock. Directly in front of the church, with smoke emerging from a chimney, a sign over the door identifies Tom King's Coffee House. King was an Eton graduate who got kicked out of King's College, Cambridge for misbehavior; his wife Moll was the daughter of a woman who kept a Covent Garden fruit and vegetable stall. Around 1720 they opened their coffeehouse in the shack shown in Hogarth's picture; the artist often dropped in there and sketched their patrons. They had a son, also named Thomas, who

17. Hogarth, *Morning*

would become a leading actor for Garrick and Sheridan, and we will meet him later on.

Inside the shack a fight has broken out; there was plenty of liquor available in addition to coffee. Swords are being brandished, and a wig is flying out the door. In the foreground a pair of gallants are fondling mildly interested prostitutes, while a woman tries to warm her hands over a fire. Meanwhile another woman holds up her hands imploringly to an imperious lady, on her way to church and paying no attention whatsoever.

In an observant commentary on this picture, an eighteenth-century visitor from Germany named Georg Christoph Lichtenberg noted, "The impressions in the foreground [just below the lady's dress] come from the iron mounting of small wooden shoes (pattens) which were then worn by the female population, and enabled them to glide a few inches above the mud of the streets. The clatter made by these little horseshoes on the London pavements is by no means disagreeable to a stranger's ear, especially since —as is mostly the case—the pedestrians are pretty." He adds that while the stern lady is putting on a show of piety, "beauty spots float about her gleaming eye like midges round a candle flame," and she carries a fashionable fan altogether unnecessary in the cold. Her youthful servant "wears slippers only; his feet are frozen anyway." The Hogarth specialist Ronald Paulson notes the contrast between the cold classical church and "the makeshift man-made hulk of Tom King's Tavern," and suggests that Hogarth is taking sides with the revelers against the church.[52]

Returning to the map and reading from west to east, we see a cluster of sites surrounding Covent Garden. The magnet for Boswell and many others was the Covent Garden Theatre at the northeast corner, where David Garrick starred before he became manager at Drury Lane close by. Soon after arriving in London Boswell went to see a comic opera, and was outraged at what happened when a couple of officers from a Scottish Highlands Regiment came in. "The mob in the upper gallery roared out, 'No Scots! No Scots! Out with them!,' hissed and pelted them with apples. My heart warmed to my countrymen, my Scotch blood boiled with indignation. I jumped up on the benches and roared out, 'Damn you, you rascals!,' hissed, and was in the greatest rage." Resentment against the Scots reflected indignation that many of them had supported Bonnie Prince Charlie in his failed attempt in 1745 to recover the English throne. The implications of that rebellion would be a frequent topic of conversation when Johnson and Boswell traveled together in Scotland in 1773.[53]

For many visitors, theater was not the only attraction at Covent Garden. The magistrate Sir John Fielding, Henry Fielding's brother, presided at the nearby Bow Street court, and described the district as "the great square of Venus." Sir John Hawkins said disapprovingly, "A playhouse, and the regions about it, are the very hotbeds of vice; how else comes it to pass that no sooner is a playhouse opened in any part of the kingdom, then it becomes surrounded by an halo of brothels?" In his capacity as magistrate at a different court Hawkins once tried a case concerning a riot in a so-called coffeehouse that was in truth "a house of lewd resort." He was especially shocked to find that the madam affected Quaker dress, "a sect who are known to discountenance vice and immorality, and even to expel from their society all persons of scandalous lives. I reproved her for her course of life and exhorted her to quit it, but could not perceive that my words made any impression on her." Hawkins was a good friend of Johnson's and a founding member of the Club.[54]

Drury Lane had been disreputable for a very long time. Historians of the language derive its name from the Middle English *druwery*, defined in the *OED* as "sexual love, lovemaking, courtship; often, illicit love, amour." In Chaucer it still had a positive spin: "Of ladies love and druerie / Anon I wol you tell." In the eighteenth century one name for syphilis was "Drury Lane ague."[55]

18. The Muffin Man

The original significance of the song "O do you know the muffin man" is obscure, but it may well be relevant that "he lives in Drury Lane." In Fielding's *Tom Jones* Sophia Western's muff has the same suggestive meaning that it does today: "Cupid, who lay in her muff, suddenly crept out." However, there were actual street vendors selling muffins, and one of them is shown in a popular series called *Twelve London Cries Done from the Life* (figure 18). At the open window two elegant ladies are being served tea. Perhaps he's scowling because they have refused his wares?[56]

Close by, in the Covent Garden piazzas, the Shakespeare Head Tavern was a headquarters for prostitution; in the next chapter we will see Boswell enjoying himself there. Adjoining that tavern was a notorious brothel run by "Mother Douglas," described by one of her customers as "a great, flabby, fat, stinking, swearing, hallowing, ranting Billingsgate bawd, very well known to most men of quality and distinction in these kingdoms."[57]

Returning one last time to the map, the official world of court and politics is located at the bottom, where Boswell had his lodgings. As he noted with satisfaction, Downing Street was close to the Horse Guards Parade. Just below that are the Parliament buildings, Westminster Abbey, and Westminster Bridge. At the time it was quite a novelty, only the second bridge over the Thames, completed as recently as 1750. The other was the old London Bridge, off to the east beyond the coverage of this map. Since the two bridges were so far apart, the usual way to cross the river was to hire a waterman with a rowboat.

CHAPTER 4

Boswell before Johnson

THE SEARCH FOR SELF

THE EXTRAORDINARY JOURNALS

We know little about Johnson's inner life when he was his early twenties. About Boswell's we know a very great deal, because he was deeply interested in it himself, and because he now began to write about it nearly every day. He had experimented with keeping a journal earlier, which was by no means a common practice. There did exist a tradition of journals with a religious theme, but few straightforward records of everyday experience. Samuel Pepys's diary is an obvious exception, but although written in the 1660s, it wasn't published until its cryptic code was cracked in the nineteenth century. The journal Boswell now kept in London covered eight months and filled seven hundred manuscript pages, with extraordinary richness of detail.

The story has often been told how Boswell's papers were believed to be lost until they unexpectedly turned up, in the early twentieth century, in a castle in Ireland where descendants of his were living. A wealthy American collector talked the owners into selling him the entire mass of material, though not before they had torn out whole swatches that they considered embarrassing. He in turn sold them to Yale University, and ever since then they have been receiving expert editorial attention in what became known as the Boswell factory. Reviewing one volume in the series forty years ago, John Updike said, "The expenditure of human time and intelligence has been on the scale of Talmudic commentary."[1]

The first volume (by now there are thirteen) was published in 1951 as *Boswell's London Journal,* edited by Frederick Pottle, who was the head of the factory and would later publish an engrossing biography of Boswell. It was at the top of the *New York Times* bestseller list for a couple of months, was offered as a dividend by the Book of the Month Club, and was the subject of a feature article in *Life* magazine entitled "Meet Mr. Boswell. He Is Fun to Know, and He Is Good for What Ails Us Now." What made him good for Americans in 1951 was his "sunny world, all laced coats and powdered hair," comforting when everyone was dreading the hydrogen bomb. President Truman took the book with him as vacation reading. Above all, though, it was popular because it was astonishingly frank about sex.

An important purpose of the journal was simply to produce an ongoing record of life as Boswell lived it: "In this way I shall preserve many things that would otherwise be lost in oblivion." During a period when he was confined by illness he lamented, "What will now become of my journal for some time? It must be a barren desert, a mere blank." And a couple of weeks later, "Nothing worth putting into my journal occurred this day. It passed away imperceptibly, like the whole life of many a human existence." On the other hand, it was easy to feel that the thing was becoming a burden—"my lagging journal, which, like a stone to be rolled up the hill, must be kept constantly going." But not bothering to write things down was distressing too. "I am fallen sadly behind in my journal," he later wrote; "I should live no more than I can record, as one should not have more corn growing than one can get in."[2]

In hindsight we can see what Boswell couldn't yet know, that in writing the journal he had found his true vocation, in the old sense of a calling. A career is a climb up the ladder of success, and he was reluctantly accepting the law as his career. He would never get further than a couple of rungs up that ladder. A vocation is chosen for its own sake. He once commented that for him, writing and drinking were both addictive. "One goes on imperceptibly, without knowing where to stop."[3]

Of crucial importance was the commitment to veracity that Boswell said his father had thrashed into him. All his life he wrote down notes, if not full narratives, as soon after an event as possible. Otherwise, "one may gradually recede from the fact till all is fiction." A modern critic has coined a term for the result: "the fact imagined." In an early journal Boswell found an apt metaphor for the telling details he wanted to preserve: "In description we omit insensibly many little touches which give life to objects. With how small a speck does a painter give life to an eye!"[4]

THE INTERIOR QUEST

What Boswell wanted above all was to establish a consistent character, reliably the same at all times, and to be admired for his stability. "I have discovered," he wrote hopefully soon after arriving in London, "that we may be in some degree whatever character we choose." But as he had to admit a few years later, "I am truly a composition of many opposite qualities." Pottle calls him "an unfinished soul."[5]

One problem was that Boswell could never resist being the life of the party, inviting companions to laugh at him as much as with him. "I was, in short, a character very different from what God intended me and I myself chose." If only he could be certain what God meant him to be, and then be it!

Settling down in London, he took a stab at defining what his ideal character might be.

> Now, when my father at last put me into an independent situation, I felt my mind regain its native dignity. I felt strong dispositions to be a Mr. Addison. Indeed, I had accustomed myself so much to laugh at everything that it required time to render my imagination solid, and give me just notions of real life and of religion. But I hoped by degrees to attain some degree of propriety. Mr. Addison's character and sentiment, mixed with a little of the gaiety of Sir Richard Steele and the manners of Mr. Digges, were the ideas which I aim to realize [i.e., make real].[6]

This is touchingly earnest, and touchingly confused. "Native dignity" was just what Boswell never had. All his life he would keep reminding himself in vain to be *retenu*—restrained and reserved. And what a curious set of role models! Collectively Addison and Steele were "Mr. Spectator," an amused, detached persona very different from the authors themselves. Steele was gregarious, had been a cavalry officer, and had fought duels. The real-life Mr. Addison was pathologically recessive, and wrote in the very first *Spectator,* "The greatest pain I can suffer is being talked to, and being stared at." Boswell liked nothing better than being talked to and stared at.

As for West Digges, that was the dashing actor he had known in Edinburgh, irresistible to women and the embodiment of the romantic highwayman Macheath in *The Beggar's Opera.* Boswell was often inclined to identify with Macheath.

Rather than thinking in terms of character, what Boswell really needed was a concept of personality, which no one had formulated yet. In Johnson's

Dictionary "personality" means merely "the existence or individuality of any-one," that is, one individual person as distinguished from another, not a clus-ter of unique characteristics. A character was expected to be consistent; a personality may seem startlingly inconsistent, and yet have a deeper unity underneath the contradictions. Boswell sensed that in himself but didn't know how to articulate it.

At this time in Western culture, a major divergence in styles of self-presentation was much in the foreground. To adopt a contrast from classical rhetoric, it was a struggle between *homo seriosus* and *homo rhetoricus.* Serious man—and serious woman—has a core of authentic self, and uses language to communicate truth. Rhetorical man exists in society, takes coloration from it, and knows who he or she is not by introspection but by feedback from other people. Language becomes a game, playfully exploited to entertain or per-suade, but not to express a "truth" that may not even exist.[7]

Boswell wanted very much to believe in an authentic core of self. Yet he was freest, happiest, and in a real sense most fully himself when he was per-forming and improvising.

We don't know when Boswell first read Hume's 1739 *Treatise of Human Nature,* but since he had been taught by Hume's close friend Smith, he may well have picked up something about it by this time. In a section entitled "Of Personal Identity," Hume declares that the only consciousness of our selves we can ever have is of the stream of sense impressions that the mind processes from moment to moment. "When I enter most intimately into what I call *myself,* I always stumble on some particular perception or other, of heat or cold, light or shade, love or hatred, pain or pleasure. I never can catch *myself* at any time without a perception, and never can observe anything but the perception."

Something must organize those impressions, no doubt, but Hume ac-knowledged frankly that he had no idea what it might be. It follows that a person is "nothing but a bundle or collection of different perceptions, which succeed each other with an inconceivable rapidity, and are in a perpetual flux and movement." In one of his later journals Boswell said the same thing: "Man's continuation of existence is a flux of ideas in the same body, like the flux of a river in the same channel." That certainly sounds like *homo rhetoricus.*[8]

Hume drew a further conclusion. Attempting to know the self through introspection is not only fruitless, but may lead to alarming anxieties. The so-lution is to stop trying. "I dine, I play a game of backgammon, I converse, and am merry with my friends; and when after three or four hours' amusement, I would return to these speculations, they appear so cold, and strained, and ridiculous, that I cannot find in my heart to enter into them any farther. Here then I find myself absolutely and necessarily determined to live, and talk, and act like other people in the common affairs of life."

One of Hume's critics objected sarcastically that in that case, "a succession of ideas and impressions may eat, and drink, and be merry." Hume, who loved to eat and drink, would have seen nothing wrong with that. We may not know the meaning of life, but we do know how to live it.[9]

There is still another way in which Hume's view of experience would be attractive to Boswell. Johnson's *Rambler* essays are full of warnings against yielding to emotion, together with injunctions to keep "reason" firmly in command. Hume's *Treatise* was a head-on challenge to that kind of ethical psychology: "Reason is, and ought to be, the slave of the passions, and can never pretend to any other office than to serve and obey them." As a young man Hume had been raised, like Boswell, in a stern Presbyterian faith, but he became a skeptical agnostic and virtually an atheist.[10]

By "passion" Hume and others were beginning to mean what they called "feeling" and we would call emotion: instinctual responses to the demands of living. In effect passion was being decriminalized and made a constructive part of existence.

Still, if Hume's account of the self might have made a lot of sense to Boswell, there are aspects of it that would not. It was no problem for Hume to let reason be the slave of the passions, because his own passions were mild. He said so himself, in a little sketch called "My Own Life" written when he knew he was dying of cancer. "I was, I say, a man of mild dispositions, of command of temper, of an open, social, and cheerful humour, capable of attachment but little susceptible of enmity, and of great moderation in all my passions." Boswell's passions were greatly immoderate.[11]

Hume liked to take a social glass; Boswell got drunk—in later years appallingly drunk. Hume seems to have had little if any sex life; Boswell compulsively picked up prostitutes and felt bad about it afterward. He needed something more than Hume's flux: he needed to construct a stable character on the Johnsonian model. Soon he would encounter Johnson in person, and would enlist him as a mentor.

It seems clear from Boswell's journals that he felt most alive—most *himself*—when he was simply relishing the present moment, not trying to understand or explain it. One such experience occurs during a chilly December evening, and we need to remember how bitterly cold it could be in London when the temperature indoors was much the same as outdoors. "It is inconceivable with what attention and spirit I manage all my concerns. I sat in all this evening calm and indulgent. I had a fire in both my rooms above stairs. I drank tea by myself for a long time. I had my feet washed with milk-warm water, I had my bed warmed, and went to sleep soft and contented." Not just one fire, when coal was expensive, but two. Not just warm water, but "milk-warm water," as if fresh from the cow. And finally, the sensual delight of feeling "soft and contented." That is what Rousseau would soon theorize as *le sentiment de l'existence,* the sensation of simply being, complete in the moment.[12]

It's worth pausing to note one element in this charming picture that Boswell fails to fill in. Who washed his feet for him? In eighteenth-century writing servants are taken so much for granted that they are usually invisible. Probably it was a maid who took care of the household and whom Boswell mentions a couple of months later: "At eight in the morning Molly lights the fire, sweeps and dresses my dining room. Then she calls me up and lets me know what o'clock it is. I lie some time in bed indulging indolence." While he is lolling there, "the maid lays a milk-white napkin upon the table and sets the things for breakfast."

Molly turns up again a month after that when Boswell stays out drinking until long after midnight, and finds the house locked when he returns. In those days it was customary to have one single key for a house, making it less likely that servants could get copies made and share them with the wrong people. "We did not part till near three, to the severe mortification of Maid Molly, who was obliged to sit up for me. Poor being!" Boswell may have been sorry, but he clearly thought it was simply her job.[13]

A FINE SWORD AND A BAD POEM

Various psychoanalytic interpretations of Boswell have been advanced, but they tend to bog down in such concepts as "diffused ego," "substitute formations," and "symbolic castration." Some less technical concepts do give valuable perspectives that Boswell couldn't have had. It makes obvious sense to say that he was always searching for father figures, and likewise that he was more than commonly narcissistic. Johnson would soon accept the role of surrogate father. As for the narcissism, there is a memorable example of it when Boswell decides to buy a sword. That was a necessary appurtenance for a gentleman, whether or not he knew how to use it; the diminutive Alexander Pope had one at his side that was not much bigger than a steak knife.

Accordingly, Boswell called on "Mr. Jefferys, sword-cutter to his Majesty"—not just any swordsmith, but the one patronized by the king—and picked out one with a hefty price of five guineas. "I determined to make a trial of the civility of my fellow-creatures, and what effect my external appearance and address would have. . . . 'Mr. Jefferys,' said I, 'I have not money here to pay for it. Will you trust me?' 'Upon my word, Sir,' said he, 'you must excuse me. It is a thing we never do to a stranger.' I bowed genteelly and said, 'Indeed, Sir, I believe it is not right.' However, I stood and looked at him, and he looked at me. 'Come, Sir,' cried he, 'I will trust you.' "[14]

This little scene reflects a complex collection of motives. There is game-playing and gambling: can I get away with it? It would be humiliating to fail. There is staginess, creating a little drama and encouraging the shopkeeper to accept his role. There is an element of class consciousness: I am a gentleman and therefore must be trusted. And then there is narcissism. The often boastful and blustering Boswell was threatened by profound insecurity, and a narcissist seeks confirmation of his insecure self-worth by provoking positive responses from other people. "I stood and looked at him, and he looked at me." The test was a success.

Conversely, negative criticism could wound Boswell to the quick. Thomas Sheridan's wife Frances was readying a play called *Elvira* for performance, and Boswell offered to write the verse prologue that one of the actors would deliver. He proudly presented it to the Sheridans and awaited the verdict. It was crushing.

> SHERIDAN. It is weighed in the balances and found light.
> BOSWELL. What, is not good?
> SHERIDAN. Indeed, I think it is very bad.

When Boswell asked for clarification, Sheridan pointed out the faults of the piece "with an insolent bitterness and a clumsy ridicule that hurt me much." Earlier in the journal Boswell had remarked, "I am hurt with the taunts of ridicule, and am unsatisfied if I do not feel myself something of a superior animal."[15]

To cheer himself up, Boswell hastened to Lady Northumberland's, where she and her friends quickly understood what he needed. "I told them my lamentable story. They were really angry, and sympathized with my vexation. I repeated my prologue, which they thought very good; and I repeated Sheridan's criticisms, which they thought were dull and stupid, and declared they always thought him a dull fellow. This had a most pleasing effect and put me again into good humour, although a little of my former uneasiness still remained." Of course they said the prologue was good. What else were they going to say?

Six weeks later *Elvira* opened, and Boswell was pleased to find that it was mediocre. His friend Dempster suggested that they boo, but he felt obliged to be quiet, "as it would look like revenge for refusing my prologue." A few days after that Boswell did get his revenge on Sheridan. "I repeated to him many severe taunts on his wife's comedy, but with so smiling a countenance that he could not show any anger. I must remark that I have a most particular art of nettling people without seeming to intend it. I seldom make use of it, but have found it very useful."[16]

Boswell's ingenuous vanity was a defense against self-doubt, and his social merriment was an escape from the threat of depression. The modern playwright Moss Hart could have been describing Boswell when he said that many an actor begins with an unhappy childhood and then discovers "that his secret goal is attainable—to be himself and yet be somebody else, and in the very act of doing so, to be loved and admired."[17]

The bouts of depression are only occasionally visible in the *London Journal,* but they show up enough to confirm that the bipolar swings continued. One winter night he wrote, "I was very low spirited and had the most dreary and discontented imaginations. All things looked black. I thought I should never be well again. I could encourage no prospect in life." Yet a week later, "this afternoon I was very high-spirited and full of ambition." Two months after that he wrote to his friend Temple, "Melancholy clouds my mind, I know not for what. But I resemble a room where somebody has by accident snuffed out the candles." Temple replied teasingly but unhelpfully, "*My* spirits are so high, and I know not for what, that I am unable to express myself. I resemble a dark room suddenly lighted up with wax tapers."[18]

One of Boswell's comments in the *London Journal* shows exceptional insight: "I am rather passive than active in life. It is difficult to make my feeling clearly understood. I may say, I act passively. That is, not with my whole heart, and thinking this or that of real consequence, but because so and so things are established and I must submit." That is what twentieth-century existentialists would call *mauvaise foi,* bad faith or inauthenticity: going through the motions mechanically because other people expect us to. Boswell added, "It is very difficult to be keen about a thing which in reality you do not regard, and consider as imaginary." All his life he would yearn for worldly success, and yet retain this sense of its ultimate hollowness.[19]

Years later Boswell elaborated these ideas impressively in his essay collection *The Hypochondriack,* describing himself in the third person: "He is distracted between indolence and shame. Every kind of labour is irksome to him. Yet he has not resolution to cease from his accustomed tasks. Though he reasons within himself that contempt is nothing, the habitual current of his feelings obliges him to shun being despised. He acts therefore like a slave, not animated by inclination but goaded by fear." Guilt is the self-punishment of conscience; shame is the dread of being found out by other people.[20]

DEATH

With the arrival of spring in 1763, Boswell yielded to morbid curiosity in a way that would be repeated throughout his life. He went to see a public hanging at Tyburn, the gallows that stood near where Marble Arch is today. As a boy he had devoured sensational *Lives of the Convicts,* and now "I had a sort of horrid eagerness to be there."

To prepare himself, he visited Newgate prison the previous day and met the condemned man, a young highwayman named Paul Lewis. "He was just a Macheath. He was dressed in a white coat and blue silk vest and silver, with his hair neatly queued and a silver-laced hat, smartly cocked. . . . He walked firmly and with a good air, with his chains rattling upon him, to the chapel." Macheath appears in chains at the end of the *Beggar's Opera.* Like American gangsters at one time, highwaymen captured the popular imagination, and they were thought to behave in a chivalrous manner as they relieved ladies of their valuables.

On the day of the execution Boswell and a friend "got up on a scaffold very near the fatal tree, so that we could clearly see all the dismal scene. There was a most prodigious crowd of spectators. I was most terribly shocked, and thrown into a very deep melancholy." What was especially horrible was that the condemned were not granted a quick and sudden drop that would break the spine. Instead they endured slow strangulation that might take half an hour to kill them. Their friends would hang on their legs to hasten the process.

"Gloomy terrors" oppressed Boswell so badly after seeing Lewis die that he begged Erskine to let him share his bed that night. The following night he was "still in horror" and stayed with Dempster.[21]

An important work on eighteenth-century crime and punishment is entitled *Albion's Fatal Tree,* taking its title from a poem by Blake that uses the same expression Boswell did; it must have been proverbial. Hard though it is to believe today, by the end of the century there were no fewer than 250 crimes for which death was the penalty (by 1850 there were only two). Nearly all were crimes against property. That included stealing anything at all from a boat on a river (but not on a canal); stealing goods worth five shillings from a shop; stealing property worth one shilling from another person; and entering land with an intent to kill game or rabbits. Children as well as adults were executed. Murderous assault, however, was not a capital offense so long as the victim survived. That reflected obvious class bias: a wealthy or noble individual might commit assault, but was not likely to pick pockets.[22]

In practice, many convicts were transported to the colonies rather than hanged. The system was thus able to claim that it tempered justice with mercy. Still, criminals knew that their lives were at risk for almost any transgression. And because public executions were supposed to be an effective deterrent to crime, they were held at Tyburn several times a year.

Johnson once made a remark that may seem callous, but needs to be explained: "The age is running mad after innovation; all the business of the world is to be done in a new way; men are to be hanged in a new way. Tyburn itself is not safe from the fury of innovation." The innovation was that increasing gentrification of the area around Tyburn made it seem unpleasant to hold executions there, so they were moved to a more constricted space at Newgate.[23]

The reason Johnson regretted the loss of the public spectacle was that he hoped it might inspire spectators to look into their own hearts. In a *Rambler* essay he quoted a Dutch physician saying that "he never saw a criminal dragged to execution without asking himself, 'Who knows whether this man is not less culpable than me?'" Johnson made another telling point. Given the proliferation of capital offenses, why wouldn't a thief forestall detection by murdering his victim and not just robbing him? "The heart of a good man cannot but recoil at the thought of punishing a slight injury with death; especially when he remembers that the thief might have procured safety by another crime, from which he was restrained only by his remaining virtue."[24]

Whether or not the spectacle deterred anybody, it was greatly appreciated as a public holiday. Hogarth depicted one such occasion (figure 19). The condemned man is standing in the cart, which already contains his coffin, while a Methodist preacher harangues him. Preceding the cart is the Ordinary of Newgate in his coach—a telling detail, since that was the prison chaplain who was officially charged with providing spiritual consolation. On top of

19. Tyburn

the gallows, the executioner is peacefully smoking a pipe. Some spectators have paid for places in a grandstand, while the others mill around in anticipation. At the lower right, a man selling cakes fails to notice that a boy is deftly picking his pocket—obviously not deterred from crime by the punishment he is about to witness.

After an execution there was a ready market for copies of the criminal's "last dying speech," usually ghostwritten of course. One of the *Twelve London Cries* series shows a ragged woman announcing her wares, with the dead man still dangling from the gallows in the distance (figure 20).

Boswell told himself that he went to executions in order to familiarize himself with death, and thereby make it less dreadful. Naturally the opposite happened, and since he had frequent nightmares about being hanged, he must have had a feeling that he himself was somehow criminal. His father the judge didn't do much to disabuse him. In May, Lord Auchinleck sent him a long and brutal letter saying how indignant James's past behavior had made him. "I by your strange conduct had come to the resolution of selling all off, from the principle that it is better to snuff a candle out than leave it to stink in a socket." That meant disinheritance. He had been deterred only by "your excellent mother, the partaker of my distresses and shame on your account."[25]

20. Last Dying Speech

SEX

Boswell seldom frequented the brothels around Covent Garden. His usual practice was to rush out into the night after having plenty to drink, pick up a streetwalker, and grapple with her briefly in one of the parks or in some dark alley. He may have enjoyed the sense of risk. On one occasion he took "a strong, jolly young damsel" onto Westminster Bridge. "The whim of doing it there with the Thames rolling below us amused me much. Yet after the brutish appetite was sated, I could not but despise myself for being so closely united with such a low wretch." That happened shortly before three in the morning, which he mentions because when he got back to his lodgings he found that this time Molly had given up waiting for him and he was locked out.[26]

At other times, Boswell convinced himself that he was just following the dictates of nature. He liked to use the expression "promiscuous concubinage," as if he were an Old Testament patriarch. When he attended church in London, he was happy to have left the warnings of Scottish Presbyterianism far behind. "What a curious, inconsistent thing is the mind of man!" he mused. "In the midst of divine service I was laying plans for having women, and yet I had the most sincere feelings of religion." Pondering this conundrum, he came up with a plausible interpretation: "I have a warm heart and a vivacious fancy. I am therefore given to love, and also to piety or gratitude to God, and to the most brilliant and showy method of public worship." "Love" was hardly the appropriate term, but he was certainly right about his emotional religiosity.[27]

Finding women was easy. The German writer Lichtenberg, whose comments on Hogarth were quoted earlier, was startled by the frank behavior of "lewd females" in the London streets. In a letter home he said, "Every ten yards one is beset, even by children of twelve years old, who by the manner of their address save one the trouble of asking whether they know what they want. They attach themselves to you like limpets, and it is often impossible to get rid of them without giving them something. Often they seize hold of you after a fashion of which I can give you the best notion by the fact that I say nothing about it." Boswell didn't want to get rid of them. He was especially pleased when a young woman "wondered at my size, and said if I ever took a girl's maidenhead, I would make her squeak."[28]

Modern studies find that most streetwalkers were not full-time prostitutes, but women who were looking for a little income when times were hard. They got off the street as soon as they could. A 1758 survey of twenty-five prostitutes around the Strand found a median age of eighteen, with several who had begun at fourteen or even younger; none were active after the age of twenty-two. No fewer than seventeen of the twenty-five were orphans, and another five had been abandoned by their parents.[29]

Occasionally, Boswell seems to have been touched by a young woman's plight. "As I was coming home this night, I felt carnal inclinations raging through my frame. I determined to gratify them. I went to St. James's Park, and like Sir John Brute, picked up a whore. For the first time did I engage in armor [a condom], which I found but a dull satisfaction. She who submitted to my lusty embraces was a young Shropshire girl, only seventeen, very well looked, her name is Elizabeth Parker. Poor being, she has a sad time of it!" Sir John Brute is a character in a Restoration comedy, *The Provoked Wife;* it was one of Garrick's favorite roles.[30]

Boswell may have assumed that Elizabeth Parker enjoyed his lusty embraces, and for once he took the trouble to learn her name. At other times he felt disgusted by his behavior, as when he picked up "the first whore I met in the park" a week later. "She was ugly and lean and her breath smelled of spirits." His did too, of course. "I never asked her name. When it was done, she slunk off. I had a low opinion of this gross practice and resolved to do it no more."[31]

It's notable that before setting out on the prowl, Boswell would always get intoxicated. Pottle says that "he let himself get drunk in order to have a defense for whoring," and another commentator says dryly, "The conscience is that part of the psyche which is soluble in alcohol."[32]

Oscar Wilde is often misquoted as saying "I can resist everything except temptation." What he did say in *The Picture of Dorian Gray* is more interesting, and highly applicable to Boswell: "The only way to get rid of a temptation is to yield to it. Resist it, and your soul grows sick with longing for the things it has forbidden to itself, with desire for what its monstrous laws have made monstrous and unlawful." But Boswell's consciousness was haunted by the Calvinist ethic that goes back to Saint Augustine, who said in the *Confessions,* "From a perverted act of will, desire had grown, and when desire is given satisfaction, habit is forged; and when habit passes unresisted, a compulsive urge sets in. By these close-knit links I was held."[33]

LOUISA

During his year in London Boswell did develop one genuine liaison, and it forms a miniature narrative. As 1762 drew to an end, he was increasingly discouraged about his brief street encounters, and declared in his journal, "In my mind there cannot be higher felicity on earth enjoyed by man than the participation of genuine reciprocal amorous affection with an amiable woman." He added that the man in a relationship should be able to "exult with a consciousness that he is the superior person. The dignity of his sex is kept up."[34]

With this in view, he called on a Covent Garden actress named Anne Lewis, just one year older than himself, whom he had known slightly in Edinburgh and referred to in his journal as Louisa, adapted from her surname. She received him politely, they chatted over tea, and he observed that "she was in a pleasing undress and looked very pretty." The next day he called again, "informing her by my looks of my passion for her." The day after that he convinced himself that his passion was real, though he used clichés to say so. "I engaged in this amour just with a view of convenient pleasure, but the god of pleasing anguish now seriously seized my breast. I felt the fine delirium of love."[35]

Two weeks after the initial encounter, Boswell was ready to bring matters to a head. "I began to take some liberties. 'Nay, Sir—now—but do consider—' 'Ah, Madam!' 'Nay, but you are an encroaching creature!' Upon this I advanced to the greatest freedom, by a sweet elevation of the charming petticoat. 'Good heaven, Sir!' 'Madam, I cannot help it. I adore you. Do you like me?' She answered me with a warm kiss, and pressing me to her bosom, sighed, 'O Mr. Boswell!' "[36]

Louisa still played hard to get, making clear that she was not a common prostitute but interested in a genuine relationship. Boswell happily played along. There were a couple of distressing setbacks. Once when he was "just making a triumphal entry" they heard the landlady coming up the stairs, and at another time she had to postpone an assignation because "nature's periodical effects on the human, or more properly female, constitution forbade it." That was something that no fictional work at the time could have mentioned.

In due course they spent a night together at the Black Lion Inn, which Boswell chose because it was the first place he stayed when he had arrived in London, and also because it was especially recommended by Digges, who had so impressed Boswell as Macheath. He made a point of registering as "Mr. and Mrs. Digges."[37]

In his account Boswell runs the gamut from expressive simplicity to preposterous clichés. First, the simplicity. Louisa demurely asked him to leave while a maid helped her to undress. "I then took a candle in my hand and walked out to the yard. The night was very dark and very cold. I experienced for some minutes the rigours of the season, and called into my mind many terrible ideas of hardships, that I might make a transition from such dreary thoughts to the most gay and delicious feelings." That is quintessential Boswell: creating a keen sensory contrast, the better to relish what is about to happen.

Then the clichés. "I came softly into the room, and in a sweet delirium slipped into bed and was immediately clasped in her snowy arms, and pressed to her milk-white bosom." There follow, in quick succession, "amorous dalliance," "luscious feast," "godlike vigour," and "supreme rapture." As Nabokov once commented, pornography is generally "the copulation of clichés."[38]

Boswell managed to perform five times in succession, and "in my own mind I was somewhat proud of my performance." Performance is what it was. He goes on to admit, "I could not help roving in fancy to the embraces of some other ladies which my lively imagination strongly pictured." He could serve as a case study for what Freud describes in "The Most Prevalent Form of Degradation in the Erotic Life." Uneasy and inhibited with women of his own class, he could feel masterful and free with servants or prostitutes.[39]

Louisa was no prostitute, but she was still a woman of easy virtue, willing to accept gifts so long as they were understood not to be pay for services rendered. It was fairly common for actresses to supplement their modest theatrical income in this way, establishing a connection with a man who would be considered their "keeper." On a return visit, Boswell explicitly "enjoyed her as an actress who had played many a fine lady's part." Both of them were acting.[40]

Boswell's self-image was splendidly reinforced by this affair, in which he was successively a gentleman caller, a pretend husband ("Mr. Digges"), and a tireless stallion. At Lady Northumberland's a couple of days later, "I strutted up and down, considering myself as a valiant man who could gratify a lady's loving desires five times in a night; and I satisfied my pride by considering that if this and all my other great qualities were known, all the women almost in the room would be making love to me."[41]

When he and Louisa next slept together, four days later, it was clear that the game was already ending. "I was permitted the rites of love with great complacency; yet I felt my passion for Louisa much gone. I felt a degree of coldness for her, and I observed an affectation about her which disgusted me." Worse was about to come. Boswell had counted on "at least a winter's safe copulation," but to his horror he began to feel "a little heat in the members of my body sacred to Cupid, very like a symptom of that distemper with which Venus, when cross, takes it into her head to plague her votaries." Less euphemistically, "too, too plain was Signor Gonorrhea." That meant weeks of confinement, together with unpleasant and even dangerous medical treatment (mercury was used). "What! thought I, can this beautiful, this sensible, and this agreeable woman be so sadly defiled? Can corruption lodge beneath so fair a form?"[42]

Returning to Louisa, he confronted her, and in his journal congratulated himself on the "excellent address" with which he introduced the topic.

> BOSWELL. Do you know that I have been very unhappy since I saw you?
> LOUISA. How so, Sir?
> BOSWELL. Why, I am afraid that you don't love me so well, nor have not such a regard for me, as I thought you had.
> LOUISA. Nay, dear Sir! (seeming unconcerned.)
> BOSWELL. Pray, Madam, have I no reason?
> LOUISA. No, indeed, Sir, you have not.
> BOSWELL. Have I *no* reason, Madam? Pray think.
> LOUISA. Sir!
> BOSWELL. Pray, Madam, in what state of health have you been for some time?
> LOUISA. Sir, you amaze me.[43]

Louisa admitted that she had once contracted gonorrhea, but declared that she had been symptom-free for a long time. Since Boswell is known to have previously had gonorrhea himself, some commentators suspect that it was just an old infection flaring up again, not a new one caught from her. But a scholar-physician who has studied the evidence thinks it did come from her, though since it was dormant she could well have been telling the truth when she thought she had recovered completely.[44]

Boswell had lent Louisa the modest sum of two guineas, and he wrote bitterly to demand it back. "I neither *paid* it for prostitution nor *gave* it in charity. . . . I want no letters. Send the money sealed up. I have nothing more to say to you." A few days later Louisa's maid turned up with a sealed envelope containing two guineas, "without a single word written. I felt a strange kind of mixed confusion. My tender heart relented. I thought I had acted too harshly to her. I imagine she might—perhaps—have been ignorant of her situation." He thought better of that, although he congratulated himself on having too much of "what Shakespeare calls the milk of human kindness," and ended the episode with the reflection "that I had come off two guineas better than I expected."[45]

As it would turn out, this illness was an early episode in a long and self-destructive sequence. Over the years the journals record at least nineteen separate attacks of urethritis, some very alarming, caused by repeated gonorrhea infections. In the end they would contribute directly to his death.

The Louisa story began in December and was over by the middle of February. Boswell was now confined to his lodgings, and reluctantly recognizing that he would never get into the Guards. What lay ahead was a journey to Holland, where he had no wish to go, in order to study law, which he had no wish to study. The picture was obviously darkening, but he had no way of knowing that three months later he would have the most important encounter of his life.

CHAPTER 5

The Fateful Meeting

Boswell had been in London for half a year, and had still not met Johnson, much though he wanted to: he had read *The Rambler* and *Rasselas,* and admired Johnson as a master of wisdom. Thomas Sheridan, from whom he took elocution lessons in Edinburgh, was known to be a friend of Johnson's, and after renewing contact with Sheridan in London Boswell assumed an introduction would soon follow. But when he suggested it, Sheridan told him bitterly that they were no longer speaking. The reason, he claimed, was the disgust he felt when Johnson accepted a government pension of £300, and yet went on criticizing the prime minister and royal family.[1]

Later on Boswell learned the full story. Johnson's was not the only pension awarded in 1762. Sheridan himself got one of £200. Lord Bute, the prime minister, was Scottish, and he was rewarding Sheridan for teaching Scots to talk like Englishmen and thereby to prosper in public careers. Johnson was indignant that someone he regarded as a mere actor should be honored in the same way as himself. When he heard about it he exclaimed, "What! have they given him a pension? Then it is time for me to give up mine." That jibe was duly communicated to Sheridan, who never forgave it. He was not mollified by hearing that Johnson added, "However, I am glad that Mr. Sheridan has a pension, for he is a very good man."[2]

Johnson didn't much mind that his friendship was over with the prickly Sheridan, who greatly disliked being called "Sherry Derry." He was amused when he heard that Sheridan resented another of his wisecracks: "Sherry is dull, naturally dull; but it must have taken him a great deal of pains to become what we now see him. Such an excess of stupidity, Sir, is not in nature."[3]

There was someone else who might connect Boswell with Johnson. A part-time actor named Thomas Davies kept a bookshop in Russell Street, close to the Covent Garden theaters (figure 21). If a description by the satirist Charles Churchill is right, Davies wasn't much of an actor—"he mouths a sentence as curs mouth a bone"—but he was companionable, and Boswell became friendly with him. Davies mentioned that Johnson often dropped in at his shop, and the chances were good that an encounter with him could happen there. And now came the moment when, as Leslie Stephen says, Johnson "at last met the predestined biographer."[4]

May 16, 1763, began for Boswell like any other day, starting with breakfast with his friend Temple. In the afternoon he stopped in at Davies's shop and accepted an invitation to sit and drink tea. Suddenly Johnson appeared. In the *Life of Johnson* Boswell presents this as a dramatic turning point in his life: "Mr. Davies, having perceived him through the glass door in the room in which we were sitting, advancing towards us, announced his aweful [i.e., awe-inspiring] approach to me, somewhat in the manner of an actor in the part of

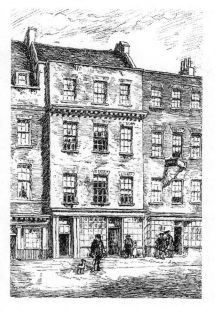

21. Davies's shop

Horatio when he addresses Hamlet on the appearance of his father's ghost: 'Look, my Lord, it comes.'" The Shakespeare allusion wasn't in Boswell's original journal. Davies probably didn't actually make the allusion at the time, and Boswell doesn't say he did. No doubt it occurred to him later as appropriate, which it certainly is. Johnson would indeed become an idealized father figure.[5]

Davies introduced Johnson to Boswell, who immediately made a conversational blunder. "I was much agitated; and recollecting his prejudice against the Scotch, of which I had heard much, I said to Davies, 'Don't tell where I come from.' 'From Scotland,' cried Davies, roguishly. 'Mr. Johnson,' said I, 'I do indeed come from Scotland, but I cannot help it.'"

What Boswell meant was that he couldn't help being a Scot, but Johnson turned the phrase to mean that far too many Scots on the make were inundating England: "'That, Sir, I find, is what a very great many of your countrymen cannot help.' This stroke stunned me a good deal, and when we had sat down, I felt myself not a little embarrassed, and apprehensive of what might come next."

It's possible that this was not the gratuitous insult it's often taken to be. Johnson liked to test people with unexpected jabs, and this one has been persuasively described as "meant to tease and shock the star-struck and thus vulnerable young man." Throughout their entire relationship Johnson enjoyed pretending that he hated Scotland and the Scots, just to get a rise out of Boswell. Usually he was putting him on.[6]

But when Boswell next spoke he made matters worse. Johnson mentioned to Davies that Garrick had refused to give him a theater ticket for his friend Anna Williams "because he knows the house will be full, and that an order would be worth three shillings." Boswell immediately put his foot in it. "Eager to take any opening to get into conversation with him, I ventured to say, 'Oh, Sir, I cannot think Mr. Garrick would grudge such a trifle to you.' 'Sir,' said he, with a stern look, 'I have known David Garrick longer than you have done, and I know no right you have to talk to me on this subject.'" Boswell acknowledged in the *Life* that it was "presumptuous in me, an entire stranger," to have any opinion about Johnson's relationship with one of his oldest friends.[7]

The exchange illustrates something interesting about Boswell's writing methods. There is nothing in the original journal entry about Garrick refusing a ticket for Anna Williams, or about Johnson's "stern look." What does exist is a marginal memorandum in Boswell's manuscript: "Mem. Garrick refusing an order to Mrs. Williams etc." So the exchange did occur, but the version in the *Life* is an expansion of the story that Boswell created from memory more than twenty years later.[8]

Boswell's faux pas and Johnson's retort might seem crushing, but Boswell was impossible to crush. He stayed on, joining the conversation only occasionally. After Johnson left Davies said, "Don't be uneasy. I can see he likes you very well."

A week later Boswell got up his courage and paid a call on Johnson in his lodgings; Davies probably told him that Johnson liked people to do that. "His brown suit of clothes looked very rusty; he had on a little old shriveled unpowdered wig, which was too small for his head; his shirt-neck and knees of his breeches were loose; his black worsted stockings ill drawn up; and he had a pair of unbuckled shoes by way of slippers. But all these slovenly particularities were forgotten the moment that he began to talk." Boswell was always vain about his own appearance, but deeply conscious that Johnson's value had nothing to do with costume.

Some other visitors soon got up to leave and Boswell did too, "but he cried, 'No, don't go away.' 'Sir,' said I, 'I am afraid that I intrude upon you. It is benevolent to allow me to sit and hear you.' He was pleased with this compliment, which I sincerely paid him." Johnson shook Boswell's hand cordially when he did leave, and he noted in his journal, "Upon my word, I am very fortunate. I shall cultivate this acquaintance."[9]

In the *Life* Boswell says, "I found that I had a very perfect idea of Johnson's figure from the portrait of him painted by Sir Joshua Reynolds soon after he had published his *Dictionary*, in the attitude of sitting in his easy chair in deep meditation, which was the first picture his friend did for him, which Sir Joshua very kindly presented to me, and from which an engraving has been made for this work."[10]

Actually that couldn't have happened. This particular portrait (figure 22) was unfinished, never shown in public or reproduced, and Boswell had not yet met Reynolds. Either he misremembered what went through his mind long before, or he simply needed to give readers of the *Life* a more positive first impression of Johnson than the uncouth, growling figure he had described in his unpublished journal. By using it as the frontispiece he could encourage readers to turn directly from the narrative to the image, which has been described as seeing Johnson "through the eyes of an admiring young stranger, an enigmatic, portentous figure." Reynolds was fourteen years younger than Johnson, and not yet a friend when he painted it.[11]

22. *Life of Johnson* frontispiece

By the time Boswell left for Holland, less than three months later, an enduring friendship had been formed. It has been well said that Johnson saw in him "a being whose human need for just what he had to give was very nearly desperate." Their relationship lasted for twenty-one years, until Johnson's death in 1784, and all that time Boswell constantly relied on him for the advice, encouragement, and love he never got from Lord Auchinleck. The great biography that developed from their relationship represents "the almost involuntary tribute of a great human weakness to a great human strength." It was far from involuntary, though. It was the one thing in Boswell's life that he ever challenged himself to do as well as he possibly could.[12]

As for Johnson, he was feeling oppressed by advancing age. He had written to a friend the previous year, when he was fifty-three, "I went down to my native town, where I found the streets much narrower and shorter than I thought I had left them, inhabited by a new race of people, to whom I was very little known. My playfellows were grown old, and forced me to suspect that I was no longer young." Now he had a young friend with whom he could enjoy relaxed sociability, at which Boswell was gifted. Many years later Johnson told him, "Boswell, I think I am easier with you than with almost anybody." Boswell was deeply moved when he heard Johnson say in company "that he reckoned the day on which he and I became acquainted one of the happiest days of his life."[13]

Boswell enjoyed playing the disciple, but there were also interesting cross-currents in their relationship. Their personal styles were so different that they represent a double helix of possibilities. Boswell was a romantic who fantasized about feudal affection between lords and their dependents, Johnson was a hardheaded pragmatist. Johnson insisted on reason and self-control, Boswell reveled in emotional "sensibility" and seized gratifications whenever he could. Johnson aspired to what he called "the grandeur of generality" and Boswell to specificity and piquant details. Johnson crafted language in the carefully assembled building blocks of the periodic style, Boswell's style was conversational and free.[14]

Soon Boswell was one of the valued friends who had a standing invitation to come by for tea at Inner Temple Lane, where Johnson occupied the second floor of the house shown here with a small portico, just above a passerby (figure 23). After leaving Gough Square in 1760 he had lived here, as his friend Arthur Murphy said, "in poverty, total idleness, and the pride of literature." It was here that he had received news in 1762 of his pension.[15]

It was fully ten years before Boswell was invited for dinner, and he was greatly surprised when it did happen. Apartment dwellers generally

23. Inner Temple Lane

didn't have kitchens, and it was normal to eat out. They sat down to "a very good soup, a boiled leg of lamb and spinach, a veal pie, and a rice pudding." Johnson mentioned that his meat pies were brought in from a public oven.[16]

When Boswell and Johnson got together for an evening, it was usually at the Mitre Tavern in Fleet Street (figure 24). On one occasion, after they had each drunk a bottle of port, Boswell cautiously asked whether Johnson might like to order more. " 'Yes,' said he, 'I think I would. I think two bottles would seem to be the quantity for us.' Accordingly we made them out." At the end of the evening Johnson "took me cordially by the hand and said, 'My dear Boswell! I do love you very much.'" That more than made up for a horrible hangover the next day. "A bottle of thick English port is a very heavy and a very inflammatory dose. This morning it was boiling in my veins." This engaging recollection from the *London Journal* didn't make it into the *Life of Johnson,* where Boswell would always try to minimize references to drinking, especially his own.[17]

ELOQUENT MORSELS OF LONDON.

THE MITRE TAVERN, FLEET STREET.

24. The Mitre Tavern

BOSWELL THE ROLE PLAYER

Boswell looked up to Johnson as a mentor, but that didn't mean he stopped picking up prostitutes. One such episode he found particularly shaming, though as usual he thought only of himself. "At night I took a streetwalker into Privy Garden and indulged sensuality. The wretch picked my pocket of my handkerchief, and then swore that she had not. When I got home I was shocked to think that I had been intimately united with a low, abandoned, perjured, pilfering creature. I determined to do so no more; but if the Cyprian fury should seize me, to participate my amorous flame with a genteel girl." Venus was born in Cyprus. What Boswell does not consider is the dismal existence of this woman whose name he doesn't know. A silk or even linen handkerchief could be fenced for a modest sum—modest, but more than he was paying her. It was worth it to her to steal it.[18]

In this final phase of the *London Journal,* two encounters are presented as narrative set pieces. Boswell thinks one of them is charming and the other embarrassing, but he feels good about himself after both. His self-knowledge only goes so far.

In the first, two weeks after meeting Johnson, Boswell played a favorite game of pretending that all women must desire him for his personal attractiveness and not his money.

I sallied forth to the Piazzas in rich flow of animal spirits and burning with fierce desire. I met two very pretty little girls who asked me to take them with me. "My dear girls," said I, "I am a poor fellow. I can give you no money. But if you choose to have a glass of wine in my company, and let us be gay and obliging to each other without money, I am your man." They agreed with great good humour. So back to the Shakespeare [Tavern] I went. "Waiter," said I, "I have got here a couple of human beings; I don't know how they'll do." "I'll look, your Honour," cried he, and with inimitable effrontery stared them in the face and then cried, "They'll do very well." "What," said I, "are they good fellow creatures? Bring them up, then." We were shown into a good room and had a bottle of sherry before us in a minute. I surveyed my seraglio and found them both good subjects for amorous play. I toyed with them and drank about and sung *Youth's the Season* and thought myself Captain Macheath; and then I solaced my existence with them, one after the other, according to their seniority.[19]

Boswell creates a theatrical scene—right around the corner from the real theaters—and the girls play along. It's obvious that since he could afford a private room and a bottle of sherry, he wasn't broke after all. Once again he is freest and happiest pretending to be someone else, and inevitably, it's Macheath. He also shared a widespread male fantasy of being the Turkish sultan in his seraglio, free to choose at whim from a stable of women.

The Shakespeare Tavern was in fact well-known as a clearinghouse for prostitutes, and for the waiter here it was all in a day's work. A pocket-size directory, with descriptions of the women's looks and erotic specialties, was published by a Shakespeare waiter as *Harris's List of Covent Garden Ladies,* updated annually. The elegant arcade of the Piazza (figure 25) leads to the entrance to the tavern at the far end. The Covent Garden playhouse was around the corner to the left, and its longtime proprietor, John Rich, lived in the house that's visible just beyond the sedan chair resting against a column.[20]

What happened two weeks later was very different. On the king's birthnight, a national holiday, Boswell "resolved to be a blackguard." In later usage that came to mean a thoroughgoing scoundrel, but Johnson defines it simply as "a cant word among the vulgar, a dirty fellow of the meanest kind." Boswell's carefully selected costume included a dark suit with powder from his wig all over it, a shirt that hadn't been cleaned for days, "and a little round hat with tarnished silver lace belonging to a disbanded officer of the Royal Volunteers." He no

25. Covent Garden Piazza

doubt acquired that on purpose as a prop. "I had in my hand an old oaken stick
battered against the pavement. And was I not a complete blackguard?"

His first move was to pick up a prostitute in St. James's Park. "I called myself a barber and agreed with her for sixpence, went to the bottom of the Park
arm in arm, and dipped my machine in the canal and performed most manfully." Sixpence was hardly any money at all. It's not clear why a retired officer
should have been a barber, but since she got her sixpence the woman was unlikely to ask questions. Boswell often liked to impersonate lower-class people,
no doubt as a way of forgetting the responsibilities of James Boswell, Esq.

He was just getting started. He went "roaring along" to a punch house in
St. Paul's Churchyard and drank three threepenny bowls, which was a lot of
punch.

In the Strand I picked up a little profligate wretch and gave her
sixpence. She allowed me entrance. But the miscreant refused me performance. I was much stronger than her, and *volens nolens* [willing or

unwilling] pushed her up against the wall. She however gave a sudden spring from me, and screaming out, a parcel of more whores and soldiers came to her relief. "Brother soldiers," said I, "should not a half-pay officer roger for sixpence? And here she has used me so and so." I got them on my side, and I abused her in blackguard style, and then left them. At Whitehall I picked up another girl to whom I called myself a highwayman, and told her I had no money and begged she would trust me. But she would not. My vanity was somewhat gratified tonight that notwithstanding of my dress, I was always taken for a gentleman in disguise. I came home about two o'clock, much fatigued.[21]

It's an ugly scene, and Boswell has no idea how ugly. Apparently he is so drunk that after first agreeing with him, the "little profligate wretch" gets scared and pushes him away. At this point he's attempting rape. Hearing her screaming, a crowd rushes up to help, and then they back off. As Boswell complacently acknowledges, the reason they do is that they realize he's a gentleman in disguise. He takes that to mean that they recognize his innate superiority. What they actually realize is that a magistrate will believe his testimony and not theirs.

Johnson must often have talked to Boswell about the plight of prostitutes, but on the one occasion when Boswell mentions that in his journal, he leaves out what was actually said. It happened a couple of months later, just a few days before he was due to leave for Holland. "As we walked along the Strand tonight, arm in arm, a woman of the town came enticingly near us. 'No,' said Mr. Johnson, 'no, my girl, it won't do.' We then talked of the unhappy situation of these wretches, and how much more misery than happiness, upon the whole, is produced by irregular love." Boswell always euphemized what he was doing as "love," a word that Johnson is very unlikely to have used.[22]

Johnson had known many prostitutes well during his down-and-out years, and in *The Rambler* he challenged his readership by impersonating an imaginary correspondent called Misella. One of her relatives seduced her, got her pregnant, kept her as a mistress for a while, and then dropped her completely. By then there was only one means of survival, however much she hated it.

In this abject state I have now passed four years, the drudge of extortion and the sport of drunkenness; sometimes the property of one man, and sometimes the common prey of accidental lewdness. . . . If those who pass their days in plenty and security could visit for an hour the dismal receptacles to which the prostitute retires from her nocturnal excursions, and see the wretches that lie crowded together, mad with intemperance, ghastly with famine, nauseous with filth, and noisome with disease; it would not be easy for any degree of abhorrence to repress the desire which they must immediately feel to rescue such numbers of human beings from a state so dreadful.

Johnson told a friend that he had known the woman whose story this was.[23]

It was usual in those days to see prostitutes as bad girls who had gone wrong, not as victims of a socioeconomic system that was officially condemned but in practice condoned. Marriages were commonly arranged between families for financial considerations, sexual attraction between spouses was seldom a consideration, and divorce was unobtainable except for those few in a position to get individual acts of Parliament. The subculture of prostitution in effect provided an outlet for male gratification, including unmarried men like Boswell, of course. Women's needs were not considered.

FAREWELL TO LONDON

For Boswell the romance of London had begun to fade. When he went up to the roof of St. Paul's to admire the view, "London gave me no great idea. I just saw a prodigious group of tiled roofs and narrow lanes opening here and there, for the streets and beauty of the buildings cannot be observed on account of the distance. The Thames and the country around, the beautiful hills of Hampstead and of Highgate looked very fine. And yet I did not feel the same enthusiasm that I have felt some time ago at viewing these rich prospects." Still, he was far from eager to embark on the year of study in Holland that he had promised his father.[24]

Two weeks before his departure, the Thames was the scene of a memorable excursion with Johnson. They took a boat on the river, and while riding along Boswell happened to ask whether a knowledge of Greek and Latin would be an advantage for everybody. Johnson acknowledged that that might not be the case: " 'For instance, this boy rows us as well without learning as if he could sing the song of Orpheus to the Argonauts, who were the first sailors.' He then called to the boy, 'What would you give, my lad, to know about the Argonauts?' 'Sir,' said the boy, 'I would give what I have.' Johnson was much pleased with his answer, and we gave him a double fare."[25]

Right after that "we landed at the Old Swan, and walked to Billingsgate, where we took oars, and moved smoothly along the silver Thames." This means that they prudently declined to "shoot" the arches of London Bridge, as some daring boatmen were willing to do, because the tidal current was too dangerous. The picture (color plate 10) shows alarming rapids as the ebbing tide pours through from beyond the bridge. The houses on the bridge, incidentally, were being demolished just at this time in order to widen the space for vehicles, but Johnson had known them well. He used to buy books from a shop there. Today the entire bridge is gone, torn down and replaced by a new one in the nineteenth century.[26]

Billingsgate was a very different milieu from the ones Boswell usually frequented. Its name became a synonym for "ribaldry, foul language," as the *Dictionary* notes, explaining that it is "a cant word borrowed from Billingsgate in London, a place where there is always a crowd of low people, and frequent brawls and foul language." That was where fishermen landed their catch and sold it; boats of any size couldn't pass beneath the bridge to get further into the city.

The picture (color plate 11) shows just such a scene. Squabbles are erupting everywhere, and a number of people have been knocked down. In the foreground a drunken fishmonger lies helpless while a kindly fisherman offers her another drink. A dog is devouring her fish.

The river below that point, known as the Pool of London, gave impressive evidence of Britain's vast international trade. An engraving made in 1757 (figure 26) shows teeming activity, with a forest of masts lining the wharves and the Tower of London in the distance. At that time the Pool was handling over 1,500 ships per year, carrying close to 250,000 tons of goods. The title of this print is *The Imports of Great Britain from France;* it was issued just after the beginning of the Seven Years War that put a temporary halt to trade with France.

In the foreground to the right are barrels of French wine, labeled as claret (red wine from Bordeaux), Burgundy, and Champagne. Wine was normally bottled at the place of destination, and there's a crate of bottles in front of the barrels. At the center of the picture, an elegantly dressed young black servant points derisively at a pair of fashionable ladies who are greeting each other with an ostentatious kiss. Several thousand blacks, freed slaves brought from the West Indies, were servants in London.[27]

At Billingsgate, Boswell says, he and Johnson took another boat. "It was a pleasant day, and when we got clear out into the country, we were charmed with the beautiful fields on each side of the river." Their little voyage ended at Greenwich, which Johnson had praised in his poem *London* twenty-five years previously:

26. The Pool of London

On Thames's banks in silent thought we stood,
Where Greenwich smiles upon the silver flood.
Struck with the seat which gave Eliza birth,
We kneel, and kiss the consecrated earth.

Queen Elizabeth was born in Greenwich. Boswell had prepared himself for this scene by bringing a copy of Johnson's poem in his pocket. "I read the passage on the banks of the Thames, and literally kissed the consecrated earth."[28]

After that they took a boat back up river and had dinner at the Turk's Head Tavern, where the Club would begin to meet later that year. Johnson said, "I must see thee go; I will go down with you to Harwich." A few days previously he had declared, "There are few people whom I take to so much as to you," and when Boswell talked about his imminent departure, "he said (with an affection that almost made me cry), 'My dear Boswell! I should be very unhappy at parting, did I think we were not to meet again.'" In the *Life* Boswell left out "almost made me cry."[29]

The reason to sail from Harwich, seventy miles to the east, was that even if the Thames had not been congested with shipping, its course was so winding that there could be long delays waiting for a favorable wind. Boswell and Johnson went down by stagecoach. During the journey, a fellow passenger boasted that in bringing up her children she "never suffered them a moment to be idle." That inspired Johnson to embarrass Boswell playfully:

> JOHNSON. "I wish, Madam, you would educate me too; for I have been an idle fellow all my life." "I am sure, Sir (said she), you have not been idle."
> JOHNSON. "Nay, Madam, it is very true; and that gentleman there (pointing to me) has been idle. He was idle at Edinburgh. His father sent him to Glasgow, where he continued to be idle. He then came to London, where he has been very idle; and now he is going to Utrecht, where he will be as idle as ever." I asked him privately how he could expose me so.
> JOHNSON. "Poh, poh! (said he) they knew nothing about you, and will think of it no more."[30]

That night they stayed at an inn, and at dinner Johnson made a comment that was sadly prophetic of Boswell's emotional troubles for the rest of his life. "A moth having fluttered round the candle and burnt itself, he laid hold of this little incident to admonish me, saying, with a sly look, and in a solemn but quiet tone, 'That creature was its own tormentor, and I believe its name was Boswell.'" Boswell did include that in the *Life*.[31]

Most memorable of all is Boswell's account of the parting when he boarded a ship for Holland.

> My revered friend walked down with me to the beach, where we embraced and parted with tenderness, and engaged to correspond by letters. I said, "I hope, Sir, you will not forget me in my absence." JOHNSON. "Nay, Sir, it is more likely you should forget me, than that I should forget you." As the vessel put out to sea, I kept my eyes upon him for a considerable time, while he remained rolling his majestic frame in his usual manner; and at last I perceived him walk back into the town, and he disappeared.[32]

CHAPTER 6

Boswell Abroad

A SOUL IN TORMENT

Boswell established himself dutifully at Utrecht, with its distinguished university, and prepared to spend a year there in accordance with his father's wishes. As a reward, he would then be permitted—which is to say, provided with funds—to make an extensive tour through Germany, Italy, and France. It was common for young gentlemen of means to devote a year or more to what was known as the Grand Tour. The idea was that they would learn languages, gain knowledge of the larger world, and if possible make connections that could be useful in later life.

At first, lonely and out of his element, Boswell fell into a catastrophic depression. Unfortunately his entire journal for this period is lost, because when he left Holland he sent it to Scotland for safekeeping, and on the way it somehow disappeared. We do, however, have letters he wrote to Temple and to other friends, and as Pottle says, they show that he was often "a soul in torment."[1]

The correspondence with Temple survives only by an extraordinary fluke. In the nineteenth century an Englishman happened to make a purchase at a shop in Boulogne, and noticed that it was wrapped in a piece of paper with the signature of James Boswell. Following up on that, he was able to retrieve no fewer than ninety-seven of Boswell's letters to Temple that had fallen into the hands of a vendor of wastepaper. Temple had saved them, of course, but after his death his son-in-law left England for France to escape his creditors. Why he took the Boswell letters with him is unknown, as is the way they got into the hands of the French wastepaper dealer.[2]

Utrecht struck Boswell at first as "a most dismal place," and he felt so desperate that he fled to a bigger city, Rotterdam. That didn't help. From there he wrote to Temple, "I sunk altogether. My mind was filled with the blackest ideas, and all my powers of reason forsook me. Would you believe it? I ran frantic up and down the streets, crying out, bursting into tears, and groaning from my innermost heart. . . . All things appeared good for nothing, all dreary. I thought I should never recover, and that now the time was come when I should really go mad."[3]

Boswell evidently wrote in similar terms to Johnson, but that letter is lost. Johnson waited three months to reply, and then complained that the letter contained "an account so hopeless of the state of your mind that it hardly admitted or deserved an answer." It may seem surprising that he could be so unsympathetic, but he probably felt that that was exactly what Boswell needed: stern advice to pull himself together. The advice was easy to give but hard to follow, as Johnson himself well knew.[4]

At any rate, Boswell was deeply grateful. He told himself in his memoranda, "Mr. Johnson's correspondence is the greatest honour you could ever imagine you could attain to." And in one of the verse exercises he had started to write he exclaimed, "Illustrious Johnson! When of thee I think / Into my little self I timid shrink."[5]

Before long Boswell began to make new friends, and the cloud lifted much of the time. But not all the time, though he was proud of putting up a good front even when suffering inwardly. In a memorandum to himself he noted, "You had no pleasure in life, and your religion was dark. Yet you was gay, and sung. You are a fine fellow. You fight bravely." Two months later he wrote to John Johnston, another trusted confidant back home, in real despair: "I have had most dreadful returns of the blackest melancholy. I have endured more than I ever did. To tell you my sufferings from a horrid imagination is scarcely possible, for I have had ideas of which to describe the frightful effects, no language has words sufficient. God preserve me from returns of the dire distemper, for indeed of late it had almost crushed me."[6]

Meanwhile Boswell must have been writing very differently to his father, though his letters home have not survived. It's clear that he wanted to give an impression of settling down well to an industrious and responsible way of life.

"Be assured," Lord Auchinleck replied, "you have no friend can sympathize so much with you as I do. God Almighty describes his pity for mankind by comparing it to that of an earthly father." He added that his own father, from whom James's affliction evidently descended, found relief from it when fully occupied with business, and was most susceptible to it when idle. That was the same advice Johnson always gave.[7]

Boswell enrolled in no formal program and could have neglected his studies if he wanted to, but in fact he pursued them conscientiously. After attending a lecture each day by a professor with whom he became friendly, he read legal texts for another three hours. In addition he took lessons in Latin, in which he was already proficient and in which university instruction was conducted, and with a tutor's help made some progress in Greek.

French was normally spoken by Boswell's Utrecht acquaintances, so he put in intensive study of that language too, writing several pages in it every day. As is often the case with gifted mimics, he had an extraordinary talent for languages. Naturally he made minor mistakes, but soon he was speaking French with ease, and even flirting:

> MME. SPAEN. I am afraid, Sir, that my hoop is in your way.
> BOSWELL. Not at all, Madame, but I fear that I am in the way of your hoop.

In addition to French, he picked up some Dutch, commenting that it was "an old, strong, rich language," all the more appealing since "I boast that I have Dutch blood in my veins." One of his great-grandmothers, a countess named Veronica van Aerssen van Sommelsdyk, had been Dutch.[8]

With vivid memories of the purgatory of venereal disease, Boswell managed to abstain from sexual encounters during the entire time he was in Holland, though he occasionally fondled streetwalkers before backing off. Besides, he felt that it was time to think about choosing a wife, whose role as consort of the future Laird of Auchinleck would be a prime consideration. There was no thought of obeying desire, which in his experience always burned out quickly.

Two young Dutch women struck him as especially eligible. One was a pretty widow who was friendly enough, but who warned him frankly that she was emotionally cold. The other was far more interesting: beautiful, extremely intelligent, and almost exactly his own age. Unlike the widow she was intensely passionate, but in a mercurial way that he found alarming; she probably reminded him too much of himself.

This remarkable person bore the majestic name of Isabella Agneta Elisabeth van Tuyll van Serooskerken, known familiarly as Belle de Zuylen (she was born in Zuylen Castle near Utrecht), and by the pen name Zélide. She had already published a novel in French, and in later life would go on to write numerous novels and plays. She composed music as well.

"She is much my superior," Boswell acknowledged in a letter to Temple, and added, "One does not like that." A Utrecht friend told him reassuringly, "She lacks good sense and consequently she goes wrong, and a man who has not half her wit and knowledge may still be above her." This he found comforting, for as the friend went on to say, "If it were not for that lack, Zélide would have an absolute power. She would have unlimited dominion over men, and would overthrow the dignity of the male sex." Boswell's insistence on male authority, like the social and political code it supported, would persist all his life.[9]

The attraction was mutual, and Zélide found Boswell much more entertaining than the stolid men in her usual circle. For some time after he left Holland they would exchange teasingly affectionate letters, but he could never resist lecturing her on the importance of religious orthodoxy—she was a freethinker—and of discreet behavior. He was especially shocked by her remark that if she turned out not to love deeply whomever she might marry, she would naturally take a lover. "I beseech you, never indulge such ideas," he replied. "Respect mankind. Respect the institutions of society." In another letter he declared pompously, "A man who has a mind and a heart like mine is rare. A woman with many talents is not so rare."[10]

After a while Zélide got sick of the whole charade, and wrote brusquely, "You are very right to say that I should be worth nothing as your wife. We are entirely in agreement on that head. I have no subaltern talents." And when he went on sending hectoring letters, describing himself as her mentor, she replied with disgust, "I was shocked and saddened to find, in a friend whom I had conceived of as a young and sensible man, the puerile vanity of a fatuous fool, coupled with the arrogant rigidity of an old Cato." Most of their correspondence is lost, which is perhaps just as well.[11]

In 1771 Zélide married a former tutor of her brother's, became Mme. de Charrière, and settled at Neuchâtel in Switzerland. There she continued to write, helped to get Rousseau's posthumous *Confessions* published in 1782, and corresponded extensively with other writers, including Benjamin Constant. She died in 1805; there is a Belle van Zuylen chair at the University of Utrecht.

BARON BOSWELL AMONG THE GERMANS

What helped the most to rescue Boswell from his depression was to be on the move; travel always cheered him up. After ten months in Holland he set out for Germany, which was not yet a unified nation, but a loose assemblage of states, principalities, margravates, and free cities, with Frederick the Great of Prussia the most powerful single ruler. (The anthem *Deutschland über Alles* does not refer to political domination; it was written in 1841 to prophesy a unified Germany that would replace the anti-liberal petty states.)

Boswell spent most of his time at a series of courts, where foreign visitors of status were welcome guests. That was considered the best way for a British traveler to make valuable contacts, and to experience the cultural centers in each region. Johnson told him before he set out, "I would go where there are courts and learned men."[12]

At each of these courts Boswell introduced himself as Baron Boswell, which he wasn't, but the term conveyed a fairly accurate sense of his position at home. In both Scotland and Germany it was a feudal title related to land ownership. In Scotland it could be inherited only by the eldest son, which means that Boswell was not yet actually a baron since his father was alive, but he would indeed succeed in due time to the "Baronry of Auchinleck." There was one inconvenient fact, though, that he preferred to ignore. The actual title of baron no longer existed, since that rank was abolished in Scotland after the union with England in 1707.[13]

Presenting himself at courts gave Boswell a good reason to acquire more fancy clothing. In Holland he had already been outfitted by a tailor with two suits, "of sea-green with silver lace, and scarlet with gold." His servant there drew up an inventory that included a blue coat with white buttons, a rose-colored coat with gold buttons, fifteen ruffled shirts, a pair of buckskin breeches and another pair in black silk, and (of course) "one sword with a silver hilt." For Germany he added to this wardrobe "a suit of summer clothes, fine camlet with a gold thread button but no lace, and against winter a complete suit of worked flowered velvet, the buttons of velvet; four pairs of laced ruffles. This I think will do." The velvet suit was in five colors. Camlet, originally woven from camel's hair, was a waterproof satiny fabric of silk and wool.[14]

All told, Boswell spent five months in Germany, starting at Berlin. Most of the time he traveled rough, and took pride in it; often he would sit on a flat board spanning the sides of an open wagon. At the end of his first week he spent the night on a table in an inn, and the night after that on a sheet laid on the floor with straw underneath, and cows and horses on either side.

"What frightened me not a little was an immense mastiff chained pretty near the head of my bed. He growled most horribly, and rattled his chain. I called for a piece of bread and made a friendship with him. Before me were two great folding doors wide open, so that I could see the beauties of the evening sky. In this way, however, did I sleep with much contentment, and much health." The reference is to mental health as much as physical. Boswell always relied on vigorous activity to cheer him up, whereas "want of motion flattened me."[15]

It was highly gratifying to be treated as a person of distinction at one provincial court after another, where the usual language was French, though Boswell began to learn some German as well. He eagerly recorded every pearl of wisdom that fell from noble lips. "On Sunday night we stood in a window with the Hereditary Prince, who said, 'It is very difficult to combine business and pleasure.'"[16]

If Boswell admired noblemen, he practically worshiped kings. A high point of the entire trip was a chance to behold Frederick the Great. "It was a glorious sight. He was dressed in a suit of plain blue, with a star in a plain hat with a white feather [i.e., the uniform of his palace guards]. He had in his hand a cane. The sun shone bright. He stood before the palace, with an air of iron confidence that could not be opposed." Boswell described the encounter afterward "with prodigious warmth" to a German general "who held me by the arm and said, 'Calm yourself, Sir.'" The adoration dwindled after Boswell was unable—much to his surprise—to get a face-to-face meeting with the king.[17]

In Wittenberg Boswell wrote to Johnson, theatrically enough, from the tomb of the Lutheran theologian Philipp Melanchthon. "My paper rests upon the gravestone of that great and good man, who was undoubtedly the worthiest of all the reformers. . . . At this tomb, my ever dear and respected friend, I vow to thee an eternal attachment. It shall be my study to do what I can to render your life happy, and if you die before me, I shall endeavour to do honour to your memory." Lytton Strachey says, "The rest of Boswell's existence was the history of that vow's accomplishment."[18]

As for sex, there still wasn't any. "Since I left England," he wrote to Temple, "I have been chaste as an anchorite." At one point he did go with friends "to a Berlin bawdy house, which I was curious to see. We found a poor little house, an old bawd, and one whore. I was satisfied with what I saw." It appears that all he did was look.[19]

Finally, after staying up writing all night, Boswell yielded to an unexpected opportunity, which he took advantage of with pidgin German.

I was quite drunk with brisk spirits, and about eight in came a woman with a basket of chocolate to sell. I toyed with her and found she was with child. Oho! a safe piece. Into my closet. "Habst er ein Man?" "Ja, in den Gards bei Potsdam." To bed directly. In a minute—over. I rose cool and astonished, half angry, half laughing. I sent her off. Bless me, have I now committed adultery? Stay, a soldier's wife is no wife [because her husband was never at home?]. Should I now torment myself with speculations on sin, and on losing in one morning the merit of a year's chastity? . . . Well, I shall not be proud. I shall be a mild and humble Christian.

A few weeks later he instructed himself: "Swear solemn with drawn sword not to be with woman *sine condom nisi* [without condom except] Swiss lass." It's not clear why he expected Swiss women to be healthy.[20]

Boswell seems to have regarded masturbation as a dangerous temptation, due to his religious upbringing and also to the medical theory that it promoted insanity. One of his notes to himself reads, "Yesterday at night, low lasciviousness. Have a care. Swear with drawn sword never *pleasure* but with a woman's aid." An example of that was an encounter with a Dresden streetwalker, avoiding penetration however:

Yet again I went with those easy street girls, and between their thighs——merely for health. I would not embrace them. First, because it was dangerous. Next, because I could not think of being so united to miscreants. Both last night and this, they picked my pocket of my handkerchief. I was angry at myself. I was obliged to own to my servant that I had been *avec les filles.* Man is sometimes low.

Once again we notice an all but invisible servant.[21]

TWO CELEBRITIES

In November it was time to move on to Switzerland, where Boswell was determined to meet, and if possible impress, two of the greatest writers then living. First would be Jean-Jacques Rousseau, who had recently fled from France to avoid arrest for political and religious writings that were considered subversive. After that would be Voltaire, the godfather of the Enlightenment, its most prolific propagandist, and a tireless campaigner against political and religious injustice.

Rousseau was living in a remote mountain village called Môtiers, near Neuchâtel, which was not yet part of Switzerland but governed by the King of Prussia. On December 3 Boswell arrived there, impressed by the snow-covered mountains, and put up at the inn. A friend who knew Rousseau had provided him with a letter of recommendation, but he always preferred to test people's response to his personal qualities. "I am above the vulgar crowd," he instructed himself. "I would have my merit fairly tried by this great judge of human nature."[22]

So he sat down at the inn and composed a letter, in French, carefully cal-culated to appeal to Rousseau, whose books he had been studying by way of preparation. "I present myself, Sir, as a man with a feeling heart, a lively but melancholy spirit. Ah, if all that I have suffered does not give me singular merit in the eyes of Monsieur Rousseau, why was I made as I am? Why did he write as he has written?"[23]

Rousseau took the bait, and although he was tormented by a chronic uri-nary condition and protested that he couldn't receive guests, the irrepressible Boswell showed up repeatedly over the course of five days. It took plenty of presumption to carry that off, but he was equal to the challenge.

> ROUSSEAU. You are irksome to me. It's my nature. I cannot
> help it.
> BOSWELL. Do not stand on ceremony with me.
> ROUSSEAU. Go away.[24]

Boswell took an immediate interest in Rousseau's lifelong companion, Thérèse Levasseur, who was forty-three but struck him as "a little, lively, neat French girl." He made a point of cultivating her, helping to ensure that he would be permitted return visits, and he complimented her cooking. "Our din-ner was as follows: 1. A dish of excellent soup. 2. A *bouilli* of beef and veal. 3. Cabbage, turnip, and carrot. 4. Cold pork. 5. Pickled trout, which he [Rous-seau] jestingly called tongue. 6. Some little dish which I forget. The dessert consisted of stoned pears and chestnuts. We had red and white wines. It was a simple, good repast." When he reached Geneva Boswell bought a garnet neck-lace and sent it to Thérèse.[25]

Not much of interest emerged in the conversations with the great man, though Boswell did elicit one striking comment: "Sir, I have no liking for the world. I live here in a world of fantasies (*chimères*), and I cannot tolerate the world as it is." Boswell may not have realized that Rousseau was quoting his own novel *Julie,* in which the heroine tells her lover that the land of chimeras is the only one worth living in.[26]

Boswell rather daringly remarked that in Scotland people might say, "Jean-Jacques, why do you allow yourself all these fantasies? You're a pretty man to put forward such claims. Come, come, settle down in society like other people." In his journal he added, "There he felt the thistle [the national symbol of Scotland]. It was just as if I had said, 'Hoot, Johnnie Rousseau man, what for hae ye sae mony figmagairies? Ye're a bonny man indeed to mauk siccan a wark; set ye up. Canna ye just live like ither fowk?' "[27]

Though intelligent, Boswell was no intellectual, and it was Rousseau the celebrity he was forcing himself upon, not Rousseau the thinker. How little he understood Rousseau's writings is revealed by a comment in the *Life of Johnson:* "His absurd preference of savage to civilized life, and other singularities, are proofs rather of a defect in his understanding than of any depravity in his heart." Boswell feeling superior to Rousseau's "understanding" is a depressing spectacle. He completely missed the point of the great *Discourse on the Origin of Inequality.* There Rousseau states clearly that even so-called savages left the state of nature long ago, and whether or not that state might have been preferable to life in society, there is no possibility of ever going back.[28]

When Boswell and Rousseau chatted on the little balcony of the house he and Thérèse were renting (figure 27), neither of them could have foreseen an event that would bring them briefly together again. A year after this visit the local Calvinist minister would stir up the villagers against the allegedly

27. Rousseau's balcony at Môtiers

unbelieving Rousseau, though that was ironic, since as he often said he was the only one of the philosophes who did believe in God. During the night the balcony was bombarded with rocks, an event that has become known as *la lapidation de Môtiers,* a sort of biblical stoning. The next day Rousseau and Thérèse would depart.

Voltaire was utterly different from the reclusive Rousseau. Born into a well-to-do Paris family as François-Marie Arouet, he became a famous poet and playwright under the pen name of Voltaire, and got rich through canny investment. He was now living in a splendid château just outside Geneva, across the border from France where he might be prosecuted for his writings. Though not an original thinker like Rousseau, Voltaire was a brilliant wit and a great popularizer of ideas, as well as a tireless crusader against political and religious oppression. He conducted a massive correspondence with people all over Europe, and welcomed visitors in a lordly but detached manner; over the years more than five hundred of them came from Britain alone. Being received by Rousseau was quite a coup for Boswell; being received by Voltaire was not.[29]

Boswell's conversations with Voltaire were casual and brief. The most interesting remark he recorded was that although Voltaire could speak English fluently, having spent a two-year exile in England at one time, he no longer used it: "To speak English one must place the tongue between the teeth, and I have lost my teeth."[30]

With his unquenchable confidence, Boswell undertook to lecture the great skeptic about the truths of Christianity. "The company went to supper. Monsieur de Voltaire and I remained in the drawing room with a great Bible before us, and if ever two mortal men disputed with vehemence, we did. Yes, upon that occasion he was one individual and I another. For a certain portion of time there was a fair opposition between Voltaire and Boswell." It did not occur to him that Voltaire, an experienced actor, was amusing himself by putting on an act. "His aged frame trembled beneath him. He cried, 'Oh, I am very sick; my head turns round,' and he let himself gently fall upon an easy chair. He recovered. I resumed our conversation."[31]

Looking back on this visit, Boswell observed complacently in his journal, "I have a pliant ease of manners which must please. I can tune myself so to the tone of any bearable man I am with that he is as much at freedom as with another self, and till I am gone, cannot imagine me a stranger." There was some truth to that, but it seems likely that neither Rousseau nor Voltaire was as impressed as Boswell imagined. In Italy he met a Genevan who told him,

"Rousseau laughed at you. Voltaire writes to any young man well-recommended and full of fire, and then forgets him, 'that English bugger.' "[32]

Some months afterward Boswell wrote to Voltaire, hoping for an extended correspondence, and received (in imperfect English) a sarcastic reply: "You seem solicitous about that pretty thing called soul. I do protest you I know nothing of it, nor wether it is, nor what it is, nor what it shall be. Young scholars and priests know all that perfectly. For my part I am but a very ignorant fellow."[33]

A little over a year later, there would be a surprising sequel to the encounter with Rousseau and Thérèse. Having been driven out of Switzerland, Rousseau accepted an invitation from David Hume to take refuge in England, and Thérèse was planning to join him there after he found a place to live. When Boswell got to Paris he heard that she was there and called on her, whereupon she asked whether she could possibly travel with him: "Mon Dieu, Monsieur, if we could go together!" He told her that that was exactly what he would like, and as it turned out, he did more than just accompany her. While they were waiting in Calais for a favorable wind, she invited him into her bed.[34]

Long afterward, when Boswell's journals were about to be sold to the collector Ralph Isham, their owner tore out numerous embarrassing passages, including the account of the voyage with Thérèse. "When Lady Talbot took a look she exclaimed, 'We can't have that sort of thing, can we?' and abruptly threw the offending pages into the fire burning in a grate. I looked on in anguish but was unable to interfere."[35]

Isham had seen the offending account, however, and he recalled that Boswell complained of Thérèse riding him "agitated, like a bad rider galloping downhill." It may be that he had had little experience of women who took an active role in sex. She also hurt his feelings by remarking that he was not the great lover he thought he was, and advised him to consider what can be accomplished with hands. All of this rests only on Isham's report, but there can be no doubt that the encounter really happened. The first surviving entry in Boswell's journal is at Dover: "Wednesday 12 February. Yesterday morning had gone to bed very early, and had done it once: thirteen in all. Was really affectionate to her."[36]

Boswell promised Thérèse never to tell anyone, and he seems to have kept his word. But it's clear that she told Rousseau. Boswell had been expecting to see much of Rousseau in England, but after delivering Thérèse, never got to see him at all. When he wrote to inquire after Rousseau's health he received the chilly answer that it wasn't good, followed by a pointed suggestion: "Permit me in turn to recommend the care of your health, and especially to have yourself bled from time to time. I believe this would do you good." The implication was that regular bleeding might diminish an overactive libido.[37]

THE WARM SOUTH

Italy was the favored destination of all young Englishmen on the Grand Tour. It could be reached only by a laborious ascent over one of the Alpine passes, in an era when most travelers still regarded mountains as ugly and dangerous obstacles, not sights worth seeing for themselves. Boswell chose the route that crossed Mont Cenis, nearly 7,000 feet high, east of Grenoble. As a teenager Rousseau had made the same crossing on foot, but well-to-do travelers like Boswell sat on an arrangement of cords strung between a pair of poles. Six men took turns carrying him, in teams of two.[38]

Boswell would spend ten months in Italy, from January through October, 1765; he made extended stays in Turin, Rome, Naples, Venice, Milan, and Siena. It was at Rome that he had his portrait painted by a young Scottish artist, George Willison (color plate 12). He chose to appear in the same scarlet-laced suit and green cloak with fox fur border that he had worn to call upon Rousseau—an odd choice, since Rousseau was an apostle of simplicity. In his notes Boswell pondered for a while whether the background of the painting should show "head or owl." The head would have been a classical bust of some kind, but he chose instead Athena's owl of wisdom, hoping no doubt that it was an auspicious omen.[39]

Sightseeing never interested Boswell. After he climbed to the summit of Mount Vesuvius, his only comment was: "Monstrous mountain. Smoke; saw hardly anything." Works of art fared little better, though he viewed them dutifully. His sole reaction to the Apollo Belvedere was "Baddish knees," and although we know from his memoranda that he saw Leonardo's *Last Supper,* he said nothing about it at all. Only people, especially female people, aroused genuine interest. "We were accompanied by a doctor from Ravenna and his wife, a rather well-shaped woman with very beautiful black hair."[40]

One person Boswell was delighted to encounter was John Wilkes, whom he had met in London when dining with Lord Eglinton at a Society of Beef-steaks that met in an upper room at the Covent Garden theater. Wilkes had become the focus of a major political controversy, when he was repeatedly elected to Parliament but refused admission because he was publishing keen criticisms of the government in a periodical called *The North Briton.* They eventually got him on charges of pornography, for an outrageous poem called *An Essay on Woman* that was privately printed for a mock-religious libertine group he belonged to called the Hell Fire Club. One of his servants gave the poem to the authorities, and Wilkes had to flee to exile abroad.

It's not known whether Boswell saw the poem, but if he did its philosophy should have appealed to him. In the *Essay on Man* Alexander Pope had called the universe "a mighty maze, but not without a plan." In Wilkes's adaptation,

> Let us (since life can little more supply
> Than just a few good fucks and then we die)
> Expatiate free o'er that loved scene of Man,
> A mighty maze, for mighty pricks to scan.[41]

"Wilkes and Liberty" had been the rallying cry of his London supporters, and from afar, many American colonists admired him. (Together with another liberal politician he inspired the name of Wilkes-Barre, Pennsylvania.) Boswell was politically conservative in most ways, but he did have romantic notions about "liberty." In London he had read each issue of the *North Briton* "with vast relish," even though the title was an implicit slap at the Scots, and he commented that "there is a poignant acrimony in it." When he got to Turin and discovered that Wilkes was there, he sent a note playfully recording a range of feelings: "I am told that Mr. Wilkes is now in Turin. As a politician, my monarchical soul abhors him. As a Scotsman I smile at him. As a friend I know him not. As a companion I love him. I believe it is not decent for me to wait upon him. Yet I wish much to see him. I shall be alone and have a tolerable dinner upon my table at one o'clock." Boswell and Wilkes immediately hit it off, and years later their friendship would produce a truly memorable encounter with Samuel Johnson.[42]

As with other languages, Boswell quickly became fluent in Italian. Exasperated by a sailor who kept postponing a voyage, he exclaimed, *Bestia bugerone! Non voglio esser più coglionato; voglio partire assolutamente questa sera. Cospetto! Si non fosse un peccato di mazzare un uomo, vi mazzarei in questo momento!*—"You big stupid bugger, I don't want to be ballocksed around anymore. I absolutely want to leave this evening. I swear to God [*cospetto*, "in the sight of God"], if it wasn't a sin to club a man to death, I'd do it right now!"[43]

In Holland and Germany Boswell had done his best to leave prostitutes alone, but in Italy he abstained no longer. Inevitably, he was reinfected with gonorrhea, and also got crab lice. "Yesterday much better. Discovered beasts. Shaved; ludicrous distress. Swear conduct. Remember family." In addition he was determined to have love affairs with ladies of fashion, which he understood were easy to manage in the warm South.[44]

Two different women in Turin turned out to be indifferent to his passionate pleas: "Ah! when we abandon ourselves to pleasures under the veil of darkness, what transports, what ecstasy will be ours! . . . O love! Baneful and delicious madness, I feel you, and am your slave." In Florence the campaign met with more success, and one woman there, Girolama Piccolomini, seems to have fallen genuinely in love, even though she recognized bitterly that he was only playing a game. After he moved on she kept sending him passionately suggestive letters: "In this very moment in which I write to you, I feel a violent resurgence of the strong impression that you made on me, and I experience the effects of that sweet memory. I am sorry that you cannot observe the excitement with which I write this letter, and the emotions I feel in this very process; but you can imagine them if you have ever been in love, as you know the strength of desire, and you know what desperate remedies must be taken when lovers are separated!"[45]

Boswell was learning languages and gaining familiarity with European culture, but he also needed to fulfill a third goal of a Grand Tour by making valuable connections. After Wilkes was permitted to return to England, he and Boswell would resume their friendship, but he was much too disreputable to advance a young man's career. In Rome Boswell established another friendship of exactly the kind he was looking for. Lord Mountstuart, four years younger than himself, was the eldest son of the Scottish Earl of Bute. Though Bute was no longer prime minister, his son was still somebody who seemed likely to become important, and could be Boswell's patron in due course. When he wrote to his father about it, Lord Auchinleck was delighted, and gave him permission to stay on in Italy longer than originally planned so that the relationship could grow firm.

Soon Boswell and Mountstuart were spending most of their time together, and in a letter to Rousseau Boswell said that his new friend told him, "Boswell, I will teach you how to live." They agreed to be traveling companions, but it soon became obvious that their temperaments were very different, and quarrels kept flaring up. Afraid of being condescended to, Boswell often gave offense by stubbornness and pride, as he eventually had to acknowledge. As for the hoped-for patronage, it never happened.[46]

In addition to resenting Mountstuart's attitude of superiority, Boswell had to deal with the contempt of his traveling tutor, a Genevan named Paul Mallet. "You know no one branch of learning," Mallet told him, accurately enough. "You never read. I don't say this to offend you, but of young men who have studied I have never found one who had so few ideas as you." The three of them quarreled constantly as they traveled along, and at one point Boswell declared, "Monsieur Mallet, if you annoy me, I shall have to crush you."[47]

CORSICA

After parting with Mountstuart, Boswell departed as well from the customary Grand Tour itinerary and made a side trip to Corsica. At that time the island was hardly ever visited by outsiders, but it was much in the news because of a rebellion against the city-state of Genoa, which had governed it since the Middle Ages. Corsican rebels held the mountainous interior, led by a charismatic general named Pasquale Paoli. If they did succeed in winning their freedom, Paoli would become their first president—a kind of Corsican George Washington.

In the *Social Contract* Rousseau had mentioned Corsica as the one place in Europe—isolated, and not yet prey to modernization—that might still become a true republic. "I have a premonition," he wrote, "that one day this little island will astonish Europe." Boswell saw his chance. His enthusiasm for "liberty" was stimulated by the thought that the Corsicans, like the Scots, were a brave people in rugged highlands defending their freedom against an outside power. And he reasoned that if he could get to know Paoli and his soldiers, he could later win fame by writing a book about them. Unlike other dreams of glory that Boswell nursed, this one would actually come to pass.[48]

Paoli was a genuinely impressive figure, and he struck Boswell as a hero right out of Plutarch's *Lives of the Noble Greeks and Romans.* In the picture reproduced here (figure 28) the female figure blowing a shell trumpet has a cap of liberty on her staff, which would become an iconic symbol after the French Revolution. A freedom fighter gazes up at her with the Moor's head emblem of Corsica behind him (it went back to a time when the island was governed by Aragon), and General Paoli presides from above.

Boswell was impressed by the big Corsican dogs, some of which always stayed close to Paoli to guard against assassins. "He treats them with great kindness, and they are strongly attached to him. Were any person to approach the general during the darkness of the night, they would instantly tear him in pieces."[49]

The Corsicans struck Boswell as resembling the ancient Spartans, whom Rousseau likewise admired for their self-discipline and loyalty to their nation.

PASCALIS de PAOLI.
Dux Corsorum pro Libertate Pugnantium.
Natus 1723.

L. de Montagna del.   J. E. Nilson fec. et excud. Aug. V.   C. Gr. et Priv. S. C. R. M.

28. Pasquale Paoli

European monarchs commonly deployed armies of hired mercenaries, whereas Rousseau was in favor of citizen militias fighting for their own land and families. Ideas like those inspired Boswell when he later wrote, in his published *Account of Corsica,* "The warlike force of Corsica principally consists in a bold and resolute militia. Every Corsican has a musket put in his hand as soon as he is able to carry it; and as there is a constant emulation in shooting, they become excellent marksmen, and will hit with a single bullet a very small mark at a great distance."[50]

The islanders' life seemed also to offer glimpses of a classical golden age. Crossing the steep mountains with Boswell, the soldiers supplemented "their best wine and some delicious pomegranates" by throwing stones into the spreading chestnut trees. "In that manner we brought down a shower of chestnuts with which we filled our pockets, and went on eating them with great relish; and when this made us thirsty, we lay down by the side of the first brook, put our mouths to the stream and drank sufficiently. It was just being for a little while one of the *prisca gens mortalium* [primitive race of mortals] who ran about in the woods eating acorns and drinking water." That was from Horace. Boswell was fond of classical references and knew forty odes of Horace by heart.[51]

A DEATH AND A REUNION

After six weeks in Corsica, during which he trekked on foot through two hundred miles of mountainous country, Boswell sailed back to Genoa and prepared to head for home. He made a leisurely progress westward along the Riviera, generally on foot or horseback while his luggage came along by boat. But the Riviera was not yet the glamorous destination it would later become. "I was surprised to find Antibes so small and so poor-looking a place."[52]

Then it was onward to Marseille, Aix, and Avignon, by stagecoach to Lyons, and finally Paris. It was now January of 1766, just short of two and a half years since Boswell had sailed from Harwich to Holland. He intended to stay in Paris for some time, but unexpectedly received shocking news that made it necessary for him to return home at once. Wilkes was in Paris by now, and had English newspapers in his lodgings. Casually picking up a copy of the *St. James's Chronicle,* Boswell was staggered to discover a report of his mother's death. He had heard that she was "indisposed" in some way, but had no idea that she might be seriously ill—we don't know with what.

He consoled himself by rushing to a brothel "as in a fever." A letter from his father confirming the loss arrived the next day. "Nothing could be a greater proof of the reality and efficacy of true religion," Lord Auchinleck wrote, "than what appeared in her conduct during the whole time of her indisposition. . . . She left us without any struggle or even a groan, and as it were fell asleep. . . . It will be needless to tell you that I expect you home with all speed. Your brother [David] remembers you with great affection. I am, my dear son, your affectionate father. ALEX. BOSWELL."[53]

"Was quite stupefied," James wrote in his journal. "Wept in bursts; prayed to her like most solemn Catholic to saint." Earlier in the journey he had already had premonitions. "I received a letter from my dear mother, which gave me great comfort, for I had not heard from her since I left England and had formed to myself dreary ideas of her being dead, or sick, or offended with me."[54]

On the twelfth of February Boswell and Thérèse arrived in Dover, and the next day she was reunited with Rousseau. Boswell found him disappointing, as he remarked in a note addressed to himself in the second person: "He seemed so oldish and weak [he was fifty-four], you had no longer your enthusiasm for him." Anyway, the only mentor he wanted to see was Samuel Johnson, and he called upon him right away. "Immediately to Johnson; received you with open arms. You kneeled, and asked blessing. Miss Williams glad of your return. When she went out, he hugged you to him like a sack, and grumbled, 'I hope we shall pass many years of regard.'"[55]

Boswell grieved for the loss of his mother, certainly, but it may also have been a relief to be free from her passive-aggressive piety. And in Johnson he had the father figure he really needed: highly moral and capable of criticism, but nonjudgmental and loving. They would indeed pass many years of regard, and Boswell would repay his debt by writing an immortal biography.

CHAPTER 7

The Club Is Born

During the relatively brief time Boswell spent with Johnson in 1763—it was less than three months—their affectionate friendship helped to cheer Johnson up. But that fall, when Boswell was in Holland, Johnson sank into an alarming depression. In part it was due to humiliation at not being able to complete the Shakespeare edition he had contracted for seven years previously. But mainly the depression reflected a welling up of obsessions that had plagued him ever since his youth.

Johnson's Oxford friend William Adams visited him at this time and "found him in a deplorable state, sighing, groaning, talking to himself, and restlessly walking from room to room. He then used this emphatical expression of the misery which he felt: 'I would consent to have a limb amputated to recover my spirits.'"[1]

Another friend, Henry Thrale, was shocked when Johnson started to make some sort of anguished confession. Henry's wife Hester later wrote, "I well remember my husband involuntarily lifted up one hand to shut his mouth, from provocation at hearing a man so wildly proclaim what he could at last persuade no one to believe; and what, if true, would have been so very unfit to reveal." She doesn't indicate what he might have intended to say, but she almost certainly guessed that it had to do with "sensuality"—sexual thoughts that Johnson believed it was sinful not to repress.[2]

Deepest of all was fear of damnation. Johnson had a custom of reviewing his inner state at Easter each year, and in April of 1764 he wrote, "My thoughts have been clouded with sensuality. . . . A kind of strange oblivion has overspread me, so that I know not what has become of the last year, and perceive that incidents and intelligence pass over me without leaving any impression. This is not the life to which heaven is promised." He brooded often about the parable of the talents, dreading eternal punishment for wasting his great gifts: "Cast ye the unprofitable servant into outer darkness; there shall be weeping and gnashing of teeth."[3]

Johnson's religion was always grounded in fear, and in the *Rambler* he had even warned his readers against not fearing *enough*. "If he who considers himself as suspended over the abyss of eternal perdition only by the thread of life, which must soon part by its own weakness, and which the wing of every minute may divide, can cast his eyes around him without shuddering with horror, or panting for security—what can he judge of himself but that he is not yet awaked to sufficient conviction?" Mr. Spectator never wrote like that.[4]

The Thrales intervened by making Johnson a welcome guest, and before long a resident, at their country estate across the Thames. Almost equally valuable was what Joshua Reynolds did. By 1764 he and Johnson were close friends, and he was well aware that socializing was essential therapy for his friend. In one of the first *Ramblers* Johnson had written, "It may be laid down as a position which will seldom deceive, that when a man cannot bear his own company there is something wrong." His readers couldn't know it, but he was talking about himself.[5]

Early in 1764, Reynolds proposed to Johnson that they form a club, made up of convivial and interesting friends who would spend an evening together once a week. They agreed that nine members would be a good number— enough to keep conversation lively and wide-ranging, even when not everyone was able to attend. Another member said later that the intention was to choose people so agreeable "that if only two of these chanced to meet for the evening, they should be able to entertain each other." They chose a Latin motto for the club, *esto perpetua,* "Let it be perpetual."[6]

After the Club began to grow in size, a rule was adopted that new members had to be chosen by unanimous election; a single blackball was enough to block a candidate. Boswell, although desperate to be elected after he returned to England in 1766, didn't get in until 1773. Club members liked him well enough, but they thought of him as a lightweight whose only merit was devotion to Johnson.

Unlike some later London clubs, this one did not have physical premises of its own, though for the first two decades it did meet regularly at the Turk's Head Tavern at 9 Gerrard Street, just off the Strand (color plate 13). The Westminster City Council has affixed a plaque outside: "Here in the former Turk's Head Tavern, DR. SAMUEL JOHNSON & JOSHUA REYNOLDS founded The Club in 1764." As the sign indicates, the building was later purchased by a charitable organization for use as a dispensary, providing medicine to the poor. The building is now occupied by the New Loon Moon Supermarket.

It's sometimes claimed that this was the very first London club, but clubs of all sorts had been active there and in other towns ever since the beginning of the century. The term came from the practice of "clubbing together" to split the charges at a coffeehouse or tavern after each meeting. In the *Dictionary* Johnson defines "club" as "an assembly of good fellows, meeting under certain conditions."

Except for Johnson and Reynolds, none of the good fellows had much public reputation at the time; they were chosen simply because the two founders liked them. Edmund Burke was then working as private secretary to a member of Parliament, and would not enter Parliament himself until two years later. Dr. Christopher Nugent was Burke's father-in-law; Anthony Chamier was a stockbroker about whom not much is known. Oliver Goldsmith was the only other professional writer; he had been turning out anonymous journalism, as Johnson once did, and was just beginning to become known by his own name. He liked to be called "Dr. Goldsmith," on the strength of some medical study in his youth, but he had no actual degree and never practiced. Johnson always addressed him as "Goldy," even though he hated the nickname—"I have often desired him," he told Boswell, "not to call me *Goldy*."7

The final three members were friends whom Johnson in particular wanted to include: a pair of young men about town, Topham Beauclerk and Bennet Langton, and the magistrate and musicologist Sir John Hawkins (figure 29).

Hawkins was stuffy and humorless, and a few years later, after quarreling with Burke, he was made to feel unwanted and dropped out (his own explanation was that he didn't care for the late hours). Johnson was loyal to old friends but didn't mind seeing him go. Years later Fanny Burney heard him say, "As to Sir John, why really I believe him to be an honest man at the *bottom;* but to be sure he is penurious, and he is mean, and it must be owned he has a degree of brutality, and a tendency to savageness, that cannot easily be

29. Sir John Hawkins

Sam: Johnson President.   JReynolds Pres.
Edm Burke   T. Beauclerk.
Christopher Nugent. M.D. Oliver Goldsmith
Bennet Langton   Ant Chamier.
            John Hawkins.

30. Facsimile signatures of the Club

defended." It is to this conversation that we owe Johnson's often quoted description of Hawkins as "an unclubbable man."[8]

    A facsimile of the signatures of the original nine members (figure 30) gives
a good sense of their individuality. The "president" was a rotating position,
chosen to preside at a given meeting.

EATING AND DRINKING

The first order of business was to get settled in a private room on the second floor of the Turk's Head Tavern, and order a satisfying dinner. Not much was recorded about particular meals they had, but we know from other sources that impressive options were available in English taverns. Some years later the two principal cooks at the nearby Crown and Anchor in the Strand published *The Universal Cook and City and Country Housekeeper,* with detailed recipes for the dishes they were prepared to present—not all at the same time, of course. The list is organized by seasons (green vegetables weren't available in winter, for example). Meats included beef, mutton, veal, pork, lamb, and rabbit. Poultry covered a still bigger range: geese, ducks, widgeons, chickens, turkeys, pigeons, woodcocks, snipes, larks, plovers, partridges, and pheasants. Fish were not neglected, either: turbot, smelts, gudgeon, eels, sturgeon, sole, and carp; and you could also get cockles, mussels, and oysters. In an era when only the well-to-do had their own cooks, a hearty tavern meal was a treat.[9]

With dinner there would be wine, of course, followed afterward by more wine. Stronger spirits were little used. Only the very poor drank gin, and although he was a Scot, Boswell didn't care for whisky. Port, not as potent as the fortified wine known as port today, was popular because it was inexpensive; French wines were subject to a higher tariff than Portuguese. Boswell mentions that the landlord of the Queen's Arms Tavern in St. Paul's Churchyard had "eight hundred dozen" bottles of "excellent old port." That would be 9,600 bottles, presumably an adequate supply for a while.[10]

There were plenty of other possibilities for drinks. Punch was based on brandy, together with lemons, oranges, and sugar. Bishop was made from hot port, sugar, nutmeg, and roasted oranges. Possets consisted of hot milk curdled in wine, with egg yolks and cinnamon or nutmeg. People liked their drinks sweet. On one occasion Boswell mentions that "every man drank his bottle of Rhenish with sugar."[11]

At various times in his life Johnson drank no alcohol, saying that he was capable of abstaining but not of moderation. He had no objection to his friends drinking, however. During one of his dry periods they persuaded him to pass judgment on a glass of claret (Bordeaux wine) "not from recollection, which might be dim, but from immediate sensation." After trying it he shook his head and said, "Poor stuff! No, Sir, claret is the liquor for boys; port, for men; but he who aspires to be a hero (smiling) must drink brandy." When he was asked on another occasion whether it was possible for a person to be happy in the present moment, he answered, "Never, but when he is drunk."[12]

The custom of hearty drinking continued well into the next century. A jolly clergyman in Thomas Love Peacock's novel *Melincourt* says, "There are two reasons for drinking: one is when you are thirsty, to cure it; the other, when you are not thirsty, to prevent it. I drink by anticipation of thirst that may be. Prevention is better than cure. What is death? Dust and ashes. There is nothing so dry. What is life? Spirit. What is spirit? Wine."[13]

It's worth mentioning that we never hear of ale or beer at the Club. It was regarded as very much an indulgence of the lower classes, though among them it was consumed in prodigious quantities. When Benjamin Franklin worked briefly in London as a printer earlier in the century, he found his fellow workers to be "great guzzlers of beer." An "alehouse boy"—there were roughly 7,000 alehouses in London—was kept on hand to fetch supplies. Franklin's companion at the press "drank every day a pint before breakfast, a pint at breakfast with his bread and cheese, a pint between breakfast and dinner, a pint at dinner, a pint in the afternoon about six o'clock, and another when he had done his day's work." The industrious Franklin, one of whose personal resolutions was "eat not to dullness, drink not to elevation," didn't approve.[14]

Beer figured, along with roast beef, as a symbol of Britishness. Hogarth's famous *Gin Lane,* with its horrific view of helpless drunks and a mother screaming while a madman impales her baby on a spike, was paired with a wholesome *Beer Street* (figure 31). Verses beneath the picture declare optimistically,

> Beer, happy Produce of our isle,
> Can sinewy Strength impart,
> And wearied with Fatigue and Toil
> Can cheer each manly Heart.

"Manly," but in the picture, a female fishmonger is holding a big mug. We can be sure of her trade because she has a basket of herrings on her head, and is perusing "A New Ballad on the Herring Fishery."

Robust and well-fed workers are resting in the evening, while roofers up above drink a toast. A lady in a sedan chair waits while her chairmen likewise pause to enjoy mugs of beer, brought out from the alehouse behind them. The only person in Beer Street who is not doing well is the pawnbroker (in *Gin Lane* a pawnbroker was prosperous). Here he is gratefully accepting a mug of beer, but he receives it through a little opening in his door because he might be arrested for debt if he came out—so poor is the pawnbroker, and so prosperous are the neighbors who don't need his services.[15]

31. Beer Street

TALKING

Above all the Club existed for conversation: not just small talk, but wide-ranging discussion on topics of all kinds. At an earlier time Hawkins had cofounded a club with Johnson known as the Ivy Lane Club. That was when he heard Johnson declare "that a tavern chair was the throne of human felicity." At a tavern the staff could be counted on to be attentive, Johnson said, and there was no host who needed to be flattered. "Wine there exhilarates my spirits, and prompts me to free conversation and an interchange of discourse with those whom I most love. I dogmatize and am contradicted, and in this conflict of opinions and sentiments I find delight."[16]

Boswell described Johnson's characteristic style of conversation as "talking for victory." Goldsmith once said, "There is no arguing with Johnson, for if his pistol misses fire, he knocks you down with the butt end of it." Boswell enjoyed that wisecrack so much that he quoted it two different times in the *Life*.[17]

When Reynolds remarked to Boswell that Johnson never hesitated to plunge into an argument, "'Yes,' said I, 'he has no formal preparation, no flourishing with his sword; he is through your body in an instant.'" Johnson would often take a position just for the fun of it. "He would begin thus," Boswell remarked to Garrick, "Why, Sir, as to the good or evil of card playing." "Now," Garrick replied, "he is thinking which side he shall take."[18]

When it was a fair fight between equals, it wasn't necessarily bullying. Leslie Stephen observes that in a culture that enjoyed competitive conversation, Johnson's putdowns were only offensive if they got really insulting. His sharp retorts, Stephen says, "were fair play under the conditions of the game, as it is fair play to kick an opponent's shins at football."[19]

Johnson especially enjoyed matching wits with Burke, who had a debater's talent for inventing arguments and an exceptional gift for persuasive language. "His stream of mind is perpetual," Johnson once said. The torrent of Burke's words and ideas was more than even Boswell could get down on paper. Johnson said memorably, "You could not stand five minutes with that man beneath a shed while it rained, but you must be convinced you had been standing with the greatest man you had ever yet seen."[20]

Once, when Johnson was ill and someone mentioned Burke, he exclaimed, "That fellow calls forth all my powers. Were I to see Burke now, it would kill me." Boswell comments, "So much was he accustomed to consider conversation as a contest, and such was his notion of Burke as an opponent." Burke himself once wrote, "He that wrestles with us strengthens our nerves and sharpens our skill. Our antagonist is our helper."[21]

Johnson liked to clinch a statement with a witty bon mot, and Boswell describes the way he would gaze about triumphantly as it took effect. This too was competitive. He told Langton that he had had a dream in which he was upset because somebody else was besting him in a contest of wit. When he woke up he realized that he himself was responsible for both sides.[22]

That's not to say that Johnson was always as witty as he intended to be, or as Boswell thought he was. On one occasion Boswell, defending the excellence of Scottish writers, protested "But, Sir, we have Lord Kames." Kames was a distinguished jurist and a good friend of Boswell's, but a writer of limited accomplishment. To this Johnson boomed out: "You *have* Lord Kames. Keep him; ha, ha, ha!"[23]

At many points in the *Life of Johnson* Boswell quotes from conversations that he heard at the Club after he did get elected. The members told him firmly that their private remarks must stay private, so he was careful to disguise their identities. He often wrote down memorable exchanges in his

32. Johnson by Charles Addams

journal, and on one occasion he gave himself the challenge of recreating an entire evening as far as possible. In the *Life* this narrative fills six pages. Nobody says anything unforgettable, but the level of intelligent discourse is high, and what is most striking is the atmosphere of relaxed thoughtfulness.

This conversation took place on April 3, 1778, five years after Boswell was elected to the Club. In the *Life* he indicates the speakers by letters of the alphabet; Reynolds for example is "P" for Painter, and Burke is "E" for Edmund. But since we have the original journal account, we can be sure who they were.[24]

The first speaker is Lord Ossory, who tells the group that he had gone to see an ancient Roman statue of a dog that was about to be sold for a thousand guineas. Ossory heard that the original dog supposedly belonged to Alcibiades, the Athenian statesman and disciple of Socrates. Johnson jumps in with a comment that is both authoritative and literal-minded: "His tail then must be docked. That was the mark of Alcibiades's dog." That surprising detail comes from Plutarch's *Lives of the Noble Greeks and Romans;* Johnson had an extraordinary memory for nearly everything he ever read.

Meanwhile Burke is shocked at the price: "A thousand guineas! The representation of no animal whatever is worth so much." Johnson disagrees, waxing philosophical:

> Sir, it is not the worth of the thing, but of the skill in forming it which is so highly estimated. Everything that enlarges the sphere of human powers, that shows man he can do what he thought he could not do, is valuable. The first man who balanced a straw upon his nose; Johnson [a well-known equestrian of that name], who rode upon three horses at a time; in short, all such men deserved the applause of mankind, not on account of the use of what they did, but of the dexterity which they exhibited.

Reynolds was present, but silent here. Apparently he didn't choose to defend the fine arts as against equestrianism and straw-balancing. He probably thought Johnson was just being provocative.

The discussion in the tavern now turns to the politically charged issue of emigration to the colonies. Was the home country being dangerously depopulated? Burke claims that emigration actually causes population to increase at home. "That sounds very much like a paradox," Gibbon comments, which it was probably meant to be. Burke and Johnson both enjoyed doing that kind of thing to stimulate debate.

By now Burke had been a member of Parliament for over a decade, and was admired as a brilliant orator, but Sheridan remarks that his speeches seldom produce the results he argues for. Burke then makes a comment that all of his biographers quote: "I believe in any body of men in England I should have been in the minority; I have always been in the minority."

The conversation turns to recent travel writers who have a low opinion of the people they encounter.

> BURKE. From the experience which I have had—and I have had a great deal—I have learnt to think *better* of mankind.
> JOHNSON. From my experience I have found them worse in commercial dealings, more disposed to cheat, than I had any notion of; but more disposed to do one another good than I had conceived.
> GIBBON. Less just, and more beneficent.
> JOHNSON. And really it is wonderful, considering how much attention is necessary for men to take care of themselves, and ward off immediate evils which press upon them, it is wonderful how much they do for others.

Reynolds mentions a man who accused a servant of theft, but was thrown in jail himself after the judge discovered that he had deliberately left money lying in the open to see whether the servant would steal it. Johnson's comment is characteristically generous: "You know, humanly speaking, there is a degree of temptation which will overcome any virtue. Now, in so far as you approach [i.e., bring] temptation to a man, you do him an injury; and if he is overcome, you share his guilt." Boswell, who seems to have kept quiet most of the time, can't resist proposing an analogy of his own: "Yes, you are his seducer; you have debauched him."

In all of this, nobody is showing off, and although Johnson sometimes talked for victory, here he is perfectly in tune with his companions. Each topic (and no doubt Boswell's written record was condensed) is pursued for a little while until everyone who wants to has offered a thought, and then somebody—often it's Burke—throws out a new topic.

What cannot be stressed enough is that this entire living episode only exists because Boswell paid close attention and wrote it all down. Sherlock Holmes says to Watson, "It may be that you are not yourself luminous, but you are a conductor of light."[25]

Over the years the Club would grow in size, first by small increments and later by large ones. Four new members were elected in the 1760s and twenty-one in the 1770s. Johnson regretted that, preferring the intimacy of the original group, but he was proud of the range of accomplishments that were represented. In 1777 he told Hester Thrale, "Our Club, Madam, is a society which can scarcely be matched in the world. We have Reynolds for painting; Goldsmith for poetry; Percy for antiquities; Nugent for physic; Chamier for trade, politics, and all money concerns; Burke for oratory; Beauclerk for polite literature; Dyer for modern history and travels; Chambers for the law; Langton for ecclesiastical history and indeed all branches of learning; Sir John Hawkins for judicature and ancient music." Admittedly, some of those named had only modest distinction, and it was years since Hawkins had been a member. Hester commented that Johnson's boast "was little less than ridiculous."[26]

A point about social status may not be obvious. At the time most people would have taken it for granted that noblemen would be invited to be members. Not a single peer was elected until Lord Ossory in 1777, the year before this conversation. Of the forty-two members who were elected during the first twenty years, only three were peers. Nearly all of the rest of the members were middle class, though that term didn't yet exist; they would then have called it "the middling sort" on a sliding scale, not a distinct "class" in the Marxist sense. Johnson's father was a provincial bookseller who also ran a tannery, Percy's a wholesale grocer, Burke's an attorney, and Reynolds's and Goldsmith's fathers were clergymen in very modest circumstances. (A complete list of Club membership through 1784, the year of Johnson's death, is given in an appendix to this book.)

C. S. Lewis once commented, "When I was a boy—a *bourgeois* boy—that term was applied to my social class by the class above it. *Bourgeois* meant 'not aristocratic, therefore vulgar.' When I was in my twenties this changed. My class was now vilified by the class below it; *bourgeois* began to mean 'not proletarian, therefore parasitic, reactionary.' Thus it has always been a reproach to assign a man to that class which has provided the world with nearly all its divines, poets, philosophers, scientists, musicians, painters, doctors, architects, and administrators."[27]

In his biography of Johnson, the novelist and poet John Wain suggests that clubs like this one played a role in London like that of cafés in twentieth-century Paris. There's some truth to that, but Simone de Beauvoir could accompany Jean-Paul Sartre to the Deux Magots. There were no women in the Club, ever, and nobody even considered it. Since Johnson greatly appreciated the company of women, that's a good reason why Hester Thrale's dinner parties at Streatham would develop into a kind of shadow club.[28]

BEYOND THE CLUB

Writing about Boswell's *Life of Johnson,* Macaulay paid tribute to the richness of the social world it conjures up:

> The clubroom is before us, at the table on which stands the omelet for Nugent [as a Catholic he wouldn't eat meat on Fridays] and the lemons for Johnson [at times he drank lemonade rather than wine]. There are assembled those heads which live forever on the canvas of Reynolds. There are the spectacles of Burke and the tall thin form of Langton, the courtly sneer of Beauclerk and the beaming smile of Garrick, Gibbon tapping his snuff box and Sir Joshua with his trumpet in his ear. In the foreground is that strange figure which is as familiar to us as the figures of those among whom we have been brought up, the gigantic body, the huge massy face seamed with the scars of disease, the brown coat, the black worsted stockings, the grey wig with the scorched foretop, the dirty hands, the nails bitten and pared to the quick.[29]

Macaulay's set piece has been aptly called "a still life reanimated as caricature." In his perspective the members of the Club become Dickensian characters, appreciated as amusingly familiar. His picture gives little sense of their full existence in London life, let alone of their professional achievements. They were great talkers because they knew and did so much, and many of them rose to accomplishments of the highest order. No fewer than seven—Johnson, Burke, Reynolds, Garrick, Gibbon, Adam Smith, and Boswell—made up a constellation of talent that has rarely if ever been equaled. Contemporaries would have added Goldsmith and Sheridan to the list of stars.[30]

Not all of these members of the Club get adequate attention in the *Life of Johnson,* where the focus is naturally on Johnson himself. Boswell deeply admired Burke, but admitted frankly that it was impossible to record the brilliance of his conversation, and besides, he had only a shallow understanding of Burke's political thought. Boswell was friendly with Reynolds, but was uninterested in painting, and although he loved going to plays he saw Garrick only as an actor, not as the pioneering director and theater manager he also was. As for Gibbon and Smith, they are practically invisible in the *Life.* Boswell hated Gibbon, and was astoundingly condescending towards his former professor

Smith. Yet each man created an enduring masterpiece, *The Decline and Fall of the Roman Empire,* and *The Wealth of Nations.*

As for the Club's lesser lights, they were lesser only from the perspective of posthumous reputation. As companions and conversationalists nearly all of them were remarkable too, which is why they were members in the first place. And several were so close to Johnson personally that they pervade the pages of the *Life.* Boswell knew them well, and when he was working on the biography, he took care to collect all the reminiscences they could give him.

Two of these were Topham Beauclerk (pronounced "Toppam Bowclare") and Bennet Langton, who had been among the original nine. Friends since Oxford and just a couple of years older than Boswell himself, they brought out an impulsive playfulness in Johnson that the adoring Boswell did not. "I love the young dogs of this age," Johnson said; "they have more wit and humour and knowledge of life than we had." Fanny Burney remarked that Beauclerk's "highest honour was that of classing himself as one of the friends of Dr. Johnson."[31]

Beauclerk (figure 33) was aristocratic, wealthy, and an entertaining though sarcastic conversationalist. Boswell once remarked, "Beauclerk has a keenness of mind which is very uncommon," and Johnson replied, "Yes, Sir; and everything comes from him so easily. It appears to me that I labor when I say a good thing." Boswell responded diplomatically, "You are loud, Sir, but it is not an effort of mind."[32]

Langton (figure 34), though inseparable from Beauclerk, was very different: deeply learned in the classics, but awkward and even muddled in conversation. He cut a striking figure, startlingly thin and six and a half feet tall. Someone compared him to a stork standing on one leg, and Burke said that when he was among a group of ladies "they were like maids dancing around a maypole."[33]

It was from Langton that Boswell acquired an especially engaging anecdote. One night Langton and Beauclerk had been drinking steadily for hours, and at three in the morning they showed up at Johnson's lodgings and thundered at his door to get him to join them. "At last he appeared in his shirt, with his little black wig on the top of his head instead of a nightcap, and a poker in his hand, imagining probably that some ruffians were coming to attack him. When he discovered who they were and was told their errand, he smiled, and with great good humour agreed to their proposal: 'What, is it you, you dogs! I'll have a frisk with you.'" Boswell tells it so vividly that it's hard to remember he wasn't there himself.[34]

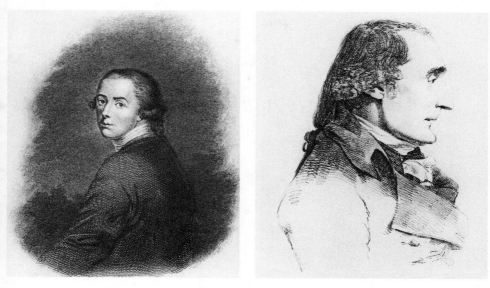

33. Topham Beauclerk   34. Bennet Langton

Another anecdote from Langton brings out a touchingly human aspect of Johnson. He had a cat called Hodge whom he used to stroke affectionately and even buy oysters for. On one occasion he told Langton about a wild young man who was running around town shooting cats, "and then, in a sort of kindly reverie, he bethought himself of his own favourite cat and said, 'But Hodge shan't be shot; no, no, Hodge shall not be shot.'" Vladimir Nabokov liked that anecdote so much that he quoted it—enigmatically—as the epigraph for his novel *Pale Fire*.[35]

CHAPTER 8

Sir Joshua Reynolds

SELF-MADE MAN

A majority of the members of the Club were self-made men, and none more than the Club's originator, Joshua Reynolds, whose rise to eminence and immense wealth was extraordinary. His father, a clergyman and schoolmaster in Devonshire, recognized his artistic talent and apprenticed him to a London painter, but at the time that career held out small prospect for worldly success.

Portrait painters, in particular, were regarded as mere journeymen slavishly reproducing people's features. Michelangelo and Raphael might have exalted reputations, but not Englishmen, and certainly not portrait painters. An influential writer on aesthetics, the Earl of Shaftesbury, said early in the century that theirs was "not a liberal art nor to be esteemed, as requiring no liberal knowledge, genius, education, converse, manners, moral science, mathematics, optics, but merely practical and vulgar." Reynolds was determined to disprove every one of those criticisms.[1]

Even in portrait painting, it was taken for granted that the only good artists came from abroad. Sir Peter Lely was originally Pieter van der Faes, a Dutchman. Sir Anthony van Dyck came from Antwerp. Sir Godfrey Kneller was born Gottfried Kniller in Germany, and it was said that "he was still Gottfried Kniller when he opened his mouth." The royal court had been German-dominated ever since George I ascended the throne in 1714, and in much the same way it was thought that only a German like Handel could compose really good music.[2]

When Reynolds was knighted in 1769 at the age of forty-six, five years after he and Johnson founded the Club, he said frankly, "Distinction is what we all seek after. The world does set a value on titles, and I go with the great stream of life." It was a real coup to be able to put "Sir" in front of his name, and his friends always referred to him as "Sir Joshua."[3]

Reynolds was known for a relaxed, genial temperament, and that didn't change when he became Sir Joshua. Johnson, speaking of his own episodes of depression, said, "Some men, and very thinking men too, have not those vexing thoughts. Sir Joshua Reynolds is the same all the year round." And Fanny Burney, painfully shy in social situations, appreciated his easy congeniality: "He is so pleasant, unaffected, and agreeable that there is no one, among those who are of celebrity, I can converse with half so easily and comfortably."[4]

35. Early self-portrait by Reynolds

A self-portrait that Reynolds painted when he was in his mid-twenties (figure 35) catches the combination of agreeable temperament and fierce ambition. It is been described as "a manifesto of the artist's aims and ambitions: Reynolds casts himself in the role of a man of vision, who uses the art of the past in order to look to the future." The art of the past was the management of light and shadow by Rembrandt, whose work he was then studying closely. He used the standard format for a head and shoulders portrait, thirty inches by twenty-five, but got an unusual effect by turning it on its side.[5]

Reynolds was an enthusiastic clubman, and the club he founded with Johnson was one of six that he attended regularly. The others were the Devonshire, the Eumelian (of which Boswell also became a member), the Thursday Night Club, the gambling club Almack's, and a Society of Dilettanti that encouraged the study of Greek and Roman art. That was its official rationale, anyway. In practice, Horace Walpole said, "The nominal qualification for membership is having been in Italy, and the real one, being drunk."[6]

Johnson once told Boswell that "Sir Joshua Reynolds was the most invulnerable man he knew, the man with whom if you should quarrel, you would find the most difficulty how to abuse." But on at least one occasion the friends did have a spat. Reynolds was praising the social advantages of drinking, and Johnson disagreed; at another time he had complained that far from improving conversation, it provoked "tumultuous, noisy, clamorous merriment." When Reynolds pressed his point Johnson suddenly burst out, "I won't argue any more with you, Sir. You are too far gone." Wounded, Reynolds replied, "I should have thought so indeed, Sir, had I made such a speech as you have now done." Johnson was chagrined: "Nay, don't be angry. I did not mean to offend you."[7]

However tactless Johnson's outburst was, everyone knew that Reynolds was indeed a heavy drinker. He never denied it. He once wrote to Boswell, who was in Scotland at the time, "I love the correspondence of *viva voce* over a bottle, with a great deal of noise and a great deal of nonsense." According to the records of the Club, on that occasion Reynolds and three others—Beauclerk, Gibbon, and Sheridan—put away eight bottles of wine, six of claret and two of port.[8]

THE OTHER PAINTER IN THE HOUSE

Reynolds liked women and was known to have had a number of affairs, but he had no inclination to tie himself down by marriage. To help with his entertaining he relied on female relatives, and especially his youngest sister Frances, who depended on him for financial support.

Frances became a talented painter herself, but Sir Joshua strongly discouraged her from competing with him, though he enlisted her to make copies of his work, and she did eventually show paintings of her own at a couple of Royal Academy exhibitions. Her principal duty was managing the household. For a long time she went along with that. In her commonplace book she advised herself, "It is unnatural in a woman to quit the private domestic path for a public one. It is this consideration that has made painting, which every person thought I pursued only for amusement, a torment as it clashed with the honourable province of family duties." Her brother undoubtedly did his best to reinforce that view.[9]

It was Frances who said that Johnson "set a higher value upon female friendship than, perhaps, most men." Often, when he called at the Reynolds's house, Sir Joshua would be busy in his studio, and Johnson and other friends would sit and drink tea with "Renny," as he affectionately nicknamed her. Once when he and Thomas Percy were there, Johnson began playfully improvising a parody of the traditional ballads Percy had collected:

> I therefore pray thee, Renny dear,
> That thou wilt give to me,
> With cream and sugar softened well,
> Another dish of tea.
>
> Nor fear that I, my gentle maid,
> Shall long detain the cup,
> When once unto the bottom I
> Have drunk the liquor up.
>
> Yet hear, alas! this mournful truth,
> Nor hear it with a frown:
> Thou canst not make the tea so fast
> As I can gulp it down.

Johnson kept on going until Percy begged him to stop.[10]

Johnson was an insatiable user of tea, as Hawkins rather wonderingly confirmed: "He was a lover of tea to an excess hardly credible; whenever it appeared, he was almost raving." Johnson published a droll defense of his habit when he happened to review a polemic entitled *An Essay on Tea, Considered as Pernicious to Health, Obstructing Industry, and Impoverishing the Nation*. He himself, he acknowledged, was "a hardened and shameless tea drinker, who has, for twenty years, diluted his meals with only the infusion of this fascinating plant, whose kettle has scarcely time to cool, who with tea amuses the evening, with tea solaces the midnights, and with tea welcomes the morning."[11]

Johnson knew that Frances was a painter, but he said to Boswell, "Miss Reynolds ought not to paint. Public practice of staring in men's faces is inconsistent with delicacy." When Boswell put that into the *Life* he omitted Frances's name and substituted for it "very indelicate in a female." Not that Johnson suspected her of the least indelicacy. When Hester Thrale was telling him not to probe his own hidden motives so painfully, she asked, "*Will* anybody's mind bear this eternal microscope that you place upon your own?" He replied, "I never saw one that would, except that of my dear Miss Reynolds— and hers is very near to purity itself." What he meant in his remark to Boswell may have been what psychologists confirm, that gazing intently into another person's eyes is likely to provoke desire.[12]

Frances continued to pester Johnson to let her paint him, and eventually he agreed. The result was a truly moving portrait (color plate 14), tender yet unsparingly honest. It captures his massive bulk, stooped posture, and fatigue, as he gazes earnestly out from the shadows. With its haunting honesty, it's a portrait that Sir Joshua would never—indeed could never—have painted of their friend.

Not everyone thought as highly of Frances as Johnson did. Hester observed, "Miss Reynolds had an odd dry manner, something between malice and simplicity." Frances also drove her friends crazy with endless vacillation. Fanny Burney said that Johnson "saw and pitied her foible, but tried to cure it in vain. It was that of living in an habitual perplexity of mind and irresolution of conduct, which to herself was restlessly tormenting, and to all around her was teasingly wearisome. Whatever she suggested or planned one day was reversed the next, though resorted to on the third, as if merely to be again rejected on the fourth, and so on, almost endlessly."[13]

Increasingly, Frances resented her brother's demands, which were not accompanied by affection or gratitude. Hester said, "He certainly does not love her as one should expect a man to love a sister he has so much reason to be proud of; perhaps she paints too well, or has learned too much Latin and is a better scholar than her brother. And upon more reflection I fancy it must be so, for if he only did not like her as an inmate, why should not he give her a genteel annuity and let her live where and how she likes? The poor lady is always miserable, always fretful; yet she seems resolved—nobly enough—not to keep her post by flattery if she cannot keep it by kindness."[14]

In the late 1770s, when their niece Mary Palmer was twenty-five and willing to take over running the London household, Frances suggested that perhaps she could live in Sir Joshua's country house at Richmond upon Thames, since he hardly ever used it—he kept it as a status symbol rather than a place where he cared to spend time. He replied, in writing, that she had no business appropriating his house. She gave up, and moved into modest lodgings of her own. Later she returned to their native Devonshire, remarking after his death that she remembered him only as "a gloomy tyrant." That was a side of the genial Sir Joshua that he didn't show to the world.[15]

THE PORTRAIT FACTORY

Reynolds loved being rich. He was able to maintain a handsome coach, which was a public expression of prosperity, and would lend it to friends to get home after his frequent dinner parties. At those he made a point of encouraging total informality, but not everyone was pleased about it. The far from punctilious Johnson complained to Boswell, "Sir, the servants, instead of doing what they are bid, stand around the table in idle clusters gaping upon the guests, and seem as unfit to attend a company as to steer a man of war." Reynolds's pupil and biographer James Northcote confirmed that there were "two or three occasional undisciplined domestics. The host left everyone at perfect liberty to scramble for himself."[16]

Johnson, who was never wealthy like Reynolds, deeply resented the attitude of haughty patricians toward working for a living. He once startled Boswell by exclaiming, "No man but a blockhead ever wrote except for money." When Boswell quoted that he called it a "strange opinion."[17]

On one occasion that Frances Reynolds recalled, Johnson felt snubbed by a duchess and suspected it was because of his unfashionable clothing. Turning to Joshua, who was sitting next to him, he exclaimed in a loud voice, "I wonder which of us two could get most money by his trade in one week, were we to work hard at it from morning till night?"[18]

The question was provocative in two ways: not just in debunking the notion that art should be above mere money, but also because discussing money at all was considered vulgar. The Thrales were shocked, for example, when the never tactful Oliver Goldsmith first dined with them and "gravely asked Mr. Thrale how much a year he got by his business." Henry answered, Hester said, "with singular propriety, 'We don't talk of those things much in company, Doctor, but I hope to have the honour of knowing you so well that I shall wonder less at the question.' "[19]

The most prestigious artistic genre was "history painting," recreating episodes from ancient history or mythology. Scenes of that kind were thought to express philosophical concepts, thereby raising painting to the status of one of the liberal arts. Reynolds knew that perfectly well, but he also knew that the way to worldly success was by painting portraits. William Blake said succinctly, "His eye is on the many, or rather on the money." Once Reynolds was well established, he charged 35 guineas for a "head" (a guinea is one pound plus one shilling) and 150 for a full-length portrait. In 1755 he had 120 sitters, and in 1758 there were 150, which brought him the enormous income of £6,000 in that single year.[20]

Reynolds had had an opportunity to study in Rome, and he believed that the great masters created ideal types, not recognizable individuals. "An history painter," he said, "paints man in general, the portrait painter, a particular man, and consequently a defective model." There was a partial solution, though. "Even in portraits, the grace, and we may add, the likeness, consists more in taking the general air than in observing the exact similitude of every feature."[21]

That sounds high minded, but there were cynics who saw it differently: Reynolds knew how to flatter his customers. What kept them crowding onto his big waiting list was a gift for likenesses that were recognizable but also subtly idealized, in the visual language of Titian and Raphael.

William Hazlitt, an accomplished portrait painter himself, enjoyed imagining the scene in Reynolds's studio. "Sir Joshua must have had a fine time with his sitters. Lords, ladies, generals, authors, opera singers, musicians, the learned and the polite, besieged his doors and found an unfailing welcome. What a rustling of silks! What a fluttering of flounces and brocades! What a cloud of powder and perfumes! What a flow of periwigs! What an exchange of civilities and of titles!" Hazlitt also caught the tactful flattery that made customers so eager to be painted by Reynolds. "By 'happy alchemy of mind,' he brought out all their good qualities and reconciled their defects, gave an air of studious ease to his learned friends, or lighted up the face of folly and fashion with intelligence and graceful smiles."[22]

Not all of Reynolds's subjects were titled, but those who weren't were celebrities, in an age when publicity was making individuals famous simply for being famous. That included a number of "courtesans"—not common prostitutes, but elegant women attached to one or more men of wealth or rank—

whose celebrity was much assisted by prints made from portraits by Reynolds. He was rumored to have had affairs with several of them.

However cynical some critics were about Reynolds's flattering portraits, he was entirely in earnest when he sought to capture "the general air" instead of an exact likeness. An excellent example of that is his portrait of Oliver Goldsmith, who was one of his dearest friends. Everyone who met Goldsmith was struck by his extreme plainness; many thought him ugly. That's evident in a portrait by Reynolds even though he made it as flattering as possible (figure 36). Frances called it a remarkable example of his skill—"giving dignity to Dr. Goldsmith's countenance, and yet preserving a strong likeness."[23]

Profile portraits were uncommon; Reynolds probably meant to recall classical coins and medals as a compliment to his friend. At the same time the image is notably informal, with shirt collar open and no wig, conveying Goldsmith's unaffected simplicity.[24]

No doubt more accurate was a sketch by Henry William Bunbury (figure 37), although neither portrait indicates that in addition to the bulging brow and receding chin, Goldsmith's face was deeply pitted by smallpox. Frances said that from head to foot "he impressed everyone at first sight with an idea of his being a low mechanic; particularly, I believe, a journeyman

36. Oliver Goldsmith by Reynolds   37. Goldsmith by Bunbury

tailor." A "mechanic" was a laborer who worked with his hands, and tailors were stereotypically stunted and awkward. During one gathering at the Reynolds's house he reported indignantly that he had been insulted by someone he ran into—"The fellow took me for a tailor!" The company had to struggle to suppress their laughter.[25]

Goldsmith affected flashy clothes as an obvious compensation. Boswell reports that when Johnson and Garrick were teasing him about it, "Well, let me tell you," Goldsmith said, "when my tailor brought home my bloom coloured coat [a light rose color], he said, 'Sir, I have a favour to beg of you. When anybody asks you who made your clothes, be pleased to mention John Filby, at the Harrow, in Water Lane.'" Johnson retorted, "Why, Sir, that was because he knew the strange colour would attract crowds to gaze at it, and thus they might hear of him, and see how well he could make a coat even of so absurd a colour."[26]

Thackeray, who was an artist as well as novelist, made an amusing sketch of the scene (figure 38). The nearsighted Johnson is engrossed in his book

38. The bloom-coloured coat

while Goldsmith struts complacently at his side. We know that he carried that cane, because he used it to thrash someone who had libeled him, and he showed up at the Club afterward with a bloody face. In the shop window above, Mr. Filby, in his cross-legged tailor's pose, looks down with satisfaction at this example of his work. The beggar urchins gaze up hopefully (one of them is playfully mimicking Goldsmith). Surely these gentlemen will be easy marks?[27]

To publicize his work Reynolds needed a house with an ample showroom as well as studio space. In 1760 he took out a lease on 40 Leicester Square, a highly fashionable address (figure 39), and spent a large sum adding on a gallery and studio. In his gallery there were many examples of his own work, and also a collection of Old Masters that he acquired over the years and that sold after his death for more than £10,000.

The large octagonal studio occupied an extension at the rear of the house. Sitters were told to expect several sessions of an hour and a half each; they were seated in an armchair that turned on casters, and Reynolds would constantly retreat to regard them from a distance. Then, as one noblewoman recalled, "he would rush up to the portrait and dash at it in a kind of fury—I sometimes thought he would make a mistake and paint on me instead of the picture."[28]

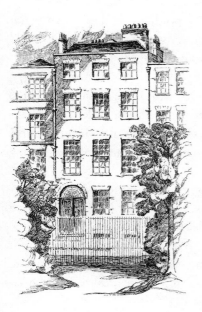

39. Reynolds's house

To manage the volume of orders, Reynolds set up a virtual factory. Once the face and head were done, so was he. All the rest would be filled in by assistants, and over the years he employed a couple of dozen of them. Some were journeymen who got paid by the day, the literal meaning of "journeyman," from the French *journée*. Others were aspiring young artists who worked in return for training in their craft. It was their role to paint the draperies, curtains, furniture, and backgrounds—in fact, everything that wasn't the head. Their work was not necessarily first-rate. The connoisseur Horace Walpole commissioned a painting of three of his nieces and called it "a most beautiful composition," but after living with it for a while became more critical. The hands in particular, he said, were "abominably bad."[29]

Reynolds was always sensitive about any suggestion that he worked too fast. When a nobleman asked how long it took him to execute a portrait, he replied, "All my life, my Lord." And as for leaving much of the work to his assistants, he saw that as grounds for pride. Lawrence Lipking says charitably, "He was paid for his play of mind."[30]

The assistants had the further job of turning out complete copies, to be sold to multiple buyers. There are, for example, five copies of a Reynolds portrait of Garrick. And a further way of disseminating his work was to employ skilled engravers and mezzotint artists to reproduce it in black-and-white prints, some of which appear in this book. Widespread sale of the prints made Reynolds's pictures familiar to a wide public abroad as well as at home.[31]

It should be added that skillfully made reproductions may give a better sense of their subjects than the original paintings now do. Reynolds could never stop experimenting with materials, and some of his favorite colors tended to fade. "Professional historians of painting," a commentator says, "would have to agree that the serious disintegration of the pigments, and the prettification of some paintings by overzealous restorers, make the mezzotints—most of them made under Reynolds's supervision and when the paints were fresh—much better records of the originals than most of the existing canvases."[32]

In addition to portraits, Reynolds sometimes did more ambitious paintings, and for those he found many of his models literally in the street. For a male figure of heroic strength, for example, he would hire a sturdy porter. Children in his pictures are always charming and sweet, even cloyingly so, but the models were not. A biographer comments, "His London street urchins, so tired that they fell asleep while they posed for him, were idealized by that radiant vision, their rags and poverty refined away."[33]

The Victorian painter William Frith happened to meet one of them in the 1830s, and asked if he had ever modeled. "Yes, once, when I was a boy. A deaf gent done it; leastways he had a trumpet, and I shouted at 'im." The man remembered that "the old gent made me take off all but my trousers, and gave me a crook to hold. There was a lamb in the picture as the old gent done." This must have been *The Child Baptist in the Wilderness.*[34]

AN ART SCHOOL AND A LECTURE SERIES

In 1768 the Royal Academy of Arts was founded, with the king as its patron, and with great pride Reynolds accepted the position of its first president. He would continue in that role until his death twenty-four years later. It was literally an academy, an art school for young aspirants, with professors of sculpture, painting, and other subjects. One of them was a friend and fellow Club member: Oliver Goldsmith had published a potboiling history of Rome, and Reynolds got him appointed as professor of ancient history.

In addition to practical training, the Royal Academy held an annual exhibition of new work by its members and other painters. In 1780 a grand new wing was completed for that purpose at Somerset House by the river, which was then a royal palace, and the annual shows there became an obligatory social scene. To modern eyes the exhibitions would look strange indeed, a mosaic of paintings jammed into every inch of the walls. In 1780 nearly five hundred works were on display, and in 1790—the last year Reynolds had paintings of his own on show—there were over seven hundred.[35]

As is obvious in a depiction of the 1787 exhibition (figure 40), most of the pictures could barely be made out from below. Few people in the crowd are even trying to see them, looking instead at each other. George, Prince of Wales, whom Reynolds assiduously cultivated, stands in the center foreground, while Reynolds gestures at a painting and holds his ear trumpet in the other hand. At the far end of the room, at the right-hand side of the bottom row, Reynolds's portrait of Boswell (color plate 30) is distantly visible.

That decorous scene may be supplemented by a Rowlandson watercolor entitled *The Exhibition Stare-Case* (color plate 15). The steep and winding staircase to the Great Room where the pictures were exhibited was notoriously challenging; three months before his death Johnson wrote proudly to his doctor that he had climbed to the top "without rest or intermission." The architect, Sir William Chambers, hoped that the effort would suggest the ascent of Mount Parnassus, but Rowlandson's picture alludes instead to a Last

40. The Royal Academy exhibition

Judgment by Rubens. In this comic descent to hell, spectators preparing to gaze solemnly at classical gods and goddesses are treated instead with a close view of English ladies in the flesh. The bewigged gentlemen at the left look on admiringly, and in a niche just beyond the stairs, Venus regards the scene with approval.[36]

Reynolds relished the prestige of his presidency of the Academy. Among its other advantages, it enabled him to become a published author. The opportunity came with a series of annual addresses that he delivered to each graduating class and later collected in book form as *Discourses on Art*. In one of them he told his audience that whatever knowledge they could not gain by reading "may be supplied by the conversation of learned and ingenious men, which is the best of all substitutes for those who have not the means or opportunities for a deep study. There are many such men in this age." He was undoubtedly thinking of his own experience in the Club, which by then had been in existence for twelve years.[37]

Reynolds greatly valued his friendship with Johnson. He told Boswell, "I acknowledge the highest obligations to him. He may be said to have formed my mind, and to have brushed off from it a deal of rubbish." Relying heavily on Johnson's views about "general truths," Reynolds invoked generality to enhance the intellectual prestige of painting, and in one lecture referred expressly to "the theory of art." That expression sounds unremarkable today, but at the time it was a challenging affirmation of intellectual value.[38]

Reynolds's emphasis on generality could seem paradoxical in practice. Committed to universal values, he always depreciated detailed representation like the costumes and Oriental rugs in Dutch paintings. So he claimed that a painter should somehow give an impression of fabric but not of any particular material. "With him, the clothing is neither woolen, nor linen, nor silk, satin, or velvet; it is drapery, it is nothing more."[39]

When Blake, who had felt condescended to by Reynolds during a brief time as a student at the Academy, read the *Discourses* he filled the margins with execrations: "Fool—A Mock—Villainy—A Lie—O Shame False— Folly!—Nonsense—I certainly do thank God that I am not like Reynolds." Partly that was due to resentment of Reynolds's domination of the art market, but partly it was an acute perception of hopeless contradictions in what Reynolds was trying to say. His not very skillful attempts to combine Lockean particularity with Platonic universality made many people wonder if he had even written the *Discourses* himself, or had just made a botch of materials that Johnson and others gave him.

Blake's comment on that is trenchant: "The contradictions in Reynolds's *Discourses* are strong presumptions that they are the work of several hands, but this is no proof that Reynolds did not write them. The man, either painter or philosopher, who learns or acquires all he knows from others must be full of contradictions."[40]

Blake had a particular axe to grind. Even while Reynolds strove to exalt oil painting to the status of an admired liberal art, he and his colleagues dismissed engraving as mindless mechanical reproduction—in spite of the superb reinterpretations of his own paintings that skilled engravers produced. Blake was a professional engraver.

On the title page of his copy of the *Discourses* Blake wrote, "This man was hired to depress art," and on the next page, "Having spent the vigour of my youth and genius under the oppression of Sir Joshua and his gang of cunning hired knaves, without employment and as much as could possibly be without bread, the reader must expect to read in all my remarks on these books nothing but indignation and resentment." That edition of the *Discourses* included an account by Edmond Malone of Reynolds's death, which provoked from Blake a deft dismissal in verse:

> When Sir Joshua Reynolds died
> All Nature was degraded;
> The King dropped a tear into the Queen's ear,
> And all his pictures faded.[41]

Among Reynolds's numerous self-portraits are two impressive ones from these years. The first (figure 41) was made in 1780 for the just completed premises of the Royal Academy. Reynolds stands in a pose adapted from Van Dyck. The composition recalls a famous Rembrandt painting, *Aristotle Contemplating a Bust of Homer,* but here the bust represents Reynolds's hero Michelangelo. An art historian comments that the picture "exudes an air of swaggering self-confidence; whether or not it was Reynolds's intention, even the shadowy bust of Michelangelo appears to nod in deference towards him." He is wearing the robe and hat that were awarded when he received an honorary doctorate from Oxford, of which he was immensely proud.[42]

41. Reynolds
self-portrait with
bust

42. Reynolds in
spectacles

The other self-portrait dates from 1788 (figure 42). It was unusual to represent people wearing spectacles, even if they normally used them in daily life as Reynolds did. Very possibly he showed himself bespectacled to suggest that he was more than just a painter: a reader, an author, even a philosopher of vision.[43]

CHAPTER 9

Edmund Burke

Of all of the members of the Club, Burke was the one who most impressively combined intellectual brilliance, literary skill, and public life. Twenty years younger than Johnson, he was the son of a Dublin lawyer who had converted from Catholicism to the Protestant Church of Ireland. Since Catholics could not attend university and were essentially barred from the professions, that was a prudential move and not resented by other Catholics. They understood that their own embattled situation could be improved by Protestant relatives.

Educated as a Protestant, Edmund was thereby eligible to enroll in Trinity College, Dublin. After graduating in 1748 he went to London to study law, but dropped it before long. To earn a living he worked as an anonymous writer, just as Johnson and Goldsmith did, and the three of them must have known each other at this time. In 1758 Burke became editor of the *Annual Register,* at a yearly salary of £100. That was a book-length collection of articles and reviews, many of them with considerable intellectual depth.

It may surprise readers today, who know Burke as a great political writer, that his breakthrough publication was a treatise on aesthetics, *A Philosophical Enquiry into the Origin of Our Ideas of the Sublime and Beautiful.* It came out in 1757, with no name on the title page, but it was immediately admired and his authorship soon became known.

Earlier theories of art emphasized imitation. In time-honored theory, the function of art was to reproduce external reality more or less exactly— Hamlet's "mirror held up to nature." Writers on art, and literary critics in particular, also tended to emphasize formal "rules" in a highly dogmatic way. Burke's emphasis was psychological, and it seemed excitingly new to readers. His subject was the emotions that works of art arouse, the same emotions that nature does. The "beautiful" was a quality that we respond to in real life, whether in a landscape or in a person. The "sublime" was also understood psychologically. In nature it took the form of overwhelming vastness and danger, as in a violent thunderstorm or a storm at sea.

The role of art, then, was not simply to reproduce the world as a mirror does. Its role was to provoke the same powerful emotions that sublime or beautiful experiences do in our lives, but with a degree of pleasurable detachment. Looking at a painting of a storm at sea, we may have an exciting sense of potential danger, but we also feel the security of knowing that it's only imaginary. We are in no danger of drowning.

The sublime was defined as a sensation of nervous tension caused by something vast and dangerous; the beautiful was delightful rather than scary, provoked by smoothness and delicacy. A discussion of "gradual variation" is illustrated by erotic responsiveness: "Observe that part of a beautiful woman where she is perhaps the most beautiful, about the neck and breasts; the smoothness, the softness, the easy and insensible swell; the variety of the surface, which is never for the smallest space the same. . . . Is not this a demonstration of that change of surface, continual, and yet hardly perceptible at any point, which forms one of the great constituents of beauty?"[1]

The gender assumptions here would have seemed natural to Burke's readers: beauty is an attribute of the female sex. But the psychological response to beauty is by no means limited to that; "gradual variation" is pleasing in any context. Similarly "smoothness," though likewise associated with the feminine, is appreciated in countless ways. "A bed smoothly laid and soft, that is, where the resistance is every way inconsiderable, is a great luxury, disposing to an universal relaxation, and inducing beyond anything else that species of it called sleep." Boswell would have appreciated that.[2]

Burke's treatise pays particular attention to sublimity and beauty in language, and he argues convincingly that we respond not just to the literal meaning of words, but also to their sounds and the associations they evoke. An ordinary horse, encountered everywhere in those days, is useful and possibly beautiful, but in no way sublime. But when Burke paraphrases the language of the King James Bible, the horse takes on symbolic power: "him whose neck is clothed with thunder, the glory of whose nostrils is terrible, who swalloweth the ground with fierceness and rage, neither believeth that it is the sound of the trumpet."

In this passage, Burke says, "the useful character of the horse entirely disappears, and the terrible and sublime blaze out together." It's not surprising that the writer who could appreciate that power in language would become one of the most compelling orators of all time.[3]

In the following year Burke married Mary Nugent, daughter of the Catholic physician Christopher Nugent, whom he would later bring with him as a founding member of the Club. Nugent was practicing at Bath at the time, and Burke had gone there to recover from ill health and mental distress of some kind. Nugent treated him successfully, and Burke thanked him in verse, speaking of him in the third person:

'Tis now two autumns since he chanced to find
A youth of body broke, infirm of mind;
He gave him all that man can ask or give:
Restored his life and taught him how to live.

Mary Nugent was still a teenager when she married Burke. It would be an enduringly happy marriage, and would produce a son, Richard or "Dick," whom his parents adored.[4]

Burke was interested in politics, but for a young Irishman without money, the only way to get ahead politically was through patronage. With that in mind he became an advisor to a member of Parliament named William Gerard Hamilton, who as it happens was Boswell's second cousin. When Fanny Burney met him years later she wrote, "This Mr. Hamilton is extremely tall and handsome; has an air of haughty and fashionable superiority, is intelligent, dry, sarcastic and clever." He acquired the nickname "Single Speech Hamilton" because his maiden speech in Parliament was so successful that apart from one disappointing attempt, he never made another speech.[5]

After some time Hamilton offered to make Burke his permanent assistant at a comfortable salary. Much to Hamilton's indignation, Burke refused. He regarded the position as a temporary rung up the ladder of success, and he believed that if it were made permanent, he would become a mere servant, forced "to give up even the possibility of liberty, and absolutely to annihilate myself forever." Burke was never given to understatement.[6]

BURKE IN CONVERSATION

When Fanny Burney met Burke for the first time in 1782, right at the apogee of his political career, she wrote to her sister, "He is tall, his figure is noble, his air commanding, his address graceful; his voice is clear, penetrating, sonorous and powerful; his language is copious, various, and eloquent; his manners are attractive; his conversation is delightful! I can give you very little of what was said, for the conversation was not *suivie* [consecutive], Mr. Burke darting from subject to subject with as much rapidity as entertainment; neither is the charm of his discourse more in the matter than the manner. All, therefore, that is related *from* him loses half its effect in not being related *by* him."[7]

Fanny's description is a reminder that although many members of the Club were excellent writers, both at the Turk's Head and elsewhere they thought of conversation as equally important. They enjoyed casual chat, but they also valued a lively exchange of experiences and opinions and ideas. Especially admired were people who could express their thoughts in compelling language. The goal was to be interesting, and at the same time socially congenial.

If Burke could be voluble, he also knew how to be quiet and attentive. The portrait reproduced here (figure 43) gives a sense of his calm thoughtfulness when he was not holding forth.

In a culture that valued epigrammatic bon mots, however, Burke did not excel. When Boswell asked, "Has not Burke a great deal of wit?" Johnson replied, "I do not think so, Sir. He is, indeed, continually attempting wit, but he fails. And I have no more pleasure in hearing a man attempting wit and failing, then in seeing a man trying to leap over a ditch and tumbling into it." Langton made a similar point, more wittily: "Burke hammered his wit upon an anvil, and the iron was cold. There were no sparks flashing and flying all about."[8]

What Burke did love was puns, but there he was going against the cultural grain. Like Addison, who had condemned them in the *Spectator* as "false wit," Johnson deplored puns, or "quibbles" as they were also known, and especially those by Shakespeare. In the preface to his edition of the plays he complained, "A quibble, poor and barren as it is, gave him such delight that he was content to purchase it by the sacrifice of reason, propriety and truth. A quibble was to him the fatal Cleopatra for which he lost the world, and was content to lose it."[9]

In the *Dictionary* Johnson defines "quibble" as "a low conceit depending on the sound of words; a pun." To illustrate usage he gives a stern statement by Isaac Watts: "Quirks or quibbles have no place in the search after truth."

43. Edmund Burke

Hester Thrale remembered that during a dinner party an Irish politician named Lord Mulgrave "heard some vile quibble of the great Edmund's and called out in his rough way, 'Why Burke! why you riot in puns today, now Johnson is not at hand.' I never saw a man so overwhelmed with anger and shame. Lord Mulgrave did not however seem to perceive it, though I did."[10]

It does seem that Burke's puns were labored. When Boswell said that if he could breathe some life into a parliamentary committee, he would be "Titan himself," Burke replied, "Aye, a *tight one.*" Boswell commented, "He loves a pun, and will make a very poor one." At other times Boswell appreciated the effort. "Burke was as usual fertile and playful. Being placed near a *ham,* he said, 'I am *Ham-Burke* (Hamburg).'" You had to be there.[11]

For Burke, punning was indeed a form of play. Someone who knew him remembered that "he would enter with cordial glee into the sports of children, rolling about with them on the carpet, and pouring out, in his gambols, the sublimest images, mingled with the most wretched puns." A musician who met him at a Royal Academy dinner was surprised "by the fun, frisk, and anecdote of Mr. Burke's conversation. I never heard anything so animated or captivating in my life, and perhaps I never shall; we laughed immoderately for nearly two hours at his eccentric and witty conversation."[12]

And there is another way of thinking about Burke's puns, even when they were dreadful. An earlier Irish master of language, Jonathan Swift, bandied them with friends as a creative game, enjoying the ways in which words could be sprung from their "correct" meanings. Swift told his friend Stella that when a political colleague set down a fringed napkin between himself and the poet Matthew Prior, "I told him I was glad to see there was such a fringeship between Mr. Prior and his Lordship. Prior swore it was the worst he ever heard; I said I thought so too."[13]

Still another great Irish writer, James Joyce, likewise adored punning. When people complained that his puns were trivial, he liked to reply, "Yes, and some of them are quadrivial." Burke would have loved that. The medieval curriculum began with three subjects known as the trivium and was followed by the quadrivium.[14]

POLITICIAN AND ORATOR

William Gerard Hamilton, despite the disagreements with Burke, did come through as a patron. He managed to arrange an official appointment for him under Lord Halifax at the Board of Trade. Whereas the job with Hamilton had been an entirely private arrangement, this was a significant bureaucratic position. It gave Burke an excellent vantage point from which to learn how government worked, and it carried an annual salary of £300—three times what he was getting from the *Annual Register.* And in 1765 he was elected to Parliament, representing a small town called Wendover thirty miles from London. That was one year after he became a founding member of the Club.

By then Burke had acquired a mansion and six-hundred-acre estate at Beaconsfield in Buckinghamshire, to the west of London. That would enable him to entertain in style, as a rising politician was expected to do. He wrote to an old friend and former schoolmate, "I have made a push, with all I could collect of my own and the aid of my friends, to cast a little root in this country. . . . It is a place exceedingly pleasant, and I propose, God willing, to become a farmer in good earnest." He did in fact work hard at learning about farming, and participated enthusiastically in modern improvements that landowners were beginning to adopt.[15]

Unfortunately, the purchase price of £20,000 was almost entirely borrowed. That would leave Burke oppressed by debt for the rest of his life,
though invulnerable to arrest so long as he remained a member of Parliament.
He had high hopes of making a killing in East India Company stock, with
what seemed to be insider advice from a close friend who had a government
appointment there. But the speculation crashed. This disaster may have influenced Burke's later hostility to the East India Company, which would bear
fruit in a crusade against colonial exploitation.

The shifting alliances and infighting in eighteenth-century politics are
bewilderingly complex, but the general picture is not. It's important to understand that unlike today, there was no party discipline to control voting in
Parliament, and no ideological platform that all members could agree upon.
Gibbon was elected to Parliament as a Whig but voted faithfully in support
of the Tory Lord North; that was because he held a government sinecure
that depended on showing loyalty. Some years later, writing to a friend, he
denounced "those foolish, obsolete, odious words, Whig and Tory."[16]

Still, from a larger perspective it's possible to tell the two main groups
apart. Whigs in general allied themselves with the financial and commercial
interests of London. For that reason they were eager to see the British Empire
expand, and supported foreign wars that promised to help it to do so. Tories
saw themselves as traditionalists, loyal to the monarchy and to the established
Church. Their strength lay among the landed gentry in the provinces, who
bitterly resented the fact that the wars were funded by taxation on their land.
But the boundary between the two types was porous. Successful merchants
often married their children into aristocratic families, and they often acquired
country estates of their own.

In 1774 Burke was elected to a more important seat, representing the commercial city of Bristol in the west. It was his firm conviction that a member of
Parliament should follow his own judgment and not that of his constituents.
In one of his most famous speeches, *Thoughts on the Present Discontents,* he
declared that a politician should be a philosopher in action, identifying appropriate means to achieve "the proper ends of government," and in another
speech he described himself as a physician whose expertise must be trusted.
"The people are the sufferers, they tell the symptoms of the complaint; but we
know the exact seat of the disease, and how to apply the remedy according to
the rules of art."[17]

In this Burke and Johnson were in agreement. The role of a true patriot
was to follow his best understanding in promoting the good of the nation,

even if that meant—as Burke had commented at the Club—that he was likely to be always in the minority. A comment of Johnson's on this point is endlessly quoted with no understanding of the original context: "Patriotism is the last refuge of a scoundrel." What Johnson had in mind was the opportunistic use of the term "patriot" by opposition politicians, who claimed that the Tory government was betraying the trust of the nation. In a polemical tract entitled *The Patriot,* he gave a generous description of what patriotism should actually be: "A patriot is he whose public conduct is regulated by one single motive, the love of his country; who, as an agent in parliament, has for himself neither hope nor fear, neither kindness nor resentment, but refers everything to the common interest."[18]

Burke's Bristol constituents were not happy with his independent stance, especially since during the six years that he represented them he visited the city only twice. So in 1780 they declined to renominate him, and another borough was found for him. By now he was making himself indispensable to Lord Rockingham, the head of a splinter group within the Whig party. A contemporary commented that he wasn't just Rockingham's right hand, he was both hands.[19]

The goal of the Rockinghams, as they were known, was to put themselves at the head of a governing coalition. In 1782 that happened, when the defeat at Yorktown brought down the administration of Lord North. This seemed to be the career breakthrough that Burke had been waiting for. He was appointed paymaster-general of the army with a magnificent salary of £4,000 a year. If the Rockingham government had endured, his debts could have been fully paid off, but after less than a year Lord Rockingham died and left his party stranded. Johnson sympathetically commented, "Mr. Burke's family is computed to have lost by this revolution twelve thousand a year. What a rise, and what a fall." Johnson's estimate reflects a belief that high officials had access to other forms of income besides their salaries.[20]

Most of the 558 members of the House of Commons never dreamed of making speeches, but star orators could hold forth for hours at a time. Persuasive eloquence was essential, and so was quickness in cut and thrust debate. Burke excelled at both. And although the debates weren't supposed to be reported in the press—that was why Johnson had to invent them in his journalistic days—the speakers could always publish their own speeches afterward, which Burke regularly did in pamphlet form.

He was immediately hailed as a master. A contemporary exclaimed, "How closely that fellow reasons in metaphor!" What Matthew Arnold said long afterward was recognized at the time: "Burke is so great because, almost alone in England, he brings thought to bear upon politics, he saturates politics with thought."[21]

All the same, many people regarded Burke as an untrustworthy Irish adventurer. After his brilliant maiden speech, Horace Walpole said that "his fame for eloquence soon rose high above the ordinary pitch," but then added a whole series of innuendos. "His name was Edmund Burke, an Irishman of a Roman Catholic family, and actually married to one of that persuasion. He had been known to the public for a few years by his *Essay on the Sublime and Beautiful* and other ingenious works, but the narrowness of his fortune had kept him down, and his best revenue had arisen from writing for booksellers."

Thomas Copeland spells out what is implied. "With an infallible eye, Walpole had managed to discern the four weakest spots in this new man's social armor. Burke was an Irishman; he was related to Roman Catholics; he was poor; he was rumored to be 'writing for booksellers.' " Even the relatively distinguished *Annual Register* still counted as hack writing that a patrician like Walpole would never have stooped to.[22]

Anti-Irish prejudice did simmer in England, and Burke was especially suspect because he campaigned against the ways in which Ireland was politically oppressed. He never lost his brogue, either, and had to face a snobbish assumption that his origins made him not quite genteel.

John Wilkes, the populist Whig whom Boswell had met in Italy, said that "Burke was eloquent, but had not the right kind of eloquence; his was a wild Irish eloquence. As Apelles's painting of a fine woman had such flesh that someone said she had fed on roses, Burke's art gives us a fine woman but fed on potatoes and whisky." Retelling this in the *Life,* Boswell didn't mention Burke by name and left out the word "Irish," but readers would have had no trouble guessing who was the "celebrated orator" distinguished by "brilliancy of imagination and exuberance of wit."[23]

Even Hester Thrale was snide. After staying with the Burkes at Beaconsfield, she wrote that both husband and wife got drunk, Burke talked obscenely, and their expensive paintings and statues were fouled by cobwebs and dirt. "Irish Roman Catholics," she added, "are always like the foreigners somehow: dirty and dressy, with their clothes hanging as if upon a peg."[24]

A favorite lie put about by Burke's opponents was that he was still secretly a Catholic, which would have disqualified him for British politics, and even that in his youth he had studied to become a Jesuit priest. Cartoonists regularly depicted him that way (figure 44). In caricatures his spectacles suggested a myopia that was not just physical.

During important debates in Parliament the visitors' gallery was often packed, especially when Burke was due to speak. When Boswell heard him there he was greatly impressed, like everyone else, but he also made a perceptive comment. "It was astonishing how all kinds of figures of speech crowded upon him. . . . It seemed to be, however, that his oratory rather tended to distinguish himself than to assist his cause. There was amusement instead of persuasion. It was like the exhibition of a favourite actor. But I would have been exceedingly happy to be him." Another picture (figure 45) gives a good sense of Burke's dramatic speaking style.[25]

Goldsmith made a similar point about Burke's speeches, in a series of imaginary epitaphs for a number of his friends.

> Here lies our good Edmund, whose genius was such,
> We scarcely can praise it or blame it too much;
> Who, born for the universe, narrowed his mind,
> And to party gave up what was meant for mankind.
> Though fraught with all learning, yet straining his throat

44. Burke as Jesuit

45. Burke as orator

> To persuade Tommy Townshend to lend him a vote;
> Who too deep for his hearers still went on refining,
> And thought of convincing, while they thought of dining.

Boswell believed that Goldsmith named Thomas Townshend because he had denounced the pension granted to Johnson.[26]

Burke's closest political ally, elected to the Club ten years after its founding, deserves mention here. That was Charles James Fox, whom caricaturists loved to depict. Even in a formal portrait (figure 46) his portly girth and jowly features are evident, and he had a perpetual five o'clock shadow.

Fox's origins and lifestyle were totally different from Burke's. The second son of a peer, he was something of a playboy, highly successful with women, and politically more radical than Burke; eventually they would fall out with each other over that. He was even Burke's rival as an orator; a contemporary spoke of "the thundering eloquence of our modern Demosthenes, Charles Fox." When they were working together they made a formidable pair.[27]

Fox, who could afford it, was a fearless gambler. When he was twenty-four his debts amounted to the fantastic sum of £140,000, which he expected to recover by future winnings. He would often play cards for twenty-four hours straight, sometimes losing £500 an hour. It was not unusual for him to rise and speak in the House of Commons after a twenty-four-hour stint at the

46. Charles James Fox

gaming table. At one point he and his brother lost £32, 000 over the course of three consecutive nights. Wealthy playboys didn't just gamble at cards, they laid impromptu wagers on anything at all. At the posh White's Club two peers bet £30,000 on which of two raindrops trickling down a window would reach the bottom first.[28]

Fox could easily have paid off Burke's debt at a stroke, but there seems to have been no thought of that. No doubt it would have been shaming for Burke to accept charity from a colleague and friend.

GOVERNMENT FOR THE PEOPLE

When Burke and Fox finally split, it was over the question of enlarging the franchise and correcting long-standing abuses in the way seats in Parliament were apportioned and controlled.

Half a century later, the campaign to do that would finally produce the Reform Bill of 1832. At this early stage, Fox occupied a relatively radical fringe of the Whig coalition—though not nearly as radical as it would later become. Burke was firmly traditionalist, in very much the way that Johnson was. They shared an ideology with most intellectuals at the time, not to mention most ordinary people, and it's important to understand what that was. In a narrow sense Burke and Johnson were not political allies, since Burke was a Whig, and Johnson always pretended to hate the Whigs (when a member of Parliament claimed that the "spirit of liberty" was being destroyed, Johnson exclaimed, "Sir, I perceive you are a vile Whig"). In a larger sense, however, they shared a similar worldview.[29]

It has been well said that Burke believed not in government by the people, but in government for the people by the entitled few. Most of the American Founders took the same view. In the next century, John Quincy Adams complained that the Jacksonian populists were wrong to claim that "democracy is the government of the whole people and nothing but the people—not the purest, not the strongest, not the wealthiest, not the wisest." Or as Johnson put it more sternly, "The vulgar are the children of the state, and must be taught like children." In those days the word "vulgar" didn't necessarily have negative connotations; in the *Dictionary* he defines it simply as "the common people."[30]

For both Johnson and Burke, the key to sustaining social order was what they called "subordination." Today that word probably suggests servility or even oppression. For them it meant a traditional structure of deference that kept society cooperative and peaceful rather than anarchic. "I am a friend to subordination," Johnson said, "as most conducive to the happiness of society. There is a reciprocal pleasure in governing and being governed."[31]

England was what would nowadays be called a minimalist state. There was no effective police, commodities were taxed but incomes were not, and there was little direct control from above. Much that we take for granted today as the responsibility of government—fire protection, highway maintenance, water supply, managing jails—was the domain of private enterprise when it existed at all.

Local needs, therefore, had to be addressed locally, by town aldermen and by country squires, who exerted great influence over their neighborhoods. Serious crimes were tried at circuit courts during the occasional visits of judges, but the rest of the time the squires acted as justices of the peace, adjudicating minor offenses in a sort of home-based legal system. Fielding's Squire Allworthy takes this responsibility very seriously; his neighbor Squire Western does not, and has to have the law patiently explained to him by an assistant.

It should be noted that the word "conservative" didn't yet have its modern connotations; those would emerge as a reaction to the French Revolution at the end of the century. But among most Whigs as well as Tories there was a shared belief that social stability depended on the majority of the population accepting their status as inevitable. Lawrence Stone says, "It was because of the underlying unity of the elites, and of the largely unquestioning habits of deference by those below, reemphasized daily in action and in prayer, reinforced by the solemn ritual of the death sentence and execution of lower-class criminals against property, that the state apparatus could remain so relatively weak in eighteenth-century England without a total collapse of social order."[32]

David Hume, who regarded himself as neither Whig nor Tory, said in an essay entitled *Of the Original Contract,* "Obedience or subjection becomes so familiar that most men never make any inquiry about its origin or cause, more than about the principle of gravity, resistance, or the most universal laws of nature." Hume thought that was a good thing, and so did Johnson and Burke.[33]

Boswell's political thinking, if thinking is the right word, was romantic in a way that was already old-fashioned. When he heard someone "mumble some stuff in favour of a republic," he went home and wrote, "Surely a regular limited royal government is the best and the most conducive to the happiness of mankind. A republic is in my opinion a most confused, vulgar system, whereas a monarchy inspires us with gay and spirited ideas." There "vulgar" does have its modern connotations.[34]

Johnson never talked like that. His position was pragmatic, and also psychologically shrewd. In a conversation with Boswell, he emphasized that the whole point about social rank was its arbitrariness. It might not be easy to agree about which people had most merit, but there was no arguing about which ones had inherited status. "What is it but opinion," Johnson said, "by which we have a respect for authority that prevents us, who are the rabble, from rising up and pulling down you who are gentlemen from your places, and saying, 'We will be gentlemen in our turn?' Now, Sir, that respect for authority is much more easily granted to a man whose father has had it, than to an upstart, and so society is more easily supported."[35]

Johnson was perfectly willing to acknowledge that in this sense he himself, despite his great accomplishments, was an "upstart" and a member of the "rabble." Boswell, as future Laird of Auchinleck, was by definition a gentleman. He proudly traced his family all the way back to the Norman Conquest. Johnson said, "I have great merit in being zealous for subordination and the honours of birth, for I can hardly tell who was my grandfather."[36]

To illustrate how deeply this code had been internalized even by people who considered themselves radicals, Johnson liked to relate a jibe of his at the dinner table of the writer Catherine Macaulay, "a great republican."

> I put on a very grave countenance and said to her, "Madam, I am now become a convert to your way of thinking. I am convinced that all mankind are upon an equal footing; and to give you an unquestionable proof, Madam, that I am in earnest, here is a very sensible, civil, well behaved fellow citizen, your footman. I desire that he may be allowed to sit down and dine with us." I thus, Sir, showed her the absurdity of the leveling doctrine. She has never liked me since. Sir, your levelers wish to level *down* as far as themselves; but they cannot bear leveling *up* to themselves. They would all have some people under them; why not then have some people above them?[37]

From the principle of subordination, it followed that a small minority deserved privileged status simply because they *had* that status. In any society, Gibbon wrote in the *Decline and Fall,* "constant and useful labor" is the lot of most people, whereas "the select few, placed by fortune above that necessity, can fill up their time by the pursuits of interest or glory, by the improvement of their estate or of their understanding, by the duties, the pleasures, and even the follies of social life."[38]

That was certainly how Gibbon understood his own place in the world. It was his good fortune to inherit a modest estate and thereby the opportunity to do his life's work without needing a job. In his *Memoirs* he acknowledged that if he had been born at the time of the Roman Empire, "My lot might have been that of a slave, a savage or a peasant; nor can I reflect without pleasure on the bounty of nature, which cast my birth in a free and civilized country, in an age of science and philosophy, in a family of honourable rank and decently endowed with the gifts of fortune."[39]

Subordination was the philosophical basis for the grim fact that the vast majority of crimes, even those punishable by death, were crimes against property. Johnson thought that the laws were much too harsh, but most intellectuals didn't. In the *Decline and Fall* Gibbon states as a truism: "Most of the crimes which disturb the internal peace of society are produced by the restraints which the necessary, but unequal, laws of property have imposed on the appetites of mankind, by confining to a few the possession of those objects that are coveted by many."[40]

Adam Smith, with whom Gibbon developed a friendship, said exactly the same thing in a series of lectures on jurisprudence. "Laws and government may be considered as a combination of the rich to oppress the poor, and preserve to themselves the inequality of the goods which would otherwise be soon destroyed by the attacks of the poor, who if not hindered by the government would soon reduce the others to an equality with themselves by open violence."[41]

Rousseau and Marx could not have put it better—except that in Smith's opinion this was a very good thing. Rousseau's great 1749 *Discourse on the Origin of Inequality*, which Smith studied closely and reacted against, describes the development of society and its legal systems as a catastrophe "which irretrievably destroyed natural liberty, established for all time the law of property and inequality, transformed adroit usurpation into irrevocable right, and for the benefit of a few ambitious men subjected the human race thenceforth to labor, servitude and misery."[42]

Most British thinkers, whether Whig or Tory, saw the essential guarantor of subordination as religion. Tories wanted the established Church of England to have special rights not because its theology was superior to others, but simply because it *was* established. "The body of the people," Burke wrote during the panic that followed the French Revolution, "must not find the principles of natural subordination by art [i.e., artfully specious arguments] routed out of their minds. They must respect that property of which they cannot partake.

They must labour to obtain what by labour can be obtained; and when they find, as they commonly do, the success disproportioned to the endeavour, they must be taught their consolation in the final proportions of eternal justice." One can't help reflecting on how nakedly all of these people declared a position which privileged people and their political allies today are careful to disguise.[43]

Conservative Whigs like Burke and Gibbon were convinced that power must be centered in a landed oligarchy. That was the class, they thought, that had the greatest stake in the good of the nation, whereas merchants and speculators were enriching themselves at the nation's expense. Burke energetically defended the privileges of the aristocracy, though he never denied that many aristocrats were complete idiots. He was defending a principle, as he saw it, not individuals.

It needs to be stressed that just as with Johnson, Burke saw his position as hardheaded and pragmatic. In 1772 he wrote to an ally in Parliament, the Duke of Richmond, "You people of great families and hereditary trusts and fortunes are not like such as I am. . . . We are but annual plants that perish with our season and leave no sort of traces behind us. You, if you are what you ought to be, are the great oaks that shade a country and perpetuate your benefits from generation to generation." Taken out of context, that might make Burke seem more reverent toward the aristocracy then he really was. Paul Langford says, "This was one of Burke's numerous attempts to get the easily distracted leaders of his party to fulfill their duties."[44]

Burke is famous for insisting on gradual change, reforming abuses but never tearing down the inherited structure in order to replace it with something entirely new. The American Founders had no thought of doing that, either. They were patricians who rejected rule from London but expected their society to continue much as it always had. "The progress of reformation," Johnson wrote in an essay, "is gradual and silent, as the extension of evening shadows." And when Boswell commented, "So, Sir, you laugh at schemes of political improvement," Johnson replied, "Why, Sir, most schemes of political improvement are very laughable things."[45]

BURKE ON REVOLUTION

For posterity, Burke's name will always be associated with the crisis that erupted in 1789, the revolution in France that overthrew the monarchy, executed tens of thousands of aristocrats, and alarmed other nations with the prospect of uprisings of their own.

There had already been foretastes in Britain of what that might be like. In 1768 there were "Wilkes and Liberty" riots in London, provoked by John Wilkes's exclusion from Parliament. Benjamin Franklin was no revolutionary at that time. In London to represent the Pennsylvania colony, he wrote home that the English people were "ungratefully abusing the best constitution, and the best king, any nation was ever blessed with." To another correspondent he added, "All respect to law and government seems to be lost among the common people, who are moreover continually inflamed by seditious scribblers to trample on authority and everything that used to keep them in order."[46]

The Wilkesite riots were short-lived, but in 1780 the much more frightening Gordon Riots broke out in London, sparked by anti-Catholic bigotry. Chapels and houses belonging to Catholics were sacked, Newgate Prison was burned, distilleries were smashed so that gin flowed in the gutters, and Henry Thrale's brewery was invaded by a dangerous mob. Fortunately his manager, John Perkins, was able to placate them with plenty of beer. There was no effective police force in those days, so the army was called out to restore order. After a week of rioting nearly a thousand people had died, hundreds of them shot by the soldiers.

This was a shocking revelation of the resentment smoldering in the mass of the population, and it terrified the ruling class. Boswell described the riots as "the most horrid series of outrage that ever disgraced a civilized country."[47]

When the French Revolution broke out in 1789, many Whigs sympathized at first with its democratic ideals, including Burke's allies Sheridan and Fox. His immediate and fierce denunciations resulted in a permanent breach with them, and by 1791 Burke was effectively a Whig no longer.

As early as 1790 Burke published his great *Reflections on the Revolution in France,* in which he foretold brilliantly how even the most well-intentioned revolution was likely to lead to a bloodbath and then the emergence of a charismatic dictator. "Some popular general, who understands the art of conciliating the soldiery, and who possesses the true spirit of command, shall draw the eyes of all men upon himself. At the moment in which that event shall happen, the person who really commands the army is your master."[48]

The very meaning of the word "revolution" was changing, under the impetus of this spectacular event in France. Johnson had defined it in the *Dictionary* as "the course of anything which returns to the point at which it began to move"—in effect, revolving. In a political context, it meant "change in the state of a government or country." That could be simply one ruler replacing another, without any significant alteration in the structure of the society as a whole. Burke helped to give "revolution" its modern meaning of drastic and wholesale change.

With his commitment to "subordination," Burke saw the social contract as an intricate web of shared associations, "a partnership not only between those who are living, but between those who are living, those who are dead, and those who are to be born." That was really the crux: denial that a people have a right to change their system of government. Thomas Paine retorted, "Mr. Burke is contending for the authority of the dead over the rights and freedom of the living. . . . As government is for the living and not for the dead, it is the living only that has any right in it." Blake said in one of his Proverbs of Hell: "Drive your cart and your plow over the bones of the dead."[49]

Modern conservatives—who resemble what used to be called liberals in the eighteenth century—have idealized Burke as their foundational thinker. It's true that many of his ideas continue to seem powerful. But it's also true that it was Paine, not Burke, who inspired the American Founders. In the 1770s Burke had defended their right not to be taxed, but never for one moment their right to govern themselves.

In the 1790s a Revolution Society began to argue that a people do indeed have a right to choose their governors, discharge them for misconduct, and if necessary frame a new government for themselves. "This new and hitherto unheard of bill of rights," Burke wrote in the *Reflections,* "though made in the name of the whole people, belongs to those gentlemen and their faction only. The body of the people of England have no share in it. They utterly disclaim it. They will resist the practical assertion of it with their lives and fortunes." Not only do they lack political rights, they would fight to the death to go on not having them.[50]

The fear that revolution might spread to Britain caused a drastic hardening in Burke's formerly humanitarian political views. A bitterly cold winter in 1794 was followed by meager harvests, resulting in a terrible famine that provoked bread riots. Some members of Parliament began to call for government assistance for people who were starving. Burke, borrowing his thinking from *The Wealth of Nations,* insisted that supply and demand must never be interfered with. He even went so far as to attribute the famine to the will of the Almighty. If the starving poor were to be relieved at all, it must be by private charity. It could never be the business of government to do that.

Burke's *Thoughts and Details on Scarcity* is pitiless in its rigor. He calls on members of Parliament "manfully to resist the very first idea, speculative or practical, that it is within the competence of government, taken as government, or even of the rich, as rich, to supply to the poor those necessaries which it has pleased the Divine Providence for a while to withhold from them. We, the people, ought to be made sensible that it is not in breaking the laws of commerce, which are the laws of nature, and consequently the laws of God, that we are to place our hope of softening the divine displeasure to remove any calamity under which we suffer, or which hangs over us."

Burke had a further suggestion, that distilling liquor should be encouraged ("beer will by no means do the business") as a way of reconciling the poor to their lot. "If not food," he explained, "it greatly alleviates the want of it."[51]

Burke was far from the only one to be horrified by the French Revolution. Paranoia swept the British propertied classes, who feared guillotines in the near future, and Burke's views were shared by nearly all of his friends. Boswell wrote to a clergyman, who seemed sympathetic to the Revolution, that it had "produced all the horrors of a barbarous anarchy." That was in 1791, when the French leaders were still high-minded reformers, two years before the outbreak of the Terror.[52]

In 1792 a British royal proclamation promised "to prosecute with severity all persons guilty of writing and publishing seditious pamphlets tending to alienate the affections of his Majesty's subjects, and to disturb the peace, order, and tranquility of the State, as well as to prohibit all illegal meetings." Concurring, the Stationers' Company declared a "determined resolution utterly to DISCOUNTENANCE and DISCOURAGE all seditious and inflammatory productions whatever." A number of journalists did go to jail, for publications that would seem only mildly radical today.[53]

CHAPTER 10

David Garrick

BREAKTHROUGH SUCCESS

Born in 1717, eight years after Johnson, Garrick grew up like him in Lichfield. The family name was originally French, De la Garrique (it's the same word as the scrubland *garrigue* in the south of France). His grandfather was a Huguenot refugee, and his father became an army officer, though not an active one. After marrying a clergyman's daughter from Lichfield he settled there on his half-pay from the army.[1]

Garrick was one of the few students—there were never more than eight—in the short-lived boarding school that Johnson had tried to establish. When that venture failed, Johnson resolved to go to London and try to make a living as an author. He was also hopeful that his tragedy *Irene,* which he had been working on for about a year, might get produced and bring him reputation. Tetty would remain behind until he got settled. Meanwhile Garrick was planning to continue his studies at a school in Rochester, beyond London, and they agreed to travel together.

Just at this time, Garrick's father died, causing a change in plan. David and his brother Peter each received £1,000, not a fortune but enough to make an independent start in the world. They decided to go into the wine trade. Peter would open a shop in Lichfield, and David would manage the business from London.

In after years Johnson and Garrick both liked to exaggerate the humbleness of their beginnings. "That was the year," Johnson declared at a dinner party where Garrick was present, "when I came to London with two-pence half-penny in my pocket, and thou, Davy, with three half-pence in thine." As for Garrick, he claimed that "we rode and tied." That would mean that they had only a single horse. One of them would ride forward for a while and then tie the horse to a post and proceed on foot. The other one would be following and would mount the horse when he reached it.[2]

It soon became obvious that Garrick had no enthusiasm for business, and he sold his share to his brother. What he wanted was to become an actor, but he knew that his family regarded that profession as disreputable—in fact, not a profession at all. If he apprenticed himself at a London theater they were likely to find out, so instead he began to learn his craft surreptitiously in a provincial troupe, using an assumed name. In 1740 his mother died, and he was finally free to follow his own wishes. No one then could have foreseen how brilliant his theatrical career would be, and still less that he would enhance the very status of actors. One day Edmund Burke would say: "He raised the character of his profession to the rank of a liberal art."[3]

Only two theaters were licensed in London, Covent Garden and the nearby Drury Lane. Ever since Elizabethan times the government had tried to suppress political satire, and there was a new wave of it in the 1730s, directed against the unpopular administration of Sir Robert Walpole. In 1737, the very year Garrick and Johnson arrived in London, Walpole passed a Licensing Act that would remain in force until 1968. It authorized the Lord Chamberlain to exert complete censorship over plays. It also put an end to the theatrical career of Henry Fielding, who had flourished with a series of satirical farces.

A few small unlicensed theaters tried to evade prosecution by pretending not to sell tickets for plays at all. One of those, known as Goodman's Fields, mounted a production of *Richard III* in 1741 that was billed as an entertainment "performed gratis by persons for their own diversion," allegedly a mere interlude from the real attraction, "a concert of vocal and instrumental music." It was Garrick's first appearance in London, and he was billed as "a gentleman who never appeared on any stage." That was an important attraction: representing him as a gentleman rather than a common player, and also as an unknown beginner. He was unknown in London all right, but he had already had valuable experience elsewhere.[4]

Richard III was a fantastic success. Garrick was immediately a star, and all who saw him declared that they had never seen such powerful acting. He was admired especially for his alarmed "start" when Richard reacts to a terrifying vision. Garrick would continue to reprise that role for the rest of his career, and his friend Hogarth created a compelling image of it (color plate 16). The majestically large painting—six feet by eight—shows a naturalistic background rather than the simple stage scenery of the time. Prints made from it were widely disseminated in a publicity campaign.

The painting depicts the night before the battle of Bosworth Field, with soldiers' tents and a campfire in the distance. Richard's armor lies tumbled on the ground, and his crown is resting on the table beside him. He has just been startled awake from a dream in which the ghosts of his victims foretell his imminent death. His hair is wild, his brow is furrowed, and he stares in horror, seizing a dagger with his left hand while warding off the imagined threat with his right.

However stylized this pose may seem to us today, people who saw Garrick perform were stunned by the realism of his "start," which seemed a spontaneous reaction of fear. They were equally impressed by the horror with which he spoke the words that followed:

> Give me another horse! Bind up my wounds!
> Have mercy, Jesu!—Soft, I did but dream.
> O coward conscience, how dost thou afflict me!
> The lights burn blue. It is now dead midnight.
> Cold fearful drops stand on my trembling flesh.
> What do I fear? Myself? There's none else by.
> Richard loves Richard; that is, I and I.[5]

Johnson had mixed feelings about this spectacular success. When they had left Lichfield together four years previously, he was an aspiring writer and Garrick was merely his young pupil, destined for the wine trade. Now Garrick was overnight the most celebrated actor in Britain, and well on the way to wealth. Within a few years he would become manager of the Drury Lane Theatre while Johnson would still be a booksellers' hack, impoverished and virtually unknown.

Long afterward, when they were both famous, Johnson was diverted by a story about a poor woman who came to London and fell upon hard times. When asked where she was from, she said Lichfield, but that there was no likelihood that anyone she used to know still existed. "I knew one David Garrick indeed, but I once heard that he turned strolling player, and is probably dead long ago. I also knew an obscure man, Samuel Johnson, very good he was too—but who can know anything of poor Johnson?" When Johnson heard about that he collected money from his friends on her behalf.[6]

As a manager Garrick proved to be a great administrator, ably assisted by another brother, George. The Drury Lane Theatre was confined within an oddly shaped plot bounded by Bridges Street, Russell Street, and Drury Lane, just east of Covent Garden where the rival theater was. Its dimensions were roughly fifty by a hundred feet, and the stage, sloping gently forward to a projecting apron, was forty-five feet wide and thirty deep. In later years ways were found to increase the seating capacity, but the building itself could never expand.[7]

The company was large, since plays had big casts and each of the two theaters alternated its way through an enormous repertory every season. Between 1747 and 1776 Drury Lane averaged sixty-eight different plays each year, and Covent Garden seventy. Actors were expected to be ready to appear in any one of these plays at short notice, and consequently they held on to specific roles as their personal property for years and even decades. When Garrick took over at Drury Lane he had a company of seventy: fifty-three actors and actresses, fifteen dancers, and two singers. In later years there were even more.[8]

Until then there had been no such thing as a director who would take charge of an entire production and rehearse the actors as an ensemble. They rehearsed themselves informally, if at all, and memorized their own parts with little or no attention to the others. Onstage they would declaim their lines oratorically and then stand at ease and ignore the action. Garrick taught his company to relate to each other with body language and eye contact, and he rehearsed the plays as a modern director would. And as actor-manager, he had complete control of an entire season.[9]

Inevitably, there was the challenge of dealing with strong egos. Thomas Davies, the sometime actor in whose bookshop Boswell met Johnson, said that "interests clash in the confined circle of a playhouse, where jealousy and distrust predominate, from very obvious reasons." That was especially true since each actor was contracted to just one of the two theaters. Davies noted, "They cannot, like those of other professions, dispose of their goods in several markets and to various purchasers."[10]

The great majority of the plays at Drury Lane, in addition to ones by Shakespeare, were familiar favorites from the Restoration and later. Garrick did put on new plays when he thought they could succeed. His friend Arthur Murphy, who became a favorite of the Thrale circle, had so many plays produced there that he has been called Drury Lane's house dramatist. Murphy's plays were well thought of in their time, but forgotten today.[11]

Though Shakespeare was immensely popular, his plays were seen only in the drastically revised versions that audiences had preferred since the late seventeenth century. When Garrick first appeared as Macbeth, James Quin, who had played the role himself, asked where on earth he got such a weird expression as "The devil damn thee black, thou cream-faced loon." Garrick suggested he take a look at Shakespeare's text.[12]

Although Garrick made modest efforts toward restoring the original texts, he fully accepted his audience's expectations. The obscene suggestions that Hamlet hurls at his mother had to go, as did "low" or comic scenes in the tragedies. The Fool disappeared from *King Lear,* the drunken porter from *Macbeth,* and the gravedigger and the fencing match from *Hamlet.*

From the perspective of posterity, an even more serious objection to the adaptations is that they not only eliminated comedy from the tragedies, they got rid of much of the tragedy as well. Hard though it may be to believe, *King Lear* was played with a happy ending, originally provided by Nahum Tate in 1681. Cordelia not only doesn't die at the end of the play, she falls in love with Edgar, marries him, and inherits Lear's kingdom. Meanwhile Lear himself settles down, together with Gloucester and Kent, in peaceful retirement. According to Murphy, this sentimental ending "can never fail to produce those gushing tears which are swelled and ennobled by a virtuous joy." Not until 1823 was the tragic ending restored, and the Fool didn't return until 1838.[13]

When Johnson later published his edition of Shakespeare, restoring the original texts, he testified eloquently to the power of the original ending of *Lear,* but accepted the verdict of his contemporaries. "In the present case the public has decided. Cordelia, from the time of Tate, has always retired with victory and felicity. And if my sensations could add anything to the general suffrage, I might relate that I was many years ago so shocked by Cordelia's death, that I know not whether I ever endured to read again the last scenes of the play till I undertook to revise them as an editor."[14]

ACTRESSES, AND A WIFE

Garrick lived for a time with Margaret ("Peg") Woffington, a beautiful actress whom he had met when touring in Dublin and who played Cordelia to his Lear. They broke up in 1744 and Woffington went on to a series of other lovers. Thomas Sheridan remembered that she once brought a sister into the green room, and when asked what the plans for her might be, she answered, "There were two things she [the sister] should never become, a whore and an actress, for she had sufficiently experienced the inconveniences of those ways of life herself."[15]

There is a lovely portrait of Woffington by Reynolds—but then, whose portrait did Reynolds not paint? She was particularly admired in cross-dressing roles, able to assume masculine poses and gestures convincingly. According to a fellow actor, "It was a most nice point to decide between the gentlemen and ladies, whether she was the finest woman or the prettiest fellow."[16]

After several further affairs of his own Garrick fell deeply in love with a young dancer named Eva Marie Veigel. Trained in her native Vienna, she came to London in her early twenties and was a great hit at Drury Lane, dancing under the name of "La Violette." They were married in 1749, and Garrick got a big laugh in *Much Ado about Nothing* with the line, "Here you may see Benedick, the married man. I may chance to have some odd quirks and remnants of wit broken on me, because I have railed so long against marriage."[17]

After they were married Eva retired from dancing, apparently by choice. She claimed to come from the Viennese aristocracy, though her origins remain highly obscure. Certainly she had been patronized by the empress Maria Theresa, and in England she was taken up by the immensely wealthy Lady Burlington. After their marriage the Garricks were regular guests at aristocratic mansions where a mere actor would not have been invited on his own. They were recognized by everyone as a deeply devoted couple, and never spent a single night apart until Garrick's death thirty years later.

As for Peg Woffington, she continued to be popular, but in 1757, when she was just forty-four, her career came to an abrupt end. She was performing as Rosalind in *As You Like It* when she suddenly cried out, "O God! O God!" and collapsed. She had suffered a stroke and never acted again.[18]

GARRICK'S ART

There are plenty of contemporary tributes to Garrick's greatness, but even from highly intelligent witnesses, they are usually too general to tell us much. When Fanny Burney was twenty she saw *Richard III* and was dazzled. "Garrick was sublimely horrible! Good heaven—how he made me shudder whenever he appeared! It is inconceivable, how terribly great he is in this character. I will never see him so disfigured again—he seemed so truly the monster he performed, that I felt myself glow with indignation every time I saw him. The applause he met with exceeds all belief of the absent. I thought at the end they would have torn the house down. Our seats shook under us." That is high praise indeed—but in what way, exactly, was Garrick sublimely horrible?[19]

Fortunately, we do have some insightful accounts of particular performances. An Irish actor named Thomas Wilkes said this about Garrick as Lear: "I never see him coming down from one corner of the stage, with his old grey hair standing, as it were, erect on his head, his face filled with horror and attention, his hands expanded, and his whole frame actuated by a dreadful solemnity, but I am astounded, and share in all his distresses. . . . I feel the dark drifting rain, and the sharp tempest." In the crude, candlelit setting of the Drury Lane stage, Garrick could make you *feel* the storm. And his delivery was wonderfully expressive. Wilkes continued, "What superlative tenderness does he discover in speaking these words, 'Pray do not mock me; for as I am a man / I take that lady to be my child Cordelia.'"[20]

The most striking phrase of all in Wilkes's description is "I never see him." You could see Garrick in the same role many times, and still be overwhelmed.

In a painting of Garrick as Lear (figure 47) the storm is made visible. The faithful Kent holds Lear's hand, and Edgar, disguised as Poor Tom, gazes back at them while lightning bolts crash in the sky. Garrick, who was just twenty-four when he first played the aging king, was concerned that his slight stature

47. Garrick as Lear

would be a handicap; he was barely five foot three. Instead he made it an asset. He seems to have been the first to conceive of Lear as a feeble, ill-used old man. For that reason there were certain heroic roles, Othello for example, that he declined to play, feeling that he couldn't be convincing.[21]

Murphy related a memorable account that he heard from Garrick about how he developed his interpretation of Lear. He happened to see a neighbor holding his two-year-old daughter by a window when she fell out into the courtyard and was killed. The man stood helplessly "screaming in agonies of grief," and afterward lost his reason. When Garrick later tried to console him, he would obsessively reenact the scene, fondling the imaginary child and then screaming in anguish. "There it was," Garrick said, "that I learned to imitate madness; I copied nature, and to that owed my success in *King Lear*."[22]

It's likely that Garrick's acting would seem artificial to us today. In important ways, however, his gifts must have been exceptional as only the greatest actors' are. He could make every thought and gesture seem perfectly spontaneous. The heroine of a Fanny Burney novel says: "I could hardly believe he had studied a written part, for every word seemed spoke from the impulse of the moment." Murphy said the same thing: when Garrick played Hamlet he seemed to be literally thinking out loud. "His voice and attitude changed with wonderful celerity, and at every pause, his face was an index to his mind."[23]

The German writer Georg Christoph Lichtenberg saw Garrick's Hamlet in 1775, and noted some fine details of the actor's technique when Hamlet sees the Ghost. His "start" at that moment was a lot like his pose as Richard III, and likewise became the subject of a popular print. But what impressed his audiences was that it seemed a *real* start, not a histrionic gesture.

Again it was Garrick's delivery that was most potent. "His whole demeanor," Lichtenberg says, "is so expressive of terror that it made my flesh creep even before he began to speak. The almost terror-struck silence of the audience, which preceded this appearance and filled one with a sense of insecurity, probably did much to enhance this effect. At last he speaks, not at the beginning but at the end of a breath, with a trembling voice: 'Angels and ministers of grace defend us!'"[24]

There's an amusing tribute to Garrick's naturalism in Fielding's *Tom Jones*, when Tom and his naïve friend Partridge go to a performance of *Hamlet*. Afterward Tom asks which of the actors he liked best, and Partridge says the one who played King Claudius. When Tom objects that Garrick is admired as the best actor who ever lived, Partridge exclaims, "He the best player! Why,

I could act as well as he myself. I am sure if I had seen a ghost, I should have looked in the very same manner and done just as he did." Partridge goes on to say what real acting is: "I have seen acting before in the country, and the king for my money. He speaks all his words distinctly, half as loud again as the other. Anybody may see he is an actor."[25]

As Goldsmith commented in a piece about traveling players, naturalistic acting would strike provincial audiences as no acting at all. "To please in town or country, the way is to cry, wring, cringe into attitudes, mark the emphasis, slap the pockets, and labour like one in the falling sickness. That is the way to work for applause."[26]

Another way in which Garrick was a master was in making each of his roles utterly individual. You knew you were watching Garrick, but what you felt most keenly was that you were watching Richard or Hamlet or Lear. An anonymous epigram made the point by contrasting Garrick with a rival actor named Spranger Barry:

> A king! aye, every inch a king,
> Such Barry doth appear;
> But Garrick's quite a different thing:
> He's every inch King Lear.[27]

What Garrick didn't have, in addition to height, was a face well suited for romantic roles. When he was playing Romeo at Drury Lane, Barry was a competing Romeo at Covent Garden. Someone who saw them both remarked that if she had been Garrick's Juliet, she would have expected him to climb up to her balcony, but if she had been Barry's, she would have climbed down herself.[28]

Most unusually, Garrick was equally great in comedy as well as tragedy, as Reynolds confirmed in a charming image (figure 48) imitating the classical "choice of Hercules" between virtue and pleasure. Tragedy, with a dagger in her belt, addresses him sternly and points up at the heavens, but the chuckling Garrick is clearly yielding to the flirtatious spirit of comedy.

One of Garrick's most popular comic roles was the tobacconist Abel Drugger in Ben Jonson's *The Alchemist* (figure 49), a victim of con men who persuade a series of dupes that they can look forward to enormous wealth. Lichtenberg comments on that performance too.

When the astrologers spell out from the stars the name Abel Drugger, henceforth to be great, the poor gullible creature says with heartfelt

48. Garrick between Tragedy and Comedy

49. Garrick as Abel Drugger

delight, "That is *my* name." Garrick makes him keep his joy to himself, for to blurt it out before everyone would be lacking in decency. So Garrick turns aside, hugging his delight to himself for a few moments, so that he actually gets those red rings round his eyes which often accompany great joy, at least when violently suppressed, and says to *himself:* "That is my name." The effect of this judicious restraint is indescribable, for one did not see him merely as a simpleton being gulled, but as a much more ridiculous creature, with an air of secret triumph, thinking himself the slyest of rogues.

Fanny Burney saw Garrick as Abel Drugger that same season. She already knew him well as a family friend, and exclaimed in her journal, "Never could I have imagined such a metamorphosis as I saw! the extreme meanness—the vulgarity—the low wit—the vacancy of countenance—the appearance of unlicked nature in all his motions—in short, never was character so well entered into, yet so opposite to his own." Garrick's brother Peter was amused when a grocer from their native Lichfield went to the play and said afterward, Partridge-like, that he couldn't believe the stories he had heard of David's wealth. "Though he is your brother, Mr. Garrick, he is one of the shabbiest, meanest, most pitiful hounds I ever saw in the whole course of my life."[29]

The year after that Boswell heard Garrick declare solemnly, "If I were to begin life again, I think I should not play those low characters." Boswell objected that he was very wrong, "for your great excellence is your variety of playing, your representing so well characters so very different." When Johnson laughed at this, Boswell asked, "Why then, Sir, did he talk so?" Johnson replied, "Why, Sir, to make you answer as you did." Boswell was surprised. "I don't know, Sir; he seemed to dip deep into his mind for the reflection." Johnson's answer shows how well he knew Garrick. "He had not far to dip, Sir: he had said the same thing, probably, twenty times before."[30]

Someone once remarked to Garrick's friend and fellow actor Tom King (it was his parents who owned the coffeehouse in figure 17, page 69 above) that since Garrick aroused such powerful emotions in his audience, he must have been feeling them himself. "Pooh," King replied, "he suffer those feelings! Why, Sir, I was playing with him one night in *Lear.* In the middle of the most passionate and affecting part, when the whole house was drowned in tears, he turned his head around to me and whispered, 'Damn me, Tom, it'll do.'"[31]

When Garrick visited Paris, the philosophes there, including Diderot, begged him to give them some examples of his acting. Realizing that not all of them were fluent in English, he chose episodes that were essentially mime, and astonished them. Fréderick Melchior Grimm, who edited the influential *Correspondance Littéraire,* was impressed by how nimbly Garrick could change from one mood to another.

> We saw him play the dagger scene from the tragedy of *Macbeth*—in a room, in his ordinary clothes, and without the benefit of theatrical illusion. His eyes followed the dagger, moving suspended through the air, and it was so beautifully done that he drew a cry of admiration from everyone present. Who could believe that the next moment the same man could give just as perfect an imitation of a pastry cook's boy, carrying a tray of pies on his head, gaping around him as he walks, dropping the tray in the gutter, staring at first stupefied at what has happened, and finally bursting into tears?[32]

Even in private life, Garrick was always on. Goldsmith caught that perfectly in one of his mock epitaphs:

> On the stage he was natural, simple, affecting;
> 'Twas only that when he was off, he was acting.
> With no reason on earth to go out of his way,
> He turned and he varied full ten times a day.
> Though secure of our hearts, yet confoundedly sick
> If they were not his own by finessing and trick,
> He cast off his friends, as a huntsman his pack,
> For he knew when he pleased he could whistle them back.[33]

Reynolds likewise thought that Garrick was one of those people whose chief concern is to make a striking impression. "An inordinate desire after fame produces an entire neglect of their old friends—or we may rather say, they never have any friends."[34]

Fanny Burney recalled a bravura performance when a footman told her father, the musicologist Charles Burney, that Sir John Hawkins was at the door. Burney was appalled. He knew and detested Hawkins, who was writing a rival history of music, and had blackballed him for election to the Club. Burney told the footman not to let him in, but it was too late: "Sir, he's at my heels! He's close to the door! He wouldn't stop!"

So in came the unwelcome guest, bundled up in a heavy greatcoat and slouched hat, and with a handkerchief over his mouth, evidently because of toothache. To the amazement of Burney and his friends, he sat calmly down in an armchair by the fire "with an air of domineering authority." While they were gazing at each other in astonishment, the intruder flung the handkerchief into the fire "and displayed to view, lustrous with vivacity, the gay features, the sparkling eyes, and laughing countenance of the inimitable imitator, David Garrick."[35]

One is irresistibly reminded of another gifted impersonator, Sherlock Holmes. "It was close upon four before the door opened, and a drunken-looking groom, ill-kempt and side-whiskered, with an inflamed face and disreputable clothes, walked into the room. Accustomed as I was to my friend's amazing powers in the use of disguises, I had to look three times before I was certain that it was indeed he."[36]

GARRICK AND JOHNSON

We recall that the very first time Boswell met Johnson he incautiously said that Garrick, whom he barely knew at the time, would surely not refuse him a favor, and Johnson sternly retorted, "I have known David Garrick longer than you have done, and I know no right you have to talk to me on this subject." Boswell had touched unknowingly upon an underlying tension between Johnson and Garrick that always threatened to surface. People who knew them thought it was mainly due to Johnson's envy of Garrick's celebrity and wealth.

There is no doubt that Johnson had Garrick in mind in one of the final *Ramblers,* when an imaginary correspondent describes a visit to an old friend who has come into prosperity. "We set out in the world together, and for a long time mutually assisted each other in our exigencies." But now "Prospero" has a mansion filled with carpets that his old friend is not allowed to walk on, and china too good for him to use. To be sure, the Rambler comments that such people "are often innocent of the pain which their vanity produces, and insult others when they have no worse purpose than to please themselves." All the same, Johnson admitted that Garrick never forgave him for the portrait of Prospero.[37]

Garrick did have a lavish lifestyle, but he was never selfish; Johnson said admiringly that he "gave away more money than any man in London." Not only did he freely help his friends, lending Burke £1,000 which he knew would never be repaid, but Murphy said that whenever Johnson asked his friends to help needy people, "he received from Garrick more than from any other person, and always more than he expected."[38]

There was not just one grand residence, but two. One was a townhouse six stories high in a brand-new development called the Adelphi, which appears at the far left in a picture of London seen from the Thames (color plate 17). St. Paul's Cathedral is at the center, and Blackfriars Bridge, completed in 1769 just two years previously, is lit by the setting sun. (The present bridge is a Victorian replacement.)

The Adelphi, which means "brothers," was an ambitious speculation by the four Adam brothers, modeled on the palace of Diocletian at Spalato (modern Split) in Dalmatia. It contained twenty-four townhouses, and because the ground sloped steeply down to the river, there were warehouses with big arched entrances below. When the Garricks moved in the chief architect, Robert Adam, lived right next door, and Topham Beauclerk was a neighbor.

Elegant furniture was ordered from Chippendale's, and a lot of it was needed, since they had no fewer than twenty-four rooms. The Adelphi was demolished in the 1930s, much to the outrage of admirers of classic architecture, but the Garricks' ornamental ceiling and marble fireplace can still be seen in the Victoria and Albert Museum.[39]

The Garricks' other residence was a country villa, such as was virtually obligatory for gentlemen of means, but unlike Burke they could afford theirs. It was on the Thames at Hampton (figure 50), with an octagonal temple to Shakespeare that Garrick had built. Inside the temple was a fine statue of Shakespeare by the distinguished sculptor Roubiliac, now in the British Museum. Garrick posed for the statue himself. There were also various miscellaneous relics, including a leather glove that Shakespeare was supposed to have worn. Garrick undoubtedly knew that Shakespeare's father was a Stratford glove maker.[40]

There is also a notable painting of the lawn in front of the house, by Johann Zoffany, a Bavarian who was one of the many foreign-born artists who made careers in London (color plate 18). Eva Garrick is seated in an elaborate chair that her husband had commissioned, allegedly from the very mulberry tree that once stood in Shakespeare's garden. When their protégée, an aspiring playwright named Hannah More, visited them, "I sat in it, but caught no ray of inspiration."[41]

Simon Schama describes this scene as "the first painted idyll of the English weekend: tea out of doors by the river, the King Charles spaniels flopped on the grass; a discreet servant ready to pour; a family friend making himself at home; and Garrick himself gesturing and speaking to his brother George, who is fishing but has turned to hear what David has to say."[42]

50. The Garricks' house at Hampton

Johnson's friends believed that another reason for his mixed feelings about Garrick was the failure of *Irene* at Drury Lane, even though Garrick did everything in his power to make it succeed, and managed to keep it going for nine nights. That was a great favor for Johnson, since the box-office take for the "third night" went to the playwright, and the sixth and ninth likewise. He earned the welcome sum of £200, as well as another £100 from Robert Dodsley, who had published *The Vanity of Human Wishes* and *Rasselas,* and had first suggested the great *Dictionary.* No doubt Dodsley wanted to help Johnson out, just as Garrick did.

Irene was written in blank verse, for which Johnson had no gift at all, and was desperately untheatrical. He thought of plays as collections of speeches that actors would recite, and had no notion of dramatic action. Garrick put in some stage business to liven things up, and Johnson took offense at that. A friend of Boswell's commented that *Irene* was "as frigid as the regions of Nova Zembla: now and then you felt a little heat like what is produced by touching ice."[43]

Johnson would never admit, however, that this disappointment hurt him. He told Boswell that he remained "as firm and unmoved" as the Monument, the two-hundred-foot-tall column by Sir Christopher Wren commemorating the Great Fire of London. He did acknowledge, however, that *Irene* wasn't very good. He was once a guest at a country house when someone tried to flatter him by reading aloud from his play. He left the room. When his host asked why, he replied, "Sir, I thought it had been better." According to Sir Walter Scott, a Mr. Pott was introduced to him as an admirer who thought *Irene* was the finest tragedy of modern times, "to which the Doctor replied, 'If Pott says so, Pott lies.' "[44]

There was also tension between Garrick and Johnson connected with the Shakespeare edition. Garrick had a valuable collection of Shakespeare quartos and other rare books, which Johnson expected to borrow when he was preparing his text. Garrick refused, for the very good reason that Johnson notoriously ruined books that he borrowed. One of Reynolds's portraits of Johnson (figure 60, page 208 below) shows him doing just that. Johnson was deeply insulted.

Besides, Johnson had a low opinion of acting in general, which his poor eyesight and hearing made it hard for him to appreciate. When Boswell asked why he didn't honor Garrick in some way in the *Preface to Shakespeare,* he replied, "I would not disgrace my page with a player. Garrick has been liberally paid for mouthing Shakespeare. He does not understand him." For some years he even objected to admitting Garrick to the Club. When Garrick hinted that he would like to be elected, Johnson complained to Boswell, "He will disturb us by his buffoonery." Garrick was finally elected in 1773, the same year as Boswell.[45]

A story about something Johnson supposedly said to Garrick became well known after the publication of the *Life of Johnson:* "I'll come no more behind your scenes, David, for the silk stockings and white bosoms of your actresses excite my amorous propensities." Boswell heard that at third hand, and there is some doubt about the trustworthiness of his sources, but if it did happen, Johnson never said "amorous propensities." That was Boswell's attempt to clean it up. According to Hume, who said that he heard it from Garrick himself, what Johnson actually said was, "The white bubbies and silk stockings of your actresses excite my genitals."[46]

Rowlandson's watercolor (figure 51) would seem to confirm that the actresses weren't much worried about modesty. And although Boswell never heard Johnson do it, there's no doubt that he sometimes talked like that. An Irish clergyman was present at a dinner where someone asked what the greatest pleasure was, and Johnson replied, "Fucking." He added that the second

51. Dressing room at
Drury Lane

best was drinking, "and therefore he wondered why there were not more drunkards, for all could drink, though not all could fuck."[47]

Whatever tensions existed between Johnson and Garrick, everyone noticed that Johnson wouldn't allow Garrick to be criticized by anyone but himself. When Boswell tried to get a rise out of him by suggesting that Garrick was too vain about his reputation, Johnson retorted, "Sir, it is wonderful how little Garrick assumes. Consider, Sir: celebrated men, such as you have mentioned, have had their applause at a distance; but Garrick had it dashed in his face, sounded in his ears, and went home every night with the plaudits of a thousand in his cranium. . . . If all this had happened to me, I should have had a couple of fellows with long poles walking before me, to knock down everybody that stood in the way."[48]

As for Garrick, it amused him to mimic Johnson's attitude toward him. Boswell remembered Garrick saying, "'Davy has some convivial pleasantry about him, but 'tis a futile fellow'; which he uttered perfectly with the tone and air of Johnson."[49]

Boswell's appreciation was that of one gifted mimic for another. Hannah More remembered an occasion when they were challenged to compete to see who could do the best Johnson impersonation. The verdict was that Garrick was the victor for poetry, but Boswell for "familiar conversation." That's amazing, actually—to surpass someone who had known Johnson much longer than he had, and was the greatest actor of the age.[50]

Johnson was not the only impression that Garrick had down perfectly. At the Burneys' house, Fanny remembered, he mentioned that he was engaged to dine with Boswell, "whom immediately, most gaily and ludicrously, he took off to the life." What wouldn't one give to know more about that Boswell impression![51]

One of Boswell's most engaging descriptions is of an affectionate encounter between Garrick and Johnson. He had invited them to dinner at his London lodgings, along with Reynolds, Goldsmith, Murphy, and Davies. "Garrick played around him with a fond vivacity, taking hold of the breasts of his coat, and, looking up in his face with a lively archness, complimented him on the good health which he seemed then to enjoy; while the sage, shaking his head, beheld him with a gentle complacency."[52]

All the same, Garrick was naturally sensitive about his relationship with Johnson. He once asked a clergyman named Percival Stockdale to try to get Johnson's frank opinion of him. So Stockdale asked Johnson, as if the thought had just occurred to him, "Do you really think that he deserves that illustrious theatrical character, and that prodigious fame, which he has acquired?" He hastened to report to Garrick what Johnson replied: "Oh, Sir, he deserves everything that he has acquired, for having seized the very soul of Shakespeare; for having embodied it in himself; and for having expanded its glory over the world." Garrick exclaimed in tears, "Oh, Stockdale! Such praise from such a man! *This* atones for all that has passed."[53]

A SAD ENDING

People aged fast in those days, as a sketch by the Drury Lane scene designer suggests (figure 52). In 1776, at the age of fifty-nine, Garrick announced that he was retiring from the stage, and gave a series of farewell performances in his most famous roles. When he played Lear for the last time, the actresses who were playing Goneril and Regan couldn't stop themselves from openly sobbing during the play.[54]

The last performance of all was not in a Shakespearean role, which he feared would be too taxing, but as Don Felix, a jealous lover in *The Wonder: A Woman Keeps a Secret* by Susanna Centlivre. When the play ended Garrick stepped forward and made a short speech of thanks to his loyal audience, and according to Murphy, "Every face in the theater was clouded with grief. Tears gushed in various parts of the house, and all concurred in one general demonstration of sorrow. The word 'farewell' resounded from every quarter, amidst the loudest bursts of applause. The people saw the theatrical sun, which had shone with transcendent lustre, go down beneath the horizon to rise no more." To his longtime friend Thomas King, Garrick afterward sent his favorite prop sword inscribed with the Ghost's words from *Hamlet:* "Farewell, remember me!"[55]

The Garricks were looking forward to a happy retirement, but it was not to be. He had been suffering bouts of serious illness for years, and as early as 1762 he wrote to his brother Peter, "I was in some alarm all the night on account of a few symptomatic creepings about my kidneys." He was right about that, although it seems that he may have been born with only one; the one he did have was being progressively damaged by infection. A haunting mezzotint made shortly before his death in 1779 (figure 53) shows the merriment gone.

52. The aging Garrick

53. Garrick in the year of his death

Schama comments, "The enormous bull-like eyes focus on the beholder with the same fierce intensity which had made the actor famous."[56] When Burney remarked a bit earlier that Garrick was looking prematurely old, Johnson replied, "Why, Sir, no man's face has had more wear and tear." Burney visited Garrick two days before he died, and was shocked to see the famously mobile face inert. "Though I saw him, he did not seem to see me—or any earthly thing. His countenance, that had never remained a moment the same in conversation, now appeared as fixed and as inanimate as a block of marble."[57]

Eva Garrick was devastated, as was her surrogate daughter Hannah More, who wrote to a friend, "My heart is almost broken! I have neither eaten nor slept since. My tears blind me as I write." Hannah hurried to try to comfort Eva. "She ran into my arms, and we both remained silent for some minutes. At last she whispered, 'I have this moment embraced his coffin, and you come next.'"[58]

No fewer than thirty-four coaches carried mourners to Westminster Abbey, four of which were allocated to members of the Club. The playwright Richard Cumberland recalled seeing "old Samuel Johnson standing beside his grave, at the foot of Shakespeare's monument, bathed in tears."[59]

CHAPTER II

The Spirit of Mirth

Garrick was the only actor in the Club, but not the only man of the theater. Just when it seemed that British playwriting was in the doldrums, two Club members came out with comedies that were immediate hits and have given pleasure to audiences ever since: Goldsmith's *She Stoops to Conquer* in 1773 and Richard Brinsley Sheridan's *The School for Scandal* in 1777.

The authors' lives were on opposite trajectories, however. Goldsmith, a founding member of the Club, died just one year after his play was produced, at the age of forty-six. Sheridan was elected to the Club in the year of his play, thanks to its extraordinary success, when he was just twenty-six. Almost immediately he gave up playwriting and went on to a long and notable career in politics.

The two London theaters were a couple of blocks apart, but had quite different performance styles. Covent Garden went in for sight gags and pratfalls, while Drury Lane was more solemn and decorous. Drury Lane was the older, designed in 1674 by Sir Christopher Wren and not much changed since then. It was known as the Theater Royal because it was originally commissioned by the king.[1]

Covent Garden, also a Theater Royal, opened in 1732 under the famous producer John Rich, whose smash hit four years previously had been John Gay's *Beggar's Opera* (it was said that it made Gay rich and Rich gay). He continued to own the theater until his death in 1761.

Garrick assumed management of Drury Lane in 1747, and when he retired in 1776, Sheridan became a part owner of that theater. By then the
building had been given an impressive classical façade by Robert Adam, and
in 1794 Sheridan replaced the entire building with a much larger structure.
That one burned down in 1809, and the theater that stands there today
opened in 1812.

As shown in a Rowlandson picture of Covent Garden (figure 54), a throng
of spectators sat in the pit on backless benches, while more affluent patrons
paid for comfortable boxes on either side of the stage. Directly below the
stage was the orchestra, playing before the show and also between the acts.
Rising at the back and sides of the theater were two levels of galleries. In this
picture, King George III and Queen Charlotte are seated in the royal box at
the far side of the stage.

There were no reserved seats, so the audience arrived early, milled around
outside until the door was thrown open, and then stampeded in to grab
places. At a popular show many of them had to settle for standing room.
There were no reserved seats even in the boxes, so the gentry would send
servants in advance to hold places for them.

On stage, sliding shutters or flats could be rolled out through grooves
from the wings, allowing frequent changes of painted backgrounds, and
also "discoveries" when the performers for the next scene would be revealed
already in place. There were few props and no attempt at realistic sets, such as
would become common in the nineteenth century.[2]

There were no spotlights, of course, but there were lamps with reflectors
that served as footlights. The rest of the theater was not darkened as it would

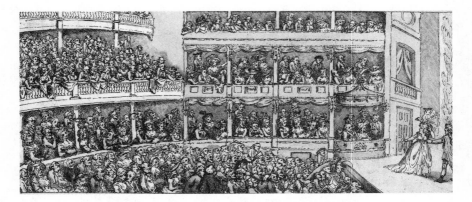

54. Covent Garden

be today. Chandeliers filled with candles illuminated the audience, which encouraged the byplay among spectators that Boswell liked to take part in.

An evening's entertainment was something of a marathon, often as long as five hours all told. There would be two principal works, first a five-act play and then a three-act musical. Last, there would be a farce or pantomime as an "afterpiece." To accommodate such a lengthy program, the show generally started around six o'clock, which meant that audience members would have dined a couple of hours before that.

Two more Rowlandson pictures, of Drury Lane this time, indicate how boisterous audiences were. In the pit (figure 55), where Boswell once did his bovine mooing, spectators are enjoying themselves while closely jammed together. The man at the far right seems to have been banged in the head. In the rear gallery (figure 56), hardly anyone is even looking at the stage. Instead young men are gazing meaningfully at fashionable ladies, and flirting if they detect encouragement.

Not only were the tragedies not very tragic during this period, the comedies weren't very comic. The fashion was for what was called sentimental comedy, or in French *comédie larmoyante,* "tearful comedy." In 1773 Goldsmith published *A Comparison between Laughing and Sentimental Comedy* in which he argued that these popular dramas weren't really comedies at all, but heartwarming fantasies in which "almost all the characters are good, and exceedingly generous." Audiences smiled through their tears but forgot how to laugh.[3]

Someone who went to one of these plays was asked whether he had hissed it. "How could I?" he replied. "A man can't hiss and yawn at the same time."[4]

55. The pit at Drury Lane

56. Drury Lane gallery

GOLDSMITH, THE GOOD-NATURED MAN

Goldsmith's first play, *The Good-Natured Man* in 1768, was sentimental in its own way. Its hero, appropriately named Honeywood, is presented as excessively good-natured, and therefore easily taken advantage of. Still, there are worse things to be. Goldsmith saw himself as a good-natured man.

His friends were far from sure that the play would be a success. They showed up in force on the first night to lend support, bringing with them a man "gifted by nature with the most sonorous, and at the same time the most contagious laugh, that ever echoed from the human lungs." There was enthusiastic applause at the end, and Goldsmith was suddenly a major playwright.[5]

One of the friends in attendance was Richard Cumberland, himself a sentimental dramatist. Goldsmith invented a mock epitaph for him:

> A flattering painter, who made it his care
> To draw men as they ought to be, not as they are.
> His gallants are all faultless, his women divine,
> And comedy wonders at being so fine.

When Cumberland read the poem he was greatly flattered. As Hester Thrale remarked, he couldn't recognize irony when it stared him in the face.[6]

Goldsmith's only other play, produced in 1773, was *She Stoops to Conquer*. It has an engaging plot, with twists and setbacks worthy of P. G. Wodehouse. Its subtitle is *The Mistakes of a Night*. Marlow, the young hero, has arrived at the country home of Kate, a well-born young woman who has been suggested to him for a spouse, although he has never met her. Unfortunately he is desperately shy with women of his own social class, so when they are introduced he can't even look her in the face. She is attracted to him, though, and comes up with a plan.

A practical joke had been played on Marlow, and he is under the misapprehension that Kate's house is an inn and her father the innkeeper. Consequently, Marlow treats him with lordly arrogance. Kate, who is playing along with the joke, pretends to be a flirtatious barmaid; in performance she traditionally affects a broad Yorkshire accent. She tells her own maid, "My chief aim is to take my gentleman off his guard, and like an invisible champion of romance, examine the giant's force before I offer to combat."[7]

Kate is witty and self-confident, a descendant of Shakespeare's comic heroines, and Marlow is charmed. Since he assumes she is a mere servant he has no problem being flirtatious in return. He tells her she is "vastly handsome," with a "sprightly malicious eye," and he proposes to investigate "the nectar of your lips." In exactly the same way, Boswell was always snatching kisses from servant girls and persuading himself that they liked it.[8]

Kate then reveals her deception, but claims to be a poor relation of the family. When he thought she was a barmaid Marlow felt free to seduce her, but now he acknowledges genuine attraction and offers to marry her, still unaware that she is wealthy. After she accepts she reveals her true status. She has, in short, stooped to conquer.

Boswell was in Edinburgh when the play opened, and wrote to Goldsmith, "I am happy to hear that you have waked the spirit of mirth which has so long lain dormant, and revived natural humor and hearty laughter." He got down to London while the play was still running. "I laughed most heartily," he recorded in his journal, "and was highly pleased at once with the excellent comedy, and with the fame and profit which my friend Goldsmith was receiving. It was really a rich evening to me." As was customary, the play was followed by a brief farce, but Boswell left before that: "I would not put the taste of Goldsmith's fruit out of my mouth."

Soon afterward Boswell went to call on the playwright. "He was not up, and I was shown into his dining room and library. When he heard that it was I, he roared from his bed, 'Boswell!' I ran to him. We had a cordial embrace."

Goldsmith was coming up in the world if he now had a dining room and library, though his expenses still left him deep in debt. A couple of weeks after that he was present at a dinner party at which Johnson declared, "I know of no comedy for many years that has so much exhilarated an audience, that has answered so much the great end of comedy—making an audience merry."[9]

A ROMANTIC STORY

The early life of Richard Brinsley Sheridan—his friends called him Dick—was lonely. His father Thomas, Boswell's elocution teacher and early London mentor, had been the successful manager of a theater in his native Dublin, but it was wrecked during a political riot and he moved to London, taking with him his wife Frances and their older son Charles. Richard, who was three at the time, was left behind in Dublin in the care of a nurse, together with his little sister Alicia, whom he called Lissy. During the next eight years he seldom saw his parents at all, and when they finally did bring him to London, they sent him to boarding school at Harrow. Lissy commented years later, "Neither he nor I were very happy, but we were fondly attached to each other. We had no one else to love."[10]

In 1764, when Richard was twelve, his parents moved to France in the hope that a benign climate would improve his mother's precarious health. Two years after that she died. His father didn't bother to let him know, and he learned about it from his Harrow headmaster.

Returning to England, Thomas Sheridan moved the family to Bath, where he intended to establish a school of elocution, but his Irishness turned out to be a fatal barrier. Young Richard, just turning twenty, plunged into a dramatic romance there. A musician whom his father knew had a daughter, Elizabeth Linley, who was not only breathtakingly beautiful but also a singer with a wonderful voice. By the time she was fourteen she was a celebrated performer, and a lovely portrait of her at that age was painted by Gainsborough.

Elizabeth and Richard fell deeply in love. Alarmed by the aggressive pursuit of her by one Captain Matthews, they eloped to France and were married there by a Catholic priest. That union would not have been recognized in England, not because of Catholicism, but because neither of them had yet reached the age of majority.

Thomas Sheridan located the couple and brought them back to Bath, and now Captain Matthews made trouble. In due course he and Richard fought a duel with swords. Matthews was wounded and called out, "I beg my life," but afterward refused to apologize as he had promised he would. Soon there was a second duel, fought after they sat up all night drinking together, and this time it was Richard who was wounded. He expected to die, but the wounds turned out not to be serious; he had been wearing a portrait miniature of Elizabeth that deflected his opponent's blade from his heart.[11]

Fintan O'Toole, in his excellent biography of Sheridan, makes clear what this melodramatic affair meant to Richard's reputation: he had established himself as a gentleman. "One sure way of proving one's right to that title was by showing a willingness to risk death in order to defend it." At Harrow he had learned to speak and carry himself like an English gentleman; now he confirmed that status, which would be essential for the public career he aspired to. He and Elizabeth were properly married by an Anglican priest, and their romantic story gave them instant celebrity.[12]

THE SILENT NIGHTINGALE

Numerous testimonies confirmed what a modern commentator on Elizabeth Linley calls "the heart-piercing timbre of her soprano voice," which could reach a note fully a fourth above the highest note on the harpsichord without the slightest strain. A cathedral organist wrote admiringly, "Her voice was remarkably sweet, and her scale just and perfect; from the lowest to the highest note the tone was the same quality. She had great flexibility of throat, and whether the passage was slow or rapid, the intervals were always precisely in tune. Her genius and sense gave a consequence to her performance which no fool with the voice of an angel could ever attain; and to those extraordinary qualifications was added a most beautiful person, expressive of the soul within."[13]

Fanny Burney was a musician's daughter and acquainted with great performers. When she heard Elizabeth in a Handel oratorio she was totally smitten. "Her voice is soft, sweet, clear and affecting, she sings with good expression, and has great fancy and even taste in her cadences." But it was her looks that were most enchanting. "Had I been, for my sins, born of the male race, I should certainly have added one more to Miss Linley's train. She is really beautiful; her complexion a clear, lovely, animated brown, with a blooming colour on her cheeks; her nose that most elegant of shapes, Grecian; fine, luxurious, easy setting hair, a charming forehead, pretty mouth, and most bewitching eyes."[14]

After their marriage Sheridan demanded that Elizabeth stop performing in public. He saw his playwriting success as merely a way to get well known before pursuing his real plan, which was to enter politics. At first she resisted. When it seemed that his first play might be a failure, she sent him a challenging note: "My dear Dick, I am delighted. I always knew that it was impossible you could make anything by writing plays, so now there is nothing for it but my beginning to sing publicly again, and we shall have as much money as we like." But Sheridan insisted that she give up for good, and she did.

From then on Elizabeth sang only occasionally, at private parties and at royal command performances such as the one Fanny Burney attended. She used to be called "the Nightingale." Now she was a silent nightingale, all the more charismatic because few people ever got to hear the legendary voice.[15]

Johnson approved of Elizabeth's withdrawal from public performance. When Boswell commented that Sheridan didn't have much money and could certainly use her income, "Johnson, with all the high spirit of a Roman senator, exclaimed, 'He resolved wisely and nobly to be sure. He is a brave man. Would not a gentleman be disgraced by having his wife singing publicly for hire?'" O'Toole draws attention to the word "gentleman" in that statement. When Sheridan launched his new career as a politician and statesman, his standing as a gentleman would be compromised if his wife were paid as a performer.[16]

It should be noted, however, that Sheridan, whose mother had been a successful author, held what would have been seen as progressive views on the status of women—at least, those women who were not married to him. At the age of twenty-two he wrote an essay on female education in which he proposed that the king should establish a university in which women would be taught astronomy, history, languages, and modern as well as ancient literature—most of which weren't offered at that time at Oxford and Cambridge, where the curriculum heavily emphasized Latin and Greek.

Perhaps Sheridan was remembering the ending of Johnson's fable *Rasselas*, in which "the princess thought that of all sublunary things, knowledge was the best; she desired first to learn all sciences, and then purposed to found a college of learned women." Johnson admired his friend Elizabeth Carter for her self-taught expertise in Greek, and after he met Fanny Burney he offered to teach her Latin. Her father forbade it. Hester Thrale noted in her journal, "Dr. Burney did not like his daughter should learn Latin, even of Johnson, who offered to teach her for friendship, because then she would have been as wise as himself forsooth, and Latin was too masculine for Misses."[17]

In 1776, shortly after Elizabeth Sheridan stopped performing, Reynolds painted her as Saint Cecilia, the patron of music (figure 57). Her angelic

57. Elizabeth Sheridan as
Saint Cecilia

children are singing from a musical score, while Elizabeth gazes intently into
the heavens where light pours down through a gust of cloud. This musical
saint is no flagrant public performer, but maternal and domestic.

THE RIVALS AND THE SCHOOL FOR SCANDAL

Sheridan wrote five plays in all, from 1775 to 1779. The first in the sequence was *The Rivals,* in which the sentimental Lydia Languish thinks it
would be noble to marry a penniless man, and her would-be lover has to
pretend to be penniless in order to win her. The plot, turning on a tangle of
mistaken identities, is far too complicated to summarize, and that was the
point, really. The anxieties of desire and frustration, leading to a potentially
fatal duel, are dispelled by freewheeling farce.

But it's not only farce. Much as Jane Austen would in her novels, Sheridan
shows romantic love rewarded in a context of practicality and good sense.

"Come, come," Lydia's lover tells her, "we must lay aside some of our romance. A little wealth and comfort may be endured after all."[18]

Sheridan excelled at memorable minor characters, who regularly steal the show in productions. His masterpiece in this regard is Mrs. Malaprop, whose name—coined by Sheridan from the French expression *mal à propos*—gave the English language a new word, "malapropism." "She's as headstrong as an allegory on the banks of the Nile," Mrs. Malaprop declares; "He is the very pineapple of politeness." She also has the imperious manner that Wilde would later give to Lady Bracknell: "You *thought*, Miss! I don't know any business you have to think at all. Thought does not become a young woman."[19]

Sheridan's masterpiece was *The School for Scandal* in 1777, which he put together from two originally separate projects. One was a satire on gossip-mongering, and the other was a moral test involving two brothers, Joseph and Charles Surface. Joseph is a hypocrite who pretends to be virtuous but in reality is a cynical seducer; Charles has a heart of gold. Sheridan may well have gotten the idea from *Tom Jones,* with Tom the lovable rogue and Blifil (who turns out to be his half-brother) the scheming hypocrite.

The gossipers take pride in their artistic skill; a character called Snake says, "Everybody allows that Lady Sneerwell can do more with a word or a look than many can with the most laboured detail, even when they happen to have a little truth on their side to support it." As for the brothers, Joseph Surface is on the point of seducing young Lady Teazle when a screen falls over and exposes his duplicity. Her honor is saved, and Joseph's hypocrisy is revealed. The "screen scene" is always deeply satisfying in performance. And then a rich uncle, who had been planning to leave his fortune to Joseph, bestows it on Charles instead.[20]

As for the scandalmongers, they are cheerfully unrepentant. Snake has played a crucial role in betraying Joseph, but only because he was paid to do it, and all he asks now is that his good deed should never be known. This is not a sentimental comedy, but it's certainly a warmhearted one. Sheridan was consciously looking back to the witty comedies of the Restoration, but his vision of the world is far sunnier than theirs.

We know a good deal about the cast for whom Sheridan wrote the play, exploiting the gifts of some exceptional actors. Having recently taken over management of Drury Lane, he inherited an experienced company that had worked with Garrick for years. The most important actor was John Palmer, who played Joseph Surface. In real life Palmer was known as Plausible Jack, because he was so persuasive that it was hard to remember that very often he was lying. Not surprisingly, his most celebrated serious role was Iago in *Othello*, though he was also a much admired Falstaff and Toby Belch. Charles Lamb saw Palmer in a later production of *The School for Scandal* and was impressed by "the gay boldness, the graceful solemn plausibility, the measured step, the insinuating voice, the downright *acted* villainy of the part."[21]

After *The School for Scandal* Palmer defected from the acting company, intending to start a rival theater of his own, which was a serious blow to Sheridan. The new venture failed when the two authorized theaters brought legal action against Palmer, and he had to ask Sheridan for his old job back. "If you could but see my heart, Mr. Sheridan," he exclaimed. Sheridan replied, "Why, Jack, you forget I wrote it."[22]

Equally effective in his own way, playing Charles Surface, was William "Gentleman" Smith. He had studied at Cambridge, moved in sophisticated circles, and conveyed an impression of utter naturalness.

The scandalmongers too were cast with care. Jane Pope, playing a character called Mrs. Candour, was remembered by Leigh Hunt as "an actress of the highest order for dry humour; one of those who convey the most laughable things with a grave face." The dopey Sir Benjamin Backbite was played by James William Dodd, brilliantly described by Lamb: "You could see the first dawn of an idea stealing slowly over his countenance, climbing up by little and little, with a painful process, till it cleared up at last to the fullness of a twilight conception—its highest meridian. A part of his forehead would catch a little intelligence, and be a long time in communicating it to the remainder." In Shakespeare Dodd was a much appreciated Osric and Andrew Aguecheek.[23]

Lady Teazle, the naïve young wife who successfully escapes seduction by Joseph Surface, was played by the celebrated beauty Frances Abington. In *Othello* and *Hamlet* she starred as Desdemona and Ophelia, and her comic roles were equally admired. Reynolds painted a ravishing portrait of her (color plate 19). It was widely believed that he was in love with her.

The School for Scandal was an enormous success. On opening night a twelve-year-old boy happened to be walking past the theater when he was terrified by a great roaring noise that made him think the building was about to topple on his head. As he wrote in a memoir long afterward, he panicked and ran for his life, "but found the next morning that the noise did not arise from the falling of the house, but from the falling of the screen in the fourth act; so violent and tumultuous were the applause and laughter." O'Toole tells the story in a chapter entitled "Bringing the House Down."[24]

Thrilled by his triumph, Sheridan spent the night getting drunk, caused a disturbance in the street, and was locked up by the night watchmen. A gentleman's wife should not perform on a public stage, but a gentleman lost no reputation by getting arrested for drunkenness.

Throughout the years—throughout the centuries, indeed—*The School for Scandal* has been a vehicle for many of the finest actors. In 1937, directed by Tyrone Guthrie, John Gielgud played Joseph Surface and Michael Redgrave was Charles, Alec Guinness was Snake, and Peggy Ashcroft was Lady Teazle. In an Old Vic production in 1949 with Laurence Olivier, Vivien Leigh was described as "a vivacious, exquisite Lady Teazle, looking like a Thomas Gainsborough portrait." The spectacular sets were designed by Cecil Beaton.[25]

Sheridan's fifth and last play was a very funny short piece called *The Critic.* In its prologue he acknowledged that it was much indebted to a popular Restoration burlesque mocking pretentious drama, *The Rehearsal.* Sheridan's play likewise involves a rehearsal, in this case of a faux Elizabethan play called *The Spanish Armada.*

Richard Cumberland came in for another jab. A character called Sir Fretful Plagiary was unmistakably based on him, and his customary costume was mimicked by the actor. Cumberland had brought his children to see *The School for Scandal* and was so jealous that he kept pinching them and exclaiming, "You should not laugh, my angels, there is nothing to laugh at." Sheridan commented that that was most ungrateful, "for I went the other night to see his tragedy, and laughed at it from beginning to end."[26]

Perhaps the metatheatrical quality of *The Critic* helps to explain why Sheridan never wrote another play, despite such splendid successes. He may have grown weary of the commercial theater, and in any case was eager to take his histrionic talents to a greater stage. In 1780 he would be elected to Parliament, where he was quickly recognized as a compelling orator as well as a leading ally of Burke and Fox, and he would continue there until 1812. He lived until 1816, four decades after his election to the Club, and long after the other members from that era were gone.

CHAPTER 12

A New Life at Streatham

STREATHAM PLACE

In 1765, a year after the Club was founded, Johnson unexpectedly found his life transformed. Through a mutual friend, the playwright Arthur Murphy, he was introduced to a wealthy brewer named Henry Thrale and his wife, Hester. The Thrales and Johnson took to each other immediately, and he became a regular dinner guest every Thursday at Streatham Place, their country estate ten miles away from the city on the south side of the Thames. Meanwhile the Club continued to meet on Fridays. Streatham soon became a kind of second club for Johnson, with a different and equally invigorating social ambience of its own.

As it turned out, that was just the beginning of the most important friendship in Johnson's life. He and Henry Thrale always treated each other with great esteem, but with Hester he formed a deep emotional bond that would prove crucial for his mental health. Two decades later, just before the end of his life, he wrote to thank her "for that kindness which soothed twenty years of a life radically wretched."[1]

The biggest change happened a year later, in 1766, when the Thrales became concerned that they had seen little of Johnson for a while. He had finally brought out the edition of Shakespeare's plays that had been stalled for almost a decade. But that only made him feel contempt for his own procrastination, as well as doubt that he would ever accomplish anything again.

When the Thrales called at his London lodgings, they were shocked to find him helpless with depression.

They immediately took action, bringing him home to live with them. From then on he was a resident at Streatham (pronounced "Strettam"), with a room of his own, and he made only occasional returns to London to check on his household of dependents at Bolt Court and to attend the Club.

The spacious mansion known as Streatham Place (color plate 20) was surrounded by a hundred acres of parkland and encircled by a gravel walk two miles in circumference. In its grounds was a little structure known as the summer house (figure 58) in which Johnson liked to read and write. By the end of his time at Streatham he would produce a late masterpiece, the *Lives of the English Poets,* which many people consider the best writing he ever did.

The Thrales were both avid readers, and had been thinking for some time about adding on a library to their house. They now did so, supplying Johnson with a liberal budget to help select the books. In the picture (figure 59) the library occupies the section with a bay window at the far right of the building; the room directly above it became Johnson's bedroom.

To decorate the library the Thrales commissioned from Reynolds portraits of a dozen of their friends. One of these, reproduced here as a print (figure 60), shows Johnson peering intently at a book—he complained that Reynolds depicted him as "blinking Sam." Someone who knew him remarked, "He

58. The summer house

59. Streatham Place

knows how to read better than anyone; he gets at the substance of a book directly; he tears out the heart of it." John Wain notes how different this image is from the portrait that Boswell chose for the frontispiece of the *Life*, in which we saw Johnson sitting at ease at his desk. Here he is "holding up to his fierce, nearsighted gaze a book that in the rapture of attention he is grasping and forcing out of shape, the covers back to back (it will never be the same again). Once again one notices the hands: large, strong, actively participating in the thrust towards knowledge and ideas, as if wisdom were a juice that could be literally squeezed out of dry paper and ink."[2]

In the portrait it's also apparent that Johnson is using his right eye only, since the left one had been virtually blind since childhood. He was heard to say that "he had not seen out of that little scoundrel for a great many years."[3]

For Johnson, Streatham meant a new life in almost every way. The Thrales loved him as well as admired him, and he knew that he was loved, after a lifetime of loneliness that was only temporarily relieved by marriage to Tetty. He was free all day long to do as he wished. And it was a life of luxury as well

60. Blinking Sam

61. Queeney Thrale

as ease, with attentive servants taking care of his needs, and a convivial dinner
every evening.

Johnson liked children, and enjoyed acting as a kind of honorary uncle
to the Thrale children. He was especially fond of the eldest, a remarkably intelligent girl named Hester after her mother, whom Johnson nicknamed
Queeney, for Queen Hester. Zoffany did an appealing picture of Queeney
just before her second birthday in 1766, embracing a family pet (figure 61).

THE THRALES

Hester Thrale was twenty-five when Johnson moved in at Streatham, one
year younger than Boswell and thirty-two years younger than Johnson. She
had grown up in a remote part of Wales, where her family had social distinction, but where her feckless father had reduced them to near poverty. Consequently, her mother was on the lookout for an affluent husband for her only

child. She found one in Henry Thrale, an Oxford graduate twelve years older than Hester, whom they met while visiting a relative near London. In 1763, at the age of twenty-two, Hester Salusbury became Mrs. Thrale, in what both sides understood to be a marriage of convenience. Henry had been turned down by eligible young women who didn't want to marry a brewer, even though his business brought him great wealth; in a good year it produced 100,000 barrels of beer, most of which was delivered to taverns. With Hester he was connecting himself with the pedigreed gentry.

Hester never complained. In fact she felt fortunate, for as she wrote in an autobiographical sketch, in Henry she got "a husband who was indeed much kinder than I counted on, to a *plain* girl who had not one attraction in his eyes, and on whom he never had thrown five minutes of his time away, in any interview unwitnessed by company, even till after our wedding day was done!!"[4]

The couple always treated each other with respect, but there was never any pretense of passion. Hester gave birth to a child almost every year, but had to accept Henry's involvement with one mistress after another. She kept her journal in a set of leather-bound volumes with the title *Thraliana* stamped in gold; Henry presented them to her in gratitude for patiently nursing him after he confessed that he had contracted a venereal disease.

Hester was diminutive—four feet eleven—and highly intelligent, witty, and socially skilled. She was also gifted at languages and a voracious reader. An engraving after her portrait by Reynolds, who became a good friend, gives a sense of her expression, both thoughtful and alert (figure 62). Streatham suited her well: between raising her children and presiding over parties, she was satisfied with her life on the whole. Also her mother came to live with them, and was the loving companion her husband could never be.

Henry was very different, both physically and temperamentally. Boswell described him as "tall, well proportioned, and stately." Hester herself said that his manner was "thoughtful and intelligent," and that he was unaffectedly courteous. A copy of his portrait, also by Reynolds (figure 63), gives a good sense of that. When he died years later Johnson composed a Latin epitaph that may be translated as: "Guileless, open, ever constant, he displayed no ostentation, whether contrived by art or wrought with care."[5]

Tragically, the family experienced an appalling toll of mortality, which was not exceptional at the time. During the space of fourteen years Hester bore eleven children, six of whom died at birth or soon afterward. She and Henry were determined to have a male heir, but only their daughters lived to adulthood. There were miscarriages as well. Later in life she said that the pleasures

62. Hester Thrale   63. Henry Thrale

of her marriage "consisted in holding my head over a basin six months in the year."[6]

A list of dates will bring home how painful, and how seemingly inevitable, child mortality was. Frances died in 1765, Ana Maria in 1770, Penelope in 1772, Lucy Elizabeth in 1773, Ralph and Frances Anna in 1775, and Henry ("Harry") in 1776.

Few of the deaths, if any, would have been likely today. Even when diseases could be accurately diagnosed, which they often weren't, the available remedies were useless or worse. When four-year-old Lucy had a serious ear infection made worse by a bout of measles, Hester called in a respected physician named Pinkstan. "He ordered sarsparilla tea and bid me do nothing else. Lucy however was fading away very fast, though everybody in the house persisted that she was well. I took her to Herbert Lawrence, who said it was the original humour repelled by Pinkstan which was fastening on her brain, but that he would try to restore it. A blister was accordingly laid on behind the ear." Predictably, it did no good at all, and after that yet another physician had the child "roughly purged" and bled with leeches. Soon afterward she died.[7]

The loss that was felt most woundingly was the death of Harry, the putative heir, in 1776 at the age of nine. He was exceptionally bright, and

Hester wrote gratefully, "He is so rational, so attentive, so good, nobody can help being pleased with him." Harry had an engaging precocity, too. When a family friend mentioned that he had personally rescued a lady on horseback from danger, "'Oh ho,' cries Harry, 'I'll warrant you'll marry her at last, as Tom Jones did Miss Sophie Western.'" Startled, his mother asked if he had actually read *Tom Jones,* which was regarded as a scandalous book at the time. "Yes, to be sure," Harry replied. "One *must* read *Tom Jones,* and *Joseph Andrews.*"[8]

On the day of his death Harry got up in good spirits and bought some pastries from a baker, but later that morning began writhing in agony. The doctor who was called in administered hot wine, whisky, and Daffy's Elixir, in which a dozen spices were suspended in brandy. Around the middle of the afternoon the boy died. It has sometimes been suggested that it was appendicitis, but the attack was too sudden and brief for that. More probably it was a virulent infection, possibly septicemia or meningitis, either of which could be cured by antibiotics today.[9]

Johnson and Boswell were in Lichfield at the time, and when the news arrived in a letter from London, Johnson cried out, "One of the most dreadful things that has happened in my time!" Boswell imagined that he must be talking about some such thing as the assassination of the king, but Johnson explained, "Mr. Thrale has lost his only son." When Boswell hinted that the reaction was rather excessive, he retorted, "This is a total extinction to their family, as much as if they were sold into captivity."[10]

Giuseppe Baretti, an Italian teacher whom Queeney adored, was present and described the immediate reaction: "Mr. Thrale, both his hands in his waistcoat pockets, sat on an armchair in a corner of the room with his body so stiffly erect, and with such a ghastly smile on his face, as was quite horrid to behold. Count Manucci [another guest] and a female servant, both as pale as ashes and as if panting for breath, were evidently spent with keeping Madam from going frantic (and well she might) every time she recovered from her fainting fits, that followed each other in a very quick succession."[11]

Later Hester wrote bleakly, "Now is not this a child to grieve after? Is not this a loss irreparable? Virtue, health, genius, knowledge and perfect bodily proportions. And now—all carried to the vault, all cold in the grave, and I left to begin the world anew." For years she had kept a pair of stockings that she knitted in the early days of her marriage. "My poor dear son wore them often, and had them on the morning that he died. I flung them in the fire so that nobody else might ever wear them after his death."[12]

A WORLD OF WOMEN

A wide range of interesting guests appeared at Streatham, many of them repeatedly, and to some extent they overlapped with the Club. Reynolds, Burke, Goldsmith, and Garrick were especially appreciated there, and the Thrales were delighted that their friendship with Johnson brought his distinguished friends into their orbit. But above all it was a world of women. As Frances Reynolds observed, Johnson enjoyed the company of women more than most men, and now he could live among them in an altogether new way, an admired celebrity but also a valued friend. With them he was flirtatious and playful in a style that Boswell probably never saw. And because Boswell himself was seldom invited to Streatham, and felt a jealous rivalry with Hester for Johnson's affection, that aspect of his life is all but invisible in the *Life of Johnson.*

The convivial ambiance at Streatham was the direct expression of Hester Thrale's personality, in ways that don't always show up clearly in written accounts. Virginia Woolf put it convincingly: "By the exercise of powers difficult to define—for to feel them one must have sat at table and noticed a thousand audacities and deftnesses and skillful combinations which die with the moment—Mrs. Thrale had the reputation of a great hostess." One thinks of the portrait of Woolf's own mother as Mrs. Ramsay in *To the Lighthouse.*[13]

What the Thrales had to offer their guests was opulent hospitality underwritten by Henry's fortune, and entertaining conversation stimulated by Hester's intelligence and wit. The dinners they gave were not just meals, they were banquets. Someone who was there in 1780 reported, "Everything was most splendid and magnificent: two courses of twenty-one dishes each, besides removes, and after that a dessert of a piece with [i.e., equal to] the dinner—fruits of all sorts, ices, creams, etc., etc., etc. without end—everything in [silver] plate, of which such a profusion, and such a sideboard, I never saw at any nobleman's." "Removes" were dishes served during a course to replace ones that had been taken away. If every dish was followed by a remove, there could have been as many as forty-two per person. As for the fruit, it was raised in the Streatham greenhouses and available year round.[14]

Maintaining a household like Streatham required a big staff. Domestic servants were in fact the single largest occupational group in eighteenth-century England. One successful lawyer at the time had eleven of them: a valet, a coachman, a postilion, a gardener, a housekeeper, a housemaid, a laundry maid, a dairy maid, a general maid, and a boy for any odd jobs left over. At Streatham there were twenty servants.[15]

Essential though these people were, we know almost nothing about any of them; they were simply taken for granted. One unforgettable portrait of six servants does exist, painted by Hogarth whose employees they were (color plate 21). David Piper, in *The English Face,* writes appreciatively of Hogarth's well-known image of a young street vendor, *The Shrimp Girl,* and then adds: "Some may find a more profound, more rounded achievement in that wonderful canvas on which, in all sobriety and humility, he set down one by one the faces of his servants. No king could hope for such sympathy combined with such veracity from his portrait-painter."[16]

Henry Thrale presided graciously at the dinner table without attempting to hold forth, which doesn't mean that he was bland. He got pleasure from encouraging lively cut and thrust among his guests. "Though entirely a man of peace," Fanny Burney commented, "and a gentleman in his character, he had a singular amusement in hearing, instigating, and provoking a war of words, alternating triumph and overthrow, between clever and ambitious colloquial combatants." That suited Johnson perfectly, of course.[17]

Many of Johnson's most memorable sayings come from the dinner parties at Streatham. One guest related what Johnson said after getting bored at a violin concert (he never cared much for music). "His friend, to induce him to take greater notice of what was going on, told him how extremely difficult it was. 'Difficult do you call it, Sir?' replied the Doctor; 'I wish it were impossible.'"[18]

Hester Thrale had a sharp tongue and was proud of it. Reynolds painted a double portrait of her and Queeney, and as was usual with him, it was softened and idealized. She complained in verse:

> In features so placid, so smooth, so serene,
> What trace of the wit, or the Welshwoman's seen?
> Of the temper sarcastic, the flattering tongue,
> The sentiment right—with th' occasion still wrong;
> What trace of the tender, the rough, the refined,
> The soul in which all contrarieties joined?[19]

Boswell heard Johnson tell Hester that she sometimes criticized people too cuttingly. With "a leering smile" Johnson added, "She is the first woman in the world, could she but restrain that wicked tongue of hers. She would be the only woman, could she but command that little whirligig." Hester seems to have taken the jibe in good part. She knew that he was only teasing, and that he greatly appreciated sharp wit in people of either sex.[20]

64. Hannah More   65. Elizabeth Montagu

A young visitor whom Johnson especially enjoyed was the Garricks' pro-tégée Hannah More (figure 64). Hannah's sister remembered an occasion when she and Johnson "were both in remarkably high spirits; it was certainly her lucky night! I never heard her say so many good things. The old genius was extremely jocular, and the young one very pleasant. You would have imagined we had been at some comedy, had you heard our peals of laughter." When they met again later, "Dr. Johnson and Hannah had a violent quarrel, till at length laughter ran so high on all sides that argument was confounded in noise." Thomas Davies said that Johnson "laughs like a rhinoceros."[21]

Garrick, himself a notable wit, once remarked of Johnson, "Rabelais and all other wits are nothing compared with him. You may be diverted by them; but Johnson gives you a forcible hug and shakes laughter out of you, whether you will or no." The forcible hug can't be preserved in writing, the bon mots can.[22]

Hannah More was at the beginning of an impressive career. In addition to poems and plays that were widely admired, she went on to do important work promoting women's education, and was the leading female member of the Society for the Abolition of the African Slave Trade. Hester Thrale thought her "the cleverest of all of us female wits," though she added, "we none of us much love the author though." Hester always preferred to be the only brilliant woman present.[23]

Another regular guest was Elizabeth Montagu (figure 65), author of a book on Shakespeare and acknowledged leader of the "Bluestockings." They were a coterie of intellectual women who didn't actually wear blue stockings, but adopted the name to indicate casual woolen stockings instead of formal silk. That was a signal that they met as intelligent friends, not as society ladies.

Johnson said, "Mrs. Montagu is a very extraordinary woman; she has a constant stream of conversation, and it is always impregnated; it has always meaning." And at another time, "She diffuses more knowledge in her conversation than any woman I know—or indeed, almost any man." Hester Thrale admired Montagu too, but appreciated a friend's comment: "That woman talks admirably well, but somehow one longs to hear the sound of one's own voice now and then."[24]

Johnson's real favorite among the women guests was Frances ("Fanny") Burney, daughter of Charles Burney, who first came to Streatham as a music teacher and would later write an important history of music. She was just twenty-five when Johnson met her in 1777, and about to publish anonymously a novel called *Evelina* that became a sensational hit. Told in letters, it traced the initiation of an inexperienced young woman into London society, with many satiric touches and eventually a romantic happy ending.

Fanny concealed her authorship at first lest the novel should turn out to be a failure, and also because she was almost pathologically shy. Knowing that, it amused Johnson to imagine her competing with the great Mrs. Montagu. Fanny recorded in her journal how he tried to egg her on:

> Dr. Johnson began to see-saw, with a countenance strongly expressive of inward fun; and after enjoying it some time in silence, he suddenly, and with great animation, turned to me and cried "*Down* with her, Burney!—*down* with her!—spare her not! attack her, fight her, and *down* with her at once! *You* are a *rising* wit—*she* is at the *top*. . . . When I was new, to vanquish the great ones was all the delight of my poor little dear soul! So at her, Burney!—At her, and *down* with her!" O how we all hollowed!

Henry Thrale suggested that Fanny should take on some less eminent writer, and Johnson retorted, "No, no—fly at the *eagle!*—*down* with Mrs. Montagu herself!"[25]

In due course Johnson himself got on Montagu's bad side, when she heard rumors that he didn't really think highly of her Shakespeare book (it was true). His comment was, "Mrs. Montagu has dropped me. Now, Sir, there are people whom one should like very well to drop, but would not wish to be dropped by."[26]

For Fanny, as everyone always called her, writing was an essential release from rigid repression; one of her sisters called her a prude. Her lively journals were addressed to "Nobody"—meaning not that she was herself a nobody, but that she expected that no one else would read them. She did sometimes share them with her sisters, and one of them later commented, "In her life she bottled it all up, and looked and generally spoke with the most refined modesty. But what was kept back, and scarcely suspected in society, wanting a safety valve, found its way to her private journal."[27]

A striking portrait of Fanny (color plate 22) was painted by a cousin named Edward Francesco Burney. He took great pains costuming his subjects, and had her wear "the black Vandyke gown, with slashed lilac sleeves, and very elegant." Wryly, she added that he insisted on turning her into a beauty: "No one would guess he ever saw me, much less that I sat for the picture called mine. Never was portrait so violently flattered. I have taken pains incredible to make him magnify the features and darken the complexion, but he is impenetrable in action, though fair and docile in promise." She soon grasped that her young cousin—she was thirty and he was twenty-two—had fallen in love with her, but it wasn't mutual.[28]

Like Hester, Fanny was tiny; Johnson liked to call her "little Burney." David Piper mentions that "height was often lent by fountains of feathers erupting from the crowns of vast-brimmed 'picture' hats." Fanny's towering hat in this portrait doesn't have feathers, but it certainly lends height.[29]

Eventually Fanny would marry for love and have a happy independent life, but for many years she was very much in her father's thrall; she was what the French call a *fille de papa.* Not born to wealth, Charles Burney maintained a comfortable lifestyle for his large family by giving music lessons from morning until night, as well as playing the organ and conducting orchestras (Handel employed him for rehearsals). Meanwhile he was working hard on his ambitious *History of Music,* whose first volume came out in 1776 and wouldn't be finished until 1789. His daughters, like Milton's, were kept hard at work as secretaries, and they were genuinely proud of his talents, which were recognized by an Oxford honorary degree. Burney had Reynolds paint him wearing his Oxford gown; and he finally got into the Club in 1784 (figure 66).

In 1775, when Fanny was twenty-three, her father began to feel alarmed at her status as an unmarried dependent. Someone she didn't care for proposed marriage, and he put heavy pressure on her to accept. She wrote imploringly to him, "To unite myself for life to a man who is not *infinitely* dear to me is what I can never, never consent to." Charles Burney relented, prompting a scene worthy of a sentimental novel:

> "I wish I could do more for thee, Fanny!" "O Sir!" cried I, "I wish for nothing!—Only let me live with you!" "My life!" cried he, kissing me kindly, "Thee shalt live with me forever, if thee wilt! Thou canst not think I meant to get rid of thee?" "I could not, Sir! I could not!" cried I, "I could not outlive such a thought." I saw his dear eyes full of tears! a mark of his tenderness which I shall never forget! "God knows," continued he, "I wish not to part with my girls! They are my greatest comfort!—only—do not be too hasty!" Thus relieved, restored to future hopes, I went to bed as light, happy and thankful as if escaped from destruction.[30]

In fact Fanny had not one papa but two, since she was close to her father's oldest friend, a reclusive country gentleman named Samuel Crisp. She called him Daddy Crisp and relied on his advice at all times. Unfortunately the two

66. Charles Burney

daddies, though delighted with the success of *Evelina,* instructed Fanny to destroy a play that Murphy and Sheridan—two accomplished men of the theater—had encouraged her to write. Called *The Witlings,* it was a clever satire on the Bluestockings, whom she regarded with cool detachment as a mutual admiration society.

The problem was that Charles Burney's income depended on giving music lessons to people in the Bluestocking milieu, hurrying from one fashionable house to another all day long—Johnson mentioned that in a single week he gave no fewer than fifty-seven lessons. He was notable for an ingratiating personality; Hester said that she liked him "but if he has any fault, it is too much obsequiousness." He was terrified to think that his standing with influential employers might be jeopardized if his daughter made fun of them, and he ordered her to drop the idea of the play. She was twenty-seven at the time, and tried to resist for a while, but he was inexorable. She did keep the manuscript, and in modern times there have been occasional attempts to produce the play.[31]

Grieving, Fanny wrote to her father (she was at Crisp's house at the time), "The fatal knell, then, is knolled! and down among the dead men sink the poor Witlings—forever and forever and forever!" She added loyally, "I am sure I speak from the bottom of a very honest heart when I most solemnly declare that upon *your* account, any disgrace would mortify and afflict me more than upon my own." But the bitterness was unmistakable. "You *have* finished it, now—in *every* sense of the word. . . . The *suppression of the piece* were words I did *not* expect—indeed, after the warm approbation of Mrs. Thrale, and the repeated commendations and flattery of Mr. Murphy, how could I?"[32]

Fanny did go on to publish further novels, which were admired by Jane Austen. She relished her fame, though she was always uneasy when strangers lavished praise on her, and acknowledged wryly that the praise was unstinting because no female novelist—not Charlotte Lennox, not Frances Sheridan—had had so great a success. "Even if Richardson or Fielding could rise from the grave, I should bid fair for supplanting them in the *popular eye,* for being a *fair female,* I am accounted *quelque chose extraordinaire.*" Not just a fair female, but a young one. "The truth is that the people, hearing I am an author, and seeing me neither as wrinkled as Mrs. Montagu, as old as Mrs. Carter, as fat as Mrs. More, nor as deformed as Mrs. Chapone [an author of conduct books], know not where to stop in their personal preference; because these are the only folks with whom they make my personal comparisons."[33]

At the National Portrait Gallery there is a 1779 painting by Richard Samuel entitled *Portraits in the Characters of the Muses in the Temple of Apollo* (color plate 23). Samuel was a young member of the Royal Academy, hoping to make an impression with this group scene. It brings together nine well-known women in the arts and literature, clothed in classical or vaguely oriental style, to celebrate their collective significance. *Evelina* had been published just one year previously, so Burney didn't make it into this pantheon.

The artist worked from portraits, but so idealized that identifying the individuals is not always easy. According to one interpretation, from left to right we are looking at Johnson's friend Elizabeth Carter and the poet Anna Letitia Barbauld. The painter Angelica Kaufman is seated at her easel, and the singer Elizabeth Linley Sheridan holds a lyre. The historian Catherine Macaulay, with a scroll, gazes at Elizabeth Montagu, next to whom is Hannah More. Standing at upper right are Charlotte Lennox—another good friend of Johnson's—and an Irish actress-playwright named Elizabeth Griffith.

Elizabeth Sheridan has a notable status in the painting. The central figure, she is the only one set apart, gazing up at the statue of the god. She seems about to sing. Each of the others, pausing to listen, was known for writing, she only for her compelling voice.

With Hester Thrale, Fanny's relationship was complicated. Charles Burney was a regular visitor at Streatham, giving music lessons to Queeney, and once Hester found out who had written *Evelina* she was wild to meet his brilliant daughter. Meanwhile Fanny herself had been longing to visit there, and when her father wrote to tell her that Hester loved *Evelina,* she wrote joyfully to her sister, "Mrs. Thrale! She, she is the goddess of my idolatry!" Soon afterward she was able to record in her journal, "I have now to write an account of the most consequential day I have spent since my birth, namely, my Streatham visit."[34]

Hester and Fanny were soon smothering each other with compliments and affection, but privately they harbored reservations. Hester couldn't resist trying to colonize her new friend, who was eleven years younger than herself. Fanny recognized that and resisted. From Hester's point of view, meanwhile, Fanny was too much a princess, receiving attentions rather than giving them, and not altogether well bred—Hester always had a vein of snobbery. "She is a graceful looking girl, but 'tis the grace of an actress, not a woman of fashion—how should it? The Burneys are, I believe, a very low race of mortals. Her conversation would be more pleasing if she thought less of herself, but her early reputation embarrasses her talk, and clouds her mind with scruples about elegancies which either come uncalled for or will not come at all."[35]

Fanny, much later, said of Hester, "She was warm-hearted, generous, sweet-tempered and full of active zeal for her friends, and of fervent devotion in religion. She was replete with wit and pleasantry, and her powers of entertainment exceeded those of almost any woman I ever knew. But her manners were flaunting, her voice was loud, and she had no peace, and allowed none to others, but in the display of her talents."[36]

Whenever Fanny felt ill, which was often, she had to be invited to stay at Streatham until she got better—apparently the coach ride back into London was thought to be too taxing.

> Fanny Burney has kept her room here in my house seven days with a fever, or something that she called a fever. I gave her every medicine and every slop with my own hand, took away her dirty cups, spoons etc., moved her tables, in short was doctor and nurse and maid—for I did not like the servants should have additional trouble, lest they should hate her for it. And now—with the true gratitude of a wit—she tells me *that the world thinks the better of me* for my civilities to her. It does! does it?

When Fanny was twenty-nine she told Hester that she was sure she would be dead within twenty years. With the iron constitution of a confirmed hypochondriac, she lived for another sixty.[37]

When Boswell did appear at Streatham, he was out of his element. Nobody there except Johnson much cared for him. He drank too much, and talked too much, and in most people's opinion doted on Johnson with unseemly spaniel-like adoration. Boswell even admitted it at a dinner party at which Johnson was expected, declaring frankly that he worshiped Johnson. The distinguished historian William Robertson remarked, "But some of you spoil him. You should not worship him. You should worship no man." Boswell's answer was, "I cannot help worshiping him. He is so much superior to other men." In the journal entry he added, "Let Robertson take this!"[38]

Fanny gave a vivid description—no doubt exaggerated—of Boswell's performance the first time she ever saw him. It was a morning visit, and as they sat down to breakfast he seemed startled that Fanny was given a seat next to Johnson. Resentfully he fetched another chair and placed himself directly behind Johnson, who didn't realize he was there.

He [Boswell] commonly forbore even answering anything that was said, or attending to anything that went forward, lest he should miss the smallest sound from that voice to which he paid such exclusive though merited homage. But the moment that voice burst forth, the attention which it excited in Mr. Boswell amounted almost to pain. His eyes goggled with eagerness, he leant his ear almost on the shoulder of the Doctor, and his mouth dropped open to catch every syllable that might be uttered. Nay, he seemed not only to dread losing a word, but to be anxious not to miss a breathing, as if hoping from it latently or mystically some information.

There was general amusement when Johnson eventually noticed Boswell, and "clapping his hand rather loudly upon his knee, he said in a tone of displeasure, 'What do you do there, Sir?—Go to the table, Sir!' Mr. Boswell instantly, and with an air of affright, obeyed."[39]

Boswell was relieved later on when Johnson assured him in a letter, "You continue to stand very high in the favour of Mrs. Thrale." When he eventually printed this letter in the *Life of Johnson,* she wrote in the margin of her copy, "Poor Mrs. Thrale was obliged to say so, in order to keep well with Johnson."[40]

A disaster that befell one of the Streatham regulars gave the Club an opportunity to exert its prestige collectively. Giuseppe Baretti was tried for murder in 1769. A couple of prostitutes had grabbed him by the genitals in the street; he struck out, they screamed, and three thugs rushed up to attack him. Panicking, he pulled out a little fruit knife from his pocket (people often carried them) and gave one of them a fatal wound. When he was arrested he sent an urgent message to the Club, in which he had several friends, and which happened to be meeting at the Turk's Head just then. Reynolds and Goldsmith accompanied him to prison in a coach. Burke and Garrick then posted bail.

At the trial, all four of them appeared as character witnesses, together with Johnson and Beauclerk. Baretti's opening statement was drafted for him by Johnson and Burke, who had gotten into a heated argument about what it should say. When someone said afterward that Johnson had shown "rather too much warmth," he agreed, and added, "Burke and I should have been of one opinion, if we had had no audience."[41]

Baretti's friends testified that he was a peaceable and even timorous man. He was also extremely nearsighted—his portrait by Reynolds (figure 67)

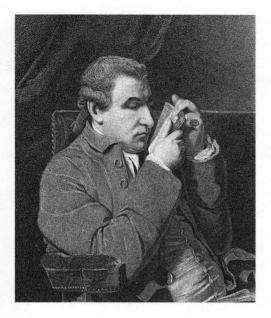

67. Giuseppe Baretti

shows him holding a book practically touching his nose—so it was believable that he didn't see clearly what was going on when he was mugged. This elicited an amusing testimony from the equally short-sighted Johnson:

> QUESTION. Was he addicted to pick up women in the street?
> DR. JOHNSON. I never knew that he was.
> QUESTION. How is he as to his eyesight?
> DR. JOHNSON. He does not see me now, nor I do not see him.

The jury found that Baretti had acted in self-defense and he was acquitted. Long afterward, eating dessert at Streatham, he remarked that the knife he was using to cut up some fruit was the same one that had killed the thug.[42]

HESTER AS THERAPIST

Hester was more than a friend and confidant to Johnson; she was effectively his therapist for years as he fought against depression. And beyond that, their relationship had a carefully concealed aspect that none of their friends seem to have suspected: psychological dependence on Johnson's part that can only be called masochistic.

In 1949 Katharine Balderston, the editor of *Thraliana,* published an essay called "Johnson's Vile Melancholy" that caused consternation among Johnson specialists, many of whom have tried to minimize its significance ever since. Her thesis was that Johnson's mental distress had twin sources: sexual thoughts that he could not dispel, and a need to be dominated and even humiliated by a woman.[43]

The most sensational piece of evidence was this. Among the belongings that were sold after Hester's death was one item with a remarkable description attached to it: "Johnson's padlock committed to my care in the year 1768." That was just two years after he moved in at Streatham. Nobody can be sure what the padlock was for, but one possibility is that Johnson feared going mad, and wanted to be restrained, as lunatics often were, if he was ever thought to be a danger to himself or others. When George III had his episodes of insanity, he was kept in manacles. In his diary in 1771 Johnson wrote, "*De pedicis et manicis insana cogitatio,*" which means "insane thoughts of shackles and handcuffs."[44]

In emphasizing the role of shackles in restraining the mentally ill, commentators have avoided a more sensational possibility: that there was something sexual about Johnson's feelings for Hester Thrale, and about the way he wanted her to treat him. There is no way of knowing what they did when they were alone together, but we do know how he talked privately with her about their relationship, and that raises plenty of questions.

For one thing, there is a strange letter that Johnson wrote to Hester in 1773, in French, probably so that servants couldn't read it. It would not have been sent by post, but handed to her at Streatham by himself or by a servant commissioned to carry it. Translated, it says, "If it seems best to you that I should remain in a certain place, I beg you to spare me the necessity of restraining myself by taking away the power to emerge from the place where you wish me to be. That will cost you no more than the trouble of turning the key in the door two times a day. It's necessary to act altogether as mistress, so that your judgment and vigilance can come to relieve my weakness." "My Mistress" was Johnson's usual term for Hester, in company as well as alone. No doubt he meant it as acknowledgment of her status in the household, but since he was calling her "*my* Mistress," not "*the* mistress," it could well suggest dependence of a deeper kind. To be sure, she often referred to Henry as "my Master," probably with an ironic edge.[45]

Hester wrote back, "If it be possible, shake off these uneasy weights, heavier to the mind by far than fetters to the body. Let not your fancy dwell thus upon confinement and severity. I am sorry you are obliged to be so much alone; I foresaw some ill consequences of your being here while my mother was dying thus." Old Mrs. Salusbury was indeed about to die, requiring constant attendance by her daughter, and several of the children were seriously ill as well.[46]

Is it possible that Johnson wanted to be restrained by his "Mistress," not just in case of a mental breakdown, but at other times? And beyond that—did he long for physical "correction"? It may be relevant that Hester's philosophy of childcare included regular beatings, and a rod lay waiting on her mantelpiece for that purpose. She exerted authority in other ways too. In her pocket she carried an ivory whistle, and when she blew it her children were expected to come to her on the run.[47]

Like many Englishmen, Johnson may have developed erotic associations in his youth from being beaten at school, where the usual practice was thrashing the bare buttocks with birch twigs. He once remarked that he regretted the decline of "flogging in our great schools" on the grounds that "less is learned there; so that what the boys get at one end, they lose at the other."[48]

Though the word "masochism" hadn't yet been coined, the phenomenon was by no means unknown. In the argot of the London underworld, "bumsitters" were ordinary prostitutes and "posture Molls" were specialists in flagellation. It's hardly likely that Johnson resorted to those, but they catered to a well-known taste. By the end of the eighteenth century plenty of libertines enjoyed it; a Paris police report noted that the philosophe Helvétius could perform his conjugal duty only if one of his wife's maids stood by simultaneously flogging him.[49]

Still, if Johnson was indeed masochistic, that needn't imply actual beating. Most immediately relevant may be what Rousseau would describe in the *Confessions,* not yet published at that time. As a boy Rousseau received a spanking from a female guardian, and to his surprise discovered that he enjoyed it and looked forward to more. She soon figured that out and never did it again.

In a brilliant analysis of the episode, Philippe Lejeune argues that what Rousseau learned was that he could experience the thrill of being reproved without actual physical contact, an erotic charge that was all the more intense for being taboo and withheld. "To be at the knees of an imperious mistress," Rousseau says in the *Confessions,* "to obey her orders, to have to beg her pardon, have been for me the sweetest delights." His word is *jouissances,* which then as now could connote orgasm. In an earlier draft he was still more specific: "I had an affection for acts of submission, confusing the posture of a suppliant lover with that of a penitent schoolboy." Jean Cocteau asked, "Is Jean-Jacques' posterior the rising sun of Freud?"[50]

There are further comments in Hester's journal that suggest how much she must have known, reluctant though she was to state it in writing. One reason Johnson was insomniac—perhaps the chief reason—was that in dreams his obsessions would invade when he was helpless to repel them. "He said to me suddenly, 'Make your boy tell you his dreams. The first corruption that entered into my heart was communicated in a dream.' 'What was it, Sir?' said I. '*Do* not ask me,' replied he with much violence, and walked away in apparent agitation. I never durst make any further inquiries." It may be significant that Johnson mentioned Hester's son but not her daughters.[51]

At another time Johnson told Hester, "The solitary mortal is certainly luxurious, probably superstitious, and possibly mad. The mind stagnates for want of employment, grows morbid, and is extinguished like a candle in foul air." Among the definitions for "luxurious" in Johnson's *Dictionary* are "lustful; libidinous," and "voluptuous; enslaved to pleasure."[52]

In 1779, when Johnson had been at Streatham for thirteen years, Hester mused in her diary that every man was likely at some time to live "under the dominion of some woman—wife, mistress, or friend. . . . Our stern philosopher Johnson trusted me about the years 1767 or 1768 [soon after he came to Streatham] with a secret far dearer to him than his life. Such however is his nobleness, and such his partiality, that I sincerely believe he has never since that day regretted his confidence, or ever looked with less kind affection on her who had him in her power."

Hester's note continues with general thoughts about men who have been dominated by women, even women who might seem quite ordinary, and then produces a startling quote: "'And yet,' says Johnson, 'a woman has such power between the ages of twenty-five and forty-five, that she may tie a man to a post and whip him if she will.'" Hester was thirty-five when she wrote that.[53]

Balderston concludes that Hester was Johnson's "unrecognized erotic object," which is to say it was her wholesomeness and virtue that he needed, not her sexuality. Far from wanting her to act out what he felt were ignoble desires, she was "to his conscious mind the revered woman, object of his awed respect and adoration, who by her very virtue could in some mysterious fashion check his abnormalities and exorcise his devils." However that may be, it's impossible to doubt a strong element of erotic attachment. Hester certainly didn't doubt it. "How many times," she wrote in 1779, "has this great, this formidable Doctor Johnson kissed my hand, aye and my foot too, and upon his knees."[54]

THE PLEASURES OF TRAVEL

Johnson's other friends probably never knew about his psychosexual involvement with Hester Thrale, but they definitely knew that he was happier at Streatham than they had ever seen him. Not only was he treated as an intimate member of the family, but the affluent Thrales liked to travel, and Johnson did too. Exploring the world beyond London always cheered him up. Hester commented that "he loved the very act of traveling," and he accompanied the Thrales on lengthy excursions to her native Wales and even to France—the only time he was ever out of England. He would have loved to go to Italy as well, and an elaborate plan was made for such a trip, but it was prevented by the death of young Harry.[55]

Travel by coach, jolting and uncomfortable though many people found it, was enjoyable for Johnson; he always made light of physical inconveniences. "In the exercise of a coach," Sir John Hawkins recalled, "he had great delight; it afforded him the indulgence of indolent postures, and as I discovered when I have had him in my own, the noise of it assisted his hearing." How exactly that could have been true remains a puzzle. Hawkins suggested that in some way the eardrum "is made more tight and springy and better reflects sounds, like a drum new-braced."[56]

What Hawkins was describing was not a stagecoach, crammed with strangers, but a private vehicle. The Thrales naturally owned one, and that meant traveling in considerable comfort in the company of friends. The journey to Wales, where Hester needed to look in on some properties she had inherited, took nearly three months, from July through September, 1774. The group consisted of Johnson, Hester, Henry, and Queeney, who was ten at the time. (Johnson kept a diary along the way, and likewise in France, but both were unfortunately perfunctory.)

There were also regular holidays closer to London. The Thrales maintained a house in the seaside resort of Brighton, for "sea bathing" and for foxhunting on the Sussex Downs; Henry kept a pack of hounds for that purpose. Johnson cheerfully took part. Hawkins remembered that "he showed himself a bold rider, for he either leaped, or broke through, many of the hedges that obstructed him." On one occasion William Gerard Hamilton was there and exclaimed, "Why, Johnson rides as well, for aught I see, as the most illiterate fellow in England."[57]

At another time, dismounting after several hours on horseback, Henry Thrale showed off by jumping over a stool. Always competitive, Johnson immediately did so too—"but in a way so strange and so unwieldy," Hester recalled, "that our terror lest he should break his bones, took from us even the power of laughing."[58]

Though an accomplished swimmer, Johnson didn't much care for the ocean. One autumn he was visiting friends in Derbyshire, not far from Lichfield, when Hester wrote to urge him to join them in Brighton: " 'Tis fine bathing, with rough breakers, and my Master longs to see you exhibit your strength in opposing them, and bids me press you to come, for he is tired of living so long without you." Johnson wrote back, "If I come, I have a great way to come to you. And then the sea is so cold, and the rooms [the public assembly rooms] are so dull. Yet I do love to hear the sea roar, and my Mistress talk. For when she talks, ye gods, how she will talk."[59]

Like the social evenings at Streatham and at the Club, these diversions offered Johnson temporary respite from his interior troubles, but never more than that. On Good Friday, 1775, half a year after returning from Wales, he wrote in his diary,

> When I look back on resolutions of improvement and amendment which have year after year been made and broken, either by negligence, forgetfulness, vicious idleness, casual interruption, or morbid infirmity; when I find that so much of my life has stolen unprofitably away, and that I can descry by retrospection scarcely a few single days properly and vigorously employed, why do I yet try to resolve again? I try because reformation is necessary and despair is criminal. I try in humble hope of the help of God.

On Easter Day two years later he was still writing, "When I survey my past life, I discover nothing but a barren waste of time with some disorders of the body, and disturbances of the mind very near to madness."[60]

Only occasionally did Johnson acknowledge an almost comic inevitability in the backsliding. In 1770 he wrote,

> Every man naturally persuades himself that he can keep his resolutions, nor is he convinced of his imbecility but by length of time and frequency of experiment. This opinion of our own constancy

is so prevalent that we always despise him who suffers his general and settled purpose to be overpowered by an occasional desire. They therefore whom frequent failures have made desperate cease to form resolutions, and they who are become cunning do not tell them.

But for him the overpowering desires were anything but occasional.[61]

CHAPTER 13

Boswell in Scotland—and Stratford

RELUCTANT LAWYER

Boswell identified deeply with the Scottish nation and with his family heritage. All the same, Edinburgh and Auchinleck became a kind of exile. London would always remain his gravitational center. Most years he would spend a couple of months there in the springtime, while the Scottish courts were adjourned and he wasn't needed at home. At those times his journals flower with lively material. But in Scotland, where life was tediously repetitive, they dwindle in interest.

There were two classes of lawyers in Scotland, known as advocates and agents (who were also called "writers"). Advocates tried cases in court. Agents couldn't do that, but they gave clients detailed advice and were likely to earn more money. Boswell was an advocate. In England he would have been called a barrister.

What Boswell did not do, but should have done, was commit himself to an apprenticeship for a number of years, thereby learning the law in depth. Perhaps he thought that an apprenticeship would be demeaning for the future Laird of Auchinleck. He persuaded himself that by attending trials and asking other lawyers questions, he would get all the expertise he needed. He admitted that it never occurred to him to study legal texts. Not surprisingly, he didn't become an especially successful advocate. For years he would make a decent income, but not nearly enough to support his family if his father hadn't continued to provide an allowance.

A real bar to professional commitment was Boswell's expectation of inheriting the estate, at which point he would be able to live comfortably as a country gentleman and also maintain a town house in Edinburgh. Lawrence Stone instances him when describing a common dilemma: eldest sons found their career prospects stalled by the certainty of an eventual inheritance, "until which time they were condemned to live a kind of shadow existence waiting for their father to die."[1]

Most of Boswell's legal cases were uninteresting. They had to do with breach of contract, or other minor issues such as disagreement over property boundaries. Frank Brady says that they often involved such small amounts of money that no one would even bother to litigate them today.[2]

Boswell further damaged his reputation with what would now be called pro bono work, defending lower-class clients whose crimes against property were punishable by death. One of those was a sheep stealer named John Reid. Boswell enjoyed the challenge of trying to win acquittals for the downtrodden, and by championing penniless outcasts, he might reassure himself that he was not in it for personal advantage. Beyond that, as with the highwaymen he went to see hanged in London, he may well have identified in some way with criminals.

Whatever oratorical gifts he possessed—he once congratulated himself on "my *Burkeish* talents"—the evidence against Reid was conclusive, and conviction followed. Boswell was present at the hanging. Reid left an eloquent statement that was afterward printed and sold for one penny:

> I return my hearty thanks to my benefactors, and in an especial manner to the honourable gentleman who has pled my cause once and again without fee or reward from me, and has further ministered to my necessities, and after all has taken every step to save my life at last. But God, that rules all things, has not seen it meet that it should be so. I wish that all his lawful undertakings in behalf of unfortunate panels [the Scottish term for "defendants"] may prosper, and that when he comes to leave the earthly bar he may find a welcome reception from the righteous Advocate at the Father's right hand; and then he will be fully rewarded for the services done to fellow men in their afflictions. Adieu, vain world.

Reid may have meant all of that sincerely, but it was Boswell who wrote it for him.[3]

There was a further complication in Boswell's practice of law, and he never articulated how he felt about that either. His own father was often one of the judges before whom he appeared. Whether or not that looked like a conflict of interest, nobody seems to have objected. In fact it actually brought him clients, who hoped that Lord Auchinleck might show favoritism. Knowing what we do about him, that probably didn't happen, but when he eventually retired from the bench, his son got less business than ever.

Sometimes Boswell questioned Johnson anxiously as to the ethics of defending someone he suspected was guilty, and Johnson always gave him the standard answer: each side in a case has a right to the best defense possible, and it is for judge and jury to decide right and wrong. Still, it's fascinating to speculate about why he kept taking these cases. He seems never to have tried to analyze it himself.

Boswell often wrote to Johnson laying out the facts of a case and begging him to write out arguments for his use. Johnson did it, though generally without enthusiasm. Some of these are printed at length in the *Life of Johnson,* but are probably not engrossing for most readers.

One in particular is interesting, though, because it reveals Johnson's views on forcing Latin grammar into the minds of unwilling schoolboys. The Reverend John Hunter, who taught him in the Lichfield grammar school, was well known for frequent beatings. Johnson's objection to that was only that the beatings tended to be arbitrary: "He used to beat us unmercifully, and he did not distinguish between ignorance and negligence; for he would beat a boy equally for not knowing a thing as for neglecting to know it. Now, Sir, if a boy could answer every question, there would be no need of a master to teach him."[4]

One case Boswell lost was a defense of a schoolmaster who had thrashed his pupils violently. During a London visit he brought it up at the Mitre, and Johnson delivered a ferocious opinion: "You must show that a schoolmaster has a prescriptive right to beat, and that an action of assault and battery cannot be admitted against him unless there is some great excess, some barbarity. This man has maimed none of his boys. They are all left with the full exercise of their corporeal faculties. In our schools in England, many boys have been maimed, yet I never heard of an action against a schoolmaster on that account." It's hard to know how literally Johnson meant that startling word "maimed." In the *Dictionary* he defined "maim" as "to deprive of any necessary part; to cripple by loss of a limb."[5]

1. Canaletto, *The Thames and the City of London from Richmond House*

2. Thomas Rowlandson, *Charing Cross*

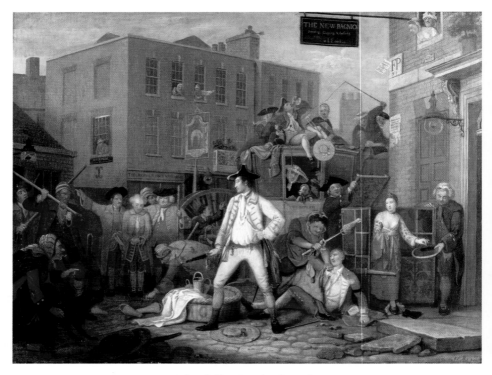

3. John Collet, *London Street Scene*

4. Maria Verelst, *Elizabeth Johnson*

5. Allan Ramsay, *Lord Auchinleck*

6. Auchinleck House

7. Thomas Rowlandson after Samuel Collings, *The Parade*

8. Balthasar Nebot, *Covent Garden*

9. Thomas Rowlandson, *Covent Garden*

10. John Boydell, *Old London Bridge*

11. Billingsgate

12. George Willison, *James Boswell*

13. The Turk's Head Tavern

14. Frances Reynolds,
   Samuel Johnson

15. Thomas Rowlandson, *The Exhibition Stare-Case*

16. William Hogarth, *Garrick as Richard III*

17. London from the Thames

18. Johann Zoffany, *The Garricks' Villa at Hampton*

19. Joshua Reynolds,
Frances Abington

20. Streatham Place

21. William Hogarth, *Six of Hogarth's Servants*

22. Edward Francesco
Burney, *Fanny Burney*

23. Richard Samuel, *Portraits in the Character of the Muses*

24. *Margaret Montgomerie Boswell* (artist not known)

25. Henry Singleton, *James Boswell and His Family*

26. The King's Library

27. Max Beerbohm, *In the Shades*

28. James Gillray, *Richard
Brinsley Sheridan*

29. James Barry, *Samuel Johnson*

30. Joshua Reynolds, *James Boswell*

31. Attributed to Johann Zoffany,
*Bennet Langton Contemplating the
Bust of Johnson*

PEGGIE

Boswell continued to pick up prostitutes and had an affair with a married woman who was estranged from her husband. (His clergyman friend Temple said approvingly, "Nothing so convenient as an eloped wife. How are you so lucky in mistresses?") But he was beginning to feel that it was high time to get married, and the Yale edition of the journal for 1766–1769 is appropriately entitled *Boswell in Search of a Wife*.[6]

A remarkable number of candidates came and went. Always susceptible, Boswell often believed he was passionately in love, but the excitement would wane quickly. Even when most smitten, he never failed to evaluate a woman's social status and financial expectations.

The wife he did find at last turned out to be someone very close to home: his first cousin, the daughter of his mother's sister, Veronica. Her name was Margaret Montgomerie (color plate 24). She grew up at Lainshaw, west of Edinburgh and not far from Auchinleck. She and James had been good friends ever since childhood, but she barely appears at all in his journal and letters until the spring of 1769, when she entered his life for good. He always called her Peggie, and she called him Jamie.

Marriage between cousins was not unusual, but there was a serious practical problem. Peggie would bring a dowry of only £1,000, which Lord Auchinleck considered far too little to set his son up in the world, and he indicated firmly that this was not a match he could approve of. The cousins were greatly attracted to each other, but they didn't expect anything to come of it. In 1768 James actually got Peggie to sign a mock legal document promising *not* to marry him, "considering that Mr. James Boswell, advocate, my cousin, is at present so much in love with me that I might certainly have him for my lawful husband if I choose it, and the said James being of a temper so inconstant that there is reason to fear he would repent of his choice in a very short time, on which account he is unwilling to trust himself in my company."[7]

At Lainshaw Boswell met a young Irish girl, Catherine Blair, who struck him as a suitable match, and he soon journeyed to Dublin to see whether that might work out. It didn't. As he wrote to his friend George Dempster, Catherine was "the sweetest, loveliest little creature that ever was born," but hopelessly childish.[8]

Meanwhile, Boswell was spending day after day in the company of Peggie, who went along on the Irish trip, presumably because she had become friendly with Catherine at Lainshaw. In a letter to Temple he admitted,

I found her both by sea and land the best companion I ever saw. I am exceedingly in love with her. I highly value her. If ever a man had his full choice of a wife, I would have it in her. But the objections are she is two years older than I. She has only a thousand pounds. My father would be violent against my marrying her, as she would bring neither money nor interest [i.e., valuable connections]. I, from a desire to aggrandize my family, think somewhat in the same manner.

Peggie of course belonged to one branch of the same family as he did, but she didn't share his romantic feelings about it.[9]

Jamie overcame these reservations, not least because Peggie was very attractive, and they were married in November 1769. Lord Auchinleck immediately took stunning revenge on his disobedient son, in a way that he had hinted he might. At the age of sixty-two, having been a widower for three years, he married a first cousin of his own named Elizabeth Boswell, who was twenty years younger than himself. And not only that: he married her in Edinburgh *on the very same day* that James and Peggie were married at Lainshaw. James felt betrayed. If there should be another son, his own inheritance might be compromised. There never was a son, but Lord Auchinleck didn't mind letting him worry about that for years. He and his new stepmother never got along.

Boswell tried hard to be a good husband, and for a while, even a faithful one. Still, there were predictable strains. Two years previously he had received a monitory letter from Girolama Piccolomini, who had been so passionately in love with him in Florence: "You have all the qualities necessary to be loved and to make another's happiness, but with all these fine attributes, I fear you also have it in you to make a wife miserable."[10]

It has been calculated that by the time of his marriage at the age of twenty-nine, Boswell had had liaisons with four actresses, three wives plus Rousseau's companion Thérèse, and three middle-class women, as well as brief encounters with over sixty prostitutes—and that's assuming he recorded them all. The prostitutes continued after he was married, and he always confessed about them to Peggie, no doubt to relieve his guilty conscience and to be forgiven.[11]

The best thing that happened to Boswell in Scotland was this marriage, to a wife whom some might consider better than he deserved. She would be loyal through thick and thin, and there would be plenty of thin. They would have five children, and with painful memories of his own childhood, he would do his best to be a supportive and loving father.

Deeply though he appreciated Peggie, whom he regularly referred to in his journal as "my valuable wife," Boswell came to recognize differences in temperament that made her unable to be the soulmate he yearned for. "Though she has excellent sense and a cheerful temper, she has not sentiments congenial with mine. She has no superstition, no enthusiasm, no vanity." She also turned out to be sexually unenthusiastic, though not possessive. "I was quite in love with her tonight. She was sensible, amiable, and all that I could wish, except being averse to hymeneal rites. I told her I must have a concubine. She said I might go to whom I pleased. She has often said so." He seems to have taken care not to infect her with venereal disease during his recurring bouts of it.[12]

The one thing Peggie could not accept was affairs with women of their own class, because those might lead to scandal. Boswell had a recurring fantasy of being a biblical patriarch, free to enjoy a host of concubines. On one occasion he "stole gently" to the room of an unnamed guest in their house. "She indulged me in amorous dalliances of much familiarity, but though I preached from the Old Testament, could not think of allowing me ingress." Peggie found out and reproved him "with so much reason and spirit that, as I candidly owned my folly, so I was impressed with proper feelings. . . . I valued and loved my wife with renewed fervour."[13]

Not surprisingly, Boswell endorsed the double standard. He states his opinion explicitly in the *Life of Johnson:* "An abandoned profligate may think that it is not wrong to debauch my wife, but shall I therefore not detest him? And if I catch him in making an attempt, shall I treat him with politeness? No, I will kick him downstairs, or run him through the body—that is, if I really love my wife, or have a true rational notion of honour."[14]

For that matter, Johnson too endorsed the double standard, though less melodramatically. His argument was that an illegitimate child would break the sequence of blood descent. "I asked him if it was not hard that one deviation from chastity should so absolutely ruin a woman. JOHNSON. Why, no, Sir; the great principle which every woman is taught is to keep her legs together." When Boswell put this exchange into the *Life*, he kept "the great principle" but left out the legs.[15]

FAMILY

Between 1773 and 1780 six children were born, at a rate of almost one per year. One died shortly after birth, but the others lived to be adults. The eldest was Veronica, followed by Euphemia and Alexander (named for Boswell's parents), James, and Elizabeth. Their nicknames in the family were Vee, Phemie, Sandy, Jamie, and Betsy. In 1786 a group portrait was painted showing three of the youngest (color plate 25). Peggie, with a formal wig and a hat matching Phemie's, has an interestingly piercing gaze. James is putting on weight, and trying to appear patriarchal.

James was deeply fond of his children and determined to deserve their love as his own father had not. It was a particular satisfaction that Veronica and Euphemia both inherited their father's musical talent; they became accomplished harpsichordists and singers. When Veronica was twelve their music teacher gave a concert for his students "at which my two daughters sung and played wonderfully well."[16]

Genuine though his affection was, Boswell didn't record much about the children in their early years. He did describe one rather challenging conversation with Veronica, who was very bright, when she was six. She still slept in her parents' room at the time.

> At night after we were in bed, Veronica spoke out from her little bed and said, "I do not believe there is a God." "Preserve me," said I, "my dear, what do you mean?" She answered, "I have *thinket* it many a time, but did not like to speak of it." I was confounded and uneasy, and tried her with the simple argument that without God there would not be all the things we see. "It is He who makes the sun shine." Said she, "It shines only on good days." Said I, "God made you." Said she, "My mother bore me." It was a strange and alarming thing to her mother and me to hear our little angel talk thus.[17]

A couple of weeks later Boswell thought it proper to impress his children with the concept of divine retribution—encouraging the same anxiety that had tormented his own childhood. "I told them in the evening so much about *black angels* or *devils* seizing bad people when they die and dragging them down to hell, a dark place (for I had not yet said anything of *fire* to them, and perhaps never will), that they were all three suddenly seized with such terror that they cried and roared out and ran to me for protection (they and I being in the drawing room) and alarmed their mother, who came upstairs in a fright." Sandy was four at the time.[18]

A few months later, however, Veronica delighted him with precocious theological acumen. She told him that when her sister Phemie said, "Christ is just like God," she replied, "He is a part of God."[19]

One family contention that concerned Peggie as well as her husband was his insistence on inheritance by males only. That meant that if their sons should die before he did, the estate would go to some remote male relative rather than to their own daughters. In addition to the rule of primogeniture, this meant drawing up an entail to specify the correct succession for all time.

In the *Wealth of Nations,* not published until a few years later, Adam Smith would vehemently criticize those arrangements. His argument was that primogeniture might have made sense in feudal times, when "every great landlord was a sort of petty prince" and security depended on keeping estates intact, but that it had negative effects in the modern world. Still less did he approve of entails. "They are founded upon the most absurd of all suppositions, the supposition that every successive generation of men have not an equal right to the earth and to all that it possesses; but that the property of the present generation should be restrained and regulated according to the fancy of those who died perhaps five hundred years ago."[20]

That is exactly what the Bennet family laments in *Pride and Prejudice:* since there is no son, the family inheritance must pass to the nearest male in the line of succession, who turns out to be the pompous and absurd Mr. Collins.

Boswell debated this issue with several advisors, including Johnson, who urged him to talk to the distinguished jurist Lord Hailes. Between them Hailes and Johnson finally persuaded him to drop his obsession and permit his daughters the right to inherit. "My wife shed tears." It turned out that the issue never arose, since their son Alexander did succeed James as Laird of Auchinleck.[21]

HYPOCHONDRIA AND ALCOHOL

Boswell's mental distress regularly returned, in a continuing cycle of elation and depression. In his mid-thirties he wrote, "I was in such spirits that I could not restrain myself from talking a great deal. . . . My wonderful spirits continued." That was followed by fondling a "fresh, plump, and comely" fifteen-year-old at a party; "my wife saw me and was offended." After dinner he sallied forth and encountered another woman, "an old dallying companion, now married," who willingly accompanied him into a field. "But I thought it wrong, so only indulged in a lesser lascivious sport."

The evening ended auspiciously. "I lay down in naked bed for a while and enjoyed my dear wife excellently. I then rose and wrote letters and had some good soup and was in a frame so firm and happy that I cannot describe it." A week later, "I was in joyous health. Bless me! How sound and vigorous am I now, in comparison with what I was once." But a few months after that: "I wretched; thought seat of reason would break." Another two weeks, and the depression lifted: "Did nothing almost. But was easy." Still another two weeks, and he was quoting Hamlet: "Flat and unprofitable." It was at this time that he began writing his series of essays entitled *The Hypochondriack*.[22]

During the episodes of depression, the sources of relief were the usual ones: "Brought out Malaga and drank it lusciously. . . . A little intoxicated. About nine went out to street. Met fine wench; with her to room in Blackfriars Wynd, and twice. Back and coffee and whist. Home near twelve. Felt no disapprobation. Wife still well." That last comment was a warning sign. Peggie was already beginning to show signs of the tuberculosis that would eventually kill her.[23]

When he was depressed, Boswell brooded on the problem of free will and determinism, which for him was no mere philosophical puzzle. He knew very well that he felt unfree, and the Calvinist insistence on predestination was hard to shake off. Johnson was no help. Anxious about his own compulsions, he didn't care to explore the topic. "Doctor Johnson shunned tonight any discussion of the perplexed question of fate and free will, which I attempted to agitate. 'Sir,' said he, 'we *know* our will is free, and there's an end on't.' "[24]

Visiting a friend, Boswell happened to pick up a treatise that argued "that every action of man was absolutely fixed and comprehended in a series of causes and effects from all eternity, so that there was an universal Necessity. . . . I was shocked by such a notion, and sunk into dreadful melancholy, so that I went out to the wood and groaned."[25]

Predictably, the drinking increased. That was all the likelier to happen in Edinburgh as contrasted with London. A Scottish writer on Boswell remarks, "For huge sustained drinking, eighteenth-century Edinburgh must have been difficult to beat at any place, at any time, in the world's history. Judges, advocates, lords, some ladies, country lairds, tradesmen and ministers consumed amounts of wine and spirits to an extent that makes one think that one is reading some saga of festivals in Valhalla."[26]

Boswell's biographers insist that he wasn't really an alcoholic, on the grounds that he could sometimes abstain. But there is no question that he often got horribly drunk and was unable the next day to remember anything that had happened. There were also episodes of falling and injuring himself severely.

On one such occasion, after consuming five bottles of claret with just one companion, "I walked off very gravely though much intoxicated. Ranged through the streets till, having run hard down the Advocates' Close, which is very steep, I found myself on a sudden bouncing down an almost perpendicular stone stair. I could not stop, but when I came to the bottom of it, fell with a good deal of violence, which sobered me much." A later fall damaged an ankle so badly that he was hobbling around for months.[27]

Soon afterward Boswell visited his old friend Temple at his rectory in Devonshire, and took a pledge for "sobriety"—the agreement being that he would never drink more than six glasses of wine at one time. Later that year he got extremely drunk at a party. When he went home he threw chairs around, breaking them, and after smashing his walking stick into pieces, he hurled it into the fire. "I have scarcely any recollection of this horrid scene, but my wife informed me of it. She was in great danger, for it seems I had aimed at her both with chairs and stick. What a monstrous account of a man! She got me to bed, where I was excessively sick." Sometimes he had to make an appearance in court after staying up all night drinking, and would barely get through it before hurrying outside to throw up.[28]

Whenever he was especially unhappy, Boswell would write to Johnson and implore him to confirm his affection. Reproduced here (figure 68) is the first page of a typical letter from these years:

> It is hard that I cannot prevail with you to write to me oftener. But I am convinced that it is in vain to push you for a private correspondence with any regularity. I must therefore look upon you as a Fountain of Wisdom from whence few rills are communicated to a distance, and which must be approached at its source, to partake fully of its virtues. I fairly own that after an absence from you for any length of time, I feel that I require a renewal of that spirit which your presence always gives me, and which makes me a better and a happier man than I imagined I could be, before I was introduced to your acquaintance.

The letter ends, "I ever am with unalterable respect and affection, my Dear Sir, your much obliged humble servant James Boswell." Johnson replied promptly, assuring Boswell of his constant affection.[29]

Naturally, Johnson got tired of having to reassure Boswell over and over again. In London five years later, he made a statement that Boswell would proudly quote in the *Life:* "My regard for you is greater almost than I have

My Dear Sir.   Edinburgh
                                                3 March 1772.

It is hard that I cannot prevail
with you to write to me oftener. But I am
convinced that it is in vain to push you
for a private correspondence with any
regularity. I must therefore look upon
you as a Fountain of Wisdom from
whence few rills are communicated
to a distance, and which must be
approached at its source, to partake
fully of its virtues.
        I fairly own that after an absence
from you for any length of time, I
feel that I require a renewal of
that spirit which your presence
allways gives me, and which makes
me a better and a happier man
                                                than

68. Boswell letter to Johnson

words to express; but I do not choose to be always repeating it. Write it down in the first leaf of your pocket-book, and never doubt of it again."[30]

Just why that should have been so is not always obvious from the documentary record, but life is much more than documents. Boswell's whimsical humorousness, enthusiasm, and gregarious charm were always a tonic for Johnson, and he knew that the pleas for advice and reassurance were wholly sincere. If Boswell found in Johnson the father he should have had, Johnson found in him the son he never had. And Boswell's admiration, which amounted really to worship, must have filled a great need for acknowledgment in Johnson.

Beyond that, Johnson may have taken vicarious pleasure in Boswell's spontaneity, uncensoredness, and defiant lustfulness. His very frivolity and triviality—his ability to *elevate* the trivial—could have been a relief from Johnson's seriousness and high morality. Likewise Boswell's childlike egotism, self-satisfaction, and self-indulgence were qualities that Johnson never allowed in himself. And if Johnson reproved him parentally, as indeed Boswell wanted him to, he also accepted and loved Boswell for who he was—a precious gift indeed.

CORSICA BOSWELL

There was one truly invigorating event during the years preceding Boswell's marriage, and that was the publication of *An Account of Corsica: The Journal of a Tour to that Island, and Memoirs of Pascal Paoli*. He had conceived the idea of writing it while he was still in Corsica. His plan was to make people aware of the plight of the brave rebels against Genoan rule, led by a general whom he regarded as a hero right out of Plutarch's *Lives*. The book would include a slightly edited version of the journal he kept when he was there, which was then a novel thing to do, and there would be ample historical and geographical details as well.

When Boswell consulted Johnson about his project, the reaction was not encouraging. "As to your history of Corsica, you have no materials which others have not, or may not have. You have, somehow or other, warmed your imagination. I wish there were some cure, like the lover's leap, for all heads of which some single idea has obtained an unreasonable and irregular possession. Mind your own affairs, and leave the Corsicans to theirs. I am, dear Sir, your most humble servant, Sam Johnson."[31]

In a way Johnson was right—the historical part of Boswell's *Account of Corsica* is cut-and-paste work. Still, Corsica was surprisingly little known, Boswell did thorough research, and many readers appreciated it. As it would turn out, that was valuable practice in skills that he would need for the far more challenging *Life of Johnson*.

The *Account* didn't come out until 1768, and in the meantime Boswell threw himself enthusiastically into a campaign to send weapons to the gallant Corsicans. He raised enough money to order thirty guns, 2,900 bullets, 5,020 grapeshot, and thirty-eight casks of gunpowder, which were duly dispatched to Paoli.[32]

He had less success trying to persuade the British government to supply the Corsicans with military aid, let alone to join in their fight. Lord Holland, who was Paymaster General of the Forces, said crisply, "Foolish as we are, we cannot be so foolish as to go to war because Mr. Boswell has been in Corsica; and yet, believe me, no better reason can be given for siding with the vile inhabitants of one of the vilest islands in the world."[33]

Over the years Boswell enjoyed publishing anonymous items in the papers, and he mounted a vigorous publicity campaign in advance of the publication of his book. A Corsican envoy in France, Signor Romanzo, was reported to have wounded an insolent nobleman who had disrespected his nation. And the *London Chronicle* published a letter from a British volunteer named Sam Jones who was fighting with the Corsicans: "I then went with my Captain to Itali wer I heerd mooch tauk of them here Corsicans, so over I gos, and faith Bob I never was better. The General on em Poli is as good a man as the King himself, whom God blis." Sam Jones never existed, and neither did Signor Romanzo.[34]

In the preface to his book Boswell declared, "I should be proud to be known as an author, and I have an ardent ambition for literary fame; for of all possessions I should imagine literary fame to be the most valuable." The book did become well known and was translated into several languages; Paoli became a symbol for resisting oppression, which is why there is a Paoli, Pennsylvania. To Boswell's extreme delight, people started referring to him as "Corsica Boswell." In a small way he now had something in common with "Dictionary Johnson." He still had no inkling, of course, of the real foundation on which his literary fame would rest.[35]

The first word of Boswell's text is "Liberty." He describes himself as "one who has been among the brave islanders, when their patriotic virtue is at its height, and who has felt as it were a communication of their spirit."

But just one year later the Corsican rebellion collapsed. Genoa ceded control of the island to France, which promptly invaded, and has continued to govern Corsica ever since. When Paoli escaped over the mountains his entourage included a lawyer named Carlo Buonaparte, whose wife gave birth three months later to Napoleon. Only in that ironic way would Rousseau's prophecy in the *Social Contract*—that one day Corsica might astonish Europe—be fulfilled.[36]

It was in London that Paoli chose to live out his exile. He would soon renew a warm relationship with Boswell, who often stayed in his house. Their friendship was mutually beneficial, since the British government gave Paoli a generous pension of £1,200, largely inspired by Boswell's book.

It gave Boswell particular pleasure to introduce his two heroes to each other. "The General spoke Italian, and Doctor Johnson English, and understood one another very well, with a little aid of interpretation from me, in which I compared myself to an isthmus which joins two great continents." The two became good friends, and saw each other often in later years.[37]

Paoli's portrait at this time (figure 69) captures the resignation of a statesman who knows he may never see his native land again. He was soon taken up by the Johnson circle and made rapid progress in English, though it was

69. Paoli in London

charmingly imperfect. Fanny Burney was amused by Paoli's account of first encountering Boswell in Corsica:

> He fetched me some letter of recommending him; but I was of the belief he might be an imposter, and I supposed, in my *mente,* he was an espy; for I look away from him, and in a moment I look to him again, and I behold his tablets! Oh! he was to the work of writing down all I say! Indeed I was angry! But soon I discover he was no imposter, and no espy, and I find I was myself the monster he was come to discern. Oh, is a very good man, I love him indeed—so cheerful! so gay! so pleasant! But at the first, oh! I was indeed angry.[38]

Actually Boswell was hardly ever so rude as to take notes like that, but he did make a practice of jotting down a few words to help his memory later, and had evidently seized what he thought was a suitable opportunity.

THE SHAKESPEARE JUBILEE

In 1769 a remarkable extravaganza was mounted at Stratford-upon-Avon, which became known as the Great Shakespeare Jubilee. It was an inspired feat of self-promotion by David Garrick, and despite exasperating setbacks it had lasting importance. Christian Deelman, whose *The Great Shakespeare Jubilee* is a highly entertaining account of the event, calls it "both ridiculous and impressive," and concludes that "it marks the point at which Shakespeare stopped being regarded as an increasingly popular and admirable dramatist, and became a god."[39]

Most of the members of the Club stayed away, regarding the event as a self-serving commercial stunt. Johnson, despite his edition of Shakespeare published four years previously, didn't care to write anything for the occasion; Garrick had to settle for an *Ode to Shakespeare* by himself. Someone who did show up, however, was Corsica Boswell. He had a wonderful time.

The original impulse for the Jubilee was casual. It occurred to the Stratford town fathers that Garrick might be charmed into giving money toward their new town hall if they offered to display in it portraits of Shakespeare and Garrick himself. They may well have heard that he had an insatiable appetite for flattery. As Goldsmith described him,

> Of praise a mere glutton, he swallowed what came,
> And the puff of a dunce, he mistook it for fame;

Till his relish grown callous, almost to disease,
Who peppered the highest was surest to please.[40]

Garrick liked the town fathers' idea, but he also saw possibilities that the stolid Stratfordians didn't. Long before this moment, as one of his biographers comments, he had come to think of himself "as Shakespeare's vicar on earth."[41]

Garrick commissioned Gainsborough to produce a double portrait: a bust of Shakespeare smiles affectionately down on Garrick, who leans toward him companionably with one arm around the pedestal of the bust. This picture and its elaborate frame ended up costing £194, equivalent to one-quarter of the entire cost of the new town hall. If the town fathers expected that Garrick was going to foot the bill, it was the first of many disappointments. "In him," Deelman says, "the Corporation had caught a bigger fish than they could handle."[42]

With his impressive organizing ability, Garrick soon developed plans for a hugely ambitious festival. The principal site was to be a big roofed rotunda newly constructed in a field by the river, where the modern Shakespeare theater stands. The view of the Avon was obscured by a row of trees, so those were all felled. Lodgings for attendees had to be arranged in the local inns, private homes, and outlying villages; even so, many people would find lodgings scarce. The Drury Lane orchestra was summoned, and the famous Thomas Arne wrote new music for the occasion.

The two highlights were to be a procession of Shakespearean characters—played by the Drury Lane actors whose roles they regularly were—and after that a masquerade ball in the rotunda. What nobody seems to have thought about was the likelihood of bad weather in September. It rained continuously for days on end, and when the river overflowed the low-lying meadow, people had to splash around in water up to their ankles. A fireworks display had been planned, but literally fizzled out. The procession was canceled. The masquerade did go forward, with something like two thousand soaking wet people crammed into the rotunda.

Garrick saved the occasion by declaiming his *Ode to Shakespeare* so masterfully that everybody who heard him burst into rapturous applause. Arne's music was also a great success. Garrick had written the lyrics, and some of them became popular afterward, especially a ballad called "Warwickshire Lads" that was frequently played in London and is still the regimental march of the Royal Warwickshire Regiment:

Of famous Will Congreve we boast too the skill,
But the Will of all Wills was a Warwickshire Will,
Warwickshire Will,
Matchless still,
For the Will of all Wills was a Warwickshire Will.

In Corsica, Boswell had acquired an authentic rebel soldier's costume, but unfortunately it had been left behind in Edinburgh. So he bustled around London getting a reproduction made. On the way to Stratford he stopped for the night in Oxford and wrote complacently to Peggie, who was still his fiancée at the time, "I assure you my Corsican dress will make a fine, striking appearance. I have that kind of weakness that, when I looked at myself in the glass last night in my Corsican dress, I could not help thinking your opinion of yourself might be still more raised: 'She has secured the constant affection and admiration of so fine a fellow.'"[43]

In Stratford Boswell developed his usual infatuations but controlled himself, determined to behave on Peggie's account. He had come to Stratford to strut about in his character as a Corsican, and he did. When he returned to London he had a drawing made, with plans to have it engraved for the *London Magazine,* as indeed it was (figure 70).

To accompany the picture, Boswell explained:

He wore a short dark-coloured coat of coarse cloth; on the front of his cap or bonnet was embroidered in gold letters VIVA LA LIBERTÀ, and on one side of it was a handsome blue feather and cockade, so that it had an elegant as well as a warlike appearance. He had also a cartridge pouch, into which was stuck a stiletto, and on his left side a pistol was hung upon the belt of his cartridge pouch. He had a fusee [flintlock rifle] slung across his shoulder, wore no powder in his hair, but had it plaited at its full length, with a knot of blue ribbons at the end of it. He had, by way of staff, a very curious vine all of one piece, with a bird finely carved upon it, emblematical of the sweet bard of Avon. He wore no mask, saying that it was not proper for a gallant Corsican. So soon as he came into the room he drew universal attention.[44]

When the whole thing was over Garrick had lost a great deal of money, probably as much as £2,000. With his usual resourcefulness he quickly made up for that. At Drury Lane he proceeded to stage the pageant that had been rained out. It was called *The Jubilee,* and it achieved a record run for any

PAUL WALE del.   I. Miller Sc.

JAMES BOSWELL Esqr.

In the Dress of an Armed Corsican Chief, as he appear'd at
Shakespeares Jubilee, at Stratford upon Avon September 1769. —

70. Corsica Boswell at Stratford

theatrical piece in the entire century, making up for the loss four times over. In its first season alone it played to packed houses ninety-one nights, and it continued to be popular thereafter.

With the advantage of a stage rather than the public streets, each group of actors was able to pause and perform, in mime, miniature scenes from the plays as well as allegorical tableaux. Garrick himself appeared as Benedick from *Much Ado,* one of his most popular roles; Sarah Siddons made her Drury Lane debut as the goddess Venus. One of the actors borrowed Boswell's Corsican costume and appeared as James Boswell. But Boswell was back in Edinburgh by then, so he lost the opportunity of applauding himself on the stage.[45]

CHAPTER 14

Among the Farthest Hebrides

The Scottish Highlands and the Hebrides Islands beyond were beginning to acquire a romantic reputation. A generation later Wordsworth would imagine a "Highland lass" reaping in a field whose singing evokes birdsong "breaking the silence of the seas / Among the farthest Hebrides." In the 1770s, however, few Englishmen or even Lowland Scots had ever gone there (Wordsworth never did either). "To the southern inhabitants of Scotland," Johnson would write, "the state of the mountains and the islands is equally unknown with that of Borneo or Sumatra."[1]

There was a reason for that neglect. Lowland Scots, Linda Colley says in her book about the concept of Britishness, "traditionally regarded their Highland countrymen as members of a different and inferior race, violent, treacherous, poverty-stricken and backward. They called them savages or aborigines." Another historian stresses the divide between two very different cultural groups. Gaelic-speaking Highlanders, living by subsistence farming on stony land, deeply resented domination by England. In the south of Scotland, "the Edinburgh-Glasgow axis of capitalist landlords, merchants, lawyers, clergy and professors" fully approved of the 1707 union of Scotland with England, and many of them pursued careers in London.[2]

Boswell was raised in the south of Scotland and absorbed its values, and he was firmly oriented toward London. All the same, the Highlands and Hebrides represented a romantic past for him, and he loved to imagine his forebears in a world in which feudal clans gave unquestioning allegiance to their hereditary chieftains. "The very Highland names, or the sound of a bagpipe," he acknowledged, "will stir my blood, and fill me with a mixture of melancholy and respect for courage."[3]

Johnson too wanted to visit the Highlands and Hebrides, but not for romantic reasons. He saw the modern world rapidly extinguishing cultural survivals from the past, and although he didn't necessarily regard that as bad, he was curious to know what life might still be like out in the Celtic fringe.

Soon after they got to know each other, Boswell planted the idea of a trip, and Johnson liked the idea. He said that when he was a boy his father had given him Martin Martin's *Description of the Western Islands of Scotland,* and he had been greatly taken with it; he agreed that one day they really ought to go.[4]

In 1773 the dream became a reality, and would produce a major book from each of them. Johnson's *A Journey to the Western Islands of Scotland,* published one year after they got back, was a brisk overview of the places they visited and the way of life they encountered. Boswell's *Journal of a Tour to the Hebrides* was not published until 1786, two years after Johnson's death. On the trip he had, as usual, kept a detailed journal, which Johnson looked at along the way and approved of greatly. This Boswell edited only lightly for publication, taking out some personal references concerning himself and softening comments on individuals who might take offense.

The resulting book was a remarkable three-dimensional image of Johnson, with numerous examples of his conversation, and it struck readers as excitingly new. Its success confirmed Boswell in his determination to incorporate material from the rest of his journals in the projected *Life of Johnson.*

Though Johnson liked the idea of the trip, still it would be a major undertaking, traveling rough in difficult country where at times there were no roads for wheeled vehicles. Fearing that they might never actually go, Boswell lobbied their friends to encourage Johnson. When he published his *Tour* he thanked Hester Thrale warmly: "To Mrs. Thrale in particular, whose enchantment over him seldom failed, I was much obliged. It was, 'I'll give thee a wind.'—'Thou art kind.'" At least that looks like warm thanks. But Boswell may have intended a submerged insult in the quotation from *Macbeth:* it's spoken by a witch.[5]

The journey took place at a symbolically significant moment for Johnson: he had just passed what was known as "the grand climacteric." The numbers seven and nine were thought to hold numerological significance, and multiplied together they give 63. That was the climacteric—a turning point when a person was exceptionally vulnerable to illness and death, but if he survived that year might live on for many more.

It was not just superstitious people who took the idea seriously. "This year I am in my grand climacteric," Adam Smith wrote to a friend, "and the state of my health has been a good deal worse than usual. I begin to flatter myself that with good pilotage I shall be able to weather this dangerous promontory of human life; after which I hope to sail in smooth water for the remainder of my days." As it turned out, he had just three years left when he wrote that.[6]

JOHNSON THE TRAVELER

In an age when travel was slow and difficult, Johnson nonetheless adored it. Hester Thrale, who had taken long trips with him to Wales and France, confirmed that "he loved the very act of traveling." Best of all was a post chaise, smaller and more comfortable than a stagecoach, in which two or three passengers sat while the driver rode one of a pair of horses. During an excursion in England, Boswell remembered, "as we were driven rapidly along in the post chaise, he said to me, 'Life has not many things better than this.'" For a modern edition of the *Life of Johnson,* Ernest Shepard—remembered best for his Winnie the Pooh illustrations—created a charming picture of Boswell and Johnson at that moment (figure 71). Like a modern convertible, the vehicle had a collapsible roof that could be lowered in good weather.[7]

71. Driving rapidly in a post-chaise

The word "post" implied speed; in the *Dictionary* Johnson defined it as "quick course or manner of traveling." That was achieved by frequent changes of horses, fresh ones being put in every ten or fifteen miles. A post road, accordingly, was one along which post houses were in place for the purpose, and the verb "to post" originally meant carrying mail in this way. Not until the nineteenth century was it used for dropping letters into a mailbox. In the eighteenth century there were no mailboxes.

It's not easy today to appreciate how fast that mode of travel seemed to people who could never experience anything faster. Someone who rode in one of the first railway trains in the nineteenth century reported breathlessly, "We went at the rate of twenty-three miles an hour. The quickness of motion is to me *frightful*. It is really flying, and it is impossible to divest yourself of the notion of instant death to all upon the least accident happening. It gave me a headache which has not left me yet."[8]

On another occasion when Boswell was traveling with Johnson, "he strongly expressed his love of driving fast in a post-chaise. 'If (said he) I had no duties, and no reference to futurity, I would spend my life in driving briskly in a post-chaise with a pretty woman; but she should be one who could understand me, and would add something to the conversation.'"[9]

Boswell shared Johnson's enthusiasm. In his journal he commented that it wasn't just velocity that cheered him, but freedom. "When a man has fairly set out in the post chaise, he is somehow flying, separated from the world and its cares, and everything appears to him in a better light than usual. There is a snugness and cheerfulness together which delight me." It would be in a post chaise that he and Johnson would begin their Scottish adventure.[10]

THE JOURNEY BEGINS

Edinburgh didn't interest Johnson much, though Boswell was eager to get reflected glory by introducing him to the literati there. The city seemed cold and provincial, and it stank. Garbage and chamber pots were freely emptied into the streets, inspiring the nickname "Auld Reekie" for the city. As they walked at dusk up the High Street to Boswell's house, there was no avoiding the stench, and "as we marched slowly along, he grumbled in my ear, 'I smell you in the dark.'"[11]

After Boswell published his *Journal of a Tour,* a series of satiric prints, engraved by Rowlandson after drawings by Samuel Collings, were published under the title *Picturesque Beauties of Boswell.* "Walking up the High Street" was the caption for one of the pictures (figure 72), in which a paunchy Boswell prances along, gazing up at his hero.

Another print in the series (figure 73) illustrates an episode just after they set out from Edinburgh toward the north. "I bought some speldings, fish (generally whitings) salted and dried in a particular manner, being dipped in the sea and dried in the sun, and eaten by the Scots by way of a relish. He had never seen them, though they are sold in London. I insisted on *scottifying* his palette, but he was very reluctant. With difficulty I prevailed with him to let a bit of one of them lie in his mouth. He did not like it." In the picture fishwives are jeering derisively while Boswell force-feeds Johnson.[12]

When Boswell published his account he made it clear that although Johnson made light of physical inconveniences, he was in his mid-sixties and far from nimble. "His person was large, robust, I may say approaching to the gigantic, and grown unwieldy from corpulency." When they paused to explore a little island while sailing across the Firth of Forth, "he stalked like a

WALKING UP THE HIGH STREET.

72. "Walking up the High Street"

73. "Scottifying the Palate"

giant among the luxuriant thistles and nettles," and Boswell compared his stout oaken walking stick to the club of Hercules.[13]

At times Johnson seemed not just gigantic, but monumental. Later on during the trip, Boswell was delighted to find a letter from Garrick awaiting him, and wrote in reply, "As I have always been accustomed to view him as a permanent London object, it would not be much more wonderful to me to see St. Paul's Church moving along where we now are." In the published version of his journal Boswell called the trip "the transit of Johnson over the Caledonian Hemisphere." He was recalling a recent voyage of Captain Cook, commissioned by the Royal Society to take an observation of the transit of Venus—a brief and rarely occurring phenomenon when Venus lines up directly between Earth and the sun, and astronomers can see it as a tiny black dot crossing the solar orb. In this analogy Johnson became a planetary body majestically traversing an entire hemisphere.[14]

They had with them a manservant who looked after both of them, Joseph Ritter, a native of Bohemia. Boswell described him as "a fine stately fellow above six feet high, who had been over a great part of Europe, and spoke many languages." He had originally engaged Joseph in Paris seven years previously and had employed him since then, though (as usual with servants) his name seldom shows up in the journals. Mentioning him in the published *Tour*, Boswell felt that some apology might be called for. "He was the best servant I ever saw. Let not my readers disdain his introduction! For Dr. Johnson gave him this character: 'Sir, he is a civil man, and a wise man.'"[15]

Proceeding northward up the east coast from Edinburgh, there was a brief pause at St. Andrews, where one of the professors said to Boswell, "Johnson is a wonderful man; he is master of every subject he handles." A physician in the Highlands said more colorfully later on, "This man is just a hogshead of sense."[16]

With his Anglican loyalties, Johnson expressed outrage that Presbyterians had destroyed the old cathedral at St. Andrews. When Boswell asked where John Knox was buried, "Dr. Johnson burst out, 'I hope in the highway. I have been looking at his reformations.'"[17]

An engraver made an image of Johnson in his traveling dress, based on Boswell's description (figure 74): "He wore a full suit of plain brown clothes,

74. Johnson's traveling dress

with twisted-hair buttons of the same colour, a large bushy greyish wig, a plain shirt, black worsted stockings, and silver buckles. Upon this tour, when journeying, he wore boots, and a very wide brown cloth greatcoat, with pockets which might have almost held the two volumes of his folio dictionary; and he carried in his hand a large English oak stick."[18]

THE HIGHLAND LANDSCAPE

Something neither Johnson nor Boswell cared about was scenery. At another time, trying to interest Johnson in a trip to Ireland, Boswell asked, "Is not the Giant's Causeway worth seeing?" Johnson replied decisively, "Worth seeing, yes; but not worth going to see."[19]

The Highlands are considered beautiful today, but Johnson didn't think so. Their appearance, he wrote, was "of matter incapable of form or usefulness, dismissed by nature from her care and disinherited of her favours, left in its original elemental state, or quickened only with one sullen power of useless vegetation." Many Englishmen regarded even the Alps as a horrible icy obstacle on the way to Italy.[20]

If the barren landscape did have any significance for Johnson, it was in freeing his mind to wander creatively.

> I sat down on a bank such as a writer of romance might have delighted to feign. I had, indeed, no trees to whisper over my head, but a clear rivulet streamed at my feet. The day was calm, the air soft, and all was rudeness, silence, and solitude. Before me, and on either side, were high hills, which, by hindering the eye from ranging, forced the mind to find entertainment for itself. Whether I spent the hour well, I know not; for here I first conceived the thought of this narration.[21]

One scene, however, was so impressive that neither Johnson nor Boswell could resist admiring it. They spent a night as guests of Lord Erroll at Slaines Castle on the coast, overlooking the sea (figure 75). Johnson noted that the castle walls "seem only a continuation of a perpendicular rock, the foot of which is beaten by the waves," and he told their host that "the prospect here was the noblest he had ever seen." Boswell added that Lord Erroll's nearest neighbor to the east was the king of Denmark.[22]

In the morning they went by carriage to the Buller (or Bullers) of Buchan. That was a deep cavern in the cliff, into which the sea rushed with a

75. Slaines Castle

violence that gave rise to the name, expressive of "boiling." With his usual contempt for danger, Johnson didn't hesitate to clamber along the narrow path shown in the picture (figure 76), even though, as he later wrote, "he that ventures to look downward sees that if his foot should slip, he must fall from his dreadful elevation upon stones on one side, or into the water on the other."

Afterward they were taken by rowboat into the Buller itself, where the looming walls were oppressive. "The interception of all lateral light caused a dismal gloom. Round us was a perpendicular rock, above us the distant sky, and below an unknown profundity of water."[23]

Proceeding westward, the travelers arrived at Fores. "This to an Englishman is classic ground," Johnson wrote, because it was there that Macbeth met the weird sisters. Boswell admired his delivery when he recited much of the play, beginning with these lines:

> How far is't called to Fores? What are these,
> So withered, and so wild in their attire?
> That look not like the inhabitants o' the earth,
> And yet are on't?

76. The Buller of Buchan

Boswell had recently purchased some land adjacent to Auchinleck known as Dalblair, and that inspired Johnson to cry out, "All hail Dalblair! hail to thee, Laird of Auchinleck!"[24]

At this point they headed southwest along the Great Glen, the sixty-mile-long geological fault that bisects Scotland, with a series of lakes (the most famous is Loch Ness) connected to each other by rivers. From this point onward, roads would be rudimentary. In Johnson's words, "We were now to bid farewell to the luxury of traveling, and to enter a country upon which perhaps no wheel has ever rolled." They acquired four horses, one for each of them and for Joseph Ritter, and another for their baggage.[25]

An incident along the way is a fine example of Boswell's gift for recreating a situation, complete with dialogue. On the shore of Loch Ness they stopped at the smoke-filled hut of an old woman. In his book Johnson described the encounter briefly. Her eighty-year-old husband was working in the woods, and two of her sons had gone to Inverness to buy oatmeal; she kept sixty goats and some chickens. "With the true pastoral hospitality, she asked us to sit down and drink whisky." The phrase "pastoral hospitality" suggests the unstinting welcome of strangers in earlier times.[26]

Boswell's account is very different:

Dr. Johnson was curious to know where she slept. I asked one of the guides, who questioned her in Erse. She answered with a tone of emotion, saying (as he told us) she was afraid we wanted to go to bed to her. This *coquetry*, or whatever it may be called, of so wretched a being was truly ludicrous.

Dr. Johnson and I afterwards were merry upon it. I said it was he who alarmed the poor woman's virtue. "No, Sir," said he, "she'll say, 'There came a wicked young fellow, a wild dog, who I believe would have ravished me, had there not been with him a grave old gentleman who repressed him; but when he gets out of the sight of his tutor, I'll warrant you he'll spare no woman he meets, young or old.'" "No, Sir," I replied, "she'll say, 'There was a terrible ruffian who would have forced me, had it not been for a civil decent young man, who, I take it, was an angel sent from heaven to protect me.'"[27]

Actually Boswell seems to have had no erotic encounters at all on the trip, under Johnson's eye as he was. At the castle of Cawdor, where Macbeth had been Thane, "I never shall forget the enchanting impression made upon my fancy by some of the ladies' maids tripping about in neat morning dresses. After seeing nothing for a long time but rusticity, their elegance delighted me, and I could have been a knight errant for them. Such is my amorous constitution." Boswell left out that final sentence in the published version of the *Tour*. This scene, too, Shepard brings engagingly to life (figure 77).[28]

At Inverness Johnson showed his playfulness. The subject of kangaroos came up—a novelty at that time, recently encountered by the British in Australia. A clergyman named Alexander Grant recalled what happened:

Johnson rose from his chair and volunteered an imitation of the animal. The company stared; and Mr. Grant said nothing could be more ludicrous than the appearance of a tall, heavy, grave-looking man like Dr. Johnson, standing up to mimic the shape and motions of a kangaroo. He stood erect, put out his hands like feelers, and gathering up the tails of his huge brown coat so as to resemble the pouch of the animal, made two or three vigorous bounds across the room.

Boswell doesn't mention this story, but that doesn't mean it didn't happen. He may have thought it too undignified.[29]

77. Boswell and the maids

BONNIE PRINCE CHARLIE

From the west coast, they sailed to the Isle of Skye, the largest of the Hebrides, where they would spend fully a month. At its nearest point the crossing from the Scottish mainland to Skye is easy, just a mile and a half away; they are connected by a bridge today.

Boswell had a strong motive for going to Skye, though he didn't say so explicitly in the published *Journal*. The route he devised for the trip might seem eccentric, if its purpose was simply to get from one place to another, but he had a different purpose in mind. They were retracing the journey in 1745–46 of Prince Charles Edward Stuart, known to the English as the Young Pretender and to Scots as Bonnie Prince Charlie. Boswell, the Lowland Scot, felt nostalgic emotion at being entertained by the chieftains of Highland clans, and imagining the romantic escape of the lost hero who was remembered as "the Wanderer."

In 1745, less than thirty years previously, the prince had left his exile in France, landed in the country of his forebears, and assembled an army to march south and recover the British crown his grandfather James II had lost in the revolution of 1688. The rebel army met a brutal defeat at the Battle of Culloden, near Inverness, remembered with bitterness in Scotland to this day. The prince escaped to France and never returned. Some of the ringleaders of the rebellion were executed, others were exiled, and still others lost their titles and lands.

More largely there was what amounted to a "pacification program" by the British troops, with houses burned to the ground all over the Highlands. A law was passed against wearing the tartan, emblematic of clan membership, with the sole exception of the Highland regiments (such as the Black Watch) in the British army. Johnson confirmed that "the plaid is rarely worn," and that he had encountered just one man "completely clothed in the ancient habit, and by him it was worn only occasionally and wantonly."[30]

People who wanted to eject the German Hanoverians from the British throne, and bring back the exiled Stuarts, were known as Jacobites, from "Jacobus," the Latin form of James. Much ink has been spilled by scholars trying to prove that Boswell and Johnson were closet Jacobites. That seems extremely unlikely. Even if they might regret what happened in 1688, they accepted that the change was permanent and that George III was the legitimate monarch. Neither of them had the slightest wish to see the disastrous civil war that would erupt if there were another attempt to bring the Stuarts back.[31]

Knowing that readers might have suspicions about Jacobite sympathies, Boswell was careful to emphasize Johnson's position. "I have heard him declare that if holding up his right hand would have secured victory at Culloden to Prince Charles's army, he was not sure he would have held it up; so little confidence had he in the right claimed by the House of Stuart, and so fearful was he of the consequences of another revolution on the throne of Great Britain."[32]

The route Boswell devised for the trip was a pilgrimage, recreating with Johnson an episode of symbolic significance. Pat Rogers entitles his account "The Rambler and the Wanderer." The most important goal was the Isle of Skye, which had played a crucial role in the prince's story, and where many residents remembered him well.[33]

There they met people who had actually been "out in the '45"—had taken an active role in the rebellion. The most memorable of those was Flora Macdonald, who at the age of twenty-four had helped Prince Charles to hide on Skye and afterward to escape. Johnson described her as "a woman of soft features, gentle manners, and elegant presence," and said that her name "will be mentioned in history, and if courage and fidelity be virtues, mentioned with honour."[34]

In her house Johnson actually spent a night in the bed the prince had used, which excited Boswell beyond his ability to express it. "To see Mr. Samuel Johnson lying in Prince Charles's bed, in the Isle of Skye, in the house of Miss Flora Macdonald, struck me with such a group of ideas as it is not easy for words to describe."[35]

A consequence of the English crackdown was a growing stream of emigration, driven partly by economic hard times but also by resentment of oppression. Between 1760 and 1775 some 40,000 Scots emigrated to America, many of them Highlanders. Boswell recorded a moving testimony. "Mrs. Mackinnon told me that last year when the ship sailed from Portree for America, the people on shore were almost distracted when they saw their relations go off; they lay down on the ground and tumbled, and tore the grass with their teeth." He did not include this in the published version of the *Tour*.[36]

Johnson asked one of their hosts whether the emigrants would stay at home if they were better treated, and "he answered with indignation that no man willingly left his native country." At a dinner on the little island of Raasay women sang in their native Gaelic. "I inquired the subjects of the songs," Johnson wrote, "and was told of one that it was a love song, and that of another that it was a farewell composed by one of the islanders that was going, in this epidemical fury of emigration, to seek his fortune in America." The American colonies were of course still British then, though not for long; Johnson thought it was disastrous to remove people from their culture and scatter them in a far off land.[37]

In his book Johnson summed up the situation trenchantly. "To hinder insurrection by driving away the people, and to govern peaceably by having no subjects, is an expedient that argues no great profundity of politics. It affords a legislator little self-applause to consider that where there was formerly an insurrection, there is now a wilderness."[38]

Three years previously, Goldsmith had published his finest poem, *The Deserted Village*. Ostensibly set in England, it really recalled the Ireland of his youth, where many people emigrated in order to escape grinding poverty. With slow, mournful eloquence he imagined them departing:

> Even now, methinks, as pondering here I stand,
> I see the rural virtues leave the land.
> Down where yon anchoring vessel spreads the sail

That idly waiting flaps with every gale,
Downward they move, a melancholy band,
Pass from the shore, and darken all the strand.[39]

SOCIETY ON THE ISLE OF SKYE

Inns were almost nonexistent on the islands. Sometimes the travelers were taken in by farmers, for whom strangers were an unusual treat; Johnson wrote that a visitor from outside "appears to them like some being of another world." They always gave their hosts a couple of shillings, gratefully received in a rural economy where very little money was in use. There was not a single shop in the whole of Skye, and the only way people could get manufactured goods was from wandering peddlers. Johnson wrote, "I have in Skye had some difficulty to find ink for a letter; and if a woman breaks her needle the work is at a stop."[40]

At farms the accommodations were naturally primitive, and Johnson took pride in indifference to physical discomfort. Just before leaving the mainland, at Glenelg, they did find an inn, but there were no beds available. In Johnson's account, "Our Highlanders at last found some hay, with which the inn could not supply them. I directed them to bring a bundle into the room, and slept upon it in my riding coat. Mr. Boswell, being more delicate, laid himself sheets with hay over and under him, and lay in linen like a gentleman."[41]

In many places the travelers were welcomed as celebrities by the local gentry, who knew about Boswell's family distinction and Johnson's literary eminence. Boswell was entertained by a little scene that occurred at Coire-chatachan on Skye. At tea, "a neat, pretty little girl" suddenly sat down on Johnson's knee, "and being bid by some of the company, put her hands around his neck and kissed him." One of the girl's descendants heard that she had done it on a bet, after her friends claimed that he was too ugly for any woman to kiss. Johnson had a quick comeback: "'Do it again,' said he, 'and let us see who will tire first.'" Boswell commented, "To see the grave philosopher—the Rambler—toying with a little Highland wench! There was a coincidence of opposed ideas."[42]

At Dunvegan on Skye, where the head of the Macleod clan resided in his ancestral castle, a less amusing episode produced a remarkable anecdote. It begins slowly, for Boswell was a skilled storyteller, and leads up gradually to the punchline. It was usual for ladies to withdraw after a meal and leave the men to continue drinking by themselves.

After the ladies were gone from table, we talked of the Highlanders not having sheets; and this led us to consider the advantage of wearing linen. JOHNSON. "All animal substances are less cleanly than vegetables. Wool, of which flannel is made, is an animal substance; flannel therefore is not so cleanly as linen. I remember I used to think tar dirty; but when I knew it to be only a preparation of the juice of the pine, I thought so no longer. It is not disagreeable to have the gum that oozes from a plum tree upon your fingers, because it is vegetable; but if you have any candle grease, any tallow upon your fingers, you are uneasy till you rub it off. I have often thought that if I kept a seraglio, the ladies should all wear linen gowns, or cotton; I mean stuffs made of vegetable substances. I would have no silk; you cannot tell when it is clean. It will be very nasty before it is perceived to be so. Linen detects its own dirtiness."

Boswell comments, "To hear the grave Dr. Samuel Johnson, that majestic teacher of moral and religious wisdom, while sitting solemn in armchair in the Isle of Skye, talk, *ex cathedra,* of his keeping a seraglio, and acknowledge that the supposition had *often* been in his thoughts, struck me so forcibly with ludicrous contrast that I could not but laugh immoderately. He was too proud to submit, even for a moment, to be the object of ridicule, and instantly retaliated with such keen sarcastic wit, and such a variety of degrading images, of every one of which I was the object, that although I can bear such attacks as well as most men, yet I found myself so much the sport of all the company that I would gladly expunge from my mind every trace of this severe retort."[43]

Johnson had revealed not only that he shared a common fantasy about the Turkish sultan in his harem, free to choose a woman at his whim, but that he had thought "often" about how he would dress them. And then, with shocking suddenness, there was the turn against Boswell for laughing at him. Boswell remembers the abuse painfully, and tells his readers so.

In his unpublished journal the narrative supplies more detail:

Mr. Macqueen asked him if he would admit me [that is, to the seraglio]. "Yes," said he, "if he were properly prepared [i.e., castrated], and he'd make a very good eunuch. He'd be a fine gay animal. He'd do his part well." "I take it," said I, "better than you would do your part." Though he treats his friends with uncommon freedom, he does not like a return. He seemed to me to be a little angry. He got off from my joke by saying, "I have not told you what was to be my part;" and then at once he returned to my office as eunuch, and expatiated upon it with such fluency that it really hurt me. He made me quite contemptible for the moment.[44]

The anecdote shows a new level of intimacy between Boswell and Johnson—and mutual vulnerability. In London Boswell had been the disciple who sat raptly at the feet of his oracle. In Scotland it was he who made all the practical and social arrangements, and who smoothed Johnson down when he got irritable. Living together for weeks on end, they were getting to know each other in a far deeper way than before. Reading Boswell's journal along the way made a difference to Johnson, too. He was surprised at how good it was. "I take great delight in reading it," he told Boswell; and later on, "This will be a great treasure to us some years hence."[45]

Completing a circuit of Skye, they returned to Armadale at its southern tip, and enjoyed a convivial evening as guests of Lady Macdonald (not Flora, but the wife of the clan chieftain). Boswell noted with pleasure, "I danced a reel tonight to the music of the bagpipe, which I never did before. It made us beat the ground with prodigious force." He added solemnly, "I thought it was better that I should engage the people of Skye by taking a cheerful glass and dancing with them, rather than play the abstract scholar." At no time in his life could Boswell have been mistaken for an abstract scholar, and he was never one to decline a cheerful glass.[46]

As a rule Johnson cared little for music, and said that the extent of his knowledge was being able to tell the difference between a bagpipe and a guitar. It turned out that he greatly enjoyed the bagpipe, however, because its piercing tone was fully audible to his defective hearing, "and he used often to stand for some time with his ear close to the great drone." As he put it himself, "I have had my dinner exhilarated by the bagpipe, at Armadale, at Dunvegan, and in Coll."[47]

At Armadale Johnson surprised Boswell in yet another way, by demonstrating an improbable gift for physical mimicry. "To my astonishment he *took off* Lady Macdonald leaning forward with a hand on each cheek and her mouth open—quite insipidity on a monument. . . . I told him it was a masterpiece and that he must have studied it much. 'Ay,' said he." A couple of weeks later he mentioned Lady Macdonald again, saying "that insipid beauty would not go a great way, and that such a woman might be cut out of a cabbage."[48]

All along Johnson had been sending regular letters to Hester Thrale that formed a kind of travelogue, planning to incorporate them in the book he was going to write. At Skye he enclosed an ode that was a touching tribute to Hester herself. It's in the lyric meter of Horace, and a manifest compliment on her mastery of Latin. The third of its five stanzas reads:

> Inter erroris salebrosa longi,
> Inter ignotae strepitus loquelae,
> Quot modis mecum, quid agat, requiro,
> Thralia dulcis!

In the translation of a nineteenth-century poet:

> Through paths that halt from stone to stone,
> Amid the din of tongues unknown,
> One image haunts my soul alone,
> Thine, gentle Thrale!

Hester would probably have preferred Johnson's *dulcis,* "sweet," to the saccharine "gentle" in the translation, but that would have spoiled the meter.[49]

HOMEWARD BOUND

The journey was nearing its end, six weeks after leaving Edinburgh. From Skye, Boswell and Johnson sailed to the island of Coll (spelled "Col" in those days) with the son of its laird, an engaging youth whom they referred to as "young Coll." This passage from Skye to Coll was by far the longest they had undertaken, and the most exposed to the western sea.

A violent storm came up and Boswell was convinced they were about to die. When he asked what he could do to help, Coll told him to hold on tight to a particular rope until further instructions. "There did I stand firm to my post, while the wind and rain beat upon me, always expecting a call to pull my rope." Only afterward did he realize that the rope did nothing at all, and that Coll was simply distracting him.[50]

"Young Coll" was one of the people with whom both Boswell and Johnson were most impressed, and a year later they were grieved to hear that he had indeed died at sea. Johnson found out just in time to add a sentence to his mention of their parting: "Here we had the last embrace of this amiable man, who, while these pages were preparing to attest his virtues, perished in the passage between Ulva and Inch Kenneth."[51]

After Coll came the Isle of Mull. Just off its southwestern tip was a tiny island called Iona, shortened from Icolmkill, that had been a center of Gaelic monasticism long ago. Very few people lived there now, and naturally there was no inn. The travelers and their host from Mull lay down on a pile of hay in a barn, and Boswell noted, "I could not help thinking in the night how curious it was to see the chief of the Macleans, Mr. Samuel Johnson, and James Boswell, Esq. lying thus."[52]

Viewing the remains of the cathedral inspired Johnson to solemn reflections. "Whatever withdraws us from the power of our senses; whatever makes the past, the distant, or the future predominate over the present, advances us in the dignity of thinking beings. . . . That man is little to be envied whose patriotism would not gain force upon the plain of Marathon, or whose piety would not grow warmer among the ruins of Iona."[53]

Boswell, with his fondness for stagey performances, went into the ruined cathedral and "read with an audible voice" a chapter from the Bible and a sermon from a book he happened to have with him. "I suppose there has not been a sermon preached in this church since the Reformation. I had a serious joy in hearing my voice while it was filled with Ogden's admirable eloquence, resounding in the ancient cathedral of Icolmkill." Boswell always did enjoy the sound of his own voice.

Before leaving he inserted a stone into the wall of a former monastery "as a talisman for chastity." No doubt that was intended as a vow. "I hoped that ever after having been in this holy place, I should maintain an exemplary conduct. One has a strange propensity to fix upon some point from whence a better course of life may be said to begin."[54]

At Inveraray, back on the mainland, Boswell had some engaging anecdotes to report. One was that they received word that a good friend, the poet and philosopher James Beattie, had been awarded a royal pension. Johnson "sat up in his bed, clapped his hands, and cried 'O brave we!'—a peculiar exclamation of his when he rejoices." Beattie often visited London and was a welcome guest at Streatham. Johnson told Boswell the previous year, "We all love Beattie. Mrs. Thrale says if ever she has another husband, she'll have Beattie." She did eventually have another husband, but not that one.[55]

The other anecdote concerned what Johnson said when, after having abstained from alcohol throughout the trip, he agreed to find out what whisky tasted like. As he accepted the glass he exclaimed, "Come, let me know what it is that makes a Scotsman happy!" Boswell adds, "He drank it all but a drop, which I begged to leave to pour into my glass, that I might say we had drunk whisky together. I proposed Mrs. Thrale should be our toast. He would not have *her* drunk in whisky."⁵⁶

Johnson's own account in the *Journey* indicates how unfamiliar whisky was in England.

> The word "whisky" signifies water, and is applied by way of eminence to "strong water," or distilled liquor. The spirit drunk in the North is drawn from barley. I never tasted it, except once for experiment at the inn in Inverary, when I thought it preferable to any English malt brandy. It was strong, but not pungent, and was free from the empyreumatic [burnt] taste or smell. What was the process I had no opportunity of inquiring, nor do I wish to improve the art of making poison pleasant.

One might assume that this experiment occurred in the evening, but not so: "Not long after the dram may be expected the breakfast."⁵⁷

The law court season in Edinburgh was about to begin, and it was time for Boswell to hurry home. In his journal he acknowledged that he badly missed his wife, which struck him as embarrassing. "Weak as it may be, I could not help having that kind of tender uneasiness which a lover has when absent from his mistress. Laugh at it who will, as not to be believed or singular, I mark it as a fact and rejoice at it, as it is the counterpart of more than ordinary conjugal felicity." That was undoubtedly true, in an era of arranged marriages. The seventeenth-century French writer La Bruyère said that he believed it might be possible, though he had never personally seen it, that a husband might be in love with his wife.⁵⁸

There was one more stop before Edinburgh, and that was at Auchinleck House, where Boswell awaited with trepidation the meeting between his mentor and his father. It did not go well.

According to Sir Walter Scott, who enjoyed picking up reminiscences from his elders, Lord Auchinleck had always looked askance at his son's friendships, which he considered unworthy of the family's distinguished rank. As Scott heard the story, Lord Auchinleck said to a friend, "There's nae hope for Jamie, mon. Jamie is gane clean gyte [insane]. What do you think, mon? He's done wi' Paoli—he's off wi' the land-louping scoundrel of a Corsican; and whose tail do you think he has pinned himself to now, mon? A *dominie,* mon—an auld dominie! he keeped a schule, and caud it an *acaadamy.*" "Dominie" is Scots for a schoolmaster, which Johnson had very briefly been in his youth.⁵⁹

At Auchinleck the laird showed Johnson a collection of medals—commemorative coins such as gentlemen often used to assemble. One of the coins, issued by Oliver Cromwell, provoked a debate about Tory veneration of the "royal martyr" Charles I. Lord Auchinleck was a vehement Whig. Boswell mentions with cautious reticence what happened next: "They became exceedingly warm and violent, and I was very much distressed by being present at such an altercation between two men, both of whom I reverenced; yet I durst not interfere. It would certainly be very unbecoming in me to exhibit my honoured father and my respected friend as intellectual gladiators for the entertainment of the public; and therefore I suppress what would, I dare say, make an interesting scene in this dramatic sketch." He may have been reluctant to record it even in his journal, since there is no trace of it there.[60]

Scott heard that when Johnson demanded to know what good Cromwell had ever done, Lord Auchinleck replied, "Good, Doctor! He gart kings ken that they had a lith in their neck" (taught kings that they had a joint in their neck). Charles I was beheaded.

As for Peggie, she did her best to entertain Johnson hospitably in Edinburgh, overlooking his habit of letting candle wax drip on the carpet, but he suspected afterward that she didn't much like him, and she frankly told Boswell so. In a footnote in the *Life* he acknowledged, "She had not that high admiration of him which was felt by most of those who knew him; and what was very natural to a female mind, she thought he had too much influence over her husband. She once, in a little warmth, made with more point than justice this remark upon that subject: 'I have seen many a bear led by a man, but I never before saw a man led by a bear.' "[61]

By the time the trip was over Boswell and Johnson had been together for one hundred and one consecutive days, nearly a quarter of the days they ever spent together. There was new intimacy and new mutual respect. On Boswell's side it is the story, as has been well said, "of one who learns to recognize the unusual powers and occasional flaws in a man whom he begins by setting on a pedestal, and ends by loving as a friend."[62]

AFTERMATH

Johnson's *Journey to the Western Islands of Scotland* was more than just a travel book. It might well be called a pioneering essay in geography and sociology, pondering for example why mountain people often resist control from outside, fragment into competing tribes or clans, and sustain endless feuds.

That anticipates the kind of thinking that Fernand Braudel would bring in the twentieth century to the mountainous regions around the Mediterranean. Ten years after the trip Johnson said, "I got an acquisition of more ideas by it than by anything that I remember. I saw quite a different system of life."[63]

Johnson always hoped to go to Italy, as he almost did with the Thrales. "A man who has not been in Italy," he said, "is always conscious of an inferiority, from his not having seen what it is expected a man should see. All our religion, almost all our law, almost all our arts, almost all that sets us above savages, has come to us from the shores of the Mediterranean." It has been suggested that the tour to the Hebrides interested him because it was absolutely the opposite: not the cradle of civilization, but an outlying region where primitive customs and lifestyles had not yet vanished. It has been described as an anti-grand tour.[64]

One passage in Johnson's book excited an angry reaction, and in turn a magisterial response from him that was much like his classic letter to Lord Chesterfield. There was a controversy at that time surrounding an allegedly ancient cycle of Gaelic poems by a bard named Ossian, translated into poetic prose by James Macpherson. Vaguely biblical in style, they struck many people as magnificent survivals from a northern Homer, and some Scottish intellectuals insisted that they were authentic. Others were certain that Macpherson had made it all up, or at most had elaborated upon fragments of folk songs.

That was Johnson's view. In a conversation on the Isle of Skye he conjectured that Macpherson must have stitched together some old fragments and then claimed to have discovered a complete epic poem, whose manuscript he always refused to show. Years before, Boswell's Scottish friend the Rev. Hugh Blair told him about an exchange when he was introduced to Johnson in London. Blair was an enthusiast for Ossian, and asked politely whether Johnson thought any man in the modern age could have written such poems. Johnson replied, "Yes, Sir, many men, many women, and many children."[65]

In the published *Journey* Johnson was just as insulting, though in a more dignified way. "The editor, or author, never could show the original; nor can it be shown by any other. To revenge reasonable incredulity by refusing evidence is a degree of insolence with which the world is not yet acquainted; and stubborn audacity is the last refuge of guilt." As for the claim of many that they had personally heard the Ossianic poems recited in their youth, Johnson said that they were simply defending their ancestors' prestige, and added, "A

Scotchman must be a very sturdy moralist, who does not love Scotland better than truth."[66]

That caused keen indignation among the Scots, including a Gaelic poet who denounced Johnson with the inventive insults known as "flyting":

> You are a slimy, yellow-bellied frog.
> You are a toad crawling along the ditches.
> You are a lizard of the waste, crawling and creeping like a reptile.

Macpherson, who was twenty-seven years younger than Johnson, sent a letter demanding a retraction and adding that only Johnson's age and infirmities could protect him from a beating.[67]

Johnson's response was to keep a stout stick by his bed in case of need, and to respond with a letter of his own that deserves to be read in full. Boswell got him to dictate his recollection of it and printed that in the *Life,* but we now have the actual text. Surprisingly, perhaps, Macpherson kept the letter.

> Mr. James Macpherson—
>
> I received your foolish and impudent note. Whatever insult is offered me I will do my best to repel, and what I cannot do for myself the law will do for me. I will not desist from detecting what I think a cheat from any fear of the menaces of a ruffian. You want me to retract. What shall I retract? I thought your book an imposture from the beginning, I think it upon yet surer reasons an imposture still. For this opinion I give the public my reasons, which I here dare you to refute.
>
> But however I may despise you, I reverence truth, and if you can prove the genuineness of the work I will confess it. Your rage I defy, your abilities since your Homer are not so formidable, and what I have heard of your morals disposes me to pay regard not to what you shall say, but to what you can prove.
>
> You may print this if you will.
>
> SAM. JOHNSON

The crack about Homer was especially deft. Macpherson had published a translation of the *Iliad* in Ossianic prose, and everyone agreed it was awful.[68]

CHAPTER 15

The Widening River

For Johnson the writer, not much happened during the decade and a half from 1765 on. After the Shakespeare edition finally came out in 1765, the *Journey to the Western Islands* nine years later was his first significant publication, apart from some brief political polemics. Then there was another hiatus until in 1779, responding to an unexpected proposal from a group of publishers, he brought out the first installment of his *Lives of the English Poets*. Those would turn out to be a career-culminating masterpiece.

This period is full of interest in the *Life of Johnson*, however, because Boswell was in London for several months most years and recorded unforgettable material. It's a salutary reminder that publications listed in a chronology are far from the whole of a writer's life. The London interludes were recurring high points for Boswell, and during each of them, as Brady says, "the journal widens like a river."[1]

One of Johnson's fundamental principles was that literature is always a selection from life, narrower and simpler than life itself, even when imaginatively powerful. In the *Preface to Shakespeare* he made a trenchant retort to Voltaire's claim that comedy and tragedy must never mix, from which it followed that since Shakespeare often disobeyed that supposed rule, his plays were by definition inferior. "Shakespeare's plays," Johnson wrote, "are not in the rigorous and critical sense either tragedies or comedies, but compositions of a distinct kind; exhibiting the real state of sublunary nature, which partakes of good and evil, joy and sorrow, mingled with endless variety of proportion and innumerable modes of combination; and expressing the course of the world, in which the loss of one is the gain of another; in which, at the same time, the reveler is hasting to his wine, and the mourner burying his friend."[2]

It's notable that Garrick, the man of the theater, was much more willing than Johnson to go along with the so-called "rules." He put together a heavily altered version of *Hamlet,* very much in line with Voltaire's criticisms, and then wrote to Voltaire himself, "Could I have been the means of bringing our Shakespeare into some favour with M. Voltaire, I should have been happy indeed! No enthusiastic missionary who had converted the emperor of China to his religion would have been prouder than I, could I have reconciled the first genius of Europe to our dramatic faith." Johnson referred in the *Preface* to "the minute and slender criticism of Voltaire."[3]

Johnson was well aware that he might seem to be lazy, and was defensive about it. Boswell said cautiously, "I wonder, Sir, you have not more pleasure in writing than in not writing." Johnson answered, "Sir, you *may* wonder."[4]

Apart from his usual procrastination, one reason to write less was that writing was no longer necessary to make ends meet. After the annual £300 pension started in 1762, he was able to live comfortably and even save money, especially since he was at Streatham much of the time. From then until his death he used his publisher William Strahan as his banker, and since Strahan kept accurate records, we know that for his final twenty-one years Johnson's total income amounted to £7,000, from which he saved £3,000 that was distributed in his will.[5]

THE CLUB GETS BIGGER—OR TOO BIG

Meanwhile, much of value was being published by other members of the Club. We have already noted Goldsmith's *She Stoops to Conquer* in 1773 and Sheridan's *School for Scandal* in 1777. Reynolds began delivering his annual *Discourses* to the Royal Academy in 1769. Most memorably, 1776 saw two permanent monuments produced by members: the first volume of Edward Gibbon's *Decline and Fall of the Roman Empire,* and Adam Smith's *The Wealth of Nations.*

The Club itself was changing, continuing to grow and losing the intimacy with which it began. The members decided that it would be a good idea to expand, and five new members were elected in 1773, including Garrick and

Boswell. There were another five the following year, including Gibbon and Burke's parliamentary ally Charles James Fox, and two more in 1775, one of whom was Smith. In 1777 still another five were added, notably Sheridan, and in 1778 another four. By then Johnson felt strongly that the whole point of the group had been forgotten; he attended only occasionally. Besides, the lively shadow club at Streatham made him need it less than he once did.

Few of the new members have left any traces for posterity. An important exception is Sir William Jones, who is hardly a household name today but richly deserved election. That happened in 1773, the same year as Boswell and Garrick. Only twenty-seven, he was already a fellow of the Royal Society (his father had been a mathematician who introduced the use of the symbol π), and he had made himself master of numerous languages, including Persian, Arabic, and Hebrew. Even as a schoolboy at Harrow he knew more Greek than the headmaster, and at Oxford he translated the *Arabian Nights* from Arabic.

A few years later Jones became a judge in Calcutta in the Bengal Supreme Court. There he got deeply interested in Indian culture, and published a re-markable range of books on its literature, music, legal system, and botany. He is best remembered today as an early proponent of the notion that a proto-language lay behind Sanskrit, Iranian, Greek, Latin, Germanic, and Celtic (he was a na-tive speaker of Welsh). That would become known as Indo-European. After all of his remarkable achievements, he was just forty-seven when he died in 1794.

Most new members, however, could not have been called distinguished at any time. One such addition in 1773 was an Irish MP with the unwieldy name of Agmondesham Vesey, a friend of Burke's whose wife was a well-known Bluestocking. Her friend Elizabeth Montagu urged Reynolds to support Vesey, which he did, but he told her that Burke himself described Vesey luke-warmly as "a man of taste, without pretensions and so without jealousy and envy."[6]

One new member who attracted Boswell's active dislike was a Scottish physician named George Fordyce, chosen one year after he was. In his journal he wrote indignantly, "I was disgusted by Fordyce, who was coarse and noisy; and as he had the Scotch accent strong, he shocked me as a kind of represen-tative of myself. He was to me as the slaves of the Spartans, when shown drunk to make that vice odious. His being a member lessens the value of the Club."[7]

Fordyce was indeed notorious for eating and drinking on an outrageous scale. On one occasion he tried to take a fashionable lady's pulse but was too shaky to accomplish it. "Drunk, by God," he muttered, and left. When he arrived to apologize the next morning, her footman handed him a message: "I know from what you said last night that you discovered my unfortunate condition. I entreat you to keep the matter a secret between us, in consideration of the enclosed." It was a banknote for one hundred pounds.[8]

Attendance at Club meetings was not mandatory, and for most members it became sporadic. In the decade from 1775 to 1785, Reynolds was the most faithful, but the greatest number of dinners he attended in any one year was sixteen, and Gibbon was next with fourteen. Johnson showed up seldom: nine times in 1778, but otherwise never more than three times in any year. He told Boswell that the Club had degenerated into "a mere miscellaneous collection of conspicuous men, without any determinate character."[9]

In 1774 Goldsmith was the first member of the Club to die, at the age of forty-six. It was a sad passing. Ill with some unspecified complaint, he took a massive dose of a patent remedy that his doctors deplored. After his death it became clear that he was deeply in debt, and some people suspected suicide. Burke burst into tears when he heard about it, and Reynolds did no work for an entire day, which for him was almost unheard of.

Johnson once visited Westminster Abbey with Goldsmith. As they stood in Poets' Corner, Johnson quoted Ovid, *Forsitan et nostrum nomen miscebitur istis*—"perhaps even our names will be mingled here." Later that day they reached Temple Bar (figure 78), where the heads of executed rebels were displayed on poles. As Johnson recalled it, Goldsmith "slyly whispered me, 'Forsitan et nostrum nomen miscebitur *istis*.'"[10]

Goldsmith did get a memorial in Westminster Abbey, and Johnson composed an epitaph for it: *Olivarii Goldsmith, Poetae, Physicii, Historici, quid nullum fere scribendi genus non tetigit, nullum quod tetigit non ornavit*—"To Oliver Goldsmith, poet, physician, historian, who left no kind of writing untouched, and touched nothing that he did not adorn."

JOHNSON'S MÉNAGE

Johnson spent a lot of time at Streatham, but by no means all of his time, and even when he was staying there he returned home regularly to look after his housemates. In 1765 he had moved from Inner Temple Lane to Johnson's Court (Boswell thought the coincidence of names appropriate) just off Fleet Street, and in 1776 to Bolt Court nearby, which would be his residence for the rest of his life (figure 79).

78. Temple Bar

79. Bolt Court

Hester Thrale regarded the entire group of Johnson's dependents as contemptible. "Blind Mrs. Williams, dropsical Mrs. Desmoulins, Black Francis and his white wife's bastard, with a wretched Mrs. White and a thing that he called Poll, shared his bounty and increased his dirt. Levet used to bleed one and blister another and be very useful, though I believe disagreeable to all." The "thing" whom Johnson called Poll was the former prostitute Poll Carmichael, mentioned earlier in this book. Robert Levet was the unlicensed physician who had acquired a great deal of practical knowledge and was beloved among the poor; to Hester he would have been merely a quack.[11]

At another time Hester referred to "a blackamoor and his wife." Francis (also known as Frank) Barber was a freed former slave from Jamaica who had been brought to England as a boy by the father of Richard Bathurst, a physician who was a good friend of Johnson's. When the younger Bathurst decided to return to the West Indies, Francis moved in with Johnson as a kind of household servant but also companion and even surrogate son. Johnson paid for Francis to get a good education, and apart from one short-lived attempt to run away to sea, he remained with Johnson for the rest of his life and was generously provided for in his will. Francis did indeed marry an English-woman.[12]

Johnson himself had no illusions about his ill-assorted companions, and Hawkins, who had known him for so many years, thought that unsentimentality was the whole point. His charity was more honorable if he got so little in return. Hawkins remembered Johnson quoting the seventeenth-century writer Jeremy Taylor: "It is no great matter to live lovingly with good-natured, humble and meek persons; but he that can do so with the froward, with the willful and the ignorant, with the peevish and perverse, he only hath true charity." Pretty much all of those terms would apply to Johnson's strange ménage.[13]

The exception was Anna Williams (figure 80), whom Johnson deeply valued for her intelligence and her willingness to chat far into the night when he dreaded going to bed. As has been mentioned, she had come to London for an operation on cataracts that didn't succeed, and became Tetty's companion before her death. She had no money and no connections, and it was a true act of charity to keep her in residence, but she also provided the companionship that he badly needed.

Johnson's friends were well aware that when they visited his lodgings they would be expected to take tea with her, as he himself customarily did. Shortly

80. Anna Williams

after first meeting him, Boswell spent an evening with him and Goldsmith, and was chagrined not to be invited to accompany Johnson home. "Dr. Goldsmith, being a privileged man, went with him this night, strutting away, and calling to me with an air of superiority, like that of an esoteric over an exoteric disciple of a sage of antiquity, 'I go to Miss Williams.' I confess I then envied him this mighty privilege of which he seemed so proud; but it was not long before I obtained the same mark of distinction."[14]

Miss or Mrs. Williams (the titles were interchangeable for unmarried women) had aspirations as an author, and in 1766 Johnson persuaded Thomas Davies to publish her *Miscellanies in Prose and Verse,* to which he contributed a number of short pieces of his own. Her poems are high-minded and competent, though in no way memorable. The little volume produced a modest profit, and that was his intention in promoting it.

After Anna Williams's death in 1783, Johnson wrote to Elizabeth Montagu, "Her curiosity was universal, her knowledge was very extensive, and she sustained forty years of misery with steady fortitude. Thirty years and more she had been my companion, and her death has left me very desolate." To his stepdaughter Lucy he said that she "had been to me for thirty years in the place of a sister; her knowledge was great and her conversation pleasing. I now live in cheerless solitude."[15]

At Streatham, meanwhile, Hester continued to be a patient therapist. But she could only relieve Johnson's anxieties, not dispel them. In 1772, after supervising a major revision of the *Dictionary,* he wrote a bleak Latin poem with a Greek title, ΓΝΩΘΙ ΣΕΑΥΤΟΝ. That was the motto of the oracle at Delphi, "Know thyself." A subtitle in Latin follows: POST LEXICON ANGLICANUM AUCTUM ET EMENDATUM—"after enlarging and correcting the English *Dictionary.*"

The poem begins by recalling that when the humanist scholar Scaliger completed a lexicon, he cursed the exhausting labor that had gone into it. And yet Johnson was finding that it was still worse to be liberated from a regular task. In the translation of his friend Arthur Murphy:

> The listless will succeeds, that worst disease,
> The rack of indolence, the sluggish ease.
> Care grows on care, and o'er my aching brain
> Black Melancholy pours her morbid train.
> No kind relief, no lenitive at hand,
> I seek at midnight clubs the social band,

> But midnight clubs, where wit with noise conspires,
> Delight no more; I seek my lonely bed,
> And call on sleep to soothe my languid head,
> But sleep from these sad lids flies far away;
> I mourn all night, and dread the coming day. . . .
> A dreary void, where fears with grief combined
> Waste all within, and desolate the mind.

The uselessness of "midnight clubs" may reflect his disappointment with the great Club itself.[16]

Perhaps the most powerful of Reynolds's portraits of Johnson is one that he made around 1769, when Johnson was turning sixty (figure 81). It shows him in an open shirt, and without his usual wig. The hands are evidently depicted in the convulsive movements that Johnson often made, as in a description by Frances Reynolds: "His gestures with his hands were equally strange. Sometimes he would hold them up with some of his fingers bent, as if he had been seized with the cramp, and sometimes at his breast in motion like those of a jockey on full speed; and often would he lift them up as high as he could stretch over his head, for some minutes." That looks very much like obsessive compulsive disorder.[17]

A ROYAL ENCOUNTER

In 1767 Johnson had a conversation with King George III that he described to his friends with reverence, and that Boswell regarded with awe. It was not difficult for someone well-placed in society to speak casually and briefly with the king, at one of the large gatherings in which he would circulate among the visitors. But to be invited to converse privately and at length was a great honor.

In 1761, one year after he came to the throne at the age of twenty-two, George III bought Buckingham House close to St. James's Palace as a private residence for Queen Charlotte, and it became known as the Queen's House. Not until the accession of Victoria in 1837, after it had been much enlarged, did it become Buckingham Palace and the official residence of the monarch. King George was well read and wanted to be known for encouraging learning, so he began amassing an exceptional collection of books covering every conceivable area: Latin and Greek classics, poetry, geography, history, mathematics, law, and so on. His librarian worked diligently to expand it, and a series of magnificent rooms were created for it in the Queen's House.

81. Johnson at sixty

Scholars and men of letters were welcome to use the library whenever they liked, which Johnson often did. Five years earlier the king had authorized his pension, and now expressed a special desire to meet him. The royal librarian, Frederick Barnard, set up the encounter. It took place in the magnificent octagonal room shown here (color plate 26); Boswell mentions the fire burning at the right.

The king asked whether Johnson was writing anything at that time, to which "he answered he was not, for he had pretty well told the world what he knew, and must now read to acquire more knowledge." He added that "he thought he had already done his part as a writer," to which the king replied, "I should have thought so too, if you had not written so well." Relating this to Boswell, Johnson commented, "No man could have paid a handsomer compliment; and it was fit for a king to pay. It was decisive."

In his courteous way, the king was acting as a traditional patron of literature, but as Alvin Kernan comments, the days of patronage were over. Johnson would write again in the future, just as he always did, only when booksellers approached him with commercial proposals. But when the time came a decade later for the *Lives of the Poets*, he certainly remembered what the king had said on this occasion: "His Majesty," Boswell wrote, "expressed a desire to have the literary biography of this country ably executed, and proposed to Dr. Johnson to undertake it. Johnson signified his readiness to comply with his Majesty's wishes."[18]

When he was gathering material for the *Life of Johnson*, Boswell took care to interview the royal librarian. No plebeian but an illegitimate son of the Prince of Wales, Barnard was impressed that the king had treated Johnson as an equal, and that Johnson had responded in kind. "During the whole of this interview Johnson talked to his Majesty with profound respect, but still in his firm manly manner, with a sonorous voice, and never in that subdued tone which is commonly used at the levee [a public reception] and in the drawing room. After the king withdrew, Johnson showed himself highly pleased with His Majesty's conversation and gracious behavior. He said to Mr. Barnard, 'Sir, they may talk of the king as they will; but he is the finest gentleman I have ever seen.'" A king of France would never have dreamt of stooping so low.[19]

Boswell knew that this interview would so interest readers that he published his account of it by itself, a year before the *Life*, as an eight-page pamphlet at the remarkably high price of half a guinea.

BOSWELL THE IMPRESARIO

Whenever Boswell was in London during these years, the *Life of Johnson* swells with incidents and conversations. In 1772 Boswell was flattered to be invited to dinner by General James Oglethorpe, then in his seventies, who had been a pioneer in prison reform and co-founder of the colony of Georgia. In his journal Boswell noted, "Mr. Johnson and Dr. Goldsmith and nobody else were the company. I felt a completion of happiness. I just sat and hugged myself in my own mind. Here I am in London, at the house of General Oglethorpe, who introduced himself to me just because I had distinguished myself; and here is Mr. Johnson, whose character is so vast; here is Dr. Goldsmith, so distinguished in literature. Words cannot describe our feelings. The finer parts are lost, as the down upon a plum; the radiance of light cannot be painted."[20]

Boswell was nothing if not social. He was in London for fifty-three days on that visit, during which he went without dinner twice, dined alone at a tavern twice, and dined with friends the other forty-nine days.[21]

It's not always realized, because Boswell's art is so deft, that he doesn't just record conversations, he helps to make them interesting while they are happening. He saw this as a lawyer's skill: "I have an admirable talent of leading the conversation; I do not mean leading as in an orchestra, by playing the first fiddle, but leading as one does in examining a witness—starting topics, and making the company pursue them."[22]

Boswell had to admit that sometimes Johnson found this tactic exasperating. Once his questioning was so persistent that "the Doctor grew enraged and said, 'Don't you consider, Sir, these are not the manners of a gentleman? I will not be baited with 'what'—'what is this? what is that? why is a cow's tail long? why is a fox's tail bushy?'" When Boswell repeated this in the *Life,* he called the questioner whom Johnson scolded "a gentleman" rather than revealing that it was himself.[23]

In her copy of the *Life,* Hester Thrale recalled a similar complaint by Johnson. "I have been put so to the question by Bozzy this morning that I am now panting for breath. One question was 'Pray, Sir, can you tell why an apple is round and a pear pointed?' Would not such talk make a man hang himself?"[24]

What Boswell really wanted was not literal answers to trivial questions, but interesting directions into which the conversation might veer. Having watched him in action, Hester understood that well: "Curiosity carried Boswell farther than it ever carried any mortal breathing. He cared not what he provoked, so as he saw what such a one would say or do."²⁵

Some of Johnson's most frequently quoted remarks emerged in just this way, during the course of otherwise unremarkable conversations. That's true, for instance, of "When a man is tired of London, he is tired of life," and likewise of "Depend upon it, Sir, when a man knows he is to be hanged in a fortnight, it concentrates his mind wonderfully."²⁶

The playwright Richard Cumberland, in his memoirs, tried to describe a quarrel between Garrick and another actor and gave up: "Why was not James Boswell present to have recorded the dialogue and the action of the scene? My stupid head only carried away the effect of it." It's striking that Cumberland mentioned "action" as well as dialogue. Boswell constantly fills in details of body language, facial expressions, and tones of voice that create genuinely dramatic scenes.²⁷

Sometimes an unexpected encounter gave Boswell the opportunity for a memorable set piece. One such occurred when he had arranged to meet Johnson at the lodgings of Robert Chambers, a lawyer friend for whom Johnson once ghostwrote a course of Oxford lectures. Johnson mentioned that Chambers had just drawn up a will for Bennet Langton, his tall and skinny friend, and then launched unexpectedly into an extraordinary performance.

He now laughed immoderately, without any reason that we could perceive, at our friend's making his will; called him the *testator,* and added, "I dare say, he thinks he has done a mighty thing. He won't stay till he gets home to his seat in the country to produce this wonderful deed: he'll call up the landlord of the first inn on the road, and after a suitable preface upon mortality and the uncertainty of life, will tell him that he should not delay making his will. And here, Sir, will he say, is my will, which I have just made, with the assistance of one of the ablest lawyers in the kingdom; and he will read it to him (laughing all the time). He believes he has made this will; but he did not make it: you, Chambers, made it for him."

Chambers was understandably offended at hearing his work taken lightly. Nevertheless, "Johnson could not stop his merriment, but continued it all the way till we got without the Temple Gate. He then burst into such a fit of laughter that he appeared to be almost in a convulsion; and in order to support himself laid hold of one of the posts at the side of the foot pavement, and sent forth peals so loud, that in the silence of the night his voice seemed to resound from Temple Bar to Fleet Ditch."[28]

In his original journal entry Boswell said that he himself took part in the teasing, calling out "Langton the testator, Langton Longshanks," which sent Johnson into still more convulsive laughter. "This tickled his fancy so much that he roared out, 'I wonder to whom he'll leave his legs?'" No doubt he was remembering that the French word for legacy is *legs* (though the "s" is silent). When they got to Johnson's lodgings in the Temple, "I accompanied him to his door, where he gave me his blessing."[29]

This strange episode has been much discussed. One interpretation is that Johnson saw comedy in a solemn attempt to defuse death by drawing up a legal document—"testator" is a pompous word. Thanks to Boswell's joke, the scene ends with the macabre thought of the legs of the spindly Langton being passed on to someone else when he no longer had need of them. For Johnson, at any rate, the explosion seems to have been cathartic. "He gave me his blessing."

It was certainly true, as Boswell says elsewhere, that Johnson could be set off by some apparently trivial thought, after which he would "laugh with a glee that was astonishing, and could hardly leave off. I have seen him do so at a small matter that struck him, and was sport to no one else. Langton told me that one night at the Club he did so while the company were all grave around him; only Garrick in his smart manner addressed him, "Mighty pleasant, Sir; mighty pleasant, Sir."[30]

After writing that, Boswell added, "Poor Langton's will was a sport of this kind." It was and it wasn't. An influential critic long ago, in a book entitled *Perilous Balance,* invoked King Lear's speech, "Hysterica passio! down, thou climbing sorrow! / Thy element's below." In *The Anatomy of Melancholy,* the treatise on mental illness that Johnson respected highly, Robert Burton noted that melancholics "have grievous passions, and immoderate perturbations of the mind, fear, sorrow, etc.; yet not so continuate, but that they are sometimes merry, apt to profuse laughter."[31]

The "perilous balance" interpretation would support an image of Johnson as a tragic figure, but maybe the comic perspective is the right one after all. There seems to have been something risible about Langton, which might make the very idea of his solemnly drawing up a will seem funny. Johnson once said to Boswell, "Sir, the earth has not a better man. But ridicule is inherent in him. There is no separating them."[32]

Hester Thrale's comment on the story confirms that. "Mr. Langton seems to stand in a very odd light among us. He is acknowledged learned, pious, and elegant of manners—yet he is always a person unrespected and commonly ridiculous. When he made his will, we were all bursting with laughter. 'Langton's will' was the *mot de guerre,* and everybody was tittering."[33]

Boswell had an even greater gift, and that was to create, and then re-create in writing, an entire dramatic scene like an impresario. The finest of these was a dinner party in 1776 at which he plotted to lure Johnson into meeting John Wilkes. Wilkes was the notorious rake, pornographer, and political pariah whom Boswell had met in Italy and continued to see in London. Wilkes and Johnson had been exchanging insults in print for years. Back in 1762, in his antigovernment periodical, the *North Briton,* Wilkes derided Johnson for accepting a government pension when his *Dictionary* had famously defined "pension" as "an allowance made to anyone without an equivalent. In England it is generally understood to mean pay given to a state hireling for treason to his country."

Beginning in 1770, Johnson began writing political tracts on behalf of the government, and many people thought they were precisely that kind of "equivalent." In *The Patriot* in 1774, he mocked Wilkes as a shallow poseur who was good at wooing voters but not much else. "No man can reasonably be thought a lover of his country for roasting an ox, or burning a boot, or attending the meeting at Mile End, or registering his name in the Lumber Troop. He may, among the drunkards, be a 'hearty fellow,' and among sober handicraftsmen a 'free spoken gentleman;' but he must have some better distinction before he is a *Patriot.*" Wilkes's supporters met in an assembly room at Mile End, just east of the City of London; the Lumber Troop was a Wilkesite club. The prime minister whom they opposed was the Earl of Bute, so it was considered witty to burn a boot in derision of him.[34]

Hogarth, whom Wilkes had also attacked, caricatured him brilliantly (figure 82). As with the French revolutionaries later on, there is a cap of liberty above his head, a symbol recalling the freeing of slaves in ancient Rome, but hanging heavily from a pole like an inverted chamber pot. Although Wilkes is fashionably dressed, his wig is curiously extended to look like devil's horns. And what most draws the eye is his cocky, knowing, leering expression. It was in fact a good likeness, capturing the lantern jaw, gap teeth, and crossed eyes that he actually had in real life. Wilkes admitted as much: "It must be allowed to be an excellent compound caricatura, or a caricature of what nature had already caricatured." Boswell was amused on the Isle of Skye when Johnson happened to sit beneath "Hogarth's print of Wilkes grinning, with the cap of liberty on a pole by him."[35]

82. John Wilkes

In conversation Johnson was still more blunt. The voters who persistently reelected Wilkes to Parliament every time he was expelled were commonly referred to as "the mob," and he agreed with the governing ministry that it was Parliament itself, not the voters, that could determine whom to seat. After the Wilkesite crisis died down he told Boswell, "Sir, had Wilkes's mob prevailed against government, this nation had died of phthiriasis." That would be an infestation of head lice.[36]

Pulling off an amicable encounter between Johnson and Wilkes was thus a daunting challenge. The first step was to secure Johnson's acceptance of the invitation by cunning indirection. Boswell's narration of how he did it, after first communicating an invitation from the publisher Charles Dilly, is very deftly handled:

> JOHNSON. Sir, I am obliged to Mr. Dilly. I will wait upon him.
> BOSWELL. Provided, Sir, I suppose, that the company which he is to have is agreeable to you.

JOHNSON. What do you mean, Sir? What do you take me for? Do you think I am so ignorant of the world, as to imagine that I am to prescribe to a gentleman what company he is to have at his table?

BOSWELL. I beg your pardon, Sir, for wishing to prevent you from meeting people whom you might not like. Perhaps he may have some of what he calls his patriotic friends with him.

JOHNSON. Well, Sir, and what then? What care I for his *patriotic friends?* Poh!

BOSWELL. I should not be surprised to find Jack Wilkes there.

JOHNSON. And if Jack Wilkes *should* be there, what is that to me, Sir? My dear friend, let us have no more of this.

"Thus I secured him," Boswell triumphantly writes.[37]

When Boswell showed up at Bolt Court on the appointed day, he was shocked to discover that Johnson had forgotten all about it. "I found him buffeting his books, covered with dust, and making no preparation for going abroad." That description incorporates a felicitous printer's error. Boswell originally wrote not the expressive word "buffeting," but "bustling among his books." It came back on a proof sheet as "buffeting among his books," which didn't quite make sense, but he evidently liked it. He struck out the irrelevant "among" and kept the "buffeting."[38]

Now there was a further obstacle. Johnson had promised to dine with Anna Williams, and refused to let her down. So Boswell went to Mrs. Williams and pleaded his case: Mr. Dilly had invited distinguished guests, and would be terribly embarrassed if Johnson did not appear.

She gradually softened to my solicitations, which were certainly as earnest as most entreaties to ladies upon any occasion, and was graciously pleased to empower me to tell Dr. Johnson that "all things considered, she thought he should certainly go." I flew back to him still in dust, and careless of what should be the event, "indifferent in his choice to go or stay;" but as soon as I had announced to him Mrs. Williams's consent, he roared, "Frank, a clean shirt!" and was very soon dressed. When I had him fairly seated in a hackney coach with me, I exulted as much as a fortune hunter who has got an heiress into a post chaise with him to set out for Gretna Green.

That was a town just across the border in Scotland, where couples who were eloping could be hastily married without the legal impediments that might have prevented them in England.

When they arrived at Dilly's and Johnson saw that Wilkes was indeed there, he sat down with his face in a book "till he composed himself." But at dinner Wilkes, who knew how to be charming, was seated beside Johnson and "gained upon him insensibly." The narration becomes irresistibly comic:

> No man ate more heartily than Johnson, or loved better what was nice and delicate. Mr. Wilkes was very assiduous in helping him to some fine veal. "Pray give me leave, Sir—it is better here—a little of the brown—some fat, Sir, a little of the stuffing—some gravy—let me have the pleasure of giving you some butter—allow me to recommend a squeeze of this orange, or the lemon perhaps may have more zest." "Sir, sir, I am obliged to you, Sir," cried Johnson, bowing, and turning his head to him with a look for some time of "surly virtue," but in a short while of complacency.

"Surly virtue" is a quote from Johnson's poem *London*.

The scene reaches its climax when it becomes clear that Wilkes and Johnson are both enjoying playing the role of congenial friends, no doubt to the wonderment of many of the guests, and they find common cause in making fun of Boswell.

> JOHNSON. You must know, Sir, I lately took my friend Boswell and showed him genuine civilized life in an English provincial town. I turned him loose at Lichfield, my native city, that he might see for once real civility; for you know he lives among savages in Scotland, and among rakes in London.
>
> WILKES. Except when he is with grave, sober, decent people like you and me.
>
> JOHNSON. (smiling). And we ashamed of him.

When Boswell recounted what had happened to his friends, Burke "pleasantly said there was nothing to equal it in the whole history of the *Corps Diplomatique*."[39]

Johnson clearly realized that Boswell had set him up, and took pleasure in collaborating with Wilkes to tease him. The upshot was that Johnson and Wilkes afterward treated each other like friends. Five years later, again at

Dilly's, Boswell observed them "literally tête-à-tête; for they were reclined upon their chairs, with their heads leaning almost close to each other, and talking earnestly in a kind of confidential whisper."[40]

Another example of Boswell's skill is more casual, but in its own way remarkable for what he made happen. Strolling one day in Butcher Row near Temple Bar (figure 83), he and Johnson happened to encounter "a decent-looking elderly man in grey clothes, and a wig of many curls," who addressed Johnson as if he knew him. It turned out that his name was Oliver Edwards, and that they had been classmates at Pembroke College, Oxford, half a century before. When they were about to part Boswell "whispered to Mr. Edwards that Dr. Johnson was going home, and that he had better accompany him now. So Edwards walked along with us, I eagerly assisting to keep up the conversation." It was not very interesting, turning on Edwards's fruit trees that the frost might have damaged, his career disappointments, and his regret at getting old. But then he came out with an unforgettable line: "You are a philosopher, Dr. Johnson. I have tried to in my time to be a philosopher; but I don't know how, cheerfulness was always breaking in."

83. Butcher Row

That artless remark is wonderful, but it also brings out an important aspect of Johnson's personality. Solemn and morose though he often was, he loved gaiety, by contrast with this defeated classmate who had launched himself into life at the same place and time. After they parted, Boswell commented that Edwards seemed to be a weak man, and Johnson replied, "Why, yes, Sir. Here is a man who has passed through life without experience."[41]

One final example illustrates not Boswell's own art, but that of another writer who realized what might be done with even a casual hint. Surely no one but Max Beerbohm would have seen anything worth mentioning in Boswell's account in the *Life* of a discussion of different styles of preaching. Johnson is pontificating:

> South is one of the best, if you except his peculiarities, and his violence and sometimes coarseness of language. Seed has a very fine style, but he is not very theological. Jortin's sermons are very elegant. Sherlock's style too is very elegant, though he has not made it his principal study. And you may add Smallridge. . . .
>
> BOSWELL. What I wish to know is, what sermons afford the best specimen of English pulpit eloquence.
>
> JOHNSON. We have no sermons addressed to the passions that are good for anything, if you mean that kind of eloquence.
>
> A CLERGYMAN (whose name I do not recollect). Were not Dodd's sermons addressed to the passions?
>
> JOHNSON. They were nothing, Sir, be they addressed to what they may.[42]

Beerbohm had the inspiration of imagining what it felt like to be that nameless clergyman, guessing that he was probably the curate at a neighboring church.

> He sits on the edge of the chair in the background. He has colourless eyes, fixed earnestly, and a face almost as pale as the clerical bands beneath his somewhat receding chin. His forehead is high and narrow, his hair mouse-coloured. His hands are clasped tight before him, the knuckles standing out sharply. This constriction does not mean that he is steeling himself to speak. He has no positive intention of speaking. Very much, nevertheless, he is wishing in the back of his mind that he *could* say something—something whereat the great Doctor would turn on him and say, after a pause for thought, "Why yes, Sir.

That is most justly observed," or "Sir, this has never occurred to me, I thank you"—thereby fixing the observer forever high in the esteem of all. And now in a flash the chance presents itself. "We have," shouts Johnson, "no sermons addressed to the passions that are good for anything." I see the curate's frame quiver with sudden impulse, and his mouth fly open, and—no, I can't bear it, I shut my eyes and ears.[43]

Surprisingly, the dim clergyman can be identified, because Hester Thrale wrote his name in the margin of her copy of the *Life of Johnson*. He was Edward Embry, thirty-three years old at the time when Johnson trampled him. He was indeed a neighbor of the Thrales, and was later appointed curate at St. Paul's in Covent Garden (the church shown by Hogarth in *Morning*, figure 17, page 69 above). Confirming Beerbohm's insight, he remained in that humble role for thirty years. Finally he rose to the status of rector, and died eight years after that. Apart from a couple of casual mentions in the journals of Hester Thrale and Fanny Burney, he remains as insubstantial as ever. The scholar who has put together what little is known concludes: " 'Fragmentary, pale, momentary, almost nothing'—so he remains, after scholarship has done what it can for him. As always, art can do more."[44]

"I like to think," Beerbohm concludes, "that he died forgiving Dr. Johnson."

Beerbohm loved the *Life of Johnson*, and he was a famously gifted parodist. In 1918, after Johnson's former house in Gough Square had become a museum in his honor, Beerbohm presented it with an inspired illustration (color plate 27). In the margin, in his characteristically minuscule handwriting, is an imaginary dialogue that skewers both Johnson and Boswell, accurately but also affectionately.

> BOSWELL: Are you not pleased, Sir, that your house in Gough Square is to be presented to the Nation?
>
> JOHNSON: Why, no, Sir. You are to consider that the purpose of a house is to be inhabited by someone. If a house be not fit for tenancy by Tom or Dick, let it be demolished or handed over without more ado to the rats, which, by frequentation, will have acquired a prescriptive right there. I conceive that in Gough Square a vast number of rats will have been disturbed and evicted. (Puffing, and rolling himself from side to side): Sir, I am sorry for the rats. Sir, the rats have a just grievance.

BOSWELL: Nevertheless, Sir, is it not well that the house of the great Samuel Johnson should be preserved? Will it not tend to diffuse happiness and to promote virtue?

JOHNSON: Nay, Sir, let us have no more of this foppishness. The house is naught. Let us not *sublimify* lath and plaster. I know not whether I profited the world whilst I was in it. I am very sure that my mere tenement will not be profitable now that I am out of it. Alas, Sir, when "tempus edax" [devouring time] has swallowed the yolk of the egg, there is no gain to be had by conservation of the eggshell.

Or (so very much was Lexiphanes a man of moods) the dialogue might run thus:

BOSWELL: Are you not pleased, Sir, that your house in Gough Square is to be presented to the Nation?

JOHNSON: Why, yes, Sir. (In a solemn, faltering tone): Nothing has pleased me half so well since the *Rambler* was translated into the Russian language and read on the banks of the Wolga.

That last remark alludes to something Johnson actually said, only a few months before his death. "He called to us with a sudden air of exultation, as the thought started into his mind, 'O! Gentlemen, I must tell you a very great thing. The Empress of Russia has ordered the *Rambler* to be translated into the Russian language; so I shall be read on the banks of the Wolga. Horace boasts that his fame would extend as far as the banks of the Rhône; now the Wolga is farther from me than the Rhône was from Horace.'"[45]

The picture is highly appropriate, too. Boswell understood very well that Johnson was much bigger than himself, and not just physically.

CHAPTER 16

Empire

An immense issue preoccupied national consciousness throughout the eighteenth century: Britain's far-flung colonies and the wars that were fought to gain and keep them. It's safe to say that everybody in this story had friends or relatives who were working in the colonies, some of whom had moved there permanently.

In Parliament, colonial affairs dominated debate for extended periods of time. Two crises in particular inspired the most brilliant rhetoric of Burke and Sheridan, as well as eliciting cranky criticism from Johnson: those were the loss of the North American colonies, and an ongoing controversy over the treatment of India. And finally, though only beginning to gain prominence, there was the moral question of slavery.

In a way, war was the norm for the British. During Johnson's lifetime there were no fewer than five different wars: the War of the Spanish Succession, the War of the Quadruple Alliance, the War of the Austrian Succession, the Seven Years War, and the War of American Independence. Between 1739 and 1783 Britain was at war for a total of twenty-four years, and at peace for twenty. The reason for all that fighting was simple. Britain was determined to dominate world trade, and defeating France and Spain was an essential step toward making that happen.

The War of the Spanish Succession, which ended with the Treaty of Utrecht in 1713 when Johnson was four years old, was fought to prevent France from putting a Bourbon ally on the Spanish throne and thereby becoming a superpower. Britain's victory in that war had immense consequences for the future. In the words of George Macaulay Trevelyan, the treaty "marked the end of danger to Europe from the old French monarchy, and it marked a change of no less significance to the world at large—the maritime, commercial and financial supremacy of Great Britain." Spain was forced to surrender a lot of territory, including Sicily, Naples, and the Spanish Netherlands, most of which went to the so-called Holy Roman Empire centered in Austria.[1]

As for Britain, it acquired the valuable fortifications at Gibraltar and parts of eastern Canada. And there was another treaty provision that would exact a dreadful human price. Britain was awarded the Asiento (from *asentir*, to acquiesce or agree), formerly held by France, that gave it a monopoly of the slave trade with the Spanish colonies in the Americas. British ships were already bringing slaves to their own colonies, so now they had an exclusive right to import slaves into the entire Western Hemisphere. In due course they would deliver a million and a half Africans to the Caribbean and to North and South America.

The biggest of all the armed conflicts was the Seven Years War, which began in 1756. On one side was Britain, allied with Portugal, Prussia, and several other German states. On the other was France, together with the Holy Roman Empire, Spain, Russia, and Sweden. It was a true world war, fought in five continents—Europe, the Americas, West Africa, India, and the Philippines. It ended with the Treaty of Paris in 1763, just as Boswell was settling down in London, which confirmed a dramatic increase in Britain's territorial holdings. Those included several Caribbean islands, the colony of Senegal in West Africa, and the Canadian region known as New France, including Quebec with its large population of French Catholics.

All that fighting had been hugely expensive. It was in part to pay for it that taxation of the American colonists was imposed, in the Townshend Acts of 1767, with what would turn out to be drastic consequences.

At the same time the British were rapidly gaining control of the Indian subcontinent, where the commercial East India Company had been established in the days of Queen Elizabeth. To protect its interests the Company began to fight skirmishes against Indian potentates and their French allies, and these developed into full-scale battles. A young bookkeeper, Robert Clive, turned out to have remarkable military abilities. In the 1750s, leading what was in effect a private army, he won a series of victories and also amassed an enormous personal fortune. A commercial organization was now the de facto government of a large part of India, and that anomalous situation provoked intense debates in Parliament, in which Burke and Sheridan would play a leading role.

IMPERIALISM

It had long been taken as obvious that a nation should acquire as many colonies as possible, and populate them with emigrants from home. In the *Dictionary* Johnson defines "to colonize" as "to plant with inhabitants; to settle with new planters, to plant with colonies," and the word "colony" means "a body of people drawn from the mother country to inhabit some distant place." That might seem to imply that nobody was living there until the colonists arrived, but of course that was never true. Increasingly, conquest was rationalized as taking what the natives didn't know how to use.

Originally the word "native" meant simply, as Johnson defines it, "one born in any place; original inhabitant." He himself was a native of Lichfield. But by now the word was acquiring negative connotations and becoming synonymous with "savage," which Johnson defines as "a man untaught and uncivilized; a barbarian." It was easier to oppress the natives, or even exterminate them, if they were seen as barbarians.

Johnson's definition of "colony" in the *Dictionary* reflected general usage, not his personal view. In one of his earliest publications, the 1744 *Life of Savage,* he denounced "the enormous wickedness of making war upon barbarous nations because they cannot resist, and of invading countries because they are fruitful." That would be his consistent position throughout his life. In an *Idler* essay in 1759—the same year as Voltaire's scathing attack on colonialism in *Candide*—he imagined the comments of an Indian chief watching an English army marching past: "Those invaders ranged over the continent slaughtering in their rage those that resisted, and those that submitted in their mirth. Of those that remained, some were buried in caverns, and condemned to dig metals for their masters; some were employed in tilling the ground, of which foreign tyrants devour the produce; and when the sword and the mines have destroyed the natives, they supply their place by human beings of another colour, brought from some distant country to perish here under toil and torture."[2]

Also in 1759, Johnson wrote an introduction for a multivolume account of voyages that he edited, *The World Displayed.* The introduction begins as a historical survey, and then erupts with moral indignation while describing Portuguese explorers who gunned down a crowd of peaceful Africans (Johnson doesn't specify where).

"The Portuguese could fear nothing from them," Johnson declares, "and had therefore no adequate provocation; nor is there any reason to believe but that they murdered the Negroes in wanton merriment, perhaps only to try how many a volley would destroy, or what would be the consternation of those that should escape." This is followed by a grim overview of the consequences of colonization (the word "colonialism" wouldn't be coined for another century). "The Europeans have scarcely visited any coast but to gratify avarice and extend corruption; to arrogate dominion without right, and practice cruelty without incentive."³

This was a not uncommon attitude among intellectuals at the time. Adam Smith, in milder and more temperate prose, said much the same thing in *The Wealth of Nations:* "Folly and injustice seem to have been the principles which presided over and directed the first project of establishing those colonies; the folly of hunting after gold and silver mines, and the injustice of coveting the possession of a country whose harmless natives, far from having ever injured the people of Europe, had received the first adventurers with every mark of kindness and hospitality."⁴

In addition to the injustice wreaked on native peoples, Johnson was shocked by the wars that were fought to acquire colonies and hold on to them. One of his most powerful pieces of writing is a 1771 pamphlet entitled *Thoughts on the Late Transactions Respecting Falkland's Islands.*

A crisis had flared up between Britain and Spain over that small archipelago, three hundred miles off the coast of Argentina. In the end war was averted (as it was not in 1982 when history repeated itself), and Johnson argued convincingly that there was no possible benefit to Britain in defending a barren territory that could produce nothing of value. Beyond that, he described with indignation what warfare is really like. His account deserves to be read at length:

> It is wonderful with what coolness and indifference the greater part of mankind see war commenced. Those that hear of it at a distance, or read of it in books, but have never presented its evils to their minds, consider it as little more than a splendid game, a proclamation, an army, a battle, and a triumph. Some, indeed, must perish in the most successful field, but they die upon the bed of honour, "resign their lives amidst the joys of conquest, and, filled with England's glory, smile in death."
>
> The life of a modern soldier is ill represented by heroic fiction. War has means of destruction more formidable than the cannon and the

sword. Of the thousands and ten thousands that perished in our late contests with France and Spain, a very small part ever felt the stroke of an enemy; the rest languished in tents and ships, amidst damps and putrefaction; pale, torpid, spiritless, and helpless; gasping and groaning, unpitied among men made obdurate by long continuance of hopeless misery; and were at last whelmed in pits, or heaved into the ocean, without notice and without remembrance. By incommodious encampments and unwholesome stations, where courage is useless and enterprise impracticable, fleets are silently dispeopled, and armies sluggishly melted away.

That was no exaggeration. In an era when there was no effective defense against infectious disease, the toll among soldiers could be staggering. In the Seven Years War, for every man who died in battle, an incredible total of eighty-eight died of disease. And Johnson's outrage is all the more impressive since he had no personal experience of war. It was his keen moral imagination that "presented its evils to his mind."[5]

The appalling quotation about smiling in death is from Joseph Addison's 1705 poem *The Campaign,* which celebrated the triumph at Blenheim of Britain's "godlike leader," the Duke of Marlborough. The poem gained a lucrative government position for the poet, and the victory gained the nation's gift of Blenheim Palace for Marlborough.

Addison (Boswell's "Mr. Spectator") was a mild-mannered individual, but his poem was bloodthirsty:

> Rivers of blood I see, and hills of slain,
> An Iliad rising out of one campaign. . . .
> A thousand villages to ashes turn,
> In crackling flames a thousand harvests burn.

Johnson's outrage at Addison's glorification of war anticipates Wilfred Owens's searing poem *Dulce et Decorum Est* and Robert Graves's bitter memoir *Goodbye to All That.*[6]

In this regard Adam Smith, the Enlightenment thinker, was less enlightened than Johnson. In his *Theory of Moral Sentiments* he wrote blandly, "In war, men become familiar with death, and are thereby necessarily cured of that superstitious horror with which it is viewed by the weak and unexperienced. They consider it merely as the loss of life." Merely![7]

IRELAND

An iniquitous example of Britain's treatment of its colonies was very close at hand, in Ireland, though technically it was a nation within Great Britain and not a colony. Its status was very different from that of Scotland. When Queen Elizabeth died in 1603, James VI of Scotland became James I of England and Scotland, and thereafter the Scottish Stuart dynasty was on the throne in London. The union of England and Scotland was ratified in 1707, when Queen Anne was the last of the Stuart monarchs, with the abolition of the Scottish Parliament and representation of Scots in London.

It took generations for the concept of a single nation to be fully accepted, but throughout the eighteenth century the concept of "Britishness" steadily gained ground. George III, whose grandfather spoke no English when he became King George I, delighted his subjects by declaring, "Born and educated in this country, I glory in the name of Briton."[8]

Ireland was never British in that sense. During the civil wars of the 1640s the Catholics in Ireland sided with the English royalists. After the royalist army fell to the Puritan rebels and Charles I was executed, Oliver Cromwell punished the Irish with a campaign of atrocities that was followed by a disastrous famine. A policy of colonization from England was then established, and it continued even after Charles II, the son of the late king, regained his throne in the Restoration of 1660.

By the end of the seventeenth century, the great majority of Catholic landowners had been dispossessed and replaced by English Protestants, most of whom were Anglicans. In the northern province of Ulster, the immigrants were Presbyterians from Scotland, laying the groundwork for bitter tensions in the ensuing centuries, and for the separation of Protestant Northern Ireland from the Irish Republic in the twentieth century.

In the world in which Burke and Goldsmith grew up, a Protestant minority known as the Ascendancy—approximately 15 percent of the Irish population—had virtually complete power over the huge Catholic majority, who were denied many basic civil rights. The administrative head in Ireland was a Lord Lieutenant appointed by the British crown, in the same way that provincial governors were sent out from England to Jamaica and Massachusetts.

Unlike the Scots, the Irish could not elect members of Parliament, and their own provincial Parliament's decisions were regularly vetoed by the British government. After the slogan "no taxation without representation" became popular in the American colonies, it was often heard in Ireland as well.[9]

A crucial way in which Ireland differed from Scotland was that it was forbidden to compete with England economically. Trade in woolen cloth had always been a mainstay of the English economy (to this day, the Speaker of the House of Lords is seated symbolically on "the woolsack"). A great deal of wool was also produced in Ireland, but they were forbidden by law to export woolen fabric, which meant that they were forced to supply the English with raw materials from which the real profit would be made.

There was a highly skilled body of weavers in Dublin, and this unfair prohibition was highlighted by Jonathan Swift in the 1720s in his *Drapier's Letters,* in which he impersonated a concerned cloth merchant. Though the Anglican Dean of St. Patrick's Cathedral, he was an Irish patriot, and is remembered as one of the first to speak for the entire people of Ireland and not just for the privileged Ascendancy.

Quoting from the Book of Joshua, Swift preached an angry sermon in St. Patrick's on the "causes of the wretched condition of Ireland." "The first cause of our misery is the intolerable hardships we lie under in every branch of our trade, by which we are become *as hewers of wood and drawers of water* to our rigorous neighbors." As for the people in the countryside, the Gaelic-speaking majority was regarded by those in power as semicivilized savages, and there was an ugly strain of racism in the way they were treated.

British policy contributed directly to episodes of economic depression, during which enormous numbers of Irish people couldn't find work. Swift wasn't exaggerating when he complained in the same sermon of "that great number of poor who, under the name of common beggars, infest our streets, and fill our ears with their continual cries and craving importunity." It was that scandal that provoked his immortal satire *A Modest Proposal,* in which he suggested that the English might as well eat Irish babies since they were already devouring Ireland in every other way.[10]

Catholicism, though not illegal, had to operate undercover. Only Protestants could attend Trinity College in Dublin and enter the professions; that was why Burke's father converted from Catholicism as the best means of supporting his family.

A series of laws known collectively as the Penal Code enforced rigid Protestant control, and growing up in that environment sensitized Burke to the nature of oppression, in ways that would deeply inform his views on America and India. In Parliament he campaigned energetically for Catholic emancipation, although he didn't live to see it happen, and he called the penal laws "as well fitted for the oppression, impoverishment, and degradation of the people, and the debasement in them of human nature itself, as ever proceeded from the perverted ingenuity of man."[11]

Johnson had many close Irish friends. Three of the original nine members of the Club—Burke, his father-in-law Nugent, and Goldsmith—were Irish, and so were Thomas Sheridan, Arthur Murphy, and others. But although Johnson was sympathetic to the plight of the Irish people, he absolutely refused to acknowledge that they deserved any political rights. As early as the twelfth century the Normans had ruled Ireland, and in the sixteenth century the Tudor monarchs consolidated British rule there. In Johnson's mind, the Irish rebellion in the seventeenth century was just that—not resistance to oppression, but sedition.

When Johnson was conversing with an Irish clergyman, Thomas Campbell, the question of Irish rights came up. With his customary overstatement Johnson declared, "Sir, you *do* owe allegiance to the British, as a *conquered* nation; and had I been minister I would have made you submit to it, and I would have done as Oliver Cromwell did, I would have burned your cities and roasted you in the flames of them." The diatribe went on for a while, and Campbell tactfully kept quiet. "After this wild rant, argument would but have enraged him; I therefore let him vibrate into calmness."[12]

AMERICA

In principle the American colonies were governed in much the same way as Ireland, with a governor sent out from London, and British troops on hand to enforce order. In practice, though, they enjoyed much more control over their own affairs, simply because they were so far away. It was not uncommon to take six weeks to cross the Atlantic, and with unfavorable winds it could be longer. Micromanaging from London was almost impossible, and the colonists had grown accustomed to a good deal of autonomy. Burke put it well: "There is a parenthesis of three thousand miles of ocean between the beginning and end of every sentence we speak of America."[13]

In the 1770s tensions rose between the colonies and the British government, and came to a head on the question of taxation. The government's position was that it cost a lot of money to defend the colonies against the French and their Indian allies, and it simply made sense for the colonists to help pay for that. The colonial position was "no taxation without representation." Burke sympathized with the colonists; Johnson emphatically did not.

Beyond the immediate issues, Johnson harbored contempt toward Americans in general, and was often provoked to denounce them. One reason for his contempt was that the settlers had stolen their land from the Indians. In 1773 he wrote to the agent for Connecticut in London, with whom he had grown friendly, "I do not much wish well to discoveries, for I am always afraid they will end in conquest and robbery."[14]

Incidentally, another colonial agent Johnson met was Benjamin Franklin, who was in London representing Pennsylvania, but there is no evidence of any conversation between them. Franklin does turn up a couple of times in Boswell's journals, but with no indication that he might be someone worth knowing. At one point Boswell mentions Franklin's humor in passing, but only to highlight one of his own similes, of which he was always so vain. Boswell had dropped in at the London lodgings of Sir John Pringle, a Scottish physician and old friend of Lord Auchinleck, and found him with Franklin playing chess. "Sir John, though a most worthy man, has a peculiar, sour manner. Franklin again is all jollity and pleasantry. I said to myself, 'Here is a fine contrast: acid and alkali.'"[15]

Johnson also thought that the settlers were mostly the dregs of British society: "They are a race of convicts, and ought to be thankful for anything we allow them short of hanging." As for the more prosperous merchants and planters, in their pursuit of wealth they were giving up all the benefits of civilization. "A man of any intellectual enjoyment will not easily go and immerse himself and posterity for ages in barbarism." A casual remark in the *Lives of the Poets* indicates Johnson's prejudice: "The eldest son was disinherited and sent to New Jersey, as wanting common understanding."[16]

As for political rights, Johnson regarded the American colonies just as he did Ireland. His claim that the Irish should have been roasted in flames was made in 1781, the year of the Battle of Yorktown. Even though he sympathized with the native Americans whose land was stolen from them, neither he nor anyone else thought of giving it back. Morally, this may be a contradiction of Johnson's views on colonialism, but in the end he was always a pragmatist.

So however the colonies were originally acquired, by now they were simply British. Most of the colonists themselves felt that way; the American Founders all grew up thinking of themselves as Englishmen. To Johnson that meant that they had the right to submit petitions, but never to rebel. And if nobody in the colonies could vote, well, that was simply how the system worked. "By his own choice," Johnson said, a settler in America "has left a country where he had a vote and little property, for another where he has great property but no vote."[17]

That was in a pamphlet entitled *Taxation No Tyranny*. It was widely believed that Johnson wrote it as payback for his government pension, and he definitely received official advice before printing it. Boswell says, "That this pamphlet was written at the desire of those who were then in power, I have no doubt; and indeed, he owned to me that it had been revised and curtailed by some of them." It was apparently originally too intemperate for even the administration to think appropriate. And the pamphlet almost certainly played a role in the award of his honorary doctorate from Oxford, where politics were always conservative.[18]

Not many people were impressed by *Taxation No Tyranny*. Boswell called it "a piece of magnificent sophistry," which is about right, and from journalists it attracted a stream of abuse. Their kindest description of Johnson was "old surly pensioner." Other writers called him a "tool of traitors," a "mercenary reptile," and a "scribbling prostitute."[19]

Perhaps surprisingly, Boswell sided with the Americans. As a lawyer, he believed that the colonial assemblies had been granted by charter the right to levy their own taxes, a commitment that ought to be honored. He also believed that the colonists were fighting for the same "liberty" that the Corsicans did. When news arrived of Cornwallis's surrender at Yorktown, he wrote to Paoli to report feelings of "joy."[20]

Since Burke was a firm supporter of the American cause, he and Johnson had a tacit agreement never to talk about it. Boswell (of course) wasn't so cautious. When Johnson "roared terribly" against the colonists, Boswell made a comment—he doesn't say what—in their favor. After that "the cloud was charged with sulphureous vapour, which was afterwards to burst in thunder." The conversation then took a different turn, to Bennet Langton's spendthrift ways, and the advisability of his living more cheaply in Lincolnshire than in London. "I said, 'All his friends must quarrel with him, which will make him go.' 'Nay, Sir,' said Dr. Johnson irritatedly, 'we'll send you to him. If your company does not drive a man out of his house, nothing will.' This was a horrible blunt shock, and I was stunned with it."

However, they soon made it up. Boswell may have been intoxicated at the time, since he next remarked that he would be happier if he could give up wine. "'Well,' said [Johnson], 'you must not drink wine and you shall not drink wine.' This he said with the most friendly, pleasing kindness." Boswell then ventured to ask Johnson why he had let the conversation wander off into a discussion of Langton's finances before belatedly delivering his insult. "'Because,' said he, 'I had nothing ready. A man cannot strike till he has his weapons.'" Boswell put most of that in the *Life,* but left out the part about the wine, and added a stage direction: "JOHNSON (smiling) Because, Sir, I had nothing ready." Boswell adds, "This was a candid and pleasant confession."[21]

It was in his speeches on America that Burke first gained his reputation as an orator. In 1773 Lord North's administration passed a Tea Act intended to relieve the near-bankrupt East India Company by granting it a monopoly to export tea duty-free to America. That would mean that tea from India would actually become cheaper in America, notwithstanding a modest tax of three pence on every pound in weight. Taxes on five other commodities—the hated Townshend duties—had been discontinued, but this one remained, not for income so much as for an assertion of principle. That was the principle that Boswell considered invalid, and in America the ensuing protests resulted in the Boston Tea Party, an ominous sign that a major confrontation might be at hand.

Burke's understanding of these issues was deepened by a position he held from 1770 to 1775, as London agent for the New York colony. In addition to a welcome salary of £500 a year, that furnished him with an informed understanding of colonial problems.

Burke's immediate response to the Tea Act was his *Speech on American Taxation,* followed in 1775 by the great *Speech on Conciliation with the Colonies.* In both of these parliamentary speeches he showed extraordinary mastery of detail, together with compelling argument. In the speech on taxation he emphasized the folly of imposing a new provocation on the nearly two million colonists whose relationship with the mother country had been developing for a century and a half. "Be content to bind America by laws of trade; you have always done it. Let this be your reason for binding their trade. Do not burden them by taxes; you were not used to do so from the beginning. Let this be your reason for not taxing. These are the arguments of states and kingdoms. Leave the rest to the schools; for there only they may be discussed with safety."

Shortly after saying that, Burke gave a histrionic performance of the kind that would become famous. Working himself up to a pitch of emotion, he seemed to be on the point of fainting. "Such is the state of America that after wading up to your eyes in blood, you could only end just where you begun; that is, to tax where no revenue is to be found, to—my voice fails me; my inclination, indeed, carries me no further; all is confusion beyond it." After a pause Burke pulled himself together, or seemed to, and addressed the Speaker again: "Well, Sir, I have recovered a little, and before I sit down I must say something to another point . . ."[22]

Burke's fertility in metaphors was much admired, and the *Speech on Taxation* has a spectacular example, criticizing William Pitt by literalizing the term "cabinet" as if it were a piece of furniture:

> He made an administration so checkered and speckled; he put together a piece of joinery so crossly indented and whimsically dovetailed; a cabinet so variously inlaid; such a piece of diversified mosaic; such a tesselated pavement without cement; here a bit of black stone, and there a bit of white; patriots and courtiers, King's friends and republicans, Whigs and Tories, treacherous friends and open enemies—that it was indeed a very curious show; but utterly unsafe to touch, and unsure to stand on. The colleagues whom he had assorted at the same boards stared at each other, and were obliged to ask, "Sir, your name?—Sir, you have the advantage of me—Mr. Such a One—I beg a thousand pardons." I venture to say, it did so happen, that persons had a single office divided between them, who had never spoke to each other in their lives, until they found themselves, they knew not how, pigging together, heads and points, in the same truckle-bed.[23]

In the *Speech on Conciliation* Burke elaborated an emotional vision of community that he would invoke for the rest of his career, a shared commitment far deeper than laws and institutions.

> Do not dream that your letters of office, and your instructions, and your suspending clauses, are the things that hold together the great contexture of this mysterious whole. These things do not make your government. Dead instruments, passive tools as they are, it is the spirit of English communion that gives all their life and efficacy to them. It is the spirit of the English constitution, which, infused through the mighty mass, pervades, feeds, unites, invigorates, vivifies every part of the empire, even down to the minutest member.[24]

Alexis de Tocqueville would say very much the same thing sixty years later in *Democracy in America,* stressing the importance of "habits of the heart." A German-born journalist in Boston, Francis Lieber, had given him the foundational idea. "Every day," Lieber told Tocqueville, "I'm more inclined to think that constitutions and political legislation are nothing in themselves.

They are the superstructure, to which only the mores and social condition of the people can give life." That formulation is altogether Burkean.

English translations misrepresent Tocqueville's "superstructure" by translating literally the French expression *oeuvres mortes,* as if the Constitution was a "dead creation." But *oeuvres mortes* is an idiom that refers to the superstructure of a ship, which would be useless without the great submerged hull, the *oeuvres vives* alive in the sea.[25]

The *Speech on Conciliation* was a triumph, as Burke's brother Richard related. "He began at half past three, and was on his legs until six o'clock. From a torrent of members rushing from the house when he sat down, I could hear the loudest, the most unanimous and the highest strains of applause, that such a performance, even from him, was never before heard in that house."[26]

It's customary today to say that the American Revolution was really no revolution at all, in the sense that the French Revolution would be. That's true; life in the new nation went along much as it always had, with the same patricians firmly in control. Still, it *was* a new nation, with a formal written constitution—something Britain has never had. "A great revolution has happened," Burke wrote in a manuscript draft. "A revolution made not by chopping and changing of power in existing states, but by appearance of the new state among mankind, of a new species, in a new part of the earth. It has made as great a change in all the relations and balances and gravitations of power, as the appearance of a new planet would in the system of our solar world."[27]

It was Burke's fate to analyze and critique British policy from the stance of an outsider. That gave him valuable perspective, but for someone eager to influence events, it was also deeply frustrating. In an extended discussion at the Club in 1778, already quoted, Sheridan commented that Burke's speeches never seemed to produce actual legislation. Burke replied that his arguments might still gradually make a difference, but he also acknowledged ruefully, "I believe in any body of men in England I should have been in the minority; I have always been in the minority."[28]

All the same, Burke was right. His ideas did gain influence, and even his opponents acknowledged his brilliance. After the war ended in 1782, he received a remarkable tribute from General John Burgoyne, whose surrender at Saratoga in 1777 had been a turning point in the American war. In addition to his military rank Burgoyne was a member of Parliament, and he said of Burke that "he reverenced him the more because he knew the real source of his attachment to proceed principally from a generous concern for the unfortunate, and a disinterested feeling for the oppressed and persecuted." As

David Bromwich says, "It is not the usual language of a defeated general in an imperial war."[29]

In an essay on Burke, Woodrow Wilson made a comment that gains force from his own experience: "The materials of his thought never appear in the same form in which he obtained them. They have been smelted and re-coined. Burke is not literary because he takes from books, but because he makes books, transmuting what he writes upon into literature. He is a master in the use of the great style. Every sentence, too, is steeped in the colors of an extraordinary imagination. The movement takes your breath and quickens your pulses."[30]

INDIA

With his personal experience of oppression in Ireland much in mind, Burke now joined in a crusade to end, or at least minimize, oppression in India. The situation there was very different from that in America. Englishmen had been living in America for generations, and continued to regard themselves as English. If they didn't yet outnumber the native Americans it was clear that they soon would. India had a huge indigenous population and an ancient civilization, dominated by the great religions of Hinduism, Buddhism, and Islam. Britain was simply exploiting the subcontinent for commercial purposes, and gradually acquired political control merely in order to support the East India Company.

When the Company was established in 1600, its royal charter was granted to "the Governor and Company of Merchants of London Trading into the East Indies." That's exactly what they were—merchants. What Adam Smith said about the Danish Virgin Islands (the United States didn't acquire them until 1918) would apply equally well to Bengal, and he probably meant it to: "The government of an exclusive company of merchants is, perhaps, the worst of all governments for any country whatever." As Linda Colley describes the dilemma, Britain "acquired too much power, too quickly, over too many people."[31]

The Rockingham Whigs, whose spokesman Burke was, decided to publicize the injustice by demanding parliamentary oversight of the East India Company. That would make India something like a colony on the model of the others around the world, instead of a cash cow controlled by de facto rulers whom nobody had appointed to that role. In 1783 they made their demand in an East India Bill, sponsored by Charles James Fox. It passed in the House of Commons but was defeated in the House of Lords.

Fox had been a member of the Club since 1774, and he and Reynolds were close friends. As a contribution to publicity, Reynolds painted an impressive portrait from which a print was made (figure 46, page 164 above). The papers below Fox's right hand were originally blank, but at the last minute he asked Reynolds to put in the inscription: "A Bill for the better regulating the affairs of the E. I. Company, &c."[32]

In the event, Fox's party lost the 1784 election, and his career would be on a decline from then on. He joined the opposition, with himself as political strategist and Burke as intellectual leader. Bromwich says, "The company of Burke made Fox a wiser man, and the company of Fox made Burke a freer mind."[33]

The next move to bring justice to India was a sensational trial in Parliament to impeach Warren Hastings, the governor general of India, on charges of gross corruption. It was launched in 1783 and would drag on with intermissions until 1791, when Hastings would finally be acquitted. Fox and Burke may have expected that. What they were really doing was raising British consciousness about what was being done far away.

Macaulay's tribute to Burke's achievement has never been surpassed. "He devoted years of intense labour to the service of a people with whom he had neither blood nor language, neither religion nor manners in common, and from whom no requital, no thanks, no applause could be expected." Burke never saw India in person, but he mastered dry documents about it in exhaustive detail, and then he transformed them. "Out of darkness and dullness and confusion, he formed a multitude of ingenious theories and vivid pictures. India and its inhabitants were not to him, as to most Englishmen, mere names and abstractions, but a real country and a real people." Macaulay himself spent five years as a civil servant in India.[34]

Burke's speech demanding impeachment of Hastings was no brief performance. It was delivered in installments over a period of four days, with a large audience in rapt attention. His fundamental point was that India was inhabited by "a people for ages civilized and cultivated, whilst we were yet in the woods." Even after the British government took over direct control from the East India Company, the administrators it sent out were ill trained and mainly interested in getting rich and returning home.[35]

As Burke's rhetoric swelled, the indictment of his country was overwhelming.

Young men (boys almost) govern there, without society and without sympathy with the natives. . . . Animated with all the avarice of age and all the impetuosity of youth, they roll in one after another, wave after wave; and there is nothing before the eyes of the natives but an endless, hopeless prospect of new flights of birds of prey and passage, with appetites continually renewing for a food that is continually wasting. . . . England has erected no churches, no hospitals, no palaces, no schools; England has built no bridges, made no high roads, cut no navigations, dug out no reservoirs. Every other conqueror of every other description has left some monument, either of state or beneficence, behind him. Were we to be driven out of India this day, nothing would remain to tell that it had been possessed, during the inglorious period of our dominion, by anything better than the orangutan or the tiger.[36]

The effect on Burke's listeners was overwhelming. Macaulay conjured up the scene in a description that became famous: "The ladies in the galleries, unaccustomed to such displays of eloquence, excited by the solemnity of the occasion, and perhaps not unwilling to display their taste and sensibility, were in a state of uncontrollable emotion. Handkerchiefs were pulled out; smelling bottles were handed round; hysterical sobs and screams were heard; and Mrs. Sheridan was carried out in a fit."[37]

This was Burke's ringing conclusion:

I impeach Warren Hastings, Esquire, of high crimes and misdemeanours.

I impeach him in the name of the Commons of Great Britain in parliament assembled, whose parliamentary trust he has betrayed.

I impeach him in the name of all the Commons of Great Britain, whose national character he has dishonoured.

I impeach him in the name of the people of India, whose laws, rights and liberties he has subverted, whose properties he has destroyed, whose country he has laid waste and desolate.

I impeach him in the name and by virtue of those eternal laws of justice which he has violated.

I impeach him in the name of human nature itself, which he has cruelly outraged, injured and oppressed, in both sexes, in every age, rank, situation and condition of life.[38]

Second only to Burke in oratory was Sheridan, shown in a contemporary image accusingly brandishing "Charges against W. Hastings" (color plate 28).

The colors are significant. Buff and blue had been adopted as a sort of uniform by the Whig party, and the rubicund cheeks and nose testify to Sheridan's notorious consumption of alcohol.

When it was his turn to hold forth he did so for nearly six hours without a pause, ending with an emotional evocation of Indian gratitude if British oppression were relieved—"the workings of the heart, the quivering lips, the trickling tears, the loud and yet tremulous joys of the millions whom your vote of this night will forever save from the cruelty of corrupted power. . . . It is with confidence, therefore, that I move you on this charge, 'that Warren Hastings be impeached.'" There was uproarious applause. Gibbon, who attended the trial, said that Sheridan "surpassed himself," and added with amusement, "Sheridan in the close of his speech sunk into Burke's arms. I called this morning—he is perfectly well. A good actor!"[39]

If the attack on Hastings failed in the short run, over time the crusade had its intended effect. Burke's arguments continued to be read in later generations, and influenced Englishmen like Macaulay and John Stuart Mill who spent time working in India. A historian pays an impressive tribute: "As the torrent of Burke's oratory poured forth in the House, sentiment became a real force which must drive any government to action. For the first time there were heard in the House expressions of regret (to become common among the humanitarians of the nineteenth century) that Europeans had ever set foot on these distant shores and imposed their wills on these alien societies. Of this humanitarianism Burke was certainly the main inspiration, and it is impossible even now to read his words without being stirred."[40]

SLAVERY

Further in the background in British social consciousness was the moral problem of slavery, but it was getting increasing attention, and calls for abolition were beginning to be heard.

In England and Ireland all slaves were freed in 1772, and in Scotland in 1778. In both cases that happened as a result of legal decisions: slave owners who had brought black servants back with them from the West Indies were compelled to set them free, on the grounds that slavery was illegal under English and Scottish law.

The Scottish case concerned a Negro named Joseph Knight whose master had brought him from Jamaica. Boswell, who thought that "the mildest and best regulated slavery" was fully acceptable, had to concede that "the sooty stranger" was legally entitled to freedom. As usual, he wrote to get Johnson's opinion, and received in reply a strong argument in favor of Knight. Much though Johnson may have disliked Rousseau, his reasoning is identical to Rousseau's in the *Social Contract:* "It is impossible not to conceive that men in their original state were equal, and very difficult to imagine how one would be subjected to another but by violent compulsion. . . . No man is by nature the property of another; the defendant is therefore by nature free." Johnson added that "the laws of Jamaica afford a Negro no redress. His colour is considered as a sufficient testimony against him. It is to be lamented that moral right should ever give way to political convenience."[41]

After quoting this eloquent statement in the *Life*, Boswell proceeded to refute it, or so he believed. "I have read, conversed, and thought much upon the subject." His reading and thinking produced this statement: "To abolish a status, which in all ages God has sanctioned and man has continued, would not only be robbery to an innumerable class of our fellow subjects, but it would be extreme cruelty to the African savages, a portion of whom it saves from massacre or intolerable bondage in their own country and introduces into a much happier state of life; especially now when their passage to the West Indies and their treatment there is humanely regulated. To abolish that trade would be to 'shut the gates of mercy on mankind.'" The quotation is from Gray's *Elegy.*[42]

Meanwhile, people in the colonies overseas could still own slaves. In the *Life* Boswell quotes two trenchant comments of Johnson's, though inserting his own opinion in between them: "When in company with some very grave men at Oxford, his toast was, 'Here's to the next insurrection of the Negroes in the West Indies.' His violent prejudice against our West Indian and American settlers appeared whenever there was an opportunity. Towards the conclusion of his *Taxation No Tyranny* he says, 'How is it that we hear the loudest *yelps* for liberty among the drivers of Negroes?'"[43]

It was true: the merchants in Bristol, whom Burke represented in Parliament, took a moderately radical position in domestic politics, but thanks to their location in the west of England with ready access to the sea, they dominated the slave trade. For them "liberty" applied to British citizens but not to all human beings. As Burke anticipated, his uncompromising opposition to slavery was a major factor in their refusal to renominate him as a candidate in 1780.

In the year the *Life* came out, Boswell published a three-hundred-line poem entitled *No Abolition of Slavery, or the Universal Empire of Love.* It was anonymous, but he was proud of it, and told all his friends he had written it. His biographer Frank Brady calls it "surely the strangest piece he ever wrote," and that's putting it mildly.[44]

After sneering references to the abolitionist crusader William Wilberforce and his allies in Parliament, Boswell declares himself "an ancient Baron of the land," extols "wise subordination's plan," and rises to a grotesquely dishonest picture of life in the Caribbean plantations:

> Lo then, in yonder fragrant isle
> Where Nature ever seems to smile,
> The cheerful gang! the Negroes see
> Perform the task of industry:
> E'en at their labour hear them sing,
> While time flies quick on downy wing.
> Finished the business of the day,
> No human beings are more gay:
> Of food, clothes, cleanly lodging sure,
> Each has his property secure.

Not just gaily singing, but secure in the possession of private property! Boswell obviously knew nothing about actual conditions in the colonies, and didn't trouble to find out.

Finally, to bring the subject as usual around to himself, Boswell segues into a description of his own amorous enslavement by some unnamed lady—

> For slavery there must ever be,
> While we have mistresses like thee!

That accounts for the Universal Empire of Love.[45]

In 1807 the slave trade in the British colonies would be abolished (by then, of course, the United States were no longer British). But if importing slaves was now illegal, slavery itself remained untouched in the empire wherever it was already in place. Not until 1833 would the Slavery Abolition Act put an end to that. Meanwhile the words of Burke, and of Sheridan too, continued to resonate. In 1830, when he was twelve years old, Frederick Douglass got hold of a collection of speeches entitled *The Columbian Orator,* and in it he found "one of Sheridan's mighty speeches" in favor of Catholic emancipation in Ireland. "What I got from Sheridan was a bold denunciation of slavery, and a powerful vindication of human rights."[46]

When the Club was founded there was an understanding that politics, if not exactly taboo, should be discussed as little as possible. One reason Johnson began attending less frequently was the accession of members, most of them little remembered today, with outspoken Whiggish sympathies that were anathema to him. Burke, though a Whig, was a very conservative one, just as Gibbon was. It's true that Johnson was passionately opposed to Burke's views on Ireland and America, but they seem to have gotten along simply by avoiding the subject. As for the trial of Warren Hastings, that didn't begin until shortly before Johnson's death.

CHAPTER 17

Adam Smith

In every European country in the eighteenth century, and especially in Britain, financial issues were increasingly in the foreground. A global empire was a source of wealth, but also a financial burden for the government that had to defend it by expensive wars. Taxation policy generated lively debate, and for the first time the British government created a large national debt. Capital for investment was raised by the sale of stocks, and in the 1770s the London Stock Exchange was established to give structure to what were previously agreements signed in coffeehouses. Meanwhile the entire economy was changing rapidly, as new industries began to emerge.

All of these issues called for a coherent science of economics. What was then known as "political economy" was only just beginning to widen its scope. Johnson's *Dictionary* gives five definitions for the word "economy," and not one of them is what we usually mean by it today. They begin with "the management of a family; the government of a household;" and continue on with "frugality; discretion of expense; laudable parsimony."

Political economy was understood by analogy: it was simply managing the finances of a nation as one would manage a household. Political economy thus meant specific financial measures adopted by a ruler or his administrators. But Adam Smith and other thinkers, particularly in France, had begun to theorize about what we mean today by "the economy"—the immense web of impersonal forces that operate with their own logic, and are never more than partially responsive to administrative actions.

Smith was elected to the Club in 1775, at the age of fifty-two, and at that time nobody could have thought of him as an economist. He got in on the strength of his 1759 *Theory of Moral Sentiments,* an attempt to show that moral values are acquired through social interaction. The book was widely read at the time, but it is very dry and abstract, and if he had done nothing else, few people today would know his name.

What Smith went on to do, of course, was to publish his masterpiece in 1776. The portrait reproduced here (figure 84) identifies him as the author of *The Wealth of Nations.* Boswell, who had been his student at Glasgow, mentioned casually that when he dropped in to see Smith in 1775, "he said that he was near finishing his book on commerce." Boswell probably thought that that was a mundane and uninteresting subject.[1]

Smith never knew his father, a minor customs official in the town of Kirkcaldy, across the Firth of Forth from Edinburgh, who died six months before he was born in 1723. His mother remained a widow, and his latest biographer comments that he was "content to spend his life with the only woman who mattered, his mother."[2]

The Author of the Wealth of Nations

84. Adam Smith

He was a studious young man, and thanks to receiving a generous fellow-ship he was able to spend six whole years at Oxford. The fellowship was originally intended to educate future Presbyterian ministers, but by his time that career was not obligatory.

After giving public lectures in Edinburgh, where he had no academic post, in 1751 Smith became Professor of Logic and Metaphysics at the University of Glasgow. A year after that he was elected Professor of Moral Philosophy, and he did indeed think of himself as concerned with human behavior in all its aspects. His lectures that Boswell heard were on rhetoric, by which was meant not just literary style, but persuasive public language in the tradition of Cicero. The emphasis was on language as a social instrument, and Smith recommended a straightforward plain style instead of the elaborate figures of speech that older rhetoricians liked to use.[3]

A few anecdotes that have survived suggest that Smith was literally an absent-minded professor, not very attentive to his immediate surroundings because his thoughts were elsewhere. At breakfast he once rolled bread and butter into a ball, dropped it into a teapot, and filled the pot with water. When he took a sip he complained it was the worst tea he had ever encountered in his life.[4]

Smith never thought of himself as a career academic, and he stopped being a professor as soon as he could. A wealthy patron could pay a tutor more handsomely than the fees he was able to collect personally from his students, which in Scotland was pretty much the only income a professor had. Accordingly, he accepted a job tutoring Lord Buccleuch, then a teenager, the stepson of the Charles Townshend who would sponsor the Townshend Acts that infuriated the Americans. It was a congenial relationship, and they remained close for years.

After 1762 Smith could have called himself "Dr. Smith," having been awarded a doctorate of laws by Glasgow, but like Johnson he didn't care to. He told his publisher, Johnson's friend William Strahan, "Call me simply Adam Smith, without any addition either before or behind." The title of "Doctor" tended to be displayed by people who needed it for prestige, Goldsmith and Burney for example.[5]

Smith's closest friend was David Hume, and what has been said of Hume is true of both: "He saw himself as a moral philosopher, a student of human action in its broadest sense, comprehending aesthetics, ethics, politics, economics, literature, law, religion, and history." In a brief autobiographical sketch at the end of his life, Hume didn't call himself a philosopher, but instead "a man of letters."[6]

Considered simply as a member of the Club, Smith seems strangely recessive, and he barely appears at all in the *Life of Johnson.* When Smith was elected, Boswell commented to his friend Temple that the Club "has lost its select merit." But then, Boswell was incorrigibly sociable and Smith was a classic introvert, at ease only with people he knew well and trusted. With them he was very different, and the philosopher Dugald Stewart commented on "the splendor of his conversation." Stopping in at the Club during occasional visits to London, surrounded by competitive talkers who loved to show off, Smith naturally kept quiet.[7]

He and Johnson never got along. Johnson called him "as dull a dog as he had ever met with." He also complained to Boswell that "Adam Smith was the most disagreeable fellow after he had drank some wine, which, he said, 'bubbled in his mouth.'" Boswell made a perceptive comment: "Smith was a man of extraordinary application, and had his mind crowded with all manner of subjects; but the force, acuteness, and vivacity of Johnson were not to be found there."

It was true also that Smith knew he had original things to say, and wanted to say them persuasively in print, not in social settings where they could be misunderstood or co-opted by others. Boswell added, "He had book-making so much in his thoughts, and was so chary of what might be turned to account in that way, that he once said to Sir Joshua Reynolds that he made it a rule when in company never to talk of what he understood."[8]

In the *Theory of Moral Sentiments* Smith described the characteristics of "the prudent man" in what was virtually a self-portrait. "As he is cautious in his actions, so he is reserved in his speech, and never rashly or unnecessarily obtrudes his opinion concerning either things or persons. . . . Though capable of friendship, he is not always much disposed to general sociality. He rarely frequents, and more rarely figures in, those convivial societies which are distinguished for the jollity and gaiety of their conversation." In short, not Johnson's kind of companion, or Boswell's either.[9]

Smith, in turn, was bemused by Johnson's eccentricities. An anonymous memoirist reported Smith saying of Johnson, "I have seen that creature bolt up in the midst of a mixed company, and without any previous notice fall upon his knees behind a chair, repeat the Lord's Prayer, and then resume his seat at table. He has played this freak over and over, perhaps five or six times in the course of an evening." That seems very hard to believe, since nobody else ever described such behavior from Johnson. If Smith did say it, he may have been deliberately exaggerating Johnson's fierce commitment to orthodox religion. Like Hume, Smith was a skeptical deist, with implications that will be taken up later.[10]

Something Johnson once said to Charles Burney suggests a tolerant view of public praying, but not encouragement of it. After his poet friend Christopher Smart had a religious conversion, he began to pray continuously, no matter where he might be. That inspired pity in Johnson: "Madness frequently discovers itself merely by unnecessary deviation from the usual mode of the world. My poor friend Smart showed the disturbance of his mind by falling upon his knees, and saying his prayers in the street, or in any other unusual place."[11]

For his own good, Smart's friends had him confined in an asylum. Johnson's comment on that was, "I did not think he ought to be shut up. His infirmities were not noxious to society. He insisted on people praying with him; and I'd as lief pray with Kit Smart as anyone else." Touchingly, a long free-verse poem that Smart wrote while insane, *Jubilate Agno,* contains this line: "Let Johnson, house of Johnson rejoice with Omphalocarpa a kind of burr. God be gracious to Samuel Johnson."[12]

Beyond their differences in temperament and religious beliefs, Smith and Johnson differed profoundly in intellectual styles. Johnson was a moralist, reflecting on how people ought to act; Smith was a social scientist, analyzing how they did act. Johnson was an essayist, writing ad hoc as opportunities turned up, and producing a very miscellaneous body of work. Smith was a theorist, and produced formal treatises, matured over many years.

THE WEALTH OF NATIONS

An Inquiry into the Nature and Causes of the Wealth of Nations was explicitly intended as a sequel to the *Theory of Moral Sentiments.* It takes for granted that human beings have moral, intellectual, and aesthetic motives as well as economic ones. Although Smith never managed to complete the great project he envisioned, *The Wealth of Nations* was to have been followed by two further books, one on literature and philosophy, and one on law and government.

Smith himself said later that *The Wealth of Nations* was "a very violent attack upon the whole commercial system of Great Britain," but it seems not to have been perceived that way. On the contrary, it was immediately recognized as a major breakthrough in understanding where national wealth comes from.[13]

The traditional view had been that people are the wealth of a nation, but only if they are productive. Those who worked hard but at a subsistence level, far from being understood as contributing in any way, were stigmatized as "the poor." Although they might deserve charity on religious grounds, economically they were considered parasites. A different but equally traditionalist view was being urged by a group of French thinkers known as the physiocrats (from a Greek word meaning "government of nature"). According to them it was land, not people, that represented the wealth of a nation, which meant that a government should actively promote agriculture. Smith spent some time in Paris and got to know the physiocrats personally, notably François Quesnay and Anne-Robert-Jacques Turgot.[14]

Smith rejected both of these positions. His groundbreaking approach was indeed to focus on commerce, as Boswell anticipated, and beyond that, on ways in which productivity could be stimulated and wages raised. If each worker could contribute to increased productivity, perhaps "the poor" need not be an unalterable underclass after all.

Famously, right at the beginning of his book, Smith gave the example of a pin factory. Rather than theorize about productivity in the abstract, he visited working factories—mostly small at that time—whose owners were putting an altogether new concept into practice. The first chapter of *The Wealth of Nations* is entitled "Of the Division of Labour." When he visited a pin factory, Smith discovered that no fewer than eighteen separate operations were involved in fabricating a simple pin. And his insight, based on practical observation, was that productivity could be enormously increased if each worker did just one or two of those operations instead of all of them.

> One man draws out the wire, another straightens it, a third cuts it, a fourth points it, a fifth grinds it at the top for receiving the head; to make the head requires two or three distinct operations; to put it on, is a peculiar business, to whiten the pins is another; it is even a trade by itself to put them into the paper [in which they were packaged for sale]; and the important business of making a pin is, in this manner, divided into about eighteen distinct operations, which in some manufactories are all performed by distinct hands, though in others the same man will sometimes perform two or three of them. I have seen a small manufactory of this kind where ten men only were employed, and where some of them consequently performed two or three distinct operations. But though they were very poor, and therefore but indifferently accommodated with

the necessary machinery, they could, when they exerted themselves, make among them about twelve pounds of pins in a day. There are in a pound upwards of four thousand pins of a middling size. Those ten persons, therefore, could make among them upwards of forty-eight thousand pins in a day.

Smith calculated that by contrast, a single person making pins by himself could turn out twenty a day at most.[15]

What made *The Wealth of Nations* so original, and what Smith meant by calling it an attack on the current economy, was that it was prophetic of the nineteenth-century factory system. In his time most production, notably of textiles, was still essentially domestic, in what was known as the "putting-out system." Employers provided materials that people would work with in their own homes. But iron and steel, and the powerful machines constructed from them, obviously could not be made at home.

When Johnson was a young man, Birmingham, where he met and married his wife, was a relatively small town. By the end of the century it was well on the way to becoming an industrial giant, the center of the metalworking industry. Matthew Boulton and James Watt established their Soho Manufactory (the original form of the word "factory") there in the 1760s, specializing in steam-driven pumps intended for mining. Within ten years they employed a workforce of eight thousand. A mile away was their Soho Foundry, located beside a canal on which shipments could be conveniently made.[16]

In 1776 Johnson visited Birmingham with Boswell and got a glimpse of the future. Boulton showed them around his factory. Boswell noted in his journal, "Boulton seemed to be a clever, fine fellow. I regretted that I did not know mechanics well enough to comprehend the description of a machine lately invented by him, which he took great pains to show me. 'I sell, Sir,' said he, 'what all the world desires to have—power.'" Boswell had only a dim appreciation of how oracular that pronouncement was. As for Johnson, he mentioned the encounter in his sketchy diary, but without enthusiasm. "We then went to Boulton's, who with great civility led us through his shops. I could not distinctly see his enginery." That apparently means that Johnson's shortsightedness prevented him from understanding the complicated machinery.[17]

Smith believed that promoting the division of labor was socially progressive, since he envisioned workers selling their labor to the highest bidder, freed from the closed-shop monopolies that had controlled most trades since the Middle Ages. If productivity increased many times over, surely everyone would get a bigger share of the profits.

History would soon show how mistaken that was, but Smith was optimistic because of a complementary strand in his theory—the "invisible hand." That meant a self-regulating logic to the market, by which the law of supply and demand always produces the best possible distribution of society's resources. When a merchant or industrialist strives to maximize his gains, "he is in this, as in many other cases, led by an invisible hand to promote an end which was no part of his intention. Nor is it always the worse for the society that it was no part of it. By pursuing his own interest he frequently promotes that of the society more effectually than when he really intends to promote it."[18]

Another comment of Smith's often gets quoted: "It is not from the benevolence of the butcher, the brewer, or the baker that we expect our dinner, but from their regard to their own interest. We address ourselves not to their humanity but to their self-love, and never talk to them of our own necessities, but of their advantages."[19]

Smith didn't place any reliance on altruistic benevolence, because he didn't believe most people had it. He wanted to show that selfishness can produce positive results in spite of itself. But he was not, as is widely assumed, an unquestioning believer in laissez-faire, a term he never used. It was just then being invented by the French physiocrats, and didn't enter regular usage in England until the 1820s.

In *The Wealth of Nations,* Smith speaks sternly of "the mean rapacity, the monopolizing spirit of merchants and manufacturers, who neither are nor ought to be the rulers of mankind." Even if personally honest, they remain "an order of men whose interest is never exactly the same with that of the public, who have generally an interest to deceive and even to oppress the public, and who accordingly have, upon many occasions, both deceived and oppressed it."[20]

It follows that government intervention, rather than laissez-faire, would often be necessary. Nevertheless, Smith didn't believe that a gap between the rich and poor was intrinsically unjust. "Civil government," he said flatly, "so far as it is instituted for the security of property, is in reality instituted for the defense of the rich against the poor, or of those who have some property against those who have none at all."[21]

It's important to emphasize that Smith never believed, as some later economists would, that economic behavior is exclusively self-interested, and still less that an abstraction called "rational man" could account for everything that happens. He was well aware that altruistic impulses, moral convictions, and ingrained habits also play important roles, and he thought he had made that clear in his *Theory of Moral Sentiments*. What he was doing in *The Wealth of Nations*, as the philosopher Hans Vaihinger argued in a classic analysis, was clarifying some essential features of economic life by proceeding *as if* egoism was always the fundamental principle.[22]

Smith's economic theory predicted that the poor would benefit, in the long run, from the operation of the free market. But that was only an assumption, and in *Adam's Fallacy* Duncan Foley calls it more "theological" than provable: a faith that the invisible hand not only orders the economy more effectively than government policies can, but also makes everyone's life better. Not for nothing was Smith's first book about moral philosophy. His concern, as Foley says, was the one that has haunted economic thinking ever since: "how to be a good person and live a good and moral life within the antagonistic, impersonal, and self-regarding social relations that capitalism imposes."[23]

CHAPTER 18

Edward Gibbon

In 1769 Goldsmith published *The Roman History, from the Foundation of the City of Rome to the Destruction of the Western Empire.* It was frankly derivative, based on easily available sources, but it was readable, and was reprinted for generations to be used in schools. Goldsmith knew that Gibbon was at work on a far more ambitious history, and in 1774 he generously proposed Gibbon for membership in the Club. No one had any objection, and he was duly elected. As it happens, that was the year of Goldsmith's death.

Just two years after that, Gibbon could not possibly have gotten into the Club. In 1776 the first volume of his *History of the Decline and Fall of the Roman Empire* came out. It was immediately recognized as a masterpiece, but there was an element of scandal. Gibbon was openly skeptical of claims that the spread of Christianity could only be explained by miraculous divine intervention. Gibbon argued that there were ample secular explanations for its success. He also questioned the historical reality of much that supposedly happened in the early years of the Church.

Johnson and Boswell both loathed Gibbon, whom they referred to as "the Infidel," and they would certainly have blackballed him if they had known what he was writing. When we look through their eyes, consequently, he is even less visible as a Club member than Adam Smith. Yet from other sources we learn that Gibbon greatly enjoyed attending, which he did more often than nearly anyone, and was engagingly talkative. Thomas Barnard, an Irish bishop who was elected a year after Gibbon, wrote years later to tell Boswell, "I always thought his familiar conversation the most valuable part of his character, as well as the most agreeable feature about him." Boswell chose not to quote that in the *Life of Johnson*.[1]

One of Gibbon's rare appearances in the *Life* comes in an account of a meeting of the Club in 1775. Johnson proclaimed in his dogmatic way that there was no point in reading history, since no skill was needed to report facts, and anything beyond facts was pointless conjecture. Boswell comments, "Mr. Gibbon, who must at that time have been employed upon his history, of which he published the first volume in the following year, was present; but did not step forth in defense of that species of writing. He probably did not like to trust himself with Johnson!" Johnson was doubtless aware of the forthcoming book and was deliberately goading Gibbon.[2]

It seems highly unlikely that Gibbon was afraid of Johnson, however. He knew, better than anyone, how often a historian has to weigh ambiguous evidence, and he always tells the reader frankly when he is offering conjectures and not facts. But he had no wish to be shouted at, let alone to be lectured on writing history by somebody who claimed it was absurdly easy. His biographer D. M. Low comments acerbically, "Mr. Gibbon could afford to bide his time and knew how to hold his tongue, an incomprehensible art for Boswell."[3]

DISCOVERING A VOCATION

Edward Gibbon was born in London in 1737, and grew up in Buriton, a little Hampshire village sixty miles to the southwest, where his family had a comfortable brick manor house. They were well off, or had been; his father was rapidly squandering an inherited fortune.

If Gibbon was born to prosperity, he was not so fortunate in his health. During his childhood he was always being treated for something or other. In his *Memoirs* he commented, "There was a time when I swallowed more physic than food, and my body is still marked with the indelible scars of lancets, issues and caustics." According to Johnson's *Dictionary,* an issue is "a vent made in a muscle for the discharge of humours," such as he himself had endured as a child. When Edward was three years old, a new baby was also christened Edward, in the obvious expectation that the first one would soon be dead. He remembered this shocking fact so vividly that he claimed that every successive boy was named Edward, though that was not actually the case.[4]

From his parents, he didn't receive much affection. His father was self-centered and remote; his mother, who was constantly pregnant, ignored her sickly eldest child—the only one of her seven children who actually survived—and died after ten years of marriage when he was nine years old.

The boy's education was haphazard, alternating between uninspiring temporary tutors and occasional episodes in schools, where he was bullied. It didn't help that he was odd looking, with a frail spindly body and an enormous head, crowned by vivid red hair (there's a lock of it in the British Museum).

Fortunately, there was one important loving adult in the boy's life. That was his mother's unmarried sister Catherine—Aunt Kitty, he called her—who lived with the family. She would stay up all night at his bedside when he was ill. In addition to giving unstinting affection, she nurtured his precocious love of reading. He adored books of historical romance that introduced him, at an early age, to some of the most memorable characters who would appear in the *Decline and Fall*—Richard the Lion Heart and his noble Saracen opponent Saladin; Tamerlane the Magnificent; Genghis Khan.

When Gibbon was fifteen his imagination was seized by a history of Rome that he happened upon, and as he recalled, "I was immersed in the passage of the Goths over the Danube when the summons of the dinner bell reluctantly dragged me from my intellectual feast." Low says that he crossed the Danube into the heart of the Roman Empire, and never came out of it again. By the end of the following year, Gibbon added, he had "exhausted all that could be learned in English of the Arabs and Persians, the Tartars and Turks." They, too, would figure largely in the *Decline and Fall*.[5]

There was an unexpected crisis, with crucial significance for the future historian, when Gibbon enrolled at Magdalen College, Oxford at the age of fifteen. That was a normal age to enter the university in those days; there were no real entrance requirements, much less competitive exams. Oxford was more like a finishing school than a modern university, with little taught except Latin and Greek (that was exactly what Johnson liked about it, of course). History was not taught at all.

Gibbon remembered his brief time at Magdalen with contempt. His tutor, he said, "well remembered that he had a salary to receive, and only forgot that he had a duty to perform." The crisis came after a single year. Suddenly, in 1753, he experienced a conversion to Roman Catholicism. As he described it long afterward, it was provoked by theological arguments, but it was undoubtedly also an act of rebellion against his father. A few years later Boswell would do the same thing.[6]

From the elder Gibbon's point of view, young Edward's conversion meant that the family stood to be financially ruined, since anti-Catholic laws would prevent him from inheriting the estate. Not until the Popery Act of 1778 were Catholics permitted to inherit and purchase land, and then only if they swore to reject the temporal authority of the Pope. That legislation was one of the triggers that provoked the anti-Catholic Gordon Riots of 1780.

Gibbon's father lost no time shipping him off to Lausanne in Switzerland, to live with a Protestant pastor there and get over his folly. The culture shock was staggering. Gibbon's host and tutor, the kindly David Pavillard, spoke no English, and the boy didn't know any French. Fortunately he had a gift for languages, and rapidly became fluent. By the time he left Lausanne, he was thinking and writing in French more easily than English.

That fluency would turn out to be invaluable for Gibbon's later work, since a vast amount of French research had never been translated into English. Still more important, it connected him with the thinking of the continental Enlightenment, which most Englishmen regarded with distrust, and his great history would have been impossible without it. While in Lausanne, he worked hard on perfecting his Latin, too. The method he used was characteristic of his disciplined work habits. He would translate a Latin text into French, wait some months until he no longer remembered the original well, and then see if he could translate it back into the original words.

By patient reasoning Pavillard managed to wean the youth from Catholicism, but his father was in no hurry to bring him home, and he remained in Lausanne for five long years. There he fell in love, apparently for the only time in his life. Suzanne Curchod was the beautiful and brilliant daughter of another Swiss pastor; she found Gibbon attractively different from her usual admirers, and they planned to get married. When his father found out about that, he was appalled all over again. He had no intention of letting his son marry a penniless foreigner, so he threatened to cut him off without a shilling, and ordered him to come home at once.

Back at Buriton, Edward pleaded his case earnestly but in vain. As he put it tersely in the *Memoirs,* "I sighed as a lover; I obeyed as a son." That statement has often been derided as dispassionate, and it's true that Gibbon was not especially passionate, but he was certainly affectionate. What it really represents is an effort to see himself objectively, trapped in a conflict between irreconcilable roles, like a character in a French classical drama. As for Suzanne, she went on to make a happy marriage with the great financier Jacques Necker, and Gibbon was their guest in Paris in later years.[7]

Gibbon's time in Buriton was now divided between two very different pursuits. One was intensive study of works of history, and he kept buying books whenever he could afford them. The other may seem surprising. In 1760 both Gibbons, father and son, enlisted as officers in the county militia. It was the midpoint of the Seven Years War, and there was much resentment of the German mercenaries the government had hired to augment its army. So Parliament passed an act to establish English militias, which would be manned by volunteers and commanded by country gentlemen. The elder Gibbon became a major and his son a captain.

Young Edward, still just twenty-three, enjoyed it. The Hampshire Militia never came close to fighting. Indeed, they never left England at all, but they did a lot of drilling, and there were convivial drunken evenings with fellow officers (one of whom happened to be John Wilkes). In the *Memoirs* Gibbon described the experience as invaluable for his later work: "The discipline and evolutions of a modern battalion gave me a clearer notion of the phalanx and the legion, and the captain of the Hampshire grenadiers (the reader may smile) has not been useless to the historian of the Roman Empire." That wry parenthesis—"the reader may smile"—is an example of his willingness to be ironic about himself, but what he says is true. He always took a keen interest in the tactics employed in ancient battles, and in the fateful consequences that flow from unwise military decisions.[8]

Gibbon's ideal of living was what used to be called epicurean: not gross sensuality, but moderate, civilized enjoyment of pleasures. He liked to recall a statement the seventeenth-century diplomat William Temple made in retirement, that the gratifications of the public world are as nothing compared with "old wood to burn, old wine to drink, old friends to converse with, and old books to read."[9]

On the issue of inherited wealth and privilege, Gibbon felt no embarrassment at all. In the *Decline and Fall* he contrasts modern civilization with primitive "barbarism." Admittedly, he says, the great majority have no choice but to work hard for a living, but they should not resent the privileged class that has a different role to play. "The select few, placed by fortune above that necessity, can fill up their time by the pursuits of interest or glory, by the improvement of their estate or of their understanding, by the duties, the pleasures, and even the follies of social life." The few are "select" not necessarily because they deserve it, but because fortune has happened to place them there.[10]

In 1764 Gibbon set off for a two-year Grand Tour of Italy; the end of his stay overlapped with the beginning of Boswell's, but they didn't meet. In his

Memoirs he traced the origin of his masterpiece to a single moment of epiphany that occurred during this tour. "It was at Rome, on 15 October, 1764, as I sat musing amidst the ruins of the Capitol while the barefooted friars were singing Vespers in the temple of Jupiter, that the idea of writing the decline and fall of the city first started to my mind."[11]

Most of the buildings of ancient Rome were long gone by then, cannibalized over the years for building stones. Those that did survive, like the grand Coliseum, were semi-ruins. The one ancient structure that remained unchanged was the awe-inspiring Pantheon, and that was because it had been repurposed as a Catholic church. And the way the Empire was replaced by the Church was exactly what Gibbon was thinking about. He believed—mistakenly, as it happens—that the church where the friars were singing vespers was located where the temple of Jupiter once stood. That had been the central symbol of the old pagan religion. And all around the church lay the ruins of the Capitol, once the nerve center of a vast empire that stretched from the Atlantic Ocean to the Middle East, and from cold, remote Britain to the then-fertile regions of North Africa.

LONDON

After nearly incredible mismanagement by Gibbon's father, the family's financial situation collapsed altogether in 1768, and he was given the thankless task of trying to repair the damage. When his father died in 1770 he didn't feel much grief. The next two years were devoted to selling off properties and restructuring debts. By 1772 he had restored order, and with quiet rejoicing moved into a townhouse in London. He was free at last to do what he felt he had been born to do. "No sooner was I settled in my house and library," he says, "than I undertook the composition of the first volume of my history."[12]

In 1774, the year of his election to the Club, Gibbon got elected to Parliament. That was something Boswell eagerly desired for himself but was never able to accomplish. What Gibbon had, and Boswell didn't, was a well-disposed patron. A cousin of Gibbon's in Cornwall, in the far southwest, controlled a seat there and made it available.

The constituency was small as well as remote, and since Gibbon could count on automatic reelection, he never went there at all. He made a joke about that, playing on the fact that he was increasingly overweight. He asked: "Why is a fat man like a Cornish borough?" The answer was: "Because he never sees his member."[13]

Like Burke, Gibbon was a conservative Whig, convinced that power should be centered in a landed oligarchy. He also acquired a lucrative government sinecure, a position in the Board of Trade for which hardly any work was required. In response he voted loyally with Lord North's Tory government on the American question, and even dedicated the *Decline and Fall* to North.

Having had a taste of military life, the historian was now experiencing politics. It began as a humiliation. He was hoping to make a name by delivering eloquent speeches, but could never screw up the courage even to try. After a few months he wrote to his closest friend, the future Lord Sheffield, "Alas, I have remained silent, chained down to my place by some invisible unknown invisible power." He was so distressed that he wrote "invisible" twice.[14]

That was in 1775, when he was nearly finished with the first volume of the *Decline and Fall*. As J. G. A. Pocock says, "Gibbon uttered in his own mind the oratory he could never pronounce in public." Still, he learned a great deal. "I had a near prospect of the characters, views, and passions of the first men of the age. The eight sessions that I sat in parliament were a school of civil prudence, the first and most essential virtue of an historian."[15]

It was at about this time that Reynolds painted Gibbon's portrait, and in a print made from it a philosopher in a toga gazes meditatively at the ruined Coliseum (figure 85). As usual Reynolds did his best to be flattering, and Gibbon certainly thought he succeeded. Years later Charles James Fox noticed him "every now and then casting a look of complacency on his own portrait by Sir Joshua Reynolds, which hung over the chimney piece—that wonderful portrait in which, while the oddness and vulgarity of the features are refined away, the likeness is perfectly preserved." Less kindly observers said that Gibbon's pudgy face resembled the rear end of a baby.[16]

With Gibbon clearly in mind, Boswell wrote in the *Life of Johnson*—published when Gibbon was still alive—"I think ridicule may be fairly used against an infidel; for instance, if he be an ugly fellow, and yet absurdly vain of his person."[17]

Gibbon's London years came to an end in 1782. By then the second and third volumes of the *Decline and Fall* were in print, with three more to go. Burke had been leading a campaign for government reform, and he got the Board of Trade abolished. There went the sinecure that had made possible Gibbon's comfortable London existence. He and Burke were good friends, but Burke could hardly exempt this particular department from his general campaign.

Gibbon understood that, and never held it against Burke, but he had no intention of withdrawing into rural isolation in Hampshire. Instead, he

85. Edward Gibbon

decided to move to Lausanne, where he could live cheaply and still have an agreeable circle of friends. With one of them, Georges Deyverdun, he shared a house in which he wrote the second half of the *Decline and Fall*. And it was there that he drafted the never-completed fragments of what became his *Memoirs* (Sheffield would stitch them into a coherent narrative after his death). It was a peaceful, unhurried existence, with enjoyable work during the day, and evenings reserved for pleasant socializing.

Gibbon's friends were increasingly concerned that he couldn't stop putting on weight, as a lithograph made at that time shows clearly (figure 86). Sheffield told him that if he lay down on his back on the floor he would be like a turtle, unable to get up again. Though always charming, he struck many people as curiously artificial. The playwright George Colman the younger, fourteen years old when he met Gibbon in Lausanne, remembered being treated with elaborate courtesy. "He tapped his snuff box, he smirked, and smiled, and rounded his periods with the same air of good breeding as if

86. Gibbon at Lausanne

he were conversing with men. His mouth, mellifluous as Plato's, was a round hole, nearly in the centre of his visage."[18]

A NEW KIND OF HISTORY

At the time of his youthful epiphany in Rome, Gibbon had thought of writing a history of just the city. By the time he tackled the project in earnest, the American colonies were breaking away, and the subject of empires and their decline had become intensely topical. To trace the long and complex story of the "decline and fall" was sure to fascinate British readers, as it fascinated Gibbon himself.

In one of his later volumes, describing Rome's struggles to hold on to its far-flung territories, Gibbon described the obstacles to maintaining an empire in terms that were altogether relevant in his own time.

There is nothing perhaps more adverse to nature and reason than to hold in obedience remote countries and foreign nations, in opposition

to their inclination and interest. An extensive empire must be supported by a refined system of policy and oppression: in the center an
absolute power, prompt in action and rich in resources; a swift and
easy communication with the extreme parts; fortifications to check
the first effort of rebellion; a regular administration to protect and
punish; and a well-disciplined army to inspire fear, without provoking
discontent and despair.[19]

Britain's power was very far from absolute, and swift and easy communication
was impossible. Of course the American colonies were not regarded as a foreign nation, but they soon would be.

Not only was Gibbon writing about a subject that was much in the news,
he was also writing a new kind of history. The philosophes of the Enlightenment, with Voltaire as their hero, believed they had achieved a breakthrough
in historiography. Instead of tedious chronicles of facts, they claimed to pen-
etrate beneath the surface to identify the essential forces that made things
happen. That was known as "philosophic history."

Gibbon wanted to get beneath the surface, certainly, but he understood
that theories without facts are empty. For that reason he supplied the *Decline
and Fall* with approximately eight thousand footnotes, some very detailed, so
that readers could be sure where he got his information, and could consider
whether he had interpreted it convincingly. Obvious though that procedure
may seem today, it was unprecedented at the time. It had never crossed Voltaire's mind to write a single footnote. "When he treats of a distant period,"
Gibbon said of Voltaire, "he is not a man to turn over musty monkish writers
to instruct himself. He follows some compilation, varnishes it over with
the magic of his style, and produces a most agreeable, superficial, inaccurate
performance."[20]

That adjective "monkish" was a red flag for intellectuals. They took it for
granted that medieval religious writers put such a biased spin on their stories
that they should simply be dismissed. Gibbon recognized the bias, but he also
knew that there had been religious writers, both Catholic and Protestant,
with the highest intellectual integrity. Those writers really did their best to
weigh evidence and present it accurately. Several of them were among his
most valued sources, as he gratefully acknowledged.

Many historians, even today, have been tempted to write as if they had
total understanding of what happened long ago. But the best historians have
always known that readers learn much more from being taken behind the

scenes, pondering the available evidence along with the author. Much of the time the evidence is far from conclusive, and then the historian's job is to help us evaluate it. Throughout the *Decline and Fall* Gibbon takes us with him on that quest.

At the beginning of his tenth chapter Gibbon sets out to describe what he calls a "calamitous period" during the middle of the third century: "The confusion of the times, and the scarcity of authentic memorials, oppose equal difficulties to the historian who attempts to preserve a clear and unbroken thread of narration. Surrounded with imperfect fragments, always concise, often obscure, and sometimes contradictory, he is reduced to collect, to compare, and to conjecture." The historian would like to establish a "clear and unbroken thread," but he shouldn't pretend to do so when it's simply not possible.[21]

Hume, who scored a big success with his *History of England* that was completed in 1761, said complacently that we read history "to see all [the] human race, from the beginning of time, pass as it were in review before us; appearing in their true colours, without any of those disguises which during their lifetime so much perplexed the judgment of the beholders." There speaks a "philosophic historian," believing that with his penetrating intelligence and objectivity, he is able to recover reality itself. By implication, an ancient Roman, despite access to a vast stream of information that is totally lost today, understood the world of Augustus or Caligula less well than an eighteenth-century British historian could.[22]

In his critique of Voltaire, Gibbon also mentions that Voltaire never possessed "the art of narrating." Dense and complex as the *Decline and Fall* is, it sustains its storytelling momentum, and the narrative is constantly enlivened by memorable incidents and characterizations. As a young army officer in India, Winston Churchill began to read seriously for the first time, and he started with the *Decline and Fall.* "I was immediately dominated both by the story and the style. All through the long glistening middle hours of the Indian day, from when we quitted stables till the evening shadows proclaimed the hour of polo, I devoured Gibbon. I rode triumphantly through it from end to end and enjoyed it all."[23]

Unlike the pompous Victorian editor of the edition he was using, Churchill added, he enjoyed the "naughty footnotes." One example will serve: "Twenty-two acknowledged concubines, and a library of sixty-two thousand volumes, attested the variety of his inclinations; and from the productions which he left behind him, it appears that the former as well as the latter were designed for use rather than for ostentation."[24]

As Churchill's absorption in the "story" suggests, in addition to its extraordinary mastery of detail, the *Decline and Fall* has many of the virtues of a great novel. Gibbon loved Fielding's *Tom Jones,* published in 1749. In his *Memoirs* he says, "The romance of *Tom Jones,* that exquisite picture of human manners, will outlive the palace of the Escurial and the imperial eagle of the House of Austria." He was perfectly right about that. In a footnote in the *Decline and Fall* he points to something Fielding had said in *Tom Jones:* "Comfort me by a solemn assurance that when the little parlor in which I sit at this instant shall be reduced to a worse furnished box, I shall be read with honor by those who never knew nor saw me, and whom I shall neither know nor see." Gibbon hoped that posterity would value the *Decline and Fall* in the same way.[25]

One reason Gibbon admired *Tom Jones* is that Fielding, a lawyer and judge by profession, makes a point of teaching us to distrust appearances. He encourages us to look for motives and connections that we originally missed, or to reconsider apparent evidence that we interpreted wrongly. Since Fielding was making up his story, he could guarantee the stable truth beneath the misleading appearances. In the *Decline and Fall,* all we have to go on is fragments of ambiguous evidence from the distant past. Sometimes the evidence seems convincing, but Gibbon reminds us that we still have to think about who wrote it down back then, and what their agenda might have been. Much of what we think we know about many characters in the story comes from enemies who hated them. Gibbon's great achievement is to help readers to construct the narrative along with him.

When the first volume of the *Decline and Fall* came out, Gibbon received a splendid personal response from a distinguished contemporary. Horace Walpole wrote to congratulate him and asked, "How can you know so much, judge so well, possess your subject and your knowledge and your power of judicious reflection so thoroughly, and yet command yourself and betray no dictatorial arrogance of decision? You have unexpectedly given the world a classic history."[26]

A modern editor of Hume's *History of England* says that Hume's style "is the fastest and smoothest vehicle in historical literature." That may be the style most appreciated today, but it's not Gibbon's, any more than it was Johnson's. Their style was periodic, and their unit was the fully crafted paragraph. "It has always been my practice," Gibbon says, "to cast a long paragraph in a single mould: to try it by my ear, to deposit it in my memory, but to suspend the action of the pen until I had given the last polish to my work."[27]

It's that art of balancing, bringing out parallels and setting antitheses against each other, that creates a coherent structure for what might otherwise be bafflingly confused. By means of Gibbon's style, Lytton Strachey says, "lucidity, balance, and precision were everywhere introduced, and the miracle of order was established over the chaos of a thousand years." In G. M. Young's metaphor, the style "has the calculated solidity of a Roman aqueduct." Gibbon's narrative marches forward on massive and equally spaced arches, while the stream flows steadily along the channel at the top.[28]

As Gibbon's narrative continued to grow, he became increasingly skeptical that clear lines of cause and effect could be extracted from the past. There are too many variables for that, and he loved to imagine what the consequences might have been if certain events had turned out differently. One such event was the Battle of Tours in 732. That was when Charles Martel defeated the Moors, and Christendom was saved "by the genius and fortune of one man" in "an encounter which would change the history of the world." But what if the Moors had won? "The Arabian fleet might have sailed, without a naval combat, into the mouth of the Thames. Perhaps the interpretation of the Koran would now be taught in the schools of Oxford, and her pulpits might demonstrate to a circumcised people the sanctity and truth of the revelation of Mahomet." J. W. Burrow observes, "Gibbon never lost the historian's indispensable attribute of wonder—a sense that things could have turned out otherwise."[29]

FAREWELL TO A LIFE'S WORK

However odd and affected Gibbon may have seemed, his mannerisms were no bar to personal and professional fulfillment. Unlike either Boswell or Johnson, he discovered very early what he felt born to accomplish, and accomplish it he did. Leslie Stephen said that he had "that peculiar balance or harmony of all the faculties which enables a man to get the very greatest possible result out of given abilities." The description is accurate, and poignant too. Stephen was the father of Virginia Woolf, and in *To the Lighthouse* he appears as the philosopher Mr. Ramsay, who anguishes over his failure to achieve what he might have done.[30]

Gibbon was fortunate, as well, to have an exceptionally optimistic temperament. When Johnson was sixty he told a friend that "he never passed that week in his life which he would wish to repeat, were an angel to make the proposal to him." Gibbon relates the story of a caliph in Córdoba who left this message at his death: "Riches and honours, power and pleasure, have waited on my call, nor does any earthly blessing appear to have been wanting to my felicity. In this situation I have diligently numbered the days of pure and genuine happiness which have fallen to my lot: they amount to FOUR-TEEN. O man! place not thy confidence in this present world!" Gibbon adds a personal footnote: "If I may speak of myself (the only person of whom I can speak with certainty), *my* happy hours have far exceeded, and far exceed, the scanty numbers of the caliph of Spain; and I shall not scruple to add that many of them are due to the pleasing labor of the present composition."[31]

After moving to Lausanne, Gibbon kept in touch with his friends back home, including a number of members of the Club. It happened that he revisited England at the time of the Warren Hastings trial, and got to hear Burke and Sheridan in their oratorical glory. Listening to one of Sheridan's speeches in Parliament, he was especially delighted by a reference to himself. Sheridan declared, "Nothing equal in criminality is to be traced, either in ancient or modern history, in the correct periods of Tacitus, or the luminous pages of Gibbon." In his *Memoirs* Gibbon wrote, "Mr. Sheridan's eloquence demanded my applause; nor could I hear without emotion the personal compliment which he paid me, in the presence of the British nation." A joke went around, however, that what Sheridan really meant to say was not "luminous," but "voluminous."[32]

Looking back at the epic achievement that had taken twenty years to complete, Gibbon wrote a quiet ending to the story that began when he heard the barefooted friars singing in the former temple of Jupiter. The scene now was Lausanne, with a view of the Alps on the far side of Lake Geneva.

> I have presumed to mark the moment of conception; I shall now commemorate the hour of my final deliverance. It was on the day, or rather the night, of the 27th of June, 1787, between the hours of eleven and twelve, that I wrote the last lines of the last page in a summer house in my garden. After laying down my pen, I took several turns in a *berceau,* or covered walk of acacias, which commands a prospect of the country, the lake, and the mountains. The air was temperate, the sky was serene, the silver orb of the moon was reflected from the waters, and all nature was silent. I will not dissemble the first emotions of joy on the recovery of my freedom, and perhaps the establishment of my fame. But my pride was soon humbled, and a sober melancholy was spread over my mind, by the idea that I had taken my everlasting leave of an old and agreeable companion, and that whatsoever might be the future date of my history, the life of the historian must be short and precarious.[33]

CHAPTER 19

Infidels and Believers

EVIDENCE AND BELIEF

Gibbon's account of the origins of Christianity in the *Decline and Fall*, though factually accurate, created an enormous scandal. Believers, which is to say most people, had a panicky reaction, and the reason why they felt so threatened makes it an interesting episode in cultural history.

Throughout the seventeenth century it was taken for granted that religious commitment rested on faith, an interior conviction of divinely revealed truth. But in the eighteenth century that premise seemed increasingly suspect to many people, because it smacked of the "enthusiasm"—from a Greek word meaning "possessed by a god"—that had energized the Puritan revolution and turned Britain upside down. Johnson defines "enthusiasm" as "a vain belief of private revelation, a vain confidence of divine favour." The definition is illustrated from Locke: "Enthusiasm is founded neither on reason nor divine revelation, but rises from the conceits of a warmed or overweening brain."[1]

A second problem with seeing faith as the guarantor of religion was that it contradicted the new philosophical orthodoxy known as empiricism. According to Locke and his successors, there is nothing in our minds that didn't come in through the senses. Like any other belief, religious belief was necessarily acquired through experience, and had to pass the test of argument and demonstration.

In his immensely popular 1690 *Essay Concerning Human Understanding,* Locke illustrated his thesis with an engaging anecdote. A Dutch ambassador in Siam used to entertain the king by describing the wonders of the land he came from. At one point, he mentioned that in winter, water would freeze solid. If the king's elephants were in Holland, they could walk right on top of a river. The king replied, "Hitherto I have believed the strange things you have told me, because I look upon you as a sober fair man; but now I am sure you lie."[2]

Naturally the king would find it incredible that at a certain temperature, a liquid would suddenly turn solid. He had never seen such a thing. But the empiricist has an effective answer: just go somewhere that does get cold enough, and you can personally verify that water freezes. Nobody expects you to take it on faith. It's not a miracle, it's a normal feature of the laws of nature.

By the middle of the eighteenth century, many people wanted their religious beliefs to be fully supported by factual proof, which they called "evidences of Christianity." One of the principal kinds of evidence was the miracles that occurred frequently when Jesus was alive, and for quite some time thereafter.

Roman Catholics believed that miracles never stopped happening. In fact, an essential criterion for canonizing individuals as saints was proof that they had caused at least two miracles, either during their lifetimes or afterward. Protestants, however, dismissed Catholic claims about recent miracles, arguing that they were either due to natural causes, or else were hoaxes. But that created a problem for Protestants. They still needed to believe that there really had been miracles during the early years of the Church, after which they ceased to happen.

But if all belief had to be grounded on empirical evidence, why wasn't the evidence for those early miracles even shakier than for the recent ones claimed by Catholics? Before saints could be canonized, Catholic investigators made sincere efforts to substantiate their alleged miracles. If Protestants sneered at those, how could they accept stories of miracles that had been handed down from fifteen hundred years earlier?

Gibbon thought they couldn't. Either all miracles were false, or else none of them were. When he was a student at Oxford, that reasoning provoked his temporary conversion to the church that said the miracles were all true.

One publication in particular created trouble for the orthodox. That was a chapter entitled "Of Miracles" in Hume's 1748 *Enquiry Concerning Human Understanding.* As a thoroughgoing empiricist, Hume took it as obvious that what we perceive with our own senses is always more reliable than what we learn from hearsay. We must always weigh probabilities, and if we haven't experienced something at first hand, we need to distrust reports that don't seem probable. Even when we hear alleged eyewitness accounts, we need to consider whether they may contradict each other, and also whether the people reporting them have an agenda of some kind.

After advancing several other arguments, Hume reaches his empiricist conclusion: "Upon the whole, it appears that no testimony for any kind of miracle has ever amounted to a probability, much less to a proof." Slyly, he concludes, "Our most holy religion is founded on faith, not on reason." He was a master of deadpan irony. He speaks of "our most holy religion," but of course he didn't believe that in the least.[3]

In the second conversation Boswell ever had with Johnson, the issue of "evidences" came up (very likely Boswell brought it up). Johnson reassured him by declaring, "The Christian religion has very strong evidences. No doubt it appears in some degree strange to reason. But in history we have many undoubted facts, against which, in reasoning *a priori*, we have more arguments than we have for them; but then, testimony has great weight, and casts the balance." In other words, objections based on the improbability of miracles are countered by the "testimony" of the early members of the Church who personally witnessed them, faced persecution for testifying to them, and had no reason to lie.[4]

The subject came up again a couple of months later, and Johnson offered a striking analogy. Without actually visiting Canada in person, he said, there was no way to be truly certain that Britain had captured it from France. The soldiers who fought there might be lying. "Now suppose you should go over and find that it is really taken, that would only satisfy yourself, for when you come home we will not believe you. We will say you have been bribed. Yet, Sir, notwithstanding all these plausible objections, we have no doubt that Canada is really ours. Such is the weight of common testimony. How much stronger are the evidences of the Christian religion?"[5]

THE SCANDALOUS FIFTEENTH AND
SIXTEENTH CHAPTERS

Gibbon ended the first volume of the *Decline and Fall* with two chapters on the rise of Christianity. It was a decision he later regretted; it might have been more prudent to save them for the second volume, published five years later. He was determined to treat the history of the Church as simply one historical phenomenon among many, not as the key to the meaning of history itself. Earlier writers claimed that an obscure and cruelly persecuted sect could never have conquered the world unless God was directly intervening in its favor. Its survival in spite of ruthless persecution was one favored kind of evidence, and so were the miracles performed on its behalf.

Gibbon's strategy was to mention the providential explanation right at the beginning, and then set it completely aside. It would have been impossible to prove that providence did *not* influence history, and he didn't try. What he did show was that "secondary causes," fully understandable in secular terms, were more than adequate to explain the success of Christianity. Those included the proselytizing zeal of the early Christians, their promise of immortality, their "pure and austere morals," and their organization as a militant body within the larger society.

It should be stressed that Gibbon never despised Christianity itself, as many of the French philosophes did. When he said that the morals of the early Church were pure, he meant it. As for Jesus, he admired him deeply, speaking of "his mild constancy in the midst of cruel and voluntary sufferings, his universal benevolence, and the sublime simplicity of his actions and character." What Gibbon did not believe was that Jesus was literally the Son of God, incarnated in human form. He thought of Jesus as a great teacher, whom later theologians reinvented as the second person of the Holy Trinity, using Greek philosophical concepts that Jesus himself never did.[6]

On the subject of immortality, Gibbon attacked the orthodox from an unexpected direction, the Old Testament. He commented that the immortality of the soul was taught in ancient India, in Egypt, and even in Gaul. So how is it that the writers of Hebrew Bible seem to have known nothing about it? "We might naturally expect that a principle so essential to religion would have been revealed in the clearest terms to the chosen people of Palestine, and that it might safely have been entrusted to the hereditary priesthood of Aaron. It is incumbent on us to adore the mysterious dispensations of Providence, when we discover that the doctrine of the immortality of the soul is omitted in the Law of Moses. . . . The hopes, as well as fears, of the Jews appear to have been confined within the narrow compass of the present life." Like Hume speaking of "our most holy religion," Gibbon says that we must "adore the mysterious dispensations of Providence," but he obviously believes no such thing.[7]

About miracles Gibbon was still more devastatingly ironic. According to the Gospels, when Christ was crucified the heavens were darkened for a space of three hours. In a footnote Gibbon observed that according to many Christian writers, the darkness covered the entire world. Yet there were pagans at the time who carefully recorded every earthquake and comet and eclipse. Why did they ignore this extraordinary event? "They omitted to mention," Gibbon says, "the greatest phenomenon to which the mortal eye has been witness since the creation of the globe."[8]

Modern theologians would not find that criticism meaningful. They would say that the Gospel writers were describing a symbolic event, not something that literally happened. But Gibbon's contemporaries needed all of the miracles to be real: they were indispensable evidence for the divine mandate of the Church.

As for the persecution of the early Christians, Gibbon had no trouble deploying evidence to show that although some episodes were certainly terrible, not many individuals were actually killed. Besides, most emperors were not persecutors at all, and during long periods Christianity was officially tolerated. Most of the dreadful stories told in later times, he argued, had to be pious fictions. He was able to quote early Church fathers who gave much less shocking accounts of persecutions than later authors did.[9]

Predictably, there was a firestorm of protest after the *Decline and Fall* was published, but Gibbon was unmoved. The only critique he bothered to answer was by a cocky young Oxford graduate who claimed to detect plagiarism and misquotation, claims that Gibbon easily refuted. In later volumes of the *Decline and Fall* he would go on to show great respect for individual leaders of the Church, but usually for their executive ability rather than their doctrines. And although he had little patience for theological controversy, he had the highest respect for the intellectual gifts of writers such as Saint Athanasius, even if he thought those gifts misapplied. He also honored the Church for caring for the poor and the sick, as the imperial government never did. But so far as doctrine was concerned, sly allusions kept up an undercurrent of attack.

One example is Gibbon's comment about the Lombards from the German hinterland who captured northern Italy in the sixth century. Following their victory, there was a period of religious competition between Christians and their pagan conquerors. The Catholics prayed for the conversion of the Lombard king, "while the more stubborn barbarians sacrificed a she-goat, or perhaps a captive, to the gods of their fathers." That provokes a wicked footnote: "Gregory the Roman supposes that they likewise adored this she-goat. I know but of one religion in which the god and the victim are the same."[10]

In the same chapter, Gibbon mentions that "a vague tradition was embraced that two Jewish teachers, a tent maker and a fisherman, had formerly been executed in the circus of Nero." Christian teaching did not consider the story of the tent maker and the fisherman a "vague tradition." The tent maker was Saint Paul and the fisherman Saint Peter, to whom Jesus said, "I will make you a fisher of men."[11]

From time to time, Gibbon also finds occasion to point out how miracles come to be believed in. During the time of the Crusaders—whom he regards as little better than land-grabbing thugs—a French priest learned in a vision that the "Holy Lance" with which Christ had been pierced at the Crucifixion was buried deep underground at Antioch. A pit was dug and turned up nothing, but the next morning a lance miraculously appeared in it. It was immediately guessed that the priest had put it there himself, and he was required to prove his veracity by a trial of fire, in which he burned to death.

Gibbon tells the story in order to draw a moral: "Yet the revelation of Antioch is gravely asserted by succeeding historians; and such is the progress of credulity that miracles, most doubtful on the spot and at the moment, will be received with implicit faith at a convenient distance of time and space." At another point Gibbon remarks that a number of early saints wrote accounts of their own lives, yet they never once mentioned the miracles that were later attributed to them.[12]

Boswell reports a discussion with Johnson about the *Decline and Fall,* in which he casts Gibbon as a virtual serpent in the garden, seducing his innocent readers. "We talked of a work much in vogue, written in a very mellifluous style, but which contained much artful infidelity. I said it was not fair to attack us thus unexpectedly. He should have warned us of our danger before we entered his garden of flowery eloquence, by advertising 'Spring-guns and man-traps set here.' " Landowners used to set man traps to catch poachers, the way the poachers themselves would trap a rabbit, and spring guns would fire when an unwary trespasser tripped over a wire attached to the trigger.[13]

THE ESTABLISHED CHURCH OF ENGLAND

For some people the philosophy known as deism was an appealing alternative to religious orthodoxy. Deists held that we can at least be certain that a divine being created the universe, simply by inspecting what would nowadays be called intelligent design: the solar system as beautifully functioning clockwork, and so on. For that reason it was called "natural religion," deducing truth from the same kinds of evidence that science did. But deists didn't claim to know anything about the nature of the deity, much less that he requires us to pray to him, promises everlasting life, and threatens torment to unbelievers.

Even people who found deism attractive feared that if it became widespread, it would weaken the morality that held society together, including its social and sexual hierarchy. A physician told Boswell, "If I thought deism the true religion, I would not say so to my wife."[14]

Johnson, like the orthodox in general, despised deism. For him, every one of the doctrines of Christianity was true, confirmed by the evidence recorded in the Bible and by later fathers of the Church. But that meant that the skepticism Johnson showed in every other context had to be firmly suppressed in this one.

To do that took tremendous determination. Hogarth once commented that Johnson not only believed the Bible, "but he fairly resolves, I think, to believe nothing *but* the Bible." In the *Life* Boswell said much the same thing: "He was so much impressed with the prevalence of falsehood, voluntary or unintentional, that I never knew any person who, upon hearing an extraordinary circumstance told, discovered more of the *incredulus odi*. He would say, with a significant look and decisive tone, 'It is not so. Do not tell this again.'" Horace's phrase means that if you tell me something incredible, "I detest and disbelieve it."[15]

On institutional religion, Johnson's position was not very different from that of Tom Jones's tutor Thwackum, whose name expresses his philosophy of education. "When I mention religion, I mean the Christian religion; and not only the Christian religion, but the Protestant religion; and not only the Protestant religion, but the Church of England." The Church of England enjoyed special privileges as the "establishment," woven into the political and social order. Its authority rested on the simple fact that it *was* established. Members of other Protestant sects—Congregationalists, Baptists, and so on—were known collectively as "Dissenters."[16]

Anomalously, in Scotland it was the Presbyterian Church that was officially established. Presbyterians in England were regarded as Dissenters.

Johnson never hesitated to say that although people were free to believe whatever they wished, they were not free in the least to publicize views that contradicted orthodoxy. "Consider, Sir. If you have children whom you wish to educate in the principles of the Church of England, and there comes a Quaker who tries to pervert them to his principles, you would drive away the Quaker. . . . Now the vulgar are the children of the state. If anyone attempts to teach them doctrines contrary to what the state approves, the magistrate may and ought to restrain him."[17]

The Church of England enjoyed a monopoly on higher education. No one could study or teach at Oxford and Cambridge who would not swear to the truth of an elaborate series of theological statements in the Prayer Book, known as the Thirty-Nine Articles. (Gibbon, whose historical research gave him deep understanding of the past theological controversies, liked to say that most believers didn't understand the meaning of the words they said as well as he did.)

Bishops had secular power, too; they sat and voted in the House of Lords, as representatives of the spiritual aristocracy. Johnson regarded that as entirely appropriate, though he admitted, "No man could now be made a bishop for his learning and piety, but because he is connected with somebody who has parliamentary interest." Many bishops accumulated great wealth. Boswell asked the Archbishop of York if it was true that he enjoyed an annual income of £6,000. He received a straightforward reply: "It is better. It is worth seven, and if there be no foolish expense, one may do all that is right and lay up money too. But I do not depend on it solely. I got a good fortune with my wife. I got £20,000, and that accumulates."[18]

Something that reformers deplored was the way clergymen were appointed to parishes, known as "livings." Those were in the gift of individual country gentlemen, who were free to make appointments entirely on their own with no outside consultation. Johnson had no problem with that, either. At one point he dictated an extended legal argument to Boswell contending that since most English churches were built long ago by lords of the manor, their descendants had every right to staff them according to their own preferences. And although it was true that few livings were now held by descendants of the original donors, the right to appoint clergymen was a form of property that could be conveyed along with the real estate itself.

Criticizing this practice, or suggesting that congregations should choose their ministers for themselves, was the type of social disruption that Johnson always feared: "Nor is any man more an enemy to public peace, than he who fills weak heads with imaginary claims, and breaks the series of civil subordination by inciting the lower classes of mankind to encroach upon the higher."[19]

Institutional religion was one thing; interior and personal religion was another. It may be that for many people at that time, religious affiliation was not much more than lip service. In a short book called *The Natural History of Religion,* Hume said, "Hear the verbal protestations of all men: nothing so certain as their religious tenets. Examine their lives: you will scarcely think that they repose the smallest confidence in them." Johnson did want to repose unquestioning confidence in them, and the result was spiritual torment.[20]

Late in Johnson's life, the philosopher and poet James Beattie—author of *An Essay on the Nature and Immutability of Truth*—admitted that he himself was "troubled with shocking impious thoughts" that he was unable to dispel. "Sir," Johnson replied, "if I was to divide my life into three parts, two of them have been filled with such thoughts." Boswell chose not to include that in the *Life.* At another time, after reading a sermon by Boswell's friend Hugh Blair, Johnson objected to the expression, "He who does not feel joy in religion is far from the kingdom of heaven." He commented grimly, "There are many good men whose fear of God predominates over their love. It may discourage. It was rashly said." His own faith has been well described as "terror-stricken orthodoxy."[21]

Six months before Johnson's death, Boswell accompanied him on a visit to William Adams, his old Oxford tutor and now master of Pembroke College. Dr. Adams said that death need not be feared since God is infinitely good.

> JOHNSON. That he is infinitely good, as far as the perfec-
> tion of his nature will allow, I certainly believe; but it is
> necessary for good upon the whole that individuals should
> be punished. As to an *individual,* therefore, he is not infi-
> nitely good; and as I cannot be *sure* that I have fulfilled the
> conditions on which salvation is granted, I am afraid I may
> be one of those who shall be damned (looking dismally).
> DR. ADAMS. What do you mean by damned?
> JOHNSON. (passionately and loudly). Sent to Hell, Sir, and
> punished everlastingly![22]

THE GREAT INFIDEL

When Boswell recorded dialogues at the Club in the *Life of Johnson,* he identified Gibbon with the initial "I," his code for "infidel." That was what he liked to call unbelievers, probably because it sounded more wicked. In the *Dictionary* Johnson defines "infidel" as "an unbeliever; a miscreant; a pagan; one who rejects Christianity." When Gibbon's narrative reaches the Crusades he has a footnote on the word "miscreant," which comes from the old French word *mécreant. A créant* is a believer, which means that a *mécreant* is simply an unbeliever. Gibbon comments, "It should seem that the zeal of our ancestors boiled higher, and they branded every unbeliever as a rascal. A similar preju-dice still lurks in the minds of many who think themselves Christians."[23]

In reality, Boswell's contempt for Gibbon was probably based more on personal dislike than on religious disagreement. David Hume was just as much an infidel as Gibbon, and Boswell was very fond of Hume, whom he often saw in Edinburgh. When they got together Boswell did argue in favor of religious belief, without accomplishing any more than he had with Vol-taire. Still, he enjoyed himself with Hume. "I had really a good chat with him this afternoon. . . . It was curious to see David such a civil, sensible, comfort-able looking man, and to recollect, 'this is the Great Infidel.'" After Boswell's marriage he even rented a house from Hume.[24]

Hume was a plump, comfortable, gregarious man, known in Paris when he had a diplomatic post there as *le bon David*. In his 1739 *Treatise of Human Nature,* he celebrated the delights of conversation: "The blood flows with a new tide; the heart is elevated; and the whole man acquires a vigor which he cannot command in his solitary and calm moments. Hence company is natu-rally so rejoicing, as presenting the liveliest of all objects, viz, a rational and thinking being like ourselves, who communicates to us all the actions of his mind; makes us privy to his inmost sentiments and affections; and lets us see, in the very instant of their production, all the emotions which are caused by any object."[25]

Hume's portrait, by his friend Allan Ramsay, captures his pleasant genial-ity (figure 87). He got along well with the leading Edinburgh intellectuals, even those who were ministers. Some held quite liberal views, and he enjoyed teasing them, warning Hugh Blair for instance that the people were "relapsing fast into the deepest stupidity, Christianity, and ignorance." The Kirk—the official Presbyterian establishment—loathed Hume, however, and made sure he could never be appointed a professor; he described a conservative clergy-man named Anderson as "the godly, spiteful, pious, splenetic, charitable, un-relenting, meek, persecuting, Christian, inhuman, peace-making, furious Anderson."[26]

Hume often told a story that he swore was true. Crossing a bog that sepa-rated Edinburgh from the New Town, where he was having a house built, he slipped into the bog and floundered there, too bulky to get out. A group of fishwives came along, but recognizing him as "the wicked unbeliever David Hume," they wouldn't help him until he had repeated the Lord's Prayer.[27]

When Johnson was in Scotland Boswell wanted to introduce him to Hume, but Johnson flatly refused. He could make peace with John Wilkes,

87. David Hume

pornographer and political pariah, but not with the Great Infidel. At bottom, we may surmise, was anxiety that the infidels might be right. If they *were* right, then Johnson would no longer have to submit to a religion of fear. With his profound feeling of unworthiness, and his conviction that sinners must be punished in the hereafter, he could not envision giving that up.

Boswell once heard Johnson make an extraordinary admission: that skepticism like Hume's had attracted him in his youth until he forcibly repelled it. "Hume, and other skeptical innovators, are vain men, and will gratify themselves at any expense. Truth will not afford sufficient food to their vanity, so they have betaken themselves to error. Truth, Sir, is a cow that will yield such people no more milk, and so they are gone to milk the bull." That is certainly witty, but what Johnson went on to say was very much in earnest, and is less often quoted: "If I could have allowed myself to gratify my vanity at the expense of truth, what fame might I have acquired! Everything which Hume has advanced against Christianity had passed through my mind long before he wrote."[28]

In 1776 it became clear that Hume was fatally ill with stomach cancer, and Boswell paid him a visit. The spectacle of an unbeliever dying in tranquility was alarming.

On Sunday forenoon the 7 of July 1776, being too late for church, I went to see Mr. David Hume, who was returned from London and

Bath, just a-dying. I found him alone, in a reclining posture in his drawing room. He was lean, ghastly, and quite of an earthy appearance. He was dressed in a suit of gray cloth with white metal [pewter] buttons, and a kind of scratch wig. He was quite different from the plump figure which he used to present. He seemed to be placid and even cheerful. He said he was just approaching to his end.[29]

Tactlessly, no doubt, Boswell insisted on talking about death, and Hume responded courteously. Much threatened by Hume's apparent equanimity, Boswell recorded the exchange at some length:

I had a strong curiosity to be satisfied if he persisted in disbelieving a future state even when he had death before his eyes. I was persuaded from what he now said, and from his manner saying it, that he did persist. I asked him if it was not possible that there might be a future state. He answered it was possible that a piece of coal put upon the fire would not burn; and he added that it was a most unreasonable fancy that we should exist forever. . . . I asked him if the thought of annihilation never gave him any uneasiness. He said not the least; no more than the thought that he had not been, as Lucretius observes. "Well," said I, "Mr. Hume, I hope to triumph over you when I meet you in a future state; and remember you are not to pretend that you was joking with all this infidelity." "No, no," said he. "But I shall have been so long there before you come that it will be nothing new." In this style of good humour and levity did I conduct the conversation. . . . I however felt a degree of horror, mixed with a sort of wild, strange, hurrying recollection of my excellent mother's pious instructions, of Doctor Johnson's noble lessons, and of my religious sentiments and affections during the course of my life. I was like a man in sudden danger eagerly seeking his defensive arms; and I could not but be assailed by momentary doubts while I had actually before me a man of such strong abilities and extensive inquiry dying in the persuasion of being annihilated. But I maintained my faith.

When Boswell reported this encounter, Johnson said flatly, "He lied. He had a vanity in being thought easy. It is more probable that he lied than that so very improbable a thing should be as a man not afraid of death; of going into an unknown state and not being uneasy at leaving all that he knew." Hume expected not to go into any "state" at all, but simply to cease to exist, just like the lump of coal. Boswell added, "The horror for death which I have always observed in Doctor Johnson appeared strong tonight. . . . He said he never had a moment in which death was not terrible to him." That was another conversation that didn't get into the *Life of Johnson*.[30]

Seven years after the farewell visit with Hume, Boswell received reassurance from his own unconscious. "Awaked after a very agreeable dream that I had found a diary kept by David Hume, from which it appeared that though his vanity made him publish treatises of skepticism and infidelity, he was in reality a Christian and a very pious man. I thought I read some beautiful passages in his diary. . . . After I awaked, it dwelt so upon my mind that I could not for some time perceive that it was only a fiction."[31]

After Hume's death Adam Smith composed a warm tribute that appeared thereafter in editions of Hume's works. Its final sentence, however, caused outrage: "Upon the whole, I have always considered him, both in his lifetime and since his death, as approaching as nearly to the idea of a perfectly wise and virtuous man, as perhaps the nature of human frailty will permit." That was a direct affront to people who thought that no unbeliever could possibly be wise and virtuous. Smith was deliberately recalling what Plato said of Socrates: "Of all those whom we knew in our time, he was the bravest and also the wisest and most upright." It was indeed a subject of debate among believers whether any non-Christians, however virtuous, could be saved.[32]

When he read Smith's tribute, Boswell wrote to Johnson that he ought to "knock Hume's and Smith's heads together," in order to "crush such noxious weeds in the moral garden." Later on, in a reprint of his Hebrides journal, he commented pompously, "When I read this sentence delivered by my old professor of moral philosophy, I could not help exclaiming with the Psalmist, 'Surely I have now more understanding than my teachers!'"[33]

Smith himself told a Danish economist, "A single, and, as I thought, a very harmless sheet of paper which I happened to write concerning the death of our late friend Mr. Hume, brought upon me ten times more abuse than the very violent attack I had made upon the whole commercial system of Great Britain."[34]

CHAPTER 20

Johnson Nearing the End

LOSS OF FRIENDS AND FAILING HEALTH

With the arrival of the 1780s, Johnson was in a pronounced physical decline and well aware of it, though he always remained as active as he could. Mentally he had lost nothing, and he surprised even himself by producing a final masterpiece, the great *Lives of the English Poets.*

Up until these last years, Johnson's robust strength never ceased to impress his friends. When he was middle aged he climbed to the top of a hill at Bennet Langton's Lincolnshire estate, where he unexpectedly declared that he intended "to take a roll down." Langton looked on in astonishment as he emptied his pockets, "and laying himself parallel with the edge of the hill, he actually descended, turning himself over and over till he came to the bottom."[1]

In 1777, on his sixty-eighth birthday, Johnson told Hester Thrale, "Age is a very stubborn disease." It was at about that time that James Barry, a young Irish artist and protégé of Burke's, captured his expression in a compelling oil study (color plate 29).[2]

Soon not just age but a whole series of specific afflictions were mounting up. In 1782 Johnson wrote to Boswell, "From the middle of January to the middle of June, I was battered by one disorder after another."[3]

There is enough evidence to allow modern specialists to make confident diagnoses. Johnson suffered from rheumatoid arthritis, asthma, and chronic bronchitis, and later on from emphysema and congestive heart failure (known then as "dropsy"). Doctors were familiar with all of these conditions, but there wasn't much they could do.

He did have the best medical care available, particularly from Dr. William Heberden. In 1780 he noted in his diary a temporary "remission of those convulsions in my breast which had distressed me for more than twenty years." That was undoubtedly angina pectoris, which Heberden himself was the first person to identify, in the *Transactions of the Royal College of Physicians* which he helped to launch: "a very singular, lingering, teasing and dangerous disease. The seat of it, and a sense of strangling and anxiety with which it is attended, have induced the author to give it the appellation of Angina Pectoris." The Latin meaning is "suffocation of the chest."[4]

There was also gout, which went almost without saying, since it was usual among gentlemen who ate rich food and consumed large quantities of alcohol. The corpulent Gibbon was a martyr to it. On one occasion Johnson wrote to Thrale that he was confined to his house by "a very serious and troublesome fit of the gout; I creep about and hang by both hands."[5]

Something else that went without saying was hypertension, not yet understood at all. The inevitable result was strokes. In 1782 Burney wrote to Johnson, "I am heartily grieved to tell you that poor Sir Joshua has had a paralytic stroke, which drew his mouth very much out of its place, and distorted his whole countenance." Happily, he made a complete recovery. That must have been what would now be called a transient ischemic attack or TIA, commonly referred to as a mini-stroke.[6]

Johnson himself had a stroke in the following year, with the same fortunate outcome. In June of 1783 he wrote to Hester to say that three days previously he had sat for his portrait (probably one by John Opie) and had gone to bed comfortably, but soon afterward was awakened by "a confusion and indistinctness in my head." He realized immediately that he had suffered a stroke and was unable to speak, but was relieved to find that he could mentally compose a prayer in Latin verse. "The lines were not very good, but I knew them not to be very good. I made them easily, and concluded myself to be unimpaired in my faculties."

The doctors, though well-meaning, were naturally of no help. "They put a blister upon my back, and two from my ear to my throat, one on a side. The blister on the back has done little, and those on the throat have not risen." The theory was that by applying irritants to the skin, blisters would develop and could then be drained, supposedly drawing "peccant humors" out of the patient.[7]

During these years Johnson began consuming opium in quantity. It was perfectly legal and freely available to combat insomnia and physical pain, and he discovered that it gave temporary relief from depression as well. "When it became habitual," Hawkins says, "it was the means of positive pleasure, and as such was resorted to by him whenever any depression of spirits made it necessary." Hawkins adds that it sometimes caused "such an exhilaration of his spirits" that people mistakenly suspected him of being drunk.[8]

Nobody knows when Johnson first used opium. It could well have been during the last years of Tetty's life, when she is known to have used it to excess. She died in 1752, and three years later, when he published the first edition of his *Dictionary,* he defined "opium" by adopting a long description from a medical textbook. "Its first effect is the making the patient cheerful, as if he had drank moderately of wine; it removes melancholy, excites boldness, and dissipates the dread of danger. . . . After the effect of a dose of opium is over, the pain generally returns in a more violent manner; the spirits, which had been elevated by it, become lower than before, and the pulse languid. An immoderate dose of opium brings on a sort of drunkenness, cheerfulness, and loud laughter at first, and after many terrible symptoms, death itself."[9]

In his later years Johnson realized he was using opium increasingly, and struggled without much success to cut back. To a concerned friend he claimed that he was keeping the habit under control, but indicated clearly enough what stimulated it: "From the retrospect of life when solitude, leisure, accident, or darkness turn my thoughts upon it, I shrink with multiplicity of horror." A modern investigation concludes that he was "a drug addict in an age that did not recognize addiction."[10]

Many people testified that during these final years Johnson seemed to mellow. Hannah More said, "He is more mild and complacent than he used to be. His sickness seems to have softened his mind, without having at all weakened it. I was struck with the mild radiance of the setting sun." He remarked to a friend, "I look upon myself to be a man very much misunderstood. I am not an uncandid, nor am I a severe man. I sometimes say more than I mean, in jest, and people are apt to believe me serious; however, I am more candid than I was when I was younger. As I know more of mankind, I expect less of them, and am ready now to call a man *a good man* upon easier terms than I was formerly."[11]

That's not to say that Johnson could ever dwindle into a kindly old gentleman. Boswell recorded an episode in 1781 when an inadvertent double entendre made by Johnson raised a laugh. Johnson mentioned that a writer they knew had married a printer's devil; apprentices in printing shops were so called because they were commonly black with ink. No doubt he cleaned her up, Johnson said, and he added, "She did not disgrace him; the woman had a bottom of good sense." That provoked the laugh, although a bishop managed to keep a straight face, and Hannah More hid hers. As for Johnson:

> His pride could not bear that any expression of his should excite ridicule when he did not intend it; he therefore resolved to assume and exercise despotic power, glanced sternly around, and called out in a strong tone, "Where is the merriment?" Then, collecting himself and looking awful, to make us feel how he could impose restraint, and as it were searching his mind for a still more ludicrous word, he slowly pronounced, "I say the woman was *fundamentally* sensible;" as if he had said, "Hear this now, and laugh if you dare." We all sat composed as at a funeral.

In the *Dictionary* Johnson defines "fundament" as "the back part of the body."[12]

That happened at Eva Garrick's house, the very first time she had entertained since her husband's death, and as Boswell and Johnson walked away they paused to look back at the Adelphi buildings. "I said to him with some emotion that I was now thinking of two friends we had lost, who once lived in the buildings behind us, Beauclerk and Garrick. 'Aye, Sir,' said he, tenderly, 'and two such friends as cannot be supplied.'"

Among the housemates at Bolt Court, death was also making inroads. One loss was Anna Williams, who had sat up night after night to drink tea with Johnson, and he missed her greatly. Another was "Doctor" Robert Levet, the unlicensed practitioner who actually had a good understanding of medicine. At a time when the profession was tightly controlled in England, he had spent five years in Paris and attended lectures by leading specialists there.[13]

When Levet died in 1782, twenty years after first moving in, Johnson wrote to a doctor who knew and liked him, "Our old friend Mr. Levet, who was last night eminently cheerful, died this morning. So has ended the long life of a very useful and very blameless man." Boswell and Hawkins both marveled at Johnson's friendship with this rather crude character, but Johnson deeply respected his generous care of the poor, and he wrote a moving elegy. It reads in part:

Well tried through many a varying year
See Levet to the grave descend;
Officious, innocent, sincere,
Of every friendless name the friend.

Yet still he fills affection's eye,
Obscurely wise, and coarsely kind;
Nor, lettered arrogance, deny
Thy praise to merit unrefined. . . .

His virtues walked their narrow round,
Nor made a pause, nor left a void;
And sure th' eternal Master found
The single talent well employed.

Boswell tells us that Johnson was haunted by the parable of the talents: "The solemn text, 'of him to whom much is given, much will be required,' seems to have been ever present to his mind in a rigorous sense." He feared deeply that he had squandered his exceptional talents. Levet had a single talent and used it well.[14]

Samuel Beckett once drafted a sketch for a play about Johnson and his domestic circle, to be called *Human Wishes,* in which an inebriated Levet makes a mute entrance after getting home very late.

> MRS. DESMOULINS. God grant all is well.
> Enter LEVET, slightly, respectably, even reluctantly drunk, in greatcoat and hat, which he does not remove, carrying a small bag. He advances unsteadily into the room and stands peering at the company. Ignored ostentatiously by Mrs. Desmoulins (knitting), Miss Carmichael (reading), Mrs. Williams (meditating), he remains a little standing as though lost in thought, then suddenly emits a single hiccup of such force that he is almost thrown off his feet. Startled from her knitting Mrs. D., from her book Miss C., from her stage meditation Mrs. W., survey him with indignation. Levet remains standing a little longer, absorbed and motionless, then on a wide tack returns cautiously to the door, which he does not close behind him. His unsteady footsteps are heard on the stairs. Between the three women, exchange of looks. Gestures of disgust. Mouths opened and shut. Finally they resume their occupations.

MRS. WILLIAMS. Words fail us.

MRS. DESMOULINS. Now this is where a writer for the stage would have us speak, no doubt.[15]

For Johnson the most serious loss was Henry Thrale, and everybody saw it coming: neither his wife nor his friends could get him to moderate his gross overeating. In 1777, when he still had four years to live, Hester noted, "Gluttony is so much the favourite vice of this age that I heard today of a waistcoat marked thus, in the manner of a barometer: Full, Very Full, Bursting—Apoplexy, Sudden Death."[16]

At dinner parties Thrale was generally torpid, and often dozed off. There was also an alarming stroke in 1779, brought on when he discovered that he was solely responsible for an enormous bond that he had signed years before, which if called in would require £220,000 that he couldn't possibly afford. He made a partial recovery, but was never really himself after that.[17]

Since 1765 Thrale had been the member of Parliament for Southwark, where his brewery was located. He never took much interest in politics, but he enjoyed the status. There was a new election in 1780 and by then he was too ill to appear in public, having recently suffered two further strokes. Hester went before the electors on his behalf and made a good impression; she would undoubtedly have been a better candidate than he. But eventually he had to show himself, and his candidacy was doomed. "His friends," she said, "now considered him as dying, his enemies as dead."[18]

By that time it was obvious that the end could not be far away. "I have no notion of health," Hester told Johnson, "for a man whose mouth cannot be sewed up." By the following April his gluttony was so compulsive that Johnson told him sternly, "Sir, after the denunciation of your physicians this morning, such eating is little better than suicide." Sure enough, three days later, after gorging himself as usual, he went to his room to rest, and Queeney found him lying there on the floor. "'What's the meaning of this?' says she in an agony—'I choose it,' replies Mr. Thrale firmly; 'I lie so o' purpose.'" Soon afterward he suffered another stroke and expired. He was just fifty-two.[19]

Johnson wrote in his diary a few days later, "I felt almost the last flutter of his pulse, and looked for the last time upon the face that for fifteen years had never been turned upon me but with respect or benignity." After the funeral he added, "With him were buried many of my hopes and pleasures." Two months after his death Fanny Burney wrote, "I have very often long and melancholy discourses with Dr. Johnson about our dear deceased master—whom indeed he regrets incessantly."[20]

A marble monument was placed in Thrale's memory in the Streatham church, with a Latin epitaph by Johnson. It said, in part, "He was ingenuous, open, always the same; in appearance he made no ostentatious display, either through vain art or excessive care. . . . Among family, associates, companions, and guests, the easy sweetness of his manners drew all men's hearts to him. Such was the happy freedom of his conversation that although he flattered none, he pleased all."

The family tomb already contained Thrale's father and his son Harry, who had died so suddenly at the age of ten. "Thus a happy and wealthy house," the epitaph concludes, "founded by the grandfather and increased by the father, fell with the grandson. Pass on, traveler; and having surveyed the reversals of human affairs, think on eternity—*abi, viator, et vicibus rerum humanarum perspectis, eternitatem cogita.*" Hester and her daughters would of course inherit Henry's fortune, but Johnson's point was that the family name would now be extinct.[21]

Boswell, who never felt comfortable with either of the Thrales, could be counted on to behave disgracefully. Just one day after the funeral, he composed a scurrilous epithalamium celebrating an imagined marriage between Hester and Johnson. He wrote it out at great speed at Reynolds's house. "Where ordinary bad taste leaves off," John Wain comments, "Boswell began." A few stanzas will confirm that:

> Convulsed in love's tumultuous throes,
> We feel the aphrodisian spasm;
> Tired Nature must at last repose,
> Then Wit and Wisdom fill the chasm.

> Nor only are our limbs entwined
> And lip in rapture glued to lip;
> Locked in embraces of the mind,
> Imagination's sweets we sip.

> While to felicity thus raised
> My bosom glows with amorous fire,
> Porter no longer shall be praised;
> 'Tis I myself am Thrale's entire.

Those last lines are packed with snide allusions. Thrale was a brewer, and porter is a kind of beer; Porter was also Tetty's surname from her first marriage. Beyond that, "entire" was also a kind of beer, and an "entire" horse was a virile stallion, as opposed to a gelding.[22]

Boswell was so delighted with this performance that he was soon reading it—or perhaps even singing it—at numerous gatherings. When Johnson heard about it there was an understandable chill, but it may be that he never saw the poem itself.

Hester, whose two youngest daughters were just four and two years old, now had to deal with the affairs of the brewery. Fortunately there was a highly competent manager, John Perkins. During Henry's lifetime she had never been allowed to get involved in the business, commenting in her journal, "The merchant's lady is never informed of her husband's circumstances any more than his whore is." Now she quickly mastered the issues, working with Perkins, but she had no intention of keeping the business going. The goal was to be rid of it.[23]

Though Johnson had no understanding of business, he had been named in the will as an executor and he was thrilled at the prospect of helping. "We are not here to sell a parcel of boilers and vats," he exclaimed, "but the potentiality of growing rich, beyond the dreams of avarice." Hester commented wryly in her journal, "If an angel from heaven had told me twenty years ago that the man I knew by the name of Dictionary Johnson should one day become partner with me in a great trade, and that we should jointly or separately sign notes, drafts, etc. for three or four thousand pounds of a morning, how unlikely it would have seemed ever to happen! 'Unlikely' is no word though—it would have seemed incredible."[24]

If anything, she thought Johnson was enjoying himself entirely too much, and she foresaw correctly that it was going to be hard "to win him from the dirty delight of seeing his name in a new character, flaming away at the bottom of bonds and leases." She referred to the business as "my golden millstone," and was immensely relieved when a brewer named Barclay bought it for the magnificent sum of £135,000. "I have by this bargain purchased peace and a stable fortune, restoration to my original rank in life, and a situation undisturbed by commercial jargon, unpolluted by commercial frauds." Barclay entered into a partnership with Perkins, and in the next century the brewery became the largest in the world. In 1955 the firm of Barclay and Perkins merged with Courage Limited; until then the label on the bottles carried a picture of Johnson, but that was replaced by the Courage cock.[25]

In 1782, when Hester was at last financially unencumbered, she decided to save money by renting Streatham Place and to travel abroad with her daughters. On October 6 Johnson dined there for the last time, recording the menu in Latin in his diary: "a roast leg of lamb with spinach chopped fine, the stuffing of flour with raisins, a sirloin of beef, and a turkey pullet (*pullum gallinae Turcicae*). . . . I took my place in no joyful mood." He ended the note, *Streathamiam quando revisam*—"When shall I see Streatham again?" The answer was, never. That night, which he spent in the house, he wrote down a brief prayer, asking "that I may with humble and sincere thankfulness remember the comforts and conveniences which I have enjoyed at this place, and that I may resign them with holy submission."[26]

A LATE MASTERPIECE

Johnson's final years at Streatham had borne unexpected fruit in a superb series of literary biographies, just when it seemed likely that his career as a writer was over. Almost everything he ever wrote was prompted by some immediate occasion, and in 1777 that had happened again. A consortium of forty booksellers decided to bring out a multivolume edition of English poets, omitting most of the ones before the Restoration but including fifty-two in all. They hired Johnson, at a modest fee, to supply brief prefaces for each poet, which was expected to be a relatively simple task. He wrote to Boswell, "I am engaged to write little lives, and little prefaces, to a little edition of the English poets." But soon he got carried away, and in his own preface he explained, "I have been led beyond my intention, I hope by the honest desire of giving useful pleasure." In his diary, though, he was characteristically hard on himself: "Sometime in March I finished the lives of the poets, which I wrote in my usual way, dilatorily and hastily, unwilling to work, and working with vigour and haste." Nearly all of it was done at Streatham, where he would often read from his manuscript to the family there.[27]

The introductions to many of the poets did remain brief, but those on Milton, Dryden, Pope, and Swift turned out to be books in their own right, divided into biography, general assessment of character, and critiques of the poems. The publishers yielded to this new reality and printed them not as prefaces but as the first ten volumes in an edition of sixty-eight. In 1781, when the entire series was finished, the introductions were reprinted by themselves and have been known ever since as *Lives of the Poets*.

Johnson had almost no input as to the choice of poets. Some were very minor indeed, and he made no effort to conceal it. On George Stepney he concludes, after a couple of perfunctory pages, "One cannot always find the reason for which the world has sometimes conspired to squander praise." About John Sheffield, Duke of Buckingham—one of several remembered mainly for having been noblemen—he says only, "His songs are upon common topics; he hopes, and grieves, and repents, and despairs, and rejoices, like any other maker of little stanzas. To be great he hardly tries; to be gay is hardly in his power."[28]

A poet named Mark Akenside still had something of a reputation then, but Johnson's refusal to analyze the poems is crushing: "When they are once found to be generally dull, all further labour may be spared, for to what use can the work be criticized that will not be read?" In conversation with Boswell he was still more blunt: "One bad ode may be suffered, but a number of them together makes one sick."[29]

One of the *Lives* provoked a break with Elizabeth Montagu. Lord Lyttelton, an extremely minor poet who had recently died and was a great favorite of hers, received the faintest possible praise: "Of his *Progress of Love* it is sufficient blame to say that it is pastoral. His blank verse in *Blenheim* has neither much force nor much elegance. His little performances, whether songs or epigrams, are sometimes sprightly and sometimes insipid." Horace Walpole wrote gleefully to a friend, "Mrs. Montagu and all her maenads intend to tear him limb from limb for despising their moppet Lord Lyttelton."[30]

The best of the *Lives* are not only superb biographies, even if underresearched, but also trenchant literary criticism from the perspective not of technical analysis but of what Johnson calls the common reader—"for by the common sense of readers, uncorrupted by literary prejudices, after all the refinements of subtlety and the dogmatism of learning, must be finally decided all claim to poetical honours." Virginia Woolf quoted that on the title page of her essay collection, *The Common Reader*.[31]

Johnson used the *Life of Cowley* to develop what was then a completely original analysis of metaphysical wit; it was he who coined the expression "the metaphysical poets." He didn't love the poems of Donne and the other metaphysicals as T. S. Eliot and the New Critics later would, but he was the first in his century to recognize their intellectual power. His objection was that it was all too intellectual. On Abraham Cowley's love poems he says, "The compositions are such as might have been written for penance by a hermit, or for hire by a philosophical rhymer who had only heard of another sex."[32]

Most literary criticism in Johnson's day relied heavily on what nowadays would be called Theory with a capital T. Johnson never forgot what literature is really for. "Works of imagination excel by their allurement and delight; by their power of attracting and detaining the attention. That book is good in vain which the reader throws away. He only is the master who keeps the mind in pleasing captivity; whose pages are perused with eagerness, and in hope of new pleasure are perused again; and whose conclusion is perceived with an eye of sorrow, such as the traveler casts upon departing day."[33]

The three poets who get the most attention are Milton, Dryden, and Pope. Johnson greatly admired all three, and wrote eloquently about their strengths. The conclusion of the *Life of Milton* is a resounding tribute: "His great works were performed under discountenance [i.e., political disfavor] and in blindness, but difficulties vanished at his touch. He was born for whatever is arduous, and his work is not the greatest of heroic poems only because it is not the first." That is to say, *Paradise Lost* is surpassed only by the *Iliad* and *Aeneid.*

Yet Johnson is willing also to say, with his hardheaded common sense, what many readers of Milton's masterpiece might endorse: "The want of human interest is always felt. *Paradise Lost* is one of the books which the reader admires and lays down, and forgets to take up again. None ever wished it longer than it is. Its perusal is a duty rather than a pleasure. We read Milton for instruction, retire harassed and overburdened, and look elsewhere for recreation; we desert our master, and seek for companions."[34]

As for the biographical sections of the *Lives,* they are filled with compelling observations on human behavior. There is a telling anecdote about Alexander Pope compulsively reading pamphlets against himself, a story that Johnson heard personally from a painter named Jonathan Richardson. One of these scurrilous pamphlets "came into the hands of Pope, who said, 'These things are my diversion.' They sat by him while he perused it, and saw his features writhen with anguish; and young Richardson said to his father, when they returned [home], that he hoped to be preserved from such diversion as had been that day the lot of Pope."[35]

That was an insight into Pope's personality, but perhaps his sensitivity to criticism helped to make possible his poetic achievement. Johnson constantly reproached himself for never trying hard enough, and his tribute to Pope is all the more moving in light of that: "Pope had genius; a mind active, ambitious, and adventurous, always investigating, always aspiring; in its widest searches still longing to go forward, in its highest flights still wishing to be higher; always imagining something greater than it knows, always endeavouring more than it can do."[36]

More than any previous works by Johnson, the *Lives* are steadily satisfying to read. Lytton Strachey praised "the easy, indolent power, the searching sense of actuality, the combined command of sanity and paradox, the immovable independence of thought. . . . As one reads, the brilliant sentences seem to come to one out of the past with the intimacy of a conversation." Another early twentieth-century writer concluded, "Johnson's last and greatest work is more than a collection of facts: it is a book of wisdom and experience, a treatise on the conduct of life, a commentary on human destiny."[37]

END OF THE IDYLL

The Thrales' marriage may not have been especially affectionate, but neither of them ever expected it to be. Between them they had worked out an agreeable way of life at Streatham, and when Henry died it was suddenly gone. Hester was free for the first time in her life, at the age of forty. What happened next was that she fell in love, though not with Johnson. There is no evidence that he himself thought such a thing could happen, though he took it for granted that their relationship would remain strong after Henry's death. While she was staying at Bath in 1783 he wrote, "Those that have loved longest, love best. . . . A friendship of twenty years is interwoven with the texture of life."[38]

The man Hester fell for was Gabriele Piozzi. One year older than herself, he had originally come to Streatham in 1778 as a singing teacher for Queeney. Their encounter at that time was anything but romantic. While he was singing and accompanying himself on the piano, with his back to the guests, she quietly slipped in behind him. And then, as Fanny Burney remembered, "she ludicrously began imitating him by squaring her elbows, elevating them with ecstatic shrugs of the shoulders, and casting up her eyes, while languishingly reclining her head; as if she were not less enthusiastically, though somewhat more suddenly, struck with the transports of harmony than himself."

Charles Burney, who had invited Piozzi, was horrified, and whispered to Hester that she had to stop. "She nodded her approbation of this admonition, and returning to her chair, quietly sat down, as she afterwards said, like a pretty little miss, for the remainder of one of the most humdrum evenings that she had ever passed." Fanny was not exaggerating when she added, "Strange, indeed, strange and most strange, the event [eventual outcome] considered, was this opening intercourse between Mrs. Thrale and Signor Piozzi. Little could she imagine that the person she was thus called away from holding up to ridicule would become, but a few years afterwards, the ideal of her fancy and the lord of her destiny!"[39]

Even before Henry died, the music teacher was making a strong impression on Hester. "Piozzi is become a prodigious favourite with me. He is so intelligent a creature, so discerning, one can't help wishing for his good opinion. His singing surpasses everybody's for taste, tenderness, and true elegance; his hand on the forte piano too is so soft, so sweet, so delicate, every tone goes to one's heart I think, and fills the mind with emotions one would not be without, though inconvenient enough sometimes."[40]

By 1783 Hester was deeply in love, and determined to marry Piozzi. The guardians who had been appointed for her daughters vehemently opposed that, on the grounds that their own chance to marry advantageously would be endangered if she married a Catholic foreigner. Music teachers were regarded as déclassé, too. Queeney, now nineteen, was particularly indignant, as Hester bitterly recorded.

> I actually groaned with anguish, threw myself on the bed in an agony, which my fair daughter beheld with frigid indifference. She had indeed never by one tender word endeavoured to dissuade me from the match, but said coldly that if I *would* abandon my children I *must;* that I should be punished by Piozzi's neglect, for she knew he hated me, and that I turned out my offspring to chance for his sake like puppies in a pond, to swim or drown according as providence pleased; that for her part she must look herself out a place like the other servants, for my face would she never see more.[41]

After a sleepless night and earnest prayer, "I flew to my daughter's bed in the morning and told her my resolution to resign my own, my dear, my favourite purposes; and to prefer my children's interest to my love." Several weeks later Hester revealed her decision to Piozzi, in the presence of a friend "to keep the meeting from being too tender, the separation from being too poignant." After that, "I flew to my dearest loveliest friend, my Fanny Burney, and poured all my sorrows into her tender bosom."[42]

That was in April of 1783. Separated from Piozzi, who went home to Italy, Hester was near despair. Fanny was no better able than Hester's daughters to imagine what overwhelming emotion could be like. A few months later Fanny told Queeney, "How *can* she suffer herself, noble-minded as she is, to be thus duped by ungovernable passions!" Fanny's own passions were always governable. "I am truly happy in being of a nature so little inflammable for love, though so ardent in friendship. To be *passive* is, as yet at least, as far as I have felt—and even that only to Mr. G. C." That was George Owen Cambridge, who was very interested in her and waiting for some definite sign before making advances. The sign never came.[43]

In the end Hester summoned her courage and defied her daughters and friends. She wrote to Piozzi to return, and in July of 1784 they were married in a Catholic ceremony, followed by an Anglican one two days later. Half a century later Fanny was still unyielding in deploring Hester's action, even though by then she herself was happily married to a Frenchman—but he was an aristocratic émigré, not a humble music teacher. Leslie Stephen commented, "An Italian musician is certainly not in the nature of things inferior to an English brewer."[44]

Fanny acknowledged that Hester had struggled against her passion, "but the subtle poison had glided into her veins so unsuspectedly, and at first so unopposedly, that the whole fabric was infected with its venom; which seemed to become a part, never to be dislodged, of its system." One of Hester's physicians thought that if she were forced to give Piozzi up, there would be "no other alternative but death or madness."[45]

Once the plan to marry Piozzi was definite, Fanny told Hester bluntly that their friendship was over. "The mother of five children, three of them as tall as herself, will never be forgiven for showing so great an ascendance of passion over reason. . . . Children—Religion, Friends, Country, Character— what on earth can compensate the loss of all these? . . . We were not born for ourselves, and I have regularly practiced, as far as occasion offered, the forbearance I recommend." Not long after that Fanny would have had to say "four children," not five, since little Henrietta died at the age of four. The surviving daughters were Queeney, now twenty; Susanna, fourteen; Sophia, thirteen, and Cecilia, seven.[46]

The Bluestockings, always scrupulously proper, were appalled. Elizabeth Montagu wrote to a friend on the day of the wedding, "I am myself convinced that the poor woman is mad, and indeed have long suspected her mind was disordered. She was the best mother, the best wife, the best friend, the most amiable member of society . . . I bring in my verdict: lunacy, in this affair."[47]

Another member of the coterie, Hester Chapone, felt the same way. "There must really be some degree of insanity in that case, for such mighty overbearing passions are not natural in a 'matron's bones.'" Everyone took it for granted that a woman in her forties should be beyond romance, and sexual passion too. The quotation is from Hamlet's cruel diatribe against his mother.[48]

Hester had to face one additional judge. When the marriage was just about to take place, she wrote to Johnson to reveal what was happening. His reply was unworthy of him, and brutal (figure 88).

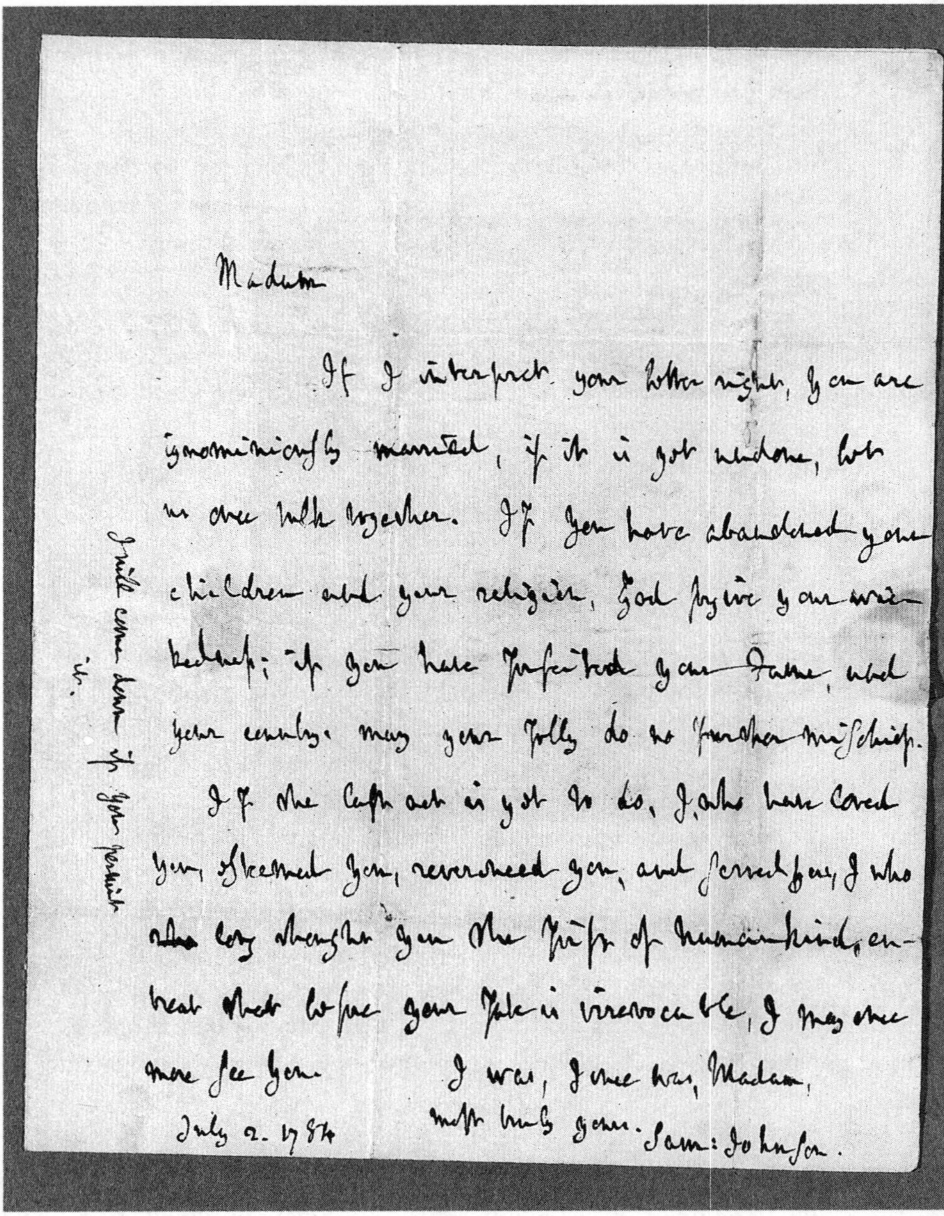

Madam

 If I interpret your letter right, you are ignominiously married, if it is yet undone, let us once talk together. If you have abandoned your children and your religion, God forgive your wickedness; if you have forfeited your fame, and your country, may your folly do no further mischief.

 If the last act is yet to do, I who have loved you, esteemed you, reverenced you, and served you, I who long thought you the first of humankind, entreat that before your fate is irrevocable, I may once more see you

July 2. 1784

  I was, I once was, Madam, most truly yours. Sam: Johnson.

88. Johnson to Hester Thrale

Madam,

If I interpret your letter right, you are ignominiously married. If it is yet undone, let us once talk together. If you have abandoned your children and your religion, God forgive your wickedness; if you have forfeited your fame [i.e., reputation] and your country, may your folly do no further mischief.

If the last act is yet to do, I, who have loved you, esteemed you, reverenced you, and served you, I who long thought you the first of humankind, entreat that before your fate is irrevocable, I may once more see you. I was, I once was, Madam, most truly yours,

SAM JOHNSON

Written vertically in the left margin is: "I will come down if you permit it." When Hester later published her letters from Johnson, she omitted this one.[49] She did, however, send a reply that is impressive in its dignity:

The birth of my second husband is not meaner than that of my first; his sentiments are not meaner; his profession is not meaner. . . . To hear that I have forfeited my fame is indeed the greatest insult I ever yet received. My fame is as unsullied as snow, or I should think it unworthy of him who must henceforward protect it. . . . You have always commanded my esteem, and enjoyed the fruits of a friendship never infringed by one harsh expression on my part. But till you have changed your opinion of Mr. Piozzi—let us converse no more. God bless you![50]

It was now Johnson's turn to be dignified, and his final letter to Hester is one of the most moving things he ever wrote. In it he echoes Dryden's translation of Virgil, in which the underworld river Styx is "the irremeable stream," meaning that there is no possibility of return. And he recalls a critical moment in the life of the romantic Mary Queen of Scots, when she put herself in the power of her cousin Queen Elizabeth, who would later have her executed.

Dear Madam,

What you have done, however I may lament it, I have no pretence to resent, as it has not been injurious to me. I therefore breathe out one sigh more of tenderness, perhaps useless, but at least sincere.

I wish that God may grant you every blessing . . . and whatever I can contribute to your happiness, I am very ready to repay for that kindness which soothed twenty years of a life radically wretched. . . .

When Queen Mary took the resolution of sheltering herself in
England, the Archbishop of St. Andrew's, attempting to dissuade her,
attended on her journey, and when they came to the irremeable stream
that separated the two kingdoms, walked by her side into the water, in
the middle of which he seized her bridle, and with earnestness proportioned to her danger and his own affection, pressed her to return. The
queen went forward.—If the parallel reaches thus far, may it go no
further. The tears stand in my eyes.

Johnson is no more able to stop Hester than the archbishop could stop the
queen, but his grief expands beyond personal grievance to an ache of cosmic
dimensions. This letter Hester did print.[51]

Still, Johnson didn't relent in his repudiation of Hester. Four months later
Fanny visited him for what would turn out to be the last time, and asked
whether he ever heard from Hester. " 'No,' cried he, 'nor write to her! I drive
her quite from my mind. She has disgraced herself, disgraced her friends and
connections, disgraced her sex, and disgraced all the expectations of mankind!
If I meet with one of her letters I burn it instantly. I have burnt all I can find.
I never speak of her, and I desire never to hear of her more.' " He had just
three weeks to live.[52]

Katharine Balderston, the scholar who first opened up the question of
Johnson's masochistic relationship to Hester, describes his state of mind in the
wake of what he felt to be a cruel desertion:

He acted like a man wounded to the quick, who could find relief
only by stamping on her memory. And he acted also like a man in a
panic, and so I believe he was. What greater blow to his ego could
he have had than to be deserted by the woman to whom he had ab-
jectly exposed his uttermost weakness? And what greater blow to his
security than to discover that the object of his idolatry, whose supposed superiority to the temptations of the flesh had been his own
bulwark, was a mere mortal with clay feet? Like Othello's, his relief
must be to loathe her.[53]

DEATH COMES FOR SAMUEL JOHNSON

Boswell saw Johnson for the last time in the summer of 1784. In June they
were together at "that respectable society," the Club, which had recently mi-
grated to a new venue. By 1783 the landlord of the Turk's Head, and also his

widow who carried on after he was gone, were both dead, and the house had reverted to private use. The Club then moved to Prince's, another tavern, in Sackville Street near Piccadilly.

The next month Boswell and Johnson dined at Reynolds's house, after which his coach took them back to Bolt Court. When Johnson invited him in, Boswell declined, "from an apprehension that my spirits would sink. We bade adieu to each other affectionately in the carriage. When he had got down upon the foot pavement, he called out 'Fare you well;' and without looking back, sprung away with a kind of pathetic briskness, if I may use that expression, which seemed to indicate a struggle to conceal uneasiness, and impressed me with a foreboding of our long, long separation." They never saw each other again.[54]

When Johnson died, Boswell was in Scotland. When it came time to narrate the final days in the *Life,* he took pains to get recollections from everyone he could, and the result is remarkably rich.

> Mr. Langton informs me that one day he found Mr. Burke and four or five more friends sitting with Johnson. Mr. Burke said to him, "I am afraid, Sir, such a number of us may be oppressive to you." "No, Sir," said Johnson, "it is not so; and I must be in a wretched state indeed when your company would not be a delight to me." Mr. Burke, in a tremulous voice, expressive of being very tenderly affected, replied, "My dear Sir, you have always been too good to me." Immediately afterwards he went away.

Langton himself was with Johnson almost constantly, and it was to him that Johnson quoted the poet Tibullus, "*Te teneam moriens deficiente manu*—dying, may I hold you with my weakening hand."[55]

Several doctors were in attendance and did what they could, which was mainly to relieve pain from increasing swelling in the legs. One of them expressed a conventional hope that Johnson was getting better, and he replied, "No, Sir; you cannot conceive with what acceleration I advance towards death." When a letter was brought to him, he remarked, "An odd thought strikes me—we shall receive no letters in the grave."[56]

There was an apt exchange of quotations with another doctor, when Johnson exclaimed, "I have been as a dying man all night," and then broke out with the words of Macbeth:

> Canst thou not minister to a mind diseased,
> Pluck from the memory a rooted sorrow,

> Raze out the written troubles of the brain,
> And with some sweet oblivious antidote
> Cleanse the stuffed bosom of that perilous stuff
> Which weighs upon the heart?

The doctor replied, "Therein the patient must minister to himself," and Johnson "expressed himself much satisfied with the application."[57]

At one point Johnson was convinced that the doctors were afraid of injuring him by cutting too deeply to drain fluid from his legs, and he seized a pair of scissors and did it ineptly for himself. "I want length of life," he exclaimed, "and you fear giving me pain, which I care not for."[58]

Several things that Johnson said near the end were especially memorable. He said to one friend, "I will be conquered; I will not capitulate," and to another, "*Jam moriturus*—I am about to die." He was recalling what gladiators used to say to the Roman emperor, *Morituri te salutamus*—"We who are about to die salute you."[59]

Most accounts of the final days made no mention of Francis Barber, yet he must have seen Johnson more than anyone else. It is to Boswell's credit that he got his brother David to go and interview Barber. David wrote back that when a Miss Morris called to ask for Johnson's blessing, "Francis went into his room, followed by the young lady, and delivered the message. The Doctor turned himself in the bed and said, 'God bless you, my dear!' These were the last words he spoke." In his will Johnson left Barber a generous bequest.[60]

Toward the end he refused opium, wanting to ensure that his mind was clear, and in the evening of December 13 he expired in a back room on the second floor, "with so little apparent pain that his attendants hardly perceived when the dissolution took place."

By way of valediction Boswell chose a statement by Johnson's friend William Gerard Hamilton—"Single Speech" Hamilton, with whom Burke worked when he first entered politics. "He has made a chasm, which not only nothing can fill up, but which nothing has a tendency to fill up. Johnson is dead. Let us go to the next best: there is nobody. No man can be said to put you in mind of Johnson."[61]

No one seems to have noticed, either then or later, that Hamilton was remembering what Johnson himself had said in the *Rambler:* "It was, perhaps, ordained by Providence, to hinder us from tyrannizing over one another, that no individual should be of such importance as to cause, by his retirement or death, any chasm in the world." Johnson was a rare exception to the rule.[62]

When the news reached Boswell in Scotland, though he of course knew that it was coming, it still staggered him. "I was stunned, and in a kind of amaze. . . . I did not shed tears. I was not tenderly affected. My feeling was just one large expanse of stupor. I knew that I should afterwards have sorer sensations."[63]

Several carriages were needed to carry members of the Club to Westminster Abbey for Johnson's funeral. Reynolds pushed hard for a statue to be erected in St. Paul's, which it duly was, but the actual burial was in the Abbey. "Who should have thought," commented Thomas Tyers, "that Garrick and Johnson would have their last sleep together?"[64]

CHAPTER 21

Boswell on the Downhill Slope

LAIRD AT LAST

When Johnson died Boswell had eleven more years to live. He was already heading downhill, and picking up speed. He never stopped dreaming of a breakthrough success in law and politics, even though he never did the things that might make that possible. His self-image was always more exalted than the image others had of him. He did acknowledge, though, that "there have been many people who built castles in the air, but I believe I am the first that ever attempted to live in them."[1]

At least Boswell finally gained a long-anticipated reward when his father died in 1782. He became the ninth Laird of Auchinleck, in a succession that stretched back to the sixteenth century. He could hardly regard his father's death as a loss. The old man remained cruel and sarcastic right up to the end. Less than a month before he died, "he spoke of poor John with contemptuous disgust. I was shocked and said, 'He's your son, and God made him.' He answered very harshly, 'If my sons are idiots, can I help it?'" Clearly he included James among the idiots.[2]

The youngest brother was David, who lived in Spain as a merchant for many years before settling in London. He was gloomy by temperament, but no idiot. John was a sad case. He inherited the family mental illness to a greater degree than James did, and spent most of his life confined under a physician's care. Whenever James made a visit, he came away distressed.

Sometimes John would refuse to speak for hours on end, and when he did speak, that only made it worse. "He asked if I was really alive, for he thought it was my ghost. I shook hands with him strongly to convince him I was not a ghost. . . . He said, 'I am confined and have lost my senses, and I am surely dying.' Poor man, my heart melted for him."[3]

When the end came for Lord Auchinleck, James's stepmother refused to let him be present. "Her hardness was amazing. I wished to go near. She said, 'It will confuse his head. Don't torture him in his last moments.' I was benumbed and stood off. Wept; for alas! There was not affection between us." If Lord Auchinleck could have known that his son would one day be a world-famous writer, he might not have cared.[4]

The new laird had new privileges, and new obligations. Early in their friendship Johnson had said, "Sir, let me tell you that to be a Scotch landlord, where you have a number of families dependent upon you and attached to you, is perhaps as high a situation as humanity can arrive at." Boswell agreed in theory, but he would not find it so gratifying in practice.[5]

He was now responsible for tenants in over a hundred farms. A few years before his father's death, Boswell had told Johnson proudly "that the Laird of Auchinleck had an elegant house, in front of which he could ride ten miles forward upon his own territories, upon which he had upwards of six hundred people attached to him, and that the family seat was rich in natural romantic beauties of rock, wood, and water." The estate was actually even more populous than that: its 27,000 acres had nearly a thousand inhabitants.

But Boswell had no interest in scenery, romantic or otherwise, and he made that statement only to reassure Johnson that he would live at Auchinleck at least part of the time when it became his own. During the same conversation he called London "a heaven upon earth," and Johnson replied, "Why, Sir, I never knew anyone who had such a *gust* for London as you have." Immediately after that came a comment that has been much quoted, "When a man is tired of London, he is tired of life."[6]

One thing Boswell did believe in was land, and after inheriting the estate he went deeply into debt to purchase large holdings adjacent to his. When a concerned friend remonstrated he exclaimed, "I should have been vexed to see an ancient appanage, a piece of, as it were, the flesh and blood of the family, in the hands of a stranger." "Appanage" was a pretentious word choice. Johnson defines it as "lands set aside by princes for the maintenance of their younger children."[7]

Fortunately, Boswell employed an able estate manager, and he was generous to his tenants. He refused to raise their rents when his costs went up, and he wouldn't evict them even when their payments were long overdue. He also tried to learn about the details of farming, though never with the enthusiasm that Burke did, and he took lessons in arithmetic—a reminder of how much was omitted from the education of eighteenth-century gentlemen.[8]

Peggie had grown up in the Scottish countryside, and she would have been happy to live at Auchinleck permanently, sixty miles from Edinburgh. They took possession in October of 1782, six weeks after Lord Auchinleck's death, and her uncertain health quickly seemed to improve. "She was wonderfully well now, and walked about Ayr as lively as when Miss Peggie Montgomerie. . . . I was quite happy to find my dear wife now so well and in so respectable a situation. It was as much as I suppose humanity has ever enjoyed. π." The sign for pi was one of his symbols for sexual relations with Peggie.[9]

James was letting himself go to seed physically. "I am too fat at present. My belly is more swelled than I ever remember it; and perhaps my humours are gross. I have a torpidity of mind that I have not often experienced. . . . I am quite sensual, and that, too, not exquisitely but rather swinishly." "Humours" were the bodily fluids which were thought to maintain health by being kept in balance.[10]

As the years went by Boswell spent less and less time at Auchinleck. He never met the young Robert Burns, who lived not far away and hoped for an introduction. Burns's wonderful *Poems, Chiefly in the Scottish Dialect* were published in 1786, but it's not clear that Boswell ever looked at them, though he loved Scottish folk songs and called them "sweet, melancholy, and natural." Perhaps he had heard that Burns held radical political views and avoided him for that reason.[11]

Like Boswell, Burns despised the dour religion of the Kirk. In 1792 he wrote a poem about the death of a minister named John Dun, who fell from his horse into a river:

> Ye Calvinists of Auchinleck,
> In mournin weeds yourselves bedeck,
> An show how much ye did respect
>   Your great divine,
> Wha fell, poor soul, and broke his neck
>   On Esk langsyne.

Dun had been Boswell's kindly tutor in his youth. When Boswell and John-son visited Auchinleck after their Hebrides tour, Dun entertained them, but the meeting did not go well. The Presbyterian minister "talked before Dr. Johnson of fat bishops and drowsy deans," and Johnson retorted, "Sir, you know no more of our church than a Hottentot."[12]

Burns's fondness for drink should surely have appealed to Boswell:

> While we sit bousing at the nappy,
> And getting fou and unco happy. . . .

(While we sit boozing on strong ale, and getting drunk and uncommon happy.) In one poem Burns glanced at Boswell's reputation as a talker:

> Alas! I'm but a nameless wight,
> Trod i' the mire out o' sight!
> But could I like Montgomeries fight,
>   Or gab like Boswell. . . .

Peggie was a Montgomerie.[13]

Burns celebrated drink and sex as pleasures that nature generously be-stows on people who don't have many other pleasures. Boswell pursued them both compulsively and reproached himself endlessly.

WOMEN

In Edinburgh there were always streetwalkers, and the journals for the 1780s contain many rueful mentions of them, though someone—presumably a scandalized descendant—tore out many pages, at one point no fewer than eighteen. What stands out especially is Peggie's long-suffering loyalty and af-fection. "Was in sound spirits, but drank so as to be intoxicated a good deal, so that I ranged an hour in the street and dallied with ten strumpets. I had however caution enough left not to run a risk with them. Told my valuable spouse when I came home. She was good-humoured and gave me excellent beef soup."[14]

Sometimes, however, his behavior was so outrageous that Peggie rebelled.

I left this my journal lying open in the dining room while I went downstairs to look for some book or paper, and my dear wife having taken it up, read the account of my life on Monday the 18, with which she was shocked, and declared that all connection between her and me was now at an end, and that she would continue to live with me only for decency and the sake of her children. I was miserably vexed and in a sort of stupor. But could say nothing for myself. I indulged some glimmering of hope, and just acquiesced in my fate for the present. I was still heated with wine.

The offending pages were among the ones that were torn out, and it's impossible to know what was so exceptionally bad. At any rate the glimmering of hope was well founded, as an entry two weeks afterward confirms: "Had Grange in my seat [at church] to hear Dr. Blair in afternoon. He and Sibthorpe dined. Supped Lady Crawford's. π."[15]

When Boswell was by himself in London he could be more daring. There was a prostitute named Betsy to whom he became so attached in 1785 that he actually tried to get her to give up her life on the streets, paying for her admission to a hospital when she had venereal disease, and offering to find her respectable employment. She told him frankly that she wasn't interested: "She said she'd be her own mistress." He recorded that he was shocked "at such an instance of depravity"—as if he himself had not been her collaborator. A few weeks later he stopped by Betsy's lodgings and "found she had gone, they could not tell whither."[16]

There was even a passionate affair during that period, with an accused forger named Margaret Caroline Rudd. She and two male accomplices had tried to cash a forged bond for £7,500 and were detected. When Boswell sought her out she had just been acquitted, to immense popular acclaim, after giving evidence against the other two who were convicted and hanged. Forgery was considered an especially heinous offense, since it was very easy: instead of using bank notes, which were issued by individual banks and not by the government, people often exchanged personal promissory notes. It was for forgery that Dr. William Dodd was executed, a clergyman whose pardon Johnson tried to obtain, and about whom he famously said, "Depend upon it, Sir, when a man knows he is to be hanged in a fortnight, it concentrates his mind wonderfully."[17]

Always fascinated by criminality, Boswell was desperately smitten with this charmer who was beautiful, sexy, and almost certainly guilty as charged. In the *Life* he mentions her (not by name) as "universally celebrated for extraordinary address and insinuation." Back in 1776, in a letter addressed to his wife but wisely sent to Temple instead, he had described Mrs. Rudd as "a sorceress, possessed of enchantment." When he told her so, she didn't contradict him. "I begged she would not enchant me too much, not change me into any other creature, but allow me to continue to be a man with some degree of reason. I was as cautious as if I had been opposite to that snake which fascinates with its eyes."[18]

During another visit to Mrs. Rudd, Boswell exclaimed, "I dare say you could make me do anything—make me commit murder." Complimenting her on her eyes and mouth—and ankles—he snatched some kisses, and the next morning departed for Edinburgh.[19]

Now, in 1785, it was Mrs. Rudd who approached Boswell, and soon they were sleeping together. At this point his journal becomes extremely elliptical, mentioning her only in passing as "M. C." (for Margaret Caroline). The connection didn't end until 1788. Among Boswell's papers is the draft of a letter he sent her: "If the Roman emperor who had exhausted delight offered a reward for the inventor of a new pleasure, how much do I owe to thee, who hast made the greatest pleasure of human life new to me!" He seems to have been genuinely in love, as he never was with Peggie's other rivals. Coincidentally, they shared the same first name. In the journals Peggie is often referred to as "M. M.," for Margaret Montgomerie.[20]

MOVING TO LONDON

Boswell kept badgering his London friends about moving there himself to practice law, but without exception they strongly discouraged the idea. The only formal requirement to become a lawyer was to prove residence at the Inner Temple by eating a stated number of dinners there; he had been doing that off and on since 1775. But English common law was very different from Scottish law, and even if he had been capable of the necessary self-discipline, it would have been very difficult in his mid-forties to acquire the expertise he would need.

On top of the professional arguments against the move, there were two personal ones. Boswell was heavily in debt, and could expect life in London to cost twice what it did in Scotland. The other concern was Peggie's health; for several years she had been showing symptoms of tuberculosis. She much preferred to live at Auchinleck, and correctly anticipated that the smoky air of London would be bad for her. Nevertheless, he could not bring himself to give up his dream.

In 1786, two years after Johnson's death, the move to London was definite, and Boswell was able to record in his journal, "Repaired to [the] Temple. Settled all dues; dined at the students' table for the last time." Immediately

afterward he was officially granted the status of barrister at law. His companions in that ceremony were twenty years younger than he. The new barristers
gave a formal dinner, as was customary. That was the high point—the only one
really—of Boswell's London career. "We had a course of fish, a course of ham,
fowls, and greens, a course of roast beef and apple pies, a dessert of cheese and
fruit, madeira, port, and as good claret as ever was drank." Reynolds was the
only member of the Club who was present.[21]

As a qualified barrister, Boswell now made efforts in two directions. One was
to listen to cases being tried before the King's Bench and to make notes for his
own instruction. (The editors of his journal say, "The notebook was Boswell's
pathetic substitute for methodical study of English law.") The other was to accompany judges and their entourage of lawyers on a twice-yearly "northern circuit," in which they heard cases successively in a number of cities, as Lord
Auchinleck had done in Scotland. Once in a while Boswell would pick up some
small legal job, but mostly he was just there for the socializing, and the travel cost
him more than he was ever paid. "Here now did I *perfectly* and *clearly* realize my
ideas of being a counsel on the Northern Circuit, and being an easy gentleman
with Lancashire ladies, with no gloom, no embarrassment."[22]

What Boswell had never done, either in Scotland or in England, was what
most new lawyers did: work for several years in the office of an established
professional, in order to gain a full understanding of the law. As an "easy
gentleman" he felt that he was far above that sort of drudgery.

The year before he moved to London, he had commissioned a formal portrait from Reynolds (color plate 30), in the expectation of paying for it once he
earned enough at the English bar. Reynolds normally charged £100 for a portrait but let Boswell have it for half as much, and eventually, when it became
clear that he would never be paid, was kind enough to make him a present of it.

When it was shown at the Royal Academy in 1787, a reviewer commented,
"This is a strong portrait, and shows an artist can do with paint more than nature hath attempted with flesh and blood, viz.—put good sense in the countenance." The editors of a recent Tate exhibition catalogue are more specific:
"Boswell must have looked all of his forty-five years. Reynolds, however, appears to have done his best to dignify a constitution ravaged by continual binge-
ing and disease, brought on by unbridled bouts of indulgence in casual sex."[23]

Boswell's biographer is more charitable. "In maturity, Boswell appears in
a blue coat, white stock, and powdered wig, steady and dignified. The face
has taken on assured and self-conscious importance. Still, some hint of cheerfulness lingers about the mouth, and the eyes remain always alert."[24]

Years later, Boswell's heirs banished the portrait to the attic. They were ashamed of his memory, since nineteenth-century readers thought he appeared in the *Life of Johnson* as a buffoonish butt. Eventually his great-granddaughter brought it back downstairs so that visitors could take potshots at it with a pistol. It is now in the National Portrait Gallery.[25]

Boswell leased a house for his family at 56 Great Queen Street, a short walk from Covent Garden where he had had such good times long before. As it happens, the teenaged William Blake had recently been an apprentice engraver a couple of doors away.

The family's two boys were put into schools, Sandy at Eton and James at Westminster, with a view to initiating them into the social class that might promote their success. The girls were still at home, or at times boarded nearby with a lady who took in a small number of pupils. Boswell had to admit that his daughters and Peggie were "long shut up in almost constant dull solitude."[26]

Peggie gave him a well-thought-out list of reasons why they ought to go back to Auchinleck, and pointed out that if he told people he was doing it for her health, it wouldn't look like admitting failure. He wrote it all down dutifully, but couldn't bear to obey. "I felt a reluctance to *descend*, as I felt it, to the narrow situation of Scotland, in which I had suffered so sadly from melancholy, fancying myself excluded from any chance of figuring in the great circle of Britain."[27]

Still, London was turning out to be a disappointment. "The truth is that *imaginary* London, gilded with all the brilliancy of warm fancy as I have viewed it, and London as a scene of real business, are quite different." It was a bit late in the day to be figuring that out.[28]

Mood swings came more frequently, too. There was a jolly party to celebrate moving into the new house, but the next day, "When I got into the streets I was so depressed that the tears run down my cheeks. . . . What a poor, wretched day!" Ten days after that, "My spirits were good as I ever remember them."[29]

LOSING PEGGIE

It was hard to deny what was slowly killing Peggie. In 1782, "she had no spitting of blood, but had a severe hollow cough in the nighttime, unless when quieted by laudanum, and sweatings every night. Also at times during the day, heats all over her body and a quick pulse. Also swellings in her legs; and she was very, very thin, and had pains shooting through her neck and breast. All these symptoms might be nervous. But both she and I dreaded the consumption, the fatal disease of her family."[30]

Johnson wrote sympathetically, "I hope that dear Mrs. Boswell will sur-mount her complaints; in losing her you would lose your anchor, and be tossed, without stability, by the waves of life." Boswell printed the letter in the *Life* and added in a footnote, "The truth of this has been proved by sad experience."[31]

In London in 1788 Peggie ran a dangerous fever, for which the treatment was useless or worse. "I called Sir George Baker again at night, and he ordered a blister on her breast and that she should be blooded again next day. Poor woman, she had said to me mournfully this afternoon, 'Oh, Mr. Boswell, I fear I'm dying.'"[32]

Yet some days later Boswell wrote, "I certainly had not that tenderness and anxiety which I once had, and could look with my mind's eye upon the event of her being removed by death with much more composure than for-merly. This I considered as humanely ordered by Providence; yet I was not without some upbraidings as if I were too selfish, from leading what may be called a life of pleasure. My enthusiasm for my family—for Auchinleck—has abated since I plunged into the wide speculative scene of English ambition."[33]

Peggie had one more year to live, during which she was never free from these alarms. And it was true that Boswell was shamefully neglectful. When he was apart from her he kept assuring himself that he loved her deeply; when he was with her he always found excuses to get away.

Death finally came in 1789, and although hardly unexpected, it was still a terrible shock. Peggie had gone back to Auchinleck and sent her husband an ominous letter. He hastened north with their daughter Veronica, who had remained with him in London, and found his wife "emaciated and dejected," and very weak. Yet he soon rushed away to take part in political canvassing, pursuing a hopeless plan of getting elected to Parliament from Ayrshire, and while drunk fell from his horse and badly injured a shoulder.

Boswell persuaded himself that Peggie had had remissions before and probably would again, and after six weeks he left. "I never shall forget her saying, 'Good journey!'" After just a week in London, during which the shoulder continued to torment him, a letter from their daughter Euphemia warned him to rush back. He and his two sons covered the distance to Auchinleck in just sixty-four hours, "but alas! our haste was all in vain. The fatal stroke had taken place before we set out."

Euphemia rushed out to meet them, weeping bitterly as she gave them the news. "O! my Temple," he wrote to his oldest friend, "what distress, what tender painful regrets, what unavailing earnest wishes to have but one week, one day, in which I might again hear her admirable conversation and assure her of my fervent attachment notwithstanding all my irregularities." He had to admit that if he had been the one who was ill, she would never have dreamed of leaving him alone. "I privately read the funeral service over her coffin in the presence of my sons, and was relieved by that ceremony a good deal."[34]

Some touching keepsakes were found among the Boswell papers, and are now in the Hyde Collection at Harvard. They include "the purse my dear wife used," her wedding ring, and a few wispy strands of her hair. There is also an envelope, now empty, labeled "two stalks of lily of the valley which my dear wife had in her hand the day before she died."

A couple of months after Peggie's death, Boswell noted a distressing dream. "I thought I was in a room into which Dr. Johnson entered suddenly, with a very angry look at me. I said to him, 'My dear Sir, you certainly have nothing to say against me.' He answered sternly: '*Have* I nothing to say against you, Sir?' I awoke uneasy and thought this applicable to my connection with E. M." Since Boswell generally used the word "connection" to indicate a sexual relationship, this may mean he was ashamed of some new liaison so soon after losing his wife. Even in dreams, Johnson, who had died five years earlier, continued to issue stern reproofs.[35]

POLITICAL HUMILIATION

Reluctantly acknowledging that he was getting nowhere as a lawyer, Boswell decided to attach himself to a powerful political patron and see what that might do. This was Lord Lonsdale, who lived in Lowther Castle in Westmoreland, in the Lake District. Lonsdale controlled no fewer than nine seats in the House of Commons, and Boswell persuaded himself that one day he might occupy one of them.

The attempt to win Lonsdale's patronage was a disaster. Though extremely wealthy, he was a penny-pinching miser with a bullying and controlling personality. He was a product of the English boarding school system, and proud of it. He related to Boswell that he and the other youngest boys had to go outdoors in the winter before dawn to pump water until their fingers were numb. Back inside, they were not allowed anywhere near the single fire at the end of the room. When the older boys needed to urinate they "would piss by the little boys' beds." Boswell was startled to find that Lonsdale recalled all of this with satisfaction. "It makes a very pernicious succession of slavery and tyranny. The big boys, recollecting what they have suffered, are barbarously severe upon the little boys; and perhaps his own domination has been in-flamed by that education."[36]

Toward the end of this nasty relationship, it even looked like there might be a duel. Once, when they were traveling together, Lonsdale told him coldly, "I suppose you thought I was to bring you into parliament. I never had any such intention. It would do you harm to be in parliament." He went on to say that Boswell "would get drunk and make a foolish speech." Lonsdale then grew even more insulting. "You have kept low company all your life. What are *you*, Sir?" Boswell retorted, "A gentleman, my Lord, a man of honour; and I hope to show myself such." To this Lonsdale replied, "You will be settled when you have a bullet in your belly."

When they arrived at an inn Boswell believed that they were on the point of fighting a duel, but the mercurial Lonsdale now acknowledged that he might have misunderstood Boswell's words, drank a glass of wine with him (usually he refused to share his wine), and after that "held out his hand and gave it me, saying, 'Boswell, forget all that is past.'"

The whole contretemps forced Boswell to acknowledge how humiliating it was to grovel. Ten days later he wrote, "I was a despicable being." He felt as if his entire personality had somehow returned to the original tabula rasa. "I was precisely as when in wretched low spirits thirty years ago, without any addition to my character from having had the friendship of Dr. Johnson and many eminent men, made the tour of Europe and Corsica in particular, and written two very successful books [his Hebrides journal had been published by then]. I was as a board on which fine figures had been painted, but which some corrosive application had reduced to its original nakedness."[37]

THE LIFE OF JOHNSON

Yet it was just at this time, when everything else was going wrong, that Boswell was completing his masterpiece. Two competitors were already in the field. One was Hester Piozzi, who was living in Italy. In 1786 her London publisher brought out her *Anecdotes of the Late Samuel Johnson during the Last Twenty Years of His Life,* which quickly became a bestseller. In it she admitted that it was "a piece of motley mosaic work," not a biography. In the *Life of Johnson,* published five years later, Boswell took pleasure in demonstrating, from other people's accounts and from his own journals, that she was slipshod in retelling conversations and often misrepresented them.[38]

The other competitor was Sir John Hawkins, whose *Life of Samuel Johnson* appeared in 1787. That was a genuine biography, by someone who had known Johnson far longer than Boswell had, and it contained much valuable material that no one else knew about. But like everything Hawkins wrote, it was exhaustingly prolix, with digressions completely unconnected to its subject, and it certainly didn't set a standard that would be hard to surpass.

It was writing the great *Life* that turned out to be Boswell's true vocation, as perhaps he had known all along. The *Journal of a Tour to the Hebrides with Samuel Johnson,* published in 1786, two years after Johnson's death, had simply been his own journal from the trip, minimally edited. Now he was determined to locate every possible kind of evidence, including hundreds of Johnson's own letters.

For once in his life, Boswell committed himself to a task with remarkable tenacity. He wrote to Temple, "You cannot imagine what labour, what perplexity, what vexation I have endured in arranging a prodigious multiplicity of materials, in supplying omissions, in searching for papers buried in different masses—and all this besides the exertion of composing and polishing. Many a time have I thought of giving it up." In the *Life* itself he said, "I have sometimes been obliged to run half over London in order to fix a date correctly, which, when I had accomplished, I well knew would obtain me no praise, though a failure would have been to my discredit."[39]

Fortunately Boswell had formed a close friendship with Edmond Malone, an Irish lawyer and scholar who was nearing completion of a major edition of Shakespeare's plays. Malone had been a member of the Club since 1782 (figure 89). Without him there would have been no *Life of Johnson.* He gave constant encouragement as well as practical advice, and he and Boswell often stayed up late into the evening working over documents. Malone also set an inspiring example. "Paid a visit to Malone. Found him, as I always have done, engaged in literature, so as to have no weariness." Malone enjoyed research so much that it invigorated him rather than tiring him.[40]

No pedant, Malone brought keen intelligence to their collaboration; Boswell referred to him in his journal as "an acute reasoner." He had to admit that the difference between him and his friend was humiliating. Finding Malone "fully occupied in historical and biographical researches" on another occasion, he acknowledged, "I had absolutely no pursuit whatever." "Pursuit" in this sense is defined by Johnson as "endeavour to attain."[41]

The *Life of Samuel Johnson, LL.D.* was published in 1791, with a dedication to Reynolds, on the twenty-eighth anniversary of Boswell's fateful

89. Edmond Malone

meeting with Johnson in Davies's shop. Its subtitle emphasized its breadth of scope: *The Whole Exhibiting a View of Literature and Literary Men in Great Britain for Near Half a Century, During Which He Flourished.*

The book is not without faults, though Boswell scholars have been reluctant to acknowledge them. The coverage of Johnson's life is very uneven, though Boswell can't be blamed for that. Little information survived from the early decades, and he did more than anyone to dig up what could be found. And of course the conversations, all of which come from Johnson's final twenty years, take up disproportionate space, but no reader would ever wish them shorter.

The real faults are two. One is a pompous literary style that Boswell thought necessary for a serious book, very different from the expressive freedom of his journals. And the other is his tendency to obtrude his own opinions on every possible subject, often telling readers that they are lucky to have them. Macaulay's verdict is severe but justified: "There is not in all his books a single remark of his own on literature, politics, religion, or society which is not either commonplace or absurd." That makes it all the more admirable that Boswell faithfully recorded what Johnson said on those subjects, which was often in direct opposition to his own views.[42]

Boswell's analogy for his project was "an Egyptian pyramid in which there will be a complete mummy of Johnson, that literary monarch." He honored

Johnson for having "embalmed so many eminent persons" in his own biographies. Those are strange analogies for a book that in fact triumphs by bringing Johnson back to life. Boswell's originality was extraordinary. No biographer before him had ever thought of including actual conversations, even if they had known their subjects personally. And few writers, then or later, have ever had Boswell's gift for creating a reality by evoking tones of voice, facial expressions, laughter, and body language. The *Life* has been admirably described as "a reenactment of Johnson."[43]

An apt analogy was proposed by an anonymous reviewer in the *Public Advertiser,* who compared the *Life of Johnson* to an opera "in which there is a *hero* with a number of *subordinate characters,* and an alternate succession of *recitative* and *airs* of various tone and effect." It was a shrewd suggestion, not less so for having been written by Boswell himself.[44]

The real reviewers treated the *Life* with the esteem it deserved. The *Critical Review,* which was the most prestigious, gives a good sense of the response:

> We have the highest respect for the vigorous, comprehensive, discriminating mind of Johnson. We listen to his solemn decisions with a kind of reverence, and even his mistakes we pass over without a censure, for to err is human. His attendant shares our regard. Lively, flippant, occasionally intelligent, and always entertaining, we can laugh with him or at him with equal ease. He is nearer our level: we never leave him but in good humour, and even sometimes, in his greatest eccentricities, we are compelled to own that we "could have better spared a better man."

"Occasionally intelligent" must have given Boswell pain, and he probably didn't find the allusion to Falstaff flattering, but on the whole this is a fair and even affectionate judgment.[45]

Jorge Luis Borges suggested that Boswell deliberately presented himself as a kind of Sancho Panza, "a sometimes stupid and loyal companion. There are characters whose role is to bring out the hero's personality. It seems impossible that Boswell didn't realize this."[46]

People who didn't like Boswell naturally didn't like the *Life.* Hester Piozzi and Hawkins were understandably insulted by the way he treated them, and Elizabeth Montagu got furious when she found confirmation in the *Life* that Johnson had never thought much of her book on Shakespeare. The hypersophisticated Horace Walpole was simply disgusted. He called Boswell "that sot," and wrote some sarcastic verses in his copy of the book:

> When boozy Bozzy belched out Johnson's sayings,
> And half the volume filled with his own brayings,
> Scotland beheld again before her pass
> A brutal bulldog coupled with an ass.[47]

Desperate for money, Boswell had been tempted to accept a flat offer of £1,000 in advance of publication, but decided to wait and see if royalties might work out better. They certainly did. A total of 1,750 sets of the two-volume work were printed, half of which sold within two weeks, and it continued to do well thereafter. At the end of 1792 he settled accounts with his publisher and printer, and joyfully recorded that he was paid £1,555, 18 shillings, and 2 pence. By the time a second edition sold out he had earned a handsome total of £2,500.[48]

DEATH COMES FOR JAMES BOSWELL

Continuing to live in London, Boswell visited Auchinleck less and less frequently after Peggie's death. In 1790 his cousin Robert Boswell, who had been looking after his financial affairs in Scotland, urged him to return and live on the estate. "To Auchinleck you must at last come," he suggested encouragingly. James replied, "So I must, alive or dead." It would be the latter.[49]

The journals, once so rich, petered out. In 1788–89 there was a gap of more than a year, and for a stretch of sixteen months in 1791–92 only a few scraps have survived. If there was any journal at all in 1795, Boswell's final year, it hasn't been found.

Life was seeming increasingly pointless. After an evening at the Club in 1793, where among others Burke and Burney were present, Boswell wrote, "I have lost my faculty of recording. . . . I had little relish even of THE CLUB. I enjoyed chiefly the wine." After attending a feast elsewhere he listed no fewer than nine varieties of alcohol he had consumed: "I drank of all the liquors—cold drink, small beer, ale, porter, cider, madeira, sherry, old hock, port, claret." If the "cold drink" was alcoholic, the total would be ten.[50]

After drinking "really too much" at the Royal Academy Club in 1793, he broke into a run on a slippery pavement, fell and damaged an elbow, and after he got home was shocked to realize he was missing £50 in bank notes that had been in his pocket. He went back to the tavern where the club had met to search for the money, without success. But the next morning his housekeeper told him she had seen him open a cabinet when he got in, and sure enough, the bank notes were there. "Strange that I was utterly unconscious of having put them there last night. But one in liquor is sometimes wonderfully cautious and cunning."[51]

On another occasion that year Boswell was stumbling home drunk when, as the *London Chronicle* reported, "he was attacked in Titchfield Street, knocked down, robbed, and left lying in the street quite stunned, so that the villain got clear off." He afterward ran a fever and was confined to bed for two weeks.[52]

Friends were beginning to find Boswell, once the most engaging of companions, downright boring. Temple came up from Devon and told him bluntly "that he had never seen anybody so idle as I was." In his own diary Temple was still more severe: "Never thinks of anyone but himself; indifferent to other people's feelings. . . . No command of his tongue; restless, no composure."[53]

John Courtenay, a member of Parliament who spent a lot of time with Boswell, Reynolds, and Malone—they called themselves "the Gang"—said in 1791, "Poor Boswell is very low and dispirited and almost melancholy mad. . . . I try all I can to rouse him, but he recurs so tiresomely and tediously to the same cursed, trite, commonplace topics about death, etc.—that we grow old, and when we are old we are not young—that I despair of effecting a cure."[54]

Valued friends continued to disappear. In 1790 Paoli, who had been so affectionate and generous, decided to return to Corsica. The island was now clearly French and would never be independent, but there were hopes that its local rights would be respected, and he was willing to reassume his eminent status there. Boswell gave him a farewell dinner, but since he wasn't keeping up his journal, there is no record of what it was like. As it turned out, Paoli's return to Corsica didn't work out, and by the end of 1795 he was back in England—but that was too late for Boswell.[55]

Another loss was especially distressing. In 1793 Boswell learned from the newspapers "that my old friend and correspondent and confidant in hypochondria, Andrew Erskine [of Grange], was dead." It later came out that he had committed suicide by filling his pockets with stones and walking into the sea. Erskine had been Boswell's friend in the early London days; it was he who said at that time, "You extract more out of me, you are more chemical to me than anybody."[56]

Worst of all was the death of Reynolds, with whom Boswell had always remained close. Reynolds had managed well enough with poor hearing, but by 1790 his eyesight was failing badly and he was forced to give up painting. It seems clear that he suffered from liver disease, due no doubt to heavy consumption of alcohol, and a malignant tumor was gradually destroying the optic nerve in one eye. That in turn provoked a detached retina, for which nothing could be done in those days. In 1792 he died, and there was a magnificent funeral in St. Paul's.[57]

The following year, while Boswell was at Auchinleck, his sixteen-year-old son Jamie wrote consolingly from London that he shouldn't brood about legal and political disappointments. People who gained distinction in those fields "have not been known to Johnson, Voltaire, Rousseau, and Garrick, Goldsmith, etc. They have not visited the patriots of Corsica. In short, would you, rather than have enjoyed so many advantages, have been a rich, though dull, plodding lawyer? You cannot expect to be both at the same time."[58]

There are two images of Boswell from these last years, both of them striking. One is a sketch by Bennet Langton's son George; an engraving made from it is reproduced here (figure 90). It captures what Fanny Burney must have meant when she said that "there was something slouching in the gait and dress of Mr. Boswell."[59]

The other is a pencil sketch by Thomas Lawrence (figure 91). A print was made from it too, and Carlyle's description is penetrating—"that cocked nose, cocked partly in triumph over his weaker fellow-creatures, partly to snuff up the smell of coming pleasure and scent it from afar; those bag-cheeks, hanging like half-filled wineskins, still able to contain more; that coarsely-protruded shelf mouth, that fat dewlapped chin." There is no denying that "wineskin" is an apt term for Boswell.[60]

Sometime in 1794 he began to write a melancholy song, but never got beyond the first two lines:

'Tis o'er, 'tis o'er, the dream is o'er,
And life's delusion is no more.[61]

On April 14, 1795, Boswell collapsed. The artist James Farington noted, "Boswell this day attended the Literary Club, and went from thence too ill to walk home." He never left his bed again, and was tormented constantly by fever, headaches, nausea, and pain. A modern physician who has studied his symptoms concludes that a lifetime of venereal disease had finally caught up with him; his kidneys were infected, and a fatal uremia ensued. He held on for a month, managing to believe that he might still get well, and on May 19 he died. He was fifty-four years old.[62]

90. Boswell by George Langton

91. Boswell by Thomas Lawrence

The ever-loyal Malone wrote to a friend, "I shall miss him more and more every day. He was in the constant habit of calling upon me almost daily, and I used to grumble sometimes at his turbulence; but now miss and regret his noise and his hilarity and his perpetual good humour, which had no bounds. Poor fellow, he has somehow stolen away from us without any notice, and without my being at all prepared for it."[63]

On June 8 James Boswell was laid to rest in the family vault at Auchinleck.

Epilogue

By the time of Boswell's death, many of the people he had known were already gone—Goldsmith, Garrick, Beauclerk, Reynolds, Thrale, Smith, and of course Johnson. Johnson was seventy-five when he died, and despite his poor health, he was the only one of them to live that long. Garrick, Reynolds, and Smith died in their sixties, Thrale at fifty-two, and Goldsmith and Beauclerk in their forties.

For those who remained, their stories can be briefly told. In the words of Sheridan's Mrs. Malaprop, "our retrospection will now be all to the future."[1]

HESTER PIOZZI

Hester Piozzi, formerly Hester Thrale, finally got to enjoy a happy life on her own terms. After Johnson's death she and her husband spent a couple of years in Italy, and then returned to England. She had no desire to rebuild bridges that other people had broken. "Mrs. Montagu," she wrote in her journal, "wants to make up with me again. I daresay she does, but I will not be taken and left, even at the pleasure of those who were much dearer and nearer to me than Mrs. Montagu." Felicity Nussbaum puts it well: "Thrale Piozzi refused to live her life as the sacrificial victim of a she-tragedy who was expected to expiate a sexual crime." George Dance made a fine likeness of her profile in 1793, when she was fifty-two (figure 92).[2]

92. Hester Piozzi

Streatham Park became available after a renter departed, and the Piozzis moved in, throwing an enormous party. It was a continuing source of bitterness, however, that Hester's daughters continued to shun her. She commented, "The Misses will be told how fine Piozzi has made their house—and will wish him and his wife dead the more, I suppose, that they may enjoy it. Was I to lose him they would come into possession instantly, for I would not live single here six weeks, and probably should not live at all three months."[3]

In 1794, weary of London, the couple moved to Hester's native Wales. Piozzi's English was still somewhat shaky. When she fell ill, he recorded in his diary, "Mrs. Piozzi she got the influenza, and find herself very ill with fever." She recovered, but before long he got worse, from gout that had afflicted him for many years.

On their anniversary in 1803 she presented him with a charming poem, running the changes on a single rhyme (Johnson had once given her a birthday poem in that style):

Accept, my love, this honest lay
Upon your twentieth wedding day.
I little hoped that life would stay
To hail the *twentieth* wedding day.
If you're grown gouty, I grown gray,
Upon our twentieth wedding day,
'Tis no great wonder; friends must say
"Why, 'twas their twentieth wedding day."[4]

In 1809 it became evident that Piozzi was nearing death. Gangrene spread through his body, and he was comatose most of the time. When he died Hester was so distraught that it was a week before she could record anything in *Thraliana*, that set of elegant blank books that Henry had given her over thirty years before. "All is over," she wrote, "and my second husband's death is the last thing recorded in my first husband's present. Cruel death!" Those are indeed the very last words in that vast, fascinating compilation.[5]

Hester lived on for another dozen years, dying at Bath in 1821. At the very end there was some rapprochement with her daughters. Queeney—who at forty-four had married an admiral much older than herself—arrived in time to be with her mother, together with her sister Sophia. "I am happy to say she knew us," Queeney wrote, "and appeared pleased at our being by her bedside; and whenever she is awake, puts out a hand to each of us." Her final gesture before expiring was characteristic, though. Looking up at her doctor, she traced the outline of a coffin in the air.[6]

Hester was buried next to Gabriele Piozzi in the churchyard in the little village of Tremeirchion, in her native Wales. In 1909 a marble plaque was placed in the church: "Hester Lynch Piozzi, Doctor Johnson's Mrs. Thrale, born 1741, died 1821. Witty, vivacious and charming, in an age of genius she ever held a foremost place." The single pub in Tremeirchion today is called the Salusbury Arms. Salusbury was Hester's maiden name.

EDMUND BURKE

After the acquittal of Warren Hastings in 1795, Burke resigned from Parliament at the age of sixty-four, having served for three decades, and was granted a royal pension in recognition of his distinguished service. In the following year one of the more radical Foxite Whigs, the young Duke of Bedford, mocked him for accepting a pension when he had campaigned in the past for financial reform. Burke had not in fact ever objected to pensions when well deserved, such as the one Johnson received, and he replied with a magnificent *Letter to a Noble Lord.*

As Burke cuttingly observed, the Duke of Bedford had done nothing whatsoever to deserve his enormous inherited wealth, and it was fortunate for him that commoners like Burke were willing to defend his privileges. "I have supported with very great zeal, and I am told with some degree of success, those opinions, or if his Grace likes another expression better, those old prejudices, which buoy up the ponderous mass of his nobility, wealth, and titles. . . . I have strained every nerve to keep the Duke of Bedford in that situation which alone makes him my superior."[7]

In the *Letter,* Burke rose for one last time to heights of rhetorical brilliance. Bedford's family, the Russells (it was they who developed Russell Square in London), originally got their start as favorites of Henry VIII. Burke imagined the young duke bloated with wealth that he owed entirely to the crown.

> The grants to the House of Russell were so enormous as not only to outrage economy, but even to stagger credibility. The Duke of Bedford is the leviathan among all the creatures of the Crown. He tumbles about his unwieldy bulk; he plays and frolics in the ocean of the royal bounty. Huge as he is, and whilst "he lies floating many a rood," he is still a creature. His ribs, his fins, his whalebone, his blubber, the very spiracles through which he spouts a torrent of brine against his origin and covers me all over with the spray—everything of him and about him is from the throne. Is it for *him* to question the dispensation of the royal favour?

Milton's Satan "lies floating many a rood." Johnson quotes this line in the *Dictionary* to illustrate the definition of "rood" as "a measure of sixteen feet and a half."[8]

Burke's feelings at the end of his life were bitter. "The storm has gone over me," he said in the *Letter,* "and I lie like one of those old oaks which the late hurricane has scattered about me. I am stripped of all my honours, I am torn up by the roots, and lie prostrate on the earth."[9]

One year later he was dead, of some kind of stomach complaint. He was buried at Beaconsfield, alongside his brother and his son. That was Richard, whom he had gotten elected to the Club in 1782, and who had just recently been elected to Parliament, but then died suddenly a few weeks afterward.

Edmund's widow, Jane Nugent Burke, lived on at Beaconsfield until 1812. The year after that there was a fire and the house burned to the ground.

RICHARD AND ELIZABETH SHERIDAN

The Sheridans' legendary love match went the way of most legendary love matches. They both took lovers, sometimes provoking jealousy and sometimes not. Richard had an overt affair with a married lady named Frances Ann Crewe, a leading beauty who was painted by both Reynolds and Gainsborough (her little son was the subject of Reynolds's charming *Master Crewe as Henry VIII*). At her Hampstead villa she often entertained Sheridan's political allies Burke and Fox, and was also friendly with the Burneys and the Thrales. Elizabeth Sheridan remained on perfectly good terms with Mrs. Crewe, and probably regarded the ménage à trois as confirmation that they had been accepted into the elite.[10]

After a while, not surprisingly, the repeated affairs took a toll and the couple separated. Elizabeth was especially disgusted by Richard's cavalier lack of discretion. On one occasion he was caught in bed at Crewe Hall not with their friend but with a governess. It was the public humiliation she objected to. To another friend she complained of "the apparent total want of feeling for me, of all sense of honor, delicacy, propriety, considering the *person,* the *place,* and the *time.*"[11]

Like Peggie Boswell, Elizabeth had shown symptoms of tuberculosis for years, and they became much worse around 1790. Although her doctors feared that pregnancy would be threatening to her health, she did get pregnant, and not by Richard but by her lover Lord Edward Fitzgerald. A baby girl was born and Elizabeth died soon afterward at the age of thirty-six. Richard was present at the deathbed and deeply moved. He and Fitzgerald agreed that he should be the one to bring up the child, but the infant fell ill and died soon afterward.

As for Sheridan's political career, it was fated to disappointment. Though losing sympathy with the French Revolution, he continued to insist on parliamentary reform, which in the charged atmosphere of the 1790s made him look like a dangerous radical. Meanwhile he had formed a close friendship with the Prince of Wales, who was just twenty-one when they met, and from whom he had good reason to expect patronage. George III suffered from recurring bouts of insanity, and the prince's supporters hoped that he would soon come to the throne or at least be named regent. That didn't happen until 1811. By then Sheridan's health was failing and he was drinking far too much. Byron, who met him during that period, wrote that "the upper part of Sheridan's face was that of a god—a forehead most expansive, and an eye of peculiar brilliancy and fire—but below he showed the satyr."[12]

By 1815 Sheridan was hopelessly broke, since a fire had destroyed the Drury Lane Theatre on which his income depended. After leaving Parliament and losing immunity to prosecution, he spent some time in a debtor's prison, even though he sold off everything he could, including Reynolds's famous portrait of Elizabeth as St. Cecilia (figure 57, page 201 above). "I shall part from this picture," he lamented, "as from drops of my heart's blood."[13]

In 1816 Sheridan died. As the author of *The Rivals* and *The School for Scandal,* he was interred in Poets' Corner in Westminster Abbey, between Handel and Johnson and close to Garrick. That would probably have disappointed him, since he had wanted to be buried next to his parliamentary colleague Fox. "Even in death," a modern commentator says, "the Whigs insisted on keeping him in his proper place."[14]

EDWARD GIBBON

In the 1790s Gibbon was living peacefully in Lausanne, tinkering with his unfinished memoirs and declaring that the French Revolution meant a new eruption of barbarism. In 1793 the death of the wife of his best friend in England, Lord Sheffield, brought him hurrying back to be of what help he could. Though by now almost frighteningly obese, he was not aware of any physical complaint more serious than his long-standing gout.

Or rather, there was something he was aware of but pretended not to be. That was a hydrocele, a grotesquely swollen testicle caused by a hernia that had developed in his Hampshire militia days, fully twenty years before. His friends did notice it, of course, but they were too tactful to comment.

Now he finally sought medical help, and several quarts of fluid were drained. The relief was only temporary. Still, he never lost his usual cheerfulness, and as late as January 14, 1794, he was talking about a journey he expected to make. Two days after that he was dead, probably from peritonitis caused by dirty surgical instruments. He was fifty-six years old.

The final sentence of Gibbon's *Memoirs,* in the composite version that Sheffield put together from his drafts, is this: "In old age, the consolation of hope is reserved for the tenderness of parents, who commence a new life in their children; the faith of enthusiasts, who sing hallelujahs above the clouds;

and the vanity of authors, who presume the immortality of their name and writings." Gibbon had no belief in eternal life above the clouds, and no children in whom part of himself could live on. For him the *Decline and Fall* was everything.[15]

BENNET LANGTON

Langton was never a public figure, and quietly faded away. Few people would know his name today if he had not been a particular friend of Johnson, and he would have thought that entirely appropriate.

One year after Johnson died Langton commissioned a painting of himself (color plate 31) gazing meditatively at an impressive bust of Johnson, in imitation of Rembrandt's *Aristotle Contemplating the Bust of Homer.* The sculptor Joseph Nollekens had made the bust in the late 1770s (figure 93), and an expert on images of Johnson thinks that this may be "the finest likeness." Johnson himself complained that he didn't appreciate the flowing hair, which the sculptor insisted would make him look like an ancient poet. It was modeled, Nollekens's biographer said, "from the flowing locks of a sturdy Irish beggar, originally a street pavior, who after he had sat an hour refused to take a shilling, stating that he could have made more by begging." But on the whole Johnson was pleased with the result, and commented later, "I think my friend Joe Nollekens can chop out a head with any of them."[16]

Langton died in 1801 at the age of sixty-four, the last remaining member of the original nine who formed the Club in 1764. His large family was generously provided for in his will—the thought of which had provoked from Johnson laughter "so loud, that in the silence of the night his voice seemed to resound from Temple Bar to Fleet Ditch."[17]

FANNY BURNEY

In 1786 Fanny was pressured by her father into accepting a position at Court which she dreaded in advance, and found miserably confining once she was there. By then she had published her second novel, *Cecilia,* and thought of herself as an established author. What she now became was Second Keeper of the Robes to Queen Charlotte, which amounted to being a domestic servant. It meant giving up her freedom and hardly ever seeing her family or friends; she was on duty seven days a week from seven in the morning until midnight. The queen herself was warm and considerate, but Fanny's

93. Johnson by Nollekens

immediate superior was a German named Mrs. Schwellenberg, the First Keeper of the Robes, who treated her with harshness little short of sadism.

All the same, there was no possibility of refusing the honor, because Charles Burney insisted on it. It seemed evident to him that his own career would benefit greatly, as well as providing financial security for Fanny. Macaulay's verdict seems just: "Dr. Burney was transported out of himself with delight. Not such are the raptures of a Circassian father who has sold his pretty daughter well to a Turkish slave merchant. . . . He seems to have thought that going to court was like going to heaven."[18]

Fanny liked the king as well as the queen, since both were unfailingly kind. Like everyone else, however, she was deeply alarmed by King George's episodes of apparent madness. One encounter with him provoked at first "the severest personal terror I ever experienced in my life," but then turned out to be deeply touching. During one of King George's episodes of so-called madness (now thought to be symptoms of a hereditary blood disorder called porphyry) Fanny was walking in the palace garden and suddenly saw him rushing toward her, having escaped from his attendants. She began to run, until the others caught up and restrained the king. Approaching her, he asked in a kind voice why she had run away. "Think of my surprise to feel him put both his hands around my two shoulders, and then kiss my cheek!" He was simply grateful for a chance to have a normal conversation with somebody he was fond of, and they chatted for several minutes until his keepers took him away.[19]

Life in this privileged purgatory went on for nearly six years, until Fanny's health was seriously affected and Charles Burney could finally entertain the possibility of letting her resign. She had fainting spells and unexplained seizures, a stabbing pain in her side, and stifled breathing. When her father grasped just how miserable she was, which he had done his best not to know until then, he authorized her to tell the queen she must leave for the sake of her health. "I was truly glad," she told her sister Susanna, "of this permission to rebel." Even rebellion required permission![20]

Soon after leaving the Court in 1791, Fanny fell in love with a charming aristocratic refugee from France, Alexandre d'Arblay, and she married him in 1793. She was forty-one at the time and had probably stopped imagining that she would ever marry. The following year their only child, named Alexander for his father, was born; he would grow up to be a fellow of Christ's College, Cambridge and an Anglican priest in London.

Meanwhile Fanny had written a third novel, *Camilla, or A Picture of Youth*, and also several plays that were never produced, apart from a single disastrous performance at Drury Lane of the oddly named *Edwy and Elgiva* (Anglo-Saxon themes were popular). Afterward she acknowledged that the play had its limitations dramatically, but she was justified in complaining that the actors didn't bother to learn their lines and ad-libbed outrageously throughout. It's interesting to speculate that her turn from comedy to tragedy may have been prompted by the depression of life at Court. Critics have noticed that these plays all deal with unjust power and abused heroines.

There was also a financial motive. Even a moderately successful playwright could expect to earn more money than a novelist. Meanwhile, Queen Charlotte gave Fanny an annual pension of £100, to be continued for life.[21]

Charles Burney never approved of Fanny's marriage. The ostensible reasons were that d'Arblay was a Roman Catholic, had lost his fortune, and at the beginning of the French Revolution had been a reformer, much like Lafayette. That hardly made him a dangerous radical, but as Fanny herself said of her father, "He is all aristocratic!" Like Johnson, Burney had fought his way into prominence from humble beginnings, and was a warm supporter of traditional hierarchy. He refused to come to his daughter's wedding.[22]

For that matter, it was probably only because he had lost his status and wealth that the aristocratic d'Arblay would marry Fanny. In France, as Betty Rizzo comments, "he would not have considered for a moment marrying an unmoneyed, unfamilied, non-Catholic professional author."[23]

For some years the d'Arblays lived in Paris, where Fanny underwent a mastectomy, without anesthesia of course. Her detailed description of the nonstop torture is horrifying to read. Happily, the operation was a success, and she would live for another twenty-nine years.

When Napoleon escaped from Elba in 1815, Fanny fled from Paris with her young son. In Brussels she heard the cannons of Waterloo booming close by. Back in England, she and her husband settled at Bath, where she had often spent time with the Thrales in years gone by. In 1818 d'Arblay died there from complications of gout. One by one the other people closest to Fanny departed this life: her brother James (a rear admiral by then) in 1821, her older sister Esther in 1832, her son Alexander in 1837, and her younger sister Charlotte in 1838. Charles Burney had died in 1814 as a lodger in the Chelsea home for military veterans, where he had been earning a modest income as an organist until symptoms of dementia incapacitated him.

Finally in 1840 it was Fanny's turn, the last of the characters in this book. She was eighty-seven. A heavily edited version of her diaries was published two years later, and in a review Macaulay marveled that someone could still have been alive so recently whose celebrity was forged so many decades before. "Thousands of reputations had, during that period, sprung up, bloomed, withered, and disappeared. . . . She lived to be a classic."[24]

THE AFTERLIFE OF THE CLUB

With inevitable mutations, the Club has remained in being right down to the present day, under the name of the London Literary Society. Among its members have been, with their years of election, Walter Scott (1818), Thomas Babington Macaulay (1839), William Ewart Gladstone (1857), Alfred Lord Tennyson (1865), Matthew Arnold (1882), Rudyard Kipling (1914), Neville Chamberlain (1929), Kenneth Clark (1941), T. S. Eliot (1942), Max Beerbohm (1942), and Harold Macmillan (1954).

Not many of the hundreds of other members' names would ring a bell with readers today. It's notable that increasingly they were chosen from politics and the peerage, not from literature and the arts, and that by the time Kipling, Beerbohm, and Eliot got in they were nearing the end of their careers. And how many names don't appear at all, who might well have been chosen if Johnson and Burke were still electing the members! No Dickens and Thackeray, no Trollope and Hardy, no Lawrence and Orwell and Auden and Larkin. There were several Conservative prime ministers, but not the greatest of them, Winston Churchill. And of course no George Eliot or Virginia Woolf. It never ceased to be a club for men.[25]

Appendix

1764   Sir Joshua Reynolds, painter and writer on art
       Samuel Johnson, writer and moralist
       Edmund Burke, parliamentary orator and political thinker
       Oliver Goldsmith, writer and soi-disant doctor
       Topham Beauclerk, man about town
       Bennet Langton, country gentleman
       Sir John Hawkins, lawyer and musicologist
       Anthony Chamier, MP and bureaucrat
       Christopher Nugent, physician and father-in-law of Burke
1765   Samuel Dyer, scholar and linguist
       Thomas Percy, clergyman and later bishop, editor of traditional ballads
1768   George Colman, playwright and theater manager
       Robert Chambers, Oxford law professor and later judge in India
1773   James Boswell, lawyer, writer, and future Scottish laird
       David Garrick, actor and theater manager
       William Jones, lawyer, linguist, and Orientalist
       Lord Charlemont, Irish statesman promoting independence
       Agmondesham Vesey, member of the Parliament of Ireland, friend of Burke
1774   Edward Gibbon, MP and historian
       Charles James Fox, parliamentary orator
       George Fordyce, Scottish chemist and physician
       George Steevens, Shakespearean scholar
       Sir Charles Bunbury, MP

1775   Adam Smith, Scottish economist and philosopher
        Thomas Barnard, Irish dean and later bishop
1777   Joseph Warton, clergyman, poet, Oxford professor of poetry
        Richard Brinsley Sheridan, playwright and parliamentary orator
        Lord Ossory, Irish peer and friend of Reynolds
        Richard Marlay, Irish clergyman and later bishop
        John Dunning, lawyer and MP
1778   Sir Joseph Banks, botanist and shipmate of Captain Cook
        William Windham, MP
        William Scott, jurist
        Earl Spencer (Viscount Althorp until 1783), politician
1780   Jonathan Shipley, bishop, friend of Benjamin Franklin
1782   Edmond Malone, Irish scholar, close friend of Boswell
        Thomas Warton, Joseph's brother, Oxford don and poet
        Edward Eliot, MP and friend of Reynolds
        Sir Charles Bingham (later Lord Lucan), Irish politician, father-in-law of Earl
           Spencer
        Richard Burke, lawyer, son of Edmund Burke
1784   Charles Burney, music teacher and performer, musicologist
        Sir William Hamilton, British envoy to Naples, antiquarian
        Henry Temple (later Lord Palmerston), politician and father of a future prime
           minister
        Richard Warren, physician

Compiled from David Cannadine et al., New Annals of the Club *(London: Henry Sotheran, 2014), 124–25.*

Short Titles

Since there are many different editions of Boswell's *Life of Johnson*, I indicate the date under which each quotation or episode appears, as well as page references to the long-standard Oxford edition. For short works, such as Johnson's *Rambler* essays or chapters in novels, it's most helpful to give chapter numbers rather than page references. All other references are given in full.

Applause of the Jury   *Boswell: The Applause of the Jury, 1782–1785,* ed. Irma S. Lustig and Frederick A. Pottle (New York: McGraw-Hill, 1981)

Bate   Walter Jackson Bate, *Samuel Johnson* (New York: Harcourt Brace, 1977)

Boswell for the Defence   *Boswell for the Defence, 1769–1774,* ed. William K. Wimsatt and Frederick A. Pottle (New York: McGraw-Hill, 1959)

Brady   Frank Brady, *James Boswell: The Later Years, 1769–1795* (New York: McGraw-Hill, 1984)

Burney *Journals*   *The Early Journals and Letters of Fanny Burney,* ed. Lars E. Troide et al. (Oxford: Clarendon, 1988–)

Dictionary   *A Dictionary of the English Language,* ed. Samuel Johnson (London, 1755)

Early Biographies   *The Early Biographies of Samuel Johnson,* ed. O. M. Brack, Jr., and Robert E. Kelley (Iowa City: University of Iowa Press, 1974)

English Experiment	*Boswell: The English Experiment, 1785–1789,* ed. Irma S. Lustig and Frederick A. Pottle (New York: McGraw-Hill, 1986)
Extremes	*Boswell in Extremes, 1776–1778,* ed. Charles M. Weis and Frederick A. Pottle (New York: McGraw-Hill, 1970)
Germany and Switzerland	*Boswell on the Grand Tour: Germany and Switzerland, 1764,* ed. Frederick A. Pottle (New York: McGraw-Hill, 1953)
Great Biographer	*Boswell: The Great Biographer, 1789–1795,* ed. Marlies K. Danziger and Frank Brady (New York: McGraw-Hill, 1989)
Hawkins	Sir John Hawkins, *The Life of Samuel Johnson,* ed. O. M. Brack, Jr. (Athens: University of Georgia Press, 2013)
Hebrides	*Boswell's Journal of a Tour to the Hebrides with Samuel Johnson, 1773,* ed. Frederick A. Pottle and Charles H. Bennett (New York: McGraw-Hill, 1961)
Holland	*Boswell in Holland, 1763–1764,* ed. Frederick A. Pottle (New York: McGraw-Hill, 1952)
In Search of a Wife	*Boswell in Search of a Wife, 1766–1769,* ed. Frank Brady and Frederick A. Pottle (New York: McGraw-Hill, 1956)
Italy, Corsica and France	*Boswell on the Grand Tour: Italy, Corsica, and France, 1765–1766,* ed. Frank Brady and Frederick A. Pottle (New York: McGraw-Hill, 1955)
Johnsonian Miscellanies	*Johnsonian Miscellanies,* ed. George Birkbeck Hill (Oxford: Clarendon, 1897)
Journey	Johnson, *A Journey to the Western Islands of Scotland,* ed. Mary Lascelles, vol. 9 in Yale *Works* (1971)
Laird of Auchinleck	*Boswell, Laird of Auchinleck, 1778–1782,* ed. Joseph W. Read and Frederick A. Pottle (New York: McGraw-Hill, 1977)
Life	Boswell, *Life of Johnson,* ed. G. B. Hill, rev. L. F. Powell, 6 vols. (Oxford: Clarendon, 1964); vol. 5 is the published version of Boswell's *Journal of a Tour to the Hebrides*
Lives	Samuel Johnson, *Lives of the English Poets,* ed. George Birkbeck Hill (Oxford: Clarendon, 1905)
London Journal	*Boswell's London Journal, 1762–1763,* ed. Frederick A. Pottle (New York: McGraw-Hill, 1950)
Ominous Years	*Boswell: The Ominous Years, 1774–1776,* ed. Charles Ryskamp and Frederick A. Pottle (New York: McGraw-Hill, 1963)

Pottle   Frederick A. Pottle, *James Boswell: The Earlier Years,*
              1740–1769 (New York: McGraw-Hill, 1966)
Thraliana   *Thraliana: The Diary of Mrs. Hester Lynch Thrale (Later*
              Mrs. Piozzi), ed. Katharine C. Balderston, 2nd ed.
              (Oxford: Clarendon, 1951)
Yale *Works* *The Yale Edition of the Works of Samuel Johnson* (1958–),
              many different editors of individual volumes

Notes

PROLOGUE

1. Johnson to Hester Thrale, Nov. 14, 1778, *Letters* 3: 140 (also quoted by Boswell, *Life* 3: 368).
2. Hawkins, 55.
3. "Boswell's *Life of Johnson*," in *Thomas Carlyle's Collected Works* (London: Chapman and Hall, 1869), 45.
4. *Life* 2: 261, May 10, 1773.
5. Joshua Reynolds to Boswell, Oct. 1, 1782, *The Correspondence of James Boswell with Certain Members of the Club*, ed. Charles N. Fifer (New York: McGraw-Hill, 1976), 127; Johnson to Boswell, July 3, 1778, *Letters* 3: 118.
6. W. H. Auden, "Young Boswell," *New Yorker*, Nov. 25, 1950, 146; *Life* 1: 421, July 5, 1763.
7. *Ominous Years*, 351; *Life* 3: 57, May 1776.
8. George Bernard Shaw, preface to *Man and Superman*.
9. *Life* 2: 106, Oct. 26, 1769.
10. Frances Reynolds, *Recollections of Dr. Johnson, Johnsonian Miscellanies* 2: 252; Hawkins, 235.
11. Lewis Carroll, *Alice in Wonderland*, ch. 1; Asa Briggs, *How They Lived: An Anthology of Original Documents Written between 1700 and 1815* (New York: Barnes and Noble, 1969), xvii.
12. Douglas Hay and Nicholas Rogers, *Eighteenth-Century English Society: Shuttles and Swords* (Oxford: Oxford University Press, 1997), 8.
13. *Life* 2: 337, April 2, 1775; Tobias Smollett, *Humphry Clinker*, ed. Lewis M. Knapp and Paul-Gabriel Boucé (Oxford: Oxford University Press, 1984), 91, 88.

14. Jerry White, *A Great and Monstrous Thing: London in the Eighteenth Century* (Cambridge: Harvard University Press, 2013), 459.

15. The interpretations of a number of commentators are reviewed by Caitlin Blackwell, *John Collet: A Commercial Comic Artist* (PhD dissertation, University of York, 2013, available online), 1: 183–91.

16. Ian Mortimer, *The Time Traveler's Guide to Medieval England: A Handbook for Visitors to the Fourteenth Century* (New York: Simon & Schuster, 2010), p. 1; George Macaulay Trevelyan, *Clio, A Muse, and Other Essays* (London: Longmans Green, 1930), 150.

17. White, *A Great and Monstrous Thing*, 85.

CHAPTER 1. JOHNSON BEFORE BOSWELL: THE YEARS OF STRUGGLE

1. *Adventurer* 111.

2. *Rambler* 95.

3. *Diaries*, Yale *Works* 1: 3; Lawrence C. McHenry, "Neurological Disorders of Dr. Samuel Johnson," *Journal of the Royal Society of Medicine* 78 (June, 1985), 488.

4. Yale *Works* 1: 3–5.

5. For further details see John Wiltshire, *Samuel Johnson in the Medical World: The Doctor and the Patient* (Cambridge: Cambridge University Press, 1991), 13–17.

6. Hester Thrale, *Anecdotes, Johnsonian Miscellanies* 1: 152, quoted also by Boswell, *Life* 1: 43.

7. Thrale, *Anecdotes, Johnsonian Miscellanies* 1: 154, 161, 163.

8. *Life* 4: 393, Dec. 2, 1784; Nathaniel's letter quoted by Pat Rogers, *The Samuel Johnson Encyclopedia* (Westport, CT: Greenwood Press, 1996), 210; Johnson to Mary Prowse, Aug. 14 and Dec. 9, 1780, *Letters* 3: 298, 320.

9. *Life* 1: 39 (1712); on the implications of "manliness" see Felicity Nussbaum, *The Autobiographical Subject: Gender and Ideology in Eighteenth-Century England* (Baltimore: Johns Hopkins University Press, 1989), 123–24.

10. *Life* 2: 407 (1775); Jonathan Swift to Charles Ford, Nov. 12, 1708, *The Correspondence of Jonathan Swift*, ed. David Woolley (Frankfurt: Peter Lang, 1999–2007), 1: 217; Edward Gibbon, *Memoirs of My Life*, ed. Georges A. Bonnard (London: Nelson, 1966), 44.

11. *Life* 1: 49 (1725).

12. *Johnsonian Miscellanies* 1: 332; Bate, 276.

13. *Johnsonian Miscellanies* 1: 149.

14. Thomas Tyers, *Early Biographies*, 78.

15. *In Rivum a Mola Stoana Lichfeldiae Diffluentem*, Yale *Works* 6: 342; John Wain, *Samuel Johnson* (New York: Viking, 1975), 298.

16. *Life* 4: 373, Nov. 1784; Nathaniel Hawthorne, *Our Old Home: A Series of English Sketches*, ed. William Charvat (Columbus: Ohio State University Press, 1970), 132. This episode is explored by Helen Deutsch, *Loving Dr. Johnson* (Chicago: University of Chicago Press, 2005), 197–207.

17. *Life* 1: 73–74, 77 (1729–30); on "rude and violent," see *The Correspondence and Other Papers of James Boswell Relating to the Making of the Life of Johnson*, ed. Marshall Waingrow, 2nd ed. (New Haven: Yale University Press, 2001), 52.

18. *Life* 1: 79 (1731).

19. *Life* 1: 272, 274 (1754); the quotation is from Alexander Pope's *Eloisa to Abelard,* line 38.

20. *Life* 1: 63–64 (1729); Frances Reynolds, *Johnsonian Miscellanies* 2: 257.

21. Hawkins, 173; Arthur Murphy, *An Essay on the Life and Genius of Samuel Johnson, Johnsonian Miscellanies* 2: 409.

22. Thomas Carlyle, *Heroes and Hero-Worship, Thomas Carlyle's Collected Works* (London: Chapman and Hall, 1869), 12: 210, 211; and *Life* 4: 304, June 12, 1784.

23. *Monthly Review* (1767), quoted by Susie I. Tucker, *Protean Shape: A Study in Eighteenth-Century Vocabulary and Usage* (London: Athlone, 1967), 27.

24. George Irwin, *Samuel Johnson: A Personality in Conflict* (Oxford: Oxford University Press, 1971), 4–5, 91.

25. Roy W. Menninger, M.D., "Johnson's Psychic Turmoil and the Women in His Life," *The Age of Johnson* 5, ed. Paul J. Korshin (New York: AMS Press, 1992), 182.

26. *Life* 2: 440, March 20, 1776; Murphy, *Johnsonian Miscellanies* 2: 409.

27. Robert Burton, *The Anatomy of Melancholy* (Oxford: Clarendon, 1989), 1: 239 (Part I, section 2, memb. 2, subsec. 6).

28. Burney *Journals* 2: 225, March 27, 1777.

29. *Portraits by Sir Joshua Reynolds,* ed. Frederick W. Hilles (New York: McGraw-Hill, 1952), 61.

30. This is not the place to go at length into the various competing interpretations, including a not entirely plausible diagnosis of Tourette syndrome. Some articles of interest include T. J. Murray, "Dr. Samuel Johnson's Movement Disorder," *British Medical Journal* (June 16, 1979), 1610–1614; Lawrence C. McHenry, "Neurological Disorders of Dr. Samuel Johnson," *Journal of the Royal Society of Medicine* 78 (June 1985), 480–90; and John G. Evans, "Psychogenic Pseudo-Tourette Syndrome: One of Dr. Johnson's Maladies?" *Journal of the Royal Society of Medicine* (Dec. 2010), 500–502.

31. *Life* 1: 94–95 (1735).

32. Thrale, *Anecdotes, Johnsonian Miscellanies* 1: 318.

33. *Life* 1: 98–99 (1736).

34. *Life* 2: 464, March 23, 1776; Thrale, *Anecdotes, Johnsonian Miscellanies* 1: 224.

35. Roy Porter, *English Society in the Eighteenth Century* (London: Penquin, 1982), 48. *Life of Savage, Lives* 2: 329.

36. *Rambler* 145.

37. John Brewer, *The Pleasures of the Imagination: English Culture in the Eighteenth Century* (Chicago: University of Chicago Press, 1997), 155; *Life* 1: 304–5 (1756).

38. *Life* 1: 111–12 (1738).

39. *Obituary and Life of Edward Cave,* Yale *Works* 19: 300–301.

40. Arthur Murphy, *An Essay on Johnson's Life and Genius, Johnsonian Miscellanies* 1: 378.

41. *Gentleman's Magazine* 11 (Jan. 1741), 46.

42. Epictetus, *Moral Discourses,* trans. Elizabeth Carter (London: Dent, 1910).

43. Montagu Pennington, *Memoirs of the Life of Mrs. Elizabeth Carter* (London: Cawthorn, 1825), 1: 39, 13, 161; Hawkins in his edition of Johnson's *Works* (1787), 11: 205.

44. *Notes of Ben Jonson's Conversations with William Drummond of Hawthornden* (London: Shakespeare Society, 1842), 40, Jan. 19, 1619.

45. Hawkins, 172.

46. John Wiltshire, "Women Writers," *Samuel Johnson in Context,* ed. Jack Lynch (Cambridge: Cambridge University Press, 2012), 402.

47. Henry Fielding, *Covent Garden Journal* 24 (March 24, 1752).

48. The full list may be seen in Richard B. Schwartz, *Daily Life in Johnson's London* (Madison: University of Wisconsin Press, 1983), 23–26; also Rogers, *Samuel Johnson Encyclopedia,* 246.

49. *Thraliana* 1: 178; Hawkins, 188.

50. *Laird of Auchinleck,* 142; Boswell to Malone, Feb. 10, 1791, *The Correspondence of James Boswell with David Garrick, Edmund Burke, and Edmond Malone* (New York: McGraw-Hill, 1986), 401. See Gay W. Brack, "Tetty and Samuel Johnson: The Romance and the Reality," *The Age of Johnson* 5, ed. Paul J. Korshin (New York: AMS Press, 1992), 147–78.

51. *Applause of the Jury,* 82, 110–13.

52. Fanny Burney to her sister Susanna, Nov. 28, 1784, *Journals and Letters,* selected by Peter Sabor and Lars E. Troide (London: Penguin, 2001), 205.

53. Johnson to Lucy Porter, Dec. 2, 1784, *Letters* 4: 444; see Brack, "Tetty and Samuel Johnson," 168–69.

54. Johnson to Thomas Warton, Dec. 21, 1754, *Letters* 1: 90.

55. Johnson to Hill Boothby, Dec. 30, 1755, Jan. 8, 1756, *Letters* 1: 117–18, 123; Thrale, *Anecdotes, Johnsonian Miscellanies* 1: 257. On Johnson's illness see Bate, 319.

56. *London,* lines 176–77; *Life* 1: 129, May 1738; T. S. Eliot, *On Poetry and Poets* (London: Faber, 1957), 173.

57. *Life* 1: 165, Feb. 1744.

58. *Life of Savage,* ed. Clarence Tracy (Oxford: Clarendon, 1971), 97. The version Johnson eventually included in the *Lives of the Poets* was considerably altered.

59. Richard Holmes, *Dr. Johnson and Mr. Savage* (New York: Vintage, 1993), 49–50, 185; see also Thomas Kaminsky, *The Early Career of Samuel Johnson* (New York: Oxford University Press, 1987), 87–89.

60. *Life of Savage,* 114, 135, 140.

61. *Life* 1: 441, July 20, 1763; *Rambler* 53.

CHAPTER 2. JOHNSON BEFORE BOSWELL: FAME AT LAST

1. *Life* 4: 326, June 22, 1784.

2. Review of Soame Jenyns, *A Free Inquiry into the Nature and Origin of Evil,* in *Samuel Johnson: The Major Works,* ed. Donald Greene (Oxford: Oxford University Press, 1984), 527; Bate, 494; Ecclesiastes 1: 2.

3. *Vanity of Human Wishes,* lines 73–76.

4. *Vanity* 345–46, 367–68.

5. *Life* 1: 202, March 1750.

6. *Life* 1: 210 (1750).

7. Bate, 496.

8. *Ominous Years,* 135, quoting Robert Orme. Boswell revised this remark more elaborately when he quoted it in the *Life* 2: 300 (1775).

9. *Rambler* 62 and 115, *Idler* 47; see James G. Basker, "Dancing Dogs, Women Preachers, and the Myth of Johnson's Misogyny," *The Age of Johnson* 3, ed. Paul J. Korshin (New York: AMS Press, 1990), 63–90.

10. "Recollections by Miss Reynolds," *Johnsonian Miscellanies* 2: 251; William Cooke, *Johnsonian Miscellanies* 2: 168; see also *Life* 4: 321–22, where Boswell gives a briefer version of the story. William Hazlitt, *Lectures on the English Comic Writers* (London: Dent, 1963), 104.

11. *Idler* 38.

12. *Thraliana* 1: 179.

13. Blaise Pascal, *Pensées,* ed. Philippe Sellier (Paris: Classiques Garnier, 1991), 392, no. 515 (my translation).

14. *Rambler* 8.

15. *Rambler* 207.

16. George Orwell, "Politics and the English Language," in *A Collection of Essays by George Orwell* (New York: Doubleday Anchor Books, 1954), 176.

17. *Adventurer* 138.

18. Richard Lanham, *Analyzing Prose* (New York: Scribner, 1983), 54.

19. *Rambler* 208.

20. Thomas Tyers, *A Biographical Sketch of Dr. Samuel Johnson, Early Biographies,* 70; "An English Saint Remembered," *The Times,* Dec. 13, 1984, p. 15.

21. "Portable" is quoted (in this context) by John Brewer, *The Pleasures of the Imagination: English Culture in the Eighteenth Century* (Chicago: University of Chicago Press, 1997), xi; Smith, *Essays on Philosophical Subjects, The Glasgow Edition of the Works and Correspondence of Adam Smith* (Oxford: Clarendon, 1976–83), 3: 232.

22. Boswell quotes Garrick's poem, originally published in newspapers, in the *Life* 1: 301 (1755).

23. *1 Henry IV,* II.iv.

24. *Preface to the Dictionary,* Yale *Works* 18: 84, 89–90.

25. *Johnsonian Miscellanies* 2: 390; Sir John Suckling, *Love's Offense.* These and other examples of "low" words are noted by Donald T. Siebert, "Bubbled, Bamboozled, and Bit: 'Low Bad' Words in Johnson's *Dictionary,*" *Studies in English Literature* 26 (1986), 485–96.

26. The anecdote comes from Robert Graves, *Goodbye to All That* (London: Penguin, 1979), 246; *Life* 2: 90, Oct. 16, 1769.

27. *Life* 2: 367, April 18, 1775.

28. *Life* 1: 287, April 1755.

29. *Preface,* 113.

30. Yale *Works* 18:59.

31. *The World* (1755 edition) 3: 270–75; Lawrence Lipking, *Samuel Johnson: The Life of an Author* (Cambridge: Harvard University Press, 1998), 12.

32. *Life* 1: 261–62 (1754–55).

33. *Vanity,* line 160.

34. Johnson to Sarah Johnson, Jan. 20, 1759, *Letters* 1: 177–78; Roy W. Menninger, M.D., "Johnson's Psychic Turmoil and the Women in His Life," *The Age of Johnson* 5, ed. Paul J. Korshin (New York: AMS Press, 1992), 184.

35. Johnson to Samuel Richardson, March 16 and 19, 1756, *Letters* 1: 132.

CHAPTER 3. BOSWELL BEFORE JOHNSON: SETTING OUT FOR THE WIDE WORLD

1. *Laird of Auchinleck*, 38.

2. *Laird of Auchinleck*, 163.

3. *London Journal*, 102; *Confession of Faith, and the Larger and Shorter Catechism, First Agreed upon by the Assembly of Divines at Westminster* (1717), 217; "Sketch of the Early Life of James Boswell, Written by Himself for Jean-Jacques Rousseau," translated from French by Pottle, 3.

4. Jacob Viner, "Man's Economic Status," *Man Versus Society in Eighteenth-Century Britain*, ed. James L. Clifford (Cambridge: Cambridge University Press, 1968), 22.

5. *Life* 1: 387 (1754); on "Scotch" and "Scottish" see Duncan Forbes, introduction to David Hume, *The History of Great Britain: The Reigns of James I and Charles I* (London: Penguin, 1970), 7.

6. Dane Love, *The History of Auchinleck* (Cunnock, Ayrshire: Carn, 1991), 64–65.

7. Letter to Monsieur de Zuylen, father of a Dutch woman whom Boswell once thought of marrying, *Holland*, 337; *English Experiment*, 246.

8. *Ominous Years*, 57.

9. *The Great Biographer*, 180.

10. *London Journal*, 192; Robert Chambers, *Traditions of Edinburgh* (Edinburgh, 1868), 245; *The Collected Works of Dugald Stewart* (London: 1854–60), 4: 230.

11. *Journal of My Jaunt, Harvest 1762, Private Papers of James Boswell from Malahide Castle*, ed. Geoffrey Scott (New York: William Rudge, 1928–34), 1: 135.

12. Ibid., 1: 60.

13. *Boswell's Book of Bad Verse*, ed. Jack Werner (London: White Lion, 1974), 161.

14. Unpublished manuscript by Boswell, mentioned by Marlies K. Danziger (ed.) in *Germany and Switzerland*, 64n.

15. *In Search of a Wife*, 99; Boswell to John Johnston, Jan. 11, 1760, *Correspondence of James Boswell and John Johnston of Grange*, ed. Ralph Walker (New Haven: Yale University Press, 1966), 28.

16. Boswell to John Johnston, Jan. 11, 1760, *Correspondence of James Boswell and John Johnston of Grange*, 7; on the University of Glasgow see Nicholas Phillipson, *Adam Smith: An Enlightened Life* (New Haven: Yale University Press, 2010), 131–32.

17. Quoted by Pottle, 572n.

18. *Grand Tour*, 169.

19. *Life* 5: 396 and note, Nov. 20, 1773.

20. *London Journal*, 281.

21. Pottle, 76.

22. *English Experiment*, 106.

23. *London Journal,* 78; "Boswell's *Life of Johnson,*" *Thomas Carlyle's Collected Works* (London: Chapman and Hall, 1869), 35.

24. Examples of the term "hipped" are in *Grand Tour,* 71, and *Laird of Auchinleck,* 360.

25. Cheyne, *The English Malady* (1733), 134–38; *Ominous Years,* 225.

26. *The Hypochondriack,* ed. Margery Bailey (Stanford: Stanford University Press, 1928), 2: 238 (1782); *Macbeth* III.ii, *Hamlet* III.i.

27. *Grand Tour,* 166.

28. *London Journal,* 41.

29. Ibid., 40–42.

30. Arthur Young, *A Six Months Tour through the North of England* (1770), 4: 581–85.

31. *London Journal,* 42–44.

32. Ibid., 50.

33. Ibid., 135.

34. Ibid., 224.

35. Smith, *Theory of Moral Sentiments* V.ii, *The Glasgow Edition of the Works and Correspondence of Adam Smith* (Oxford: Clarendon, 1976–83), 1: 203.

36. "A Constitutional and Political English Catechism, Necessary for All Families," *Gentleman's Magazine* 36 (1766), 232.

37. *London Journal,* 66.

38. *Applause of the Jury,* 77; *Extremes,* 69; Vic Gatrell, *City of Laughter: Sex and Satire in Eighteenth-Century London* (New York: Walker, 2006), 364; *Life* 4: 23 (1780).

39. *London Journal,* 53, 65, 198.

40. Ibid., 238, 181; the friend was Lord Eglinton.

41. Ibid., 181, 201.

42. Adam Sisman, *Boswell's Presumptuous Task: The Making of the Life of Dr. Johnson* (New York: Farrar, Straus and Giroux, 2001), 281; *London Journal,* 98.

43. *London Journal,* 272, 282.

44. Ibid., 169.

45. Ibid., 52, 255.

46. Pat Rogers, "Conversation," *Samuel Johnson in Context,* ed. Jack Lynch (Cambridge: Cambridge University Press, 2012), 153; Fintan O'Toole, *A Traitor's Kiss: The Life of Richard Brinsley Sheridan* (New York: Farrar, Straus and Giroux, 1998), xiv.

47. *Life* 1: 389–90 (1763).

48. *London Journal,* 74.

49. Ibid., 94.

50. Ibid., 289; Richard Altick, *The Shows of London* (Cambridge: Harvard University Press, 1978), 52.

51. *London Journal,* 86–87.

52. *The World of Hogarth: Lichtenberg's Commentaries on Hogarth's Engravings,* trans. Innes and Gustav Herdan (Boston: Houghton Mifflin, 1966), 275–78; Ronald Paulson, *Hogarth: His Life, Art and Times* (New Haven: Yale University Press, 1974), 177–79.

53. *London Journal,* 71–72.

54. Fielding is quoted by Jerry White, *A Great and Monstrous Thing: London in the Eighteenth Century* (Cambridge: Harvard University Press, 2013), 361; Hawkins, 48.

55. Geoffrey Chaucer, *Sir Thopas,* line 184; see Burford, *Wits, Wenchers and Wantons* (London: Robert Hale, 1986), 13.

56. Fielding, *Tom Jones,* VII.x.

57. Charles Hanbury Williams, quoted by White, *A Great and Monstrous Thing,* 366.

CHAPTER 4. BOSWELL BEFORE JOHNSON: THE SEARCH FOR SELF

1. John Updike, "Through the Mid-Life Crisis with James Boswell, Esq.," *Hugging the Shore: Essays and Criticism* (New York: Knopf, 1983), 334.

2. Bertrand H. Bronson, "Boswell's Boswell," *Johnson Agonistes and Other Essays* (Berkeley: University of California Press, 1965), 60; *London Journal,* 40, 166, 188, 324; *Ominous Years,* 265.

3. *The Hypochondriack,* ed. Margery Bailey (Stanford: Stanford University Press, 1928), 1: 341 (1780).

4. *Laird of Auchinleck,* 307; William K. Wimsatt, "The Fact Imagined: James Boswell," *Hateful Contraries: Studies in Literature and Criticism* (Lexington: University of Kentucky Press, 1965), 165–83; *In Search of a Wife,* 292.

5. *London Journal,* 47; *In Search of a Wife,* 226; Pottle, 53.

6. *London Journal,* 62.

7. I draw these terms from Richard A. Lanham (who in turn adapted them from Werner Jaeger), *The Motives of Eloquence: Literary Rhetoric in the Renaissance* (New Haven: Yale University Press, 1976), ch. 1.

8. Hume, *A Treatise of Human Nature* I.iv.6; *Ominous Years,* 212.

9. Thomas Reid, quoted by S. A. Grave, *The Scottish Philosophy of Common Sense* (Oxford: Clarendon, 1960), 98n.

10. Hume, *Treatise* II.iii.

11. Hume, "My Own Life," in *Essays Moral, Political, and Literary,* ed. Eugene F. Miller (Indianapolis: Liberty Classics, 1987), xl.

12. *London Journal,* 81.

13. Ibid., 183, 220–21.

14. Ibid., 60.

15. Ibid., 151, 61.

16. Ibid., 178, 182.

17. Moss Hart, *Act One: An Autobiography* (New York: Random House, 1959), 6.

18. *London Journal,* 192, 199; Boswell to Temple, April 25, 1763, and Temple to Boswell, April 26, *Correspondence of James Boswell and William Johnson Temple, 1756–1795,* ed. Thomas Crawford (New Haven: Yale University Press, 1997), 34–35.

19. *London Journal,* 77–79.

20. Ibid., 77; *The Hypochondriack,* 2: 41 (1780).

21. *London Journal,* 251–54.

22. See Jacob Viner, "Man's Economic Status," *Man Versus Society in Eighteenth-Century Britain,* ed. James L. Clifford (Cambridge: Cambridge University Press, 1968), 38–39;

see also *Albion's Fatal Tree: Crime in Society in Eighteenth-Century England,* ed. Douglas Hay et al. (London: Verso, 2011).

23. *Life* 4: 188 (1783).

24. *Rambler* 114.

25. *London Journal,* appendix, 337–42.

26. *London Journal,* 255–56.

27. *London Journal,* 304, 54–55.

28. *Lichtenberg's Visits to England, as Described in His Letters and Diaries,* trans. Margaret L. Mare (New York: Benjamin Blom, 1938), 65; *London Journal,* 49–50.

29. Lawrence Stone, *The Family, Sex and Marriage in England, 1500–1800* (New York: Harper and Row, 1977), 618.

30. *London Journal,* 227.

31. Ibid., 231.

32. Pottle, 321; William B. Ober, M.D., *Boswell's Clap and Other Essays: Medical Analyses of Literary Men's Afflictions* (Carbondale: Southern Illinois University Press, 1979), 14.

33. Oscar Wilde, *The Picture of Dorian Gray,* ch. 2; Augustine, *Confessions* VIII.v.10, as translated by Peter Brown, *Augustine of Hippo: A Biography,* 2nd ed. (Berkeley: University of California Press, 2000), 167.

34. *London Journal,* 84.

35. Ibid., 85, 89.

36. Ibid., 115.

37. Ibid., 117, 126.

38. Ibid., 138–39; Vladimir Nabokov, *Lolita* (New York: Vintage, 1997), afterword, 313.

39. *London Journal,* 139.

40. Ibid., 149.

41. Ibid., 142.

42. Ibid., 145, 149, 155–56.

43. Ibid., 158–59.

44. Ober, *Boswell's Clap,* 6–7.

45. *London Journal,* 140, 175, 187. The implications of this episode are well explored by David M. Weed, "Sexual Positions: Men of Pleasure, Economy, and Dignity in Boswell's *London Journal,*" *Eighteenth-Century Studies* 31 (1997–98), 225–31.

CHAPTER 5. THE FATEFUL MEETING

1. *London Journal,* 54.

2. *Life* 1: 386 (1763).

3. Ibid., 1: 453, July 28, 1763.

4. Charles Churchill, *The Rosciad,* line 322; Leslie Stephen, *Studies of a Biographer* (New York: Putnam, 1907), 113.

5. *London Journal,* 260; *Life* 1: 392, May 16, 1763. On differences between the early and the later version of the episode, see William R. Siebenschuh, *Fictional Techniques and Factual Works* (Athens: University of Georgia Press, 1983), 56–62.

6. John A. Vance, "The Laughing Johnson," *Boswell's Life of Johnson: New Questions, New Answers,* ed. John A. Vance (Athens: University of Georgia Press, 1985), 208.

7. *Life* 1: 392, May 16, 1763.

8. See William R. Siebenschuh, "Boswell's Second Crop of Memory: A New Look at the Role of Memory in the Making of the *Life*," *Boswell's Life of Johnson: New Questions, New Answers*, 94.

9. *Life* 1: 396, May 24, 1763.

10. *Life* 1: 392.

11. Derek Hudson, *Sir Joshua Reynolds: A Personal Study* (London: Geoffrey Bles, 1958), 187; and see Bruce Redford, *Designing the Life of Johnson* (Oxford: Oxford University Press, 2002), 139–41.

12. Bertrand H. Bronson, "Boswell's Boswell," *Johnson Agonistes and Other Essays* (Berkeley: University of California Press, 1965), 75–76.

13. Johnson to Giuseppe Baretti, July 20, 1762, *Letters* 1: 206; *Ominous Years*, 110.

14. "Grandeur of generality": *Life of Cowley, Lives* 1: 45.

15. Murphy, *Johnsonian Miscellanies* 1: 416.

16. *Life* 2: 215, April 11, 1773.

17. *London Journal*, 303.

18. Ibid., 280.

19. Ibid., 263–64.

20. See Hugh Phillips, *Mid-Georgian London* (London: Collins, 1964), 139. *Harris's List of Covent Garden Ladies* has been edited by Hallie Rubenhold (London: Doubleday, 2012), and the milieu is very fully described by her in *The Covent Garden Ladies: Pimp General Jack and the Extraordinary Story of Harris's List* (London: Tempus, 2005).

21. *London Journal*, 272–73.

22. Ibid., 327.

23. *Rambler* 170–71; *Johnsonian Miscellanies* 2: 213n.

24. *London Journal*, 310.

25. Ibid., 329; I follow the slightly different version in the *Life* 1: 458, July 30, 1763.

26. Johnson mentions "the booksellers on the bridge" in a letter of Jan. 6, 1784, *Life* 4: 257.

27. Source for figures about shipping: https://en.wikipedia.org/wiki/Pool_of_London.

28. *London*, lines 21–24; *London Journal*, 329–30.

29. *London Journal*, 331, 321; *Life* 1:451 (July 21, 1763).

30. *Life* 1: 465, Aug. 5, 1763.

31. Ibid., 1: 470, Aug. 5, 1763.

32. Ibid., 1: 472, Aug. 5, 1763. The *London Journal* breaks off before these final conversations. They were evidently reconstructed from brief notes that were never expanded at the time; see *James Boswell's Life of Johnson: An Edition of the Original Manuscript*, ed. Marshall Waingrow (New Haven: Yale University Press, 1994), 1: 328n.

CHAPTER 6. BOSWELL ABROAD

1. *Holland*, preface, xiii.

2. See Adam Sisman, *Boswell's Presumptuous Task: The Making of the Life of Dr. Johnson* (New York: Farrar, Straus and Giroux, 2001), 297.

3. *Holland,* 7.

4. Ibid., 89.

5. Ibid., 92, 202.

6. Ibid., 215, 279–80.

7. Ibid., 219.

8. Ibid., 99, 115, 133.

9. Ibid., 227, 230.

10. Ibid., 313, 328.

11. Ibid., 305, 331.

12. *London Journal,* 284.

13. On the technical status of baronries see *Germany and Switzerland,* 163n.

14. *Holland,* 37, 270, 395–96; the five colors are mentioned in *Germany and Switzerland,* 146.

15. Ibid., 11, 64.

16. Ibid., 62.

17. Ibid., 24, 31.

18. Ibid., 118–19; Lytton Strachey, *Portraits in Miniature and Other Essays* (New York: Harcourt, Brace, 1931), 88.

19. *Germany and Switzerland,* 37, 82.

20. Ibid., 91, 130n.

21. Ibid., 285n, 136.

22. Ibid., 217.

23. Ibid., 218.

24. Ibid., 229.

25. Ibid., 229, 258–59.

26. Ibid., 223–24, 260; Jean-Jacques Rousseau, *Julie, ou La Nouvelle Héloïse,* VI.viii (my translation).

27. *Germany and Switzerland,* 260.

28. *Life* 2: 12, Feb. 16, 1766.

29. Gavin de Beer and André-Michel Rousseau, "Voltaire's British Visitors," *Studies in Voltaire and the Eighteenth Century* 49 (1967), 99.

30. *Germany and Switzerland,* 280.

31. Ibid., 293.

32. Ibid, 304–5; *Italy and France,* 94.

33. *Germany and Switzerland,* 320–21.

34. Ibid., 275.

35. Quoted by Frederick A. Pottle, *Pride and Negligence: The History of the Boswell Papers* (New York: McGraw-Hill, 1982), 97–100. In this latest of his discussions of Isham's story, Pottle mentions several apparent inconsistencies that had made him wonder if it was partly made up after the fact, but seems inclined to give it credence on the whole. See also David Buchanan, *The Treasure of Auchinleck: The Story of the Boswell Papers* (New York: McGraw-Hill, 1974), 334–41.

36. *Italy, Corsica, and France,* 279.

37. Rousseau to Boswell, Aug. 4, 1766, *Correspondance Complète de Jean-Jacques Rousseau,* ed. R. A. Leigh (Oxford: Voltaire Foundation, 1998), 30: 203 (my translation).

38. *Italy, Corsica, and France,* 22.
39. Ibid., 10, 94.
40. Ibid., 55, 84, 42n, 90.
41. John Wilkes, *An Essay on Woman,* ed. Arthur H. Cash (New York: AMS Press, 2000), 97.
42. *London Journal,* 187; *Italy, Corsica, and France,* 20.
43. *Italy, Corsica, and France,* 209; I have somewhat altered Pottle's translation.
44. Ibid., 74.
45. Ibid., 40, 264.
46. Ibid., 9.
47. Ibid., 92–93, 98.
48. Rousseau, *The Social Contract,* II.x (my translation). On Corsica and Scotland, see Murray Pittock, *James Boswell* (Aberdeen: AHRC Centre for Irish and Scottish Studies, 2007).
49. James Boswell, *An Account of Corsica,* ed. James T. Boulton and T. O. McLoughlin (Oxford: Oxford University Press, 2006), 200. The Plutarchan vision of Paoli is explored by William C. Dowling, *The Boswellian Hero* (Athens: University of Georgia Press, 1979).
50. *Account of Corsica,* 110.
51. *Italy, Corsica, and France,* 159–60.
52. Ibid., 236.
53. Ibid., 273–74.
54. Ibid., 272, 23.
55. Ibid., 281.

CHAPTER 7. THE CLUB IS BORN

1. *Life* 1: 483, spring 1764.
2. Thrale, *Anecdotes, Johnsonian Miscellanies* 1: 234.
3. *Diaries,* Yale *Works* 1: 77–78; Matthew 25: 30.
4. *Rambler* 110.
5. *Rambler* 5.
6. Thomas Percy, *The Life of Dr. Goldsmith, Miscellaneous Works* (London, 1801), 1: 70.
7. *Life* 2: 258, May 7, 1773.
8. Burney *Journals* 3: 77, August 1778 (a slightly different version of this conversation is sometimes quoted from the *Memoirs* that she published half a century later, in which she tinkered a bit with the style). On Hawkins withdrawing from the Club, see Hawkins, 255–56.
9. John Francis Collingwood and John Woollams, *The Universal Cook and City and Country Housekeeper* (1792).
10. *Boswell for the Defence,* 163.
11. *London Journal,* 297; see Richard B. Schwartz, *Daily Life in Johnson's London* (Madison: University of Wisconsin Press, 1983), 71–72.
12. *London Journal,* 303 (toned down somewhat in the *Life* 1: 434); *Life* 3: 381, April 7, 1779; *Life* 2: 350–51, April 10, 1775.

13. Thomas Love Peacock, *Melincourt* (1817), ch. 16, 121.

14. *The Autobiography of Benjamin Franklin,* ed. Leonard Labaree et al. (New Haven: Yale University Press, 1964), 99–100, 149. On the number of alehouses, Jerry White, *A Great and Monstrous Thing: London in the Eighteenth Century* (Cambridge: Harvard University Press, 2013), 328.

15. See Ronald Paulson, *Hogarth: Art in Politics, 1750–64* (London: Lutterworth, 1993), 24–25.

16. Hawkins, 55–56.

17. *Life* 2: 100, Oct. 26, 1769; 4: 274, May 15, 1784; 5: 292, Oct. 5, 1772.

18. *Life* 2: 365, April 18, 1775; 3: 24, April 5, 1776.

19. Leslie Stephen, *Samuel Johnson* (New York: Harper, 1879), 61.

20. *Life* 2: 450, March 20, 1776; Hester Thrale, *Anecdotes, Johnsonian Miscellanies* 1: 290.

21. *Life* 2: 450; Edmund Burke, *Reflections on the Revolution in France,* ed. Conor Cruise O'Brien (London: Penguin, 1969), 278.

22. *Life* 4: 5–6 (1780).

23. *Life* 2: 53, spring 1768.

24. The conversation appears in the *Life* at 3: 231–37, April 3, 1778; the journal version is in *Extremes,* 234–39.

25. Arthur Conan Doyle, *The Hound of the Baskervilles,* ch. 1.

26. *Thraliana* 1: 188.

27. C. S. Lewis, *Studies in Words* (Cambridge: Cambridge University Press, 1967), 21.

28. John Wain, *Samuel Johnson* (New York: Viking, 1974), 120.

29. Thomas Babington Macaulay, *Critical and Historical Essays,* ed. Hugh Trevor-Roper (New York: McGraw-Hill, 1965), 115.

30. Helen Deutsch, *Loving Dr. Johnson* (Chicago: University of Chicago Press, 2005), 109.

31. *London Journal,* 319; Frances Burney, *Memoirs of Doctor Burney* (London: Moxon, 1832), 2: 106.

32. *Hebrides,* 53; *Life* 5: 76–77, Aug. 21, 1773.

33. *Johnsonian Miscellanies* 2: 390; *Laird of Auchinleck,* 336. On Langton's height, see *Correspondence of James Boswell with Certain Members of the Club, Including . . . Bennet Langton* (New York: McGraw-Hill, 1976), lxix.

34. *Life* 1: 250 (1753).

35. *Life* 4: 197 (1783).

CHAPTER 8. SIR JOSHUA REYNOLDS

1. Anthony Ashley Cooper, 3rd Earl of Shaftesbury, *Second Characters, or the Language of Forms,* ed. Benjamin Rand (Cambridge: Cambridge University Press, 1914), 135.

2. Jerry White, *A Great and Monstrous Thing: London in the Eighteenth Century* (Cambridge: Harvard University Press, 2013), 140.

3. Quoted by Derek Hudson, *Sir Joshua Reynolds: A Personal Study* (London: Geoffrey Bles, 1958), 94.

4. Hudson, 64; *Life* 3: 5, March 29, 1776; Burney *Journals* 5: 213, Dec. 1782.

5. Martin Postle et al., *Joshua Reynolds: The Creation of Celebrity* (London: Tate Publishing, 2005), 74.

6. Richard Wendorf, *Sir Joshua Reynolds: The Painter in Society* (Cambridge: Harvard University Press, 1996), 53; Walpole quoted by Ian McIntyre, *Joshua Reynolds: The Life and Times of the First President of the Royal Academy* (London: Allen Lane, 2003), 173.

7. *Life* 5: 102, Aug. 24, 1773; 3: 41, April 12, 1776; 3: 329, April 28, 1778.

8. McIntyre, 357.

9. Quoted by Kate Chisholm, *Wits and Wives: Doctor Johnson and the Company of Women* (London: Chatto and Windus, 2011), 173.

10. Yale *Works* 6: 269–70.

11. Hawkins, 214; review of Jonas Hanway (1757), *Samuel Johnson: The Major Works,* ed. Donald Greene (Oxford: Oxford University Press, 1984), 509.

12. *Ominous Years,* 149; *Life* 2: 362, April 18, 1775; *Anecdotes, Johnsonian Miscellanies,* 1: 207.

13. *Thraliana* 1: 268; Frances Burney, *Memoirs of Doctor Burney* (London: Moxon, 1832), 1: 332.

14. *Thraliana* 1: 79.

15. Hudson, 148. The various relationships in the Reynolds ménage are interestingly surveyed by Wendorf, 65–82.

16. *Life* 4: 312, June 1784; James Northcote, *The Life of Sir Joshua Reynolds,* 2nd ed. (London: Colburn, 1818), 2: 96.

17. *Life* 3: 19, April 5, 1776.

18. *Recollections by Miss Reynolds, Johnsonian Miscellanies* 2: 261.

19. *Thraliana* 1: 83.

20. Annotations to Reynolds's *Discourses, The Complete Poetry and Prose of William Blake,* ed. David V. Erdman (Berkeley: University of California Press, 1982), 655; on Reynolds's sales, see Hudson, 52–56.

21. Reynolds, *Discourses on Art,* ed. Stephen O. Mitchell (Indianapolis: Library of Liberal Arts, 1965), no. 4, 53 and 41.

22. William Hazlitt, "On Sitting for One's Picture," *Complete Works,* ed. P. P. Howe (London: Dent, 1930–34), 12: 110–11. The phrase Hazlitt quotes comes from a poem by Matthew Green called *The Spleen.*

23. *Recollections by Miss Reynolds, Johnsonian Miscellanies* 2: 269.

24. See Postle, "'The Modern Apelles': Joshua Reynolds and the Creation of Celebrity," *Joshua Reynolds: The Creation of Celebrity,* 19, and *Portraits by Sir Joshua Reynolds,* ed. Frederick W. Hilles (New York: McGraw-Hill, 1952), 28.

25. *Johnsonian Miscellanies* 2: 269.

26. *Life* 2: 83, Oct. 16, 1769.

27. On the cane, see *Life* 2: 209n, April 3, 1773, and 501, Appendix B.

28. Hudson, 75–76.

29. Hudson, 161; McIntyre, 370.

30. William Cotton, *Sir Joshua Reynolds and His Works* (London: J. R. Smith, 1856), 140; Lawrence Lipking, *The Ordering of the Arts in Eighteenth-Century England* (Princeton: Princeton University Press, 1970), 177.

31. Tim Clayton, "'Figures of Fame': Reynolds and the Printed Image," *Joshua Reynolds: The Creation of Celebrity*, ed. Postle, 49–59.
32. Herman W. Liebert, *Lifetime Likenesses of Samuel Johnson* (Los Angeles: Clark Memorial Library, 1974), 48; on the fading colors, see McIntyre, 202.
33. Hudson, 151.
34. McIntyre, 312–13.
35. Mark Hallett, "Reynolds, Celebrity and the Exhibition Space," *Joshua Reynolds: The Creation of Celebrity*, ed. Postle, 44.
36. Johnson to William Heberden, Oct. 13, 1784, *Letters* 4: 418.
37. *Discourse* 7, p. 93.
38. *Portraits by Sir Joshua Reynolds,* ed. Hilles, 74; *Discourse* 10, p. 145.
39. *Discourse* 4, p. 44.
40. Blake, *Complete Poetry and Prose,* 639.
41. Ibid., 635–36, 641.
42. Postle, 82.
43. Ibid., 86.

CHAPTER 9. EDMUND BURKE

1. Edmund Burke, *A Philosophical Inquiry into the Origin of Our Ideas of the Sublime and Beautiful,* III.xv.
2. Ibid., IV.xx.
3. Ibid., II.v; Job 39: 19–25.
4. Quoted by Jesse Norman, *Edmund Burke: The First Conservative* (New York: Basic Books, 2013), 21.
5. Burney *Journals* 3: 429, Nov. 15, 1779.
6. Quoted by David Bromwich, *The Intellectual Life of Edmund Burke: From the Sublime and Beautiful to American Independence* (Cambridge: Harvard University Press, 2014), 112.
7. Fanny Burney to Susanna Burney, July 9, 1782, Burney *Journals* 5: 70.
8. *Life* 1: 453, July 28, 1763; *Boswelliana: The Commonplace Book of James Boswell* (London: Grampian Club, 1874), 328.
9. *Spectator* 61; *Preface to Shakespeare,* Yale *Works* 7: 74.
10. *Thraliana* 1: 27.
11. *Ominous Years,* 121; *English Experiment,* 186.
12. *Memoirs of the Life of Sir James Mackintosh,* ed. R. J. Mackintosh (London: Edward Moxon, 1835), 1: 92; *Recollections of R. J. S. Stevens, an Organist in Georgian London,* ed. Mark Argent (Carbondale: Southern Illinois University Press, 1992), 67.
13. Jonathan Swift, *Journal to Stella,* ed. Harold Williams (Oxford: Blackwell, 1948), 1: 250.
14. Marshall McLuhan adopted the joke for the title of an essay, "James Joyce: Trivial and Quadrivial," *Thought* 28 (1953), 75–98.
15. Burke to Richard Shackleton, May 1, 1768, *The Correspondence of Edmund Burke* (Cambridge: Cambridge University Press, 1958–1978), 1: 351.

16. Edward Gibbon to Lord Sheffield, Aug. 7, 1790, *Letters,* ed. J. E. Norton (New York: Macmillan, 1956), 3: 195.

17. *Thoughts on the Present Discontents* and *Speech on Economical Reform, The Writings and Speeches of Edmund Burke,* ed. Paul Langford and William B. Todd (Oxford: Oxford University Press, 1981), 2: 317; 3: 547.

18. *Life* 2: 348, April 7, 1775; *The Patriot, Yale Works* 10: 390.

19. Copeland, *Our Eminent Friend Edmund Burke* (New Haven: Yale University Press, 1949), 74, quoting Lord Buckinghamshire.

20. Johnson to John Taylor, July 22, 1782, *Letters* 4: 62.

21. *Johnsonian Miscellanies* 1: 174n; "The Function of Criticism at the Present Time," *The Works of Matthew Arnold* (London: Macmillan, 1903), 3: 15.

22. Copeland, 92.

23. *Laird of Auchinleck,* 96; *Life* 4: 104, May 8, 1781.

24. *Thraliana* 1: 475 and note.

25. *Boswell for the Defence,* 165–66.

26. *Retaliation,* lines 29–36; *Life* 4: 318, June 1784.

27. Thomas Davies, *Memoirs of the Life of David Garrick* (London: Longman, Hurst, Rees, and Orme, 1808), 1: 198.

28. Richard B. Schwartz, *Daily Life in Johnson's London* (Madison: University of Wisconsin Press, 1983), 74; Vic Gatrell, *City of Laughter: Sex and Satire in Eighteenth-Century London* (New York: Walker, 2006), 128.

29. *Life* 2: 170, March 31, 1772.

30. Bromwich, *The Intellectual Life of Edmund Burke,* 159; John Quincy Adams, *The Social Compact, Exemplified in the Constitution of the Commonwealth of Massachusetts* (Providence: Knowles and Vose, 1842), 31; *Life* 2: 14, spring 1766.

31. *Life* 4: 408, June 25, 1763.

32. Lawrence Stone, *The Family, Sex and Marriage 1500–1800* (New York: Harper and Row, 1977), 223; on the evolving connotations of "conservatism," see Hannah Arendt, *On Revolution* (London: Penguin, 1973), 44.

33. Hume, *Essays Moral, Political, and Literary,* ed. Eugene F. Miller (Indianapolis: Liberty Classics, 1987), 470.

34. *London Journal,* 226–27.

35. *Life* 2: 153, March 21, 1772; see Nicholas Hudson, *Samuel Johnson and the Making of Modern England* (Cambridge: Cambridge University Press, 2003), 24–25.

36. *Life* 2: 261, May 10, 1773.

37. *Life* 1: 447–48, July 21, 1763.

38. Edward Gibbon, *The History of the Decline and Fall of the Roman Empire,* ed. David Womersley (London: Penguin, 1994), ch. 9, 1: 237.

39. *Memoirs of My Life,* ed. Georges A. Bonnard (London: Nelson, 1966), 24.

40. *Decline and Fall,* ch. 4, 1: 109.

41. Smith, *Lectures on Jurisprudence, The Glasgow Edition of the Works and Correspondence of Adam Smith* (Oxford: Clarendon, 1976–83), 5: 7.

42. Jean-Jacques Rousseau, *A Discourse on Inequality,* trans. Maurice Cranston (London: Penguin, 1984), 122.

43. Edmund Burke, *Reflections on the Revolution in France,* ed. Conor Cruise O'Brien (London: Penguin, 1969), 372.

44. Burke to the Duke of Richmond, Nov. 1772, *Correspondence* 2: 377; Paul Langford, "Edmund Burke," *Oxford Dictionary of National Biography,* online edition, page 6.

45. *Adventurer* 137, Yale *Works* 2: 489; *Life* 2: 102, Oct. 26, 1769.

46. Benjamin Franklin to John Ross and to Joseph Galloway, May 14, 1768, *The Works of Benjamin Franklin,* ed. Jared Sparks (Boston: Tappan and Whittemore, 1840), 7: 401–3.

47. *Life* 3: 427, May 25, 1780.

48. *Reflections,* 342.

49. *Reflections,* 194–95; Thomas Paine, *The Rights of Man,* in *Common Sense and Other Political Writings,* ed. Nelson F. Adkins (New York: Liberal Arts Press, 1953), 77, 80; William Blake, *The Marriage of Heaven and Hell,* plate 7.

50. *Reflections,* 99.

51. *Thoughts and Details on Scarcity, The Writings and Speeches of Edmund Burke,* ed. Paul Langford and William B. Todd (Oxford: Oxford University Press, 1981), 9: 136–40.

52. Boswell to the Rev. Andrew Kippis, July 11, 1791, *Great Biographer,* 149.

53. The royal proclamation and Stationers' Company resolution are quoted by Michael Phillips, "Blake and the Terror 1792–93," *The Library,* sixth series, no. 16 (December 1994), 266, 272.

CHAPTER 10. DAVID GARRICK

1. Alan Kendall, *David Garrick: A Biography* (New York: St. Martin's, 1985), 12.

2. *Life* 1: 101 (1737).

3. Quoted by Kendall, 58.

4. Allardyce Nicoll, *The Garrick Stage: Theaters and Audience in the Eighteenth Century* (Manchester: Manchester University Press, 1980), 3–7.

5. *Richard III* V.iii. Modern editors sometimes give the final words as "I am I," depending upon which quarto of the play they follow.

6. *Thraliana* 1: 495.

7. Ian McIntyre, *Garrick* (London: Penguin, 2000), 140.

8. Mark S. Auburn, "Theater in the Age of Garrick and Sheridan," *Sheridan Studies,* ed. James Morwood and David Crane (Cambridge: Cambridge University Press, 1995), 17–20; Nora Nachumi, "Theater," *Samuel Johnson in Context,* ed. Jack Lynch (Cambridge: Cambridge University Press, 2012), 367–74.

9. Auburn, 19–20.

10. McIntyre, 138; Thomas Davies, *Memoirs of the Life of David Garrick* (London: Longman, Hurst, Rees, and Orme, 1808), 2: 345.

11. On Murphy and Garrick, see Vanessa Cunningham, *Shakespeare and Garrick* (Cambridge: Cambridge University Press, 2008), 14.

12. T. Davies, 1: 153.

13. *The Works of Arthur Murphy* (1786), 6: 271.

14. Yale *Works* 8: 704.

15. *The Early Life and Diaries of William Windham,* ed. Robert Ketton-Cremer (London: Faber, 1930), 79.

16. *The Life of Mr. James Quinn, Comedian* (1766), 67–68.

17. McIntyre, 164; *Much Ado about Nothing* II.iii.

18. Tate Wilkinson, *Memoirs of His Own Life* (1790), 1: 118–19.

19. Burney *Journals* 1: 225, May 30, 1771.

20. *A General View of the Stage* (1759), 234–35. This work has sometimes been attributed to Samuel Derrick, but was definitely by the Irish author Thomas Wilkes: see William H. Miller, "The Authorship of *A General View of the Stage,*" *Modern Language Notes* 8 (1941), 612–14.

21. See Oliver Ford Davies, *Playing Lear* (London: Nick Hearn, 2003), 64.

22. Arthur Murphy, *The Life of David Garrick* (Dublin: Wogan, 1801), 20–21.

23. Frances Burney, *Evelina,* ed. Edward A. Bloom and Vivien Jones (Oxford: Oxford University Press, 2002), volume I, letter 10, p. 27; Murphy, *Life of David Garrick,* 31.

24. *Lichtenberg's Visits to England, as Described in His Letters and Diaries,* trans. Margaret L. Mare (New York: Benjamin Blom, 1938), 3–4.

25. Henry Fielding, *Tom Jones,* XVI.vi.

26. Goldsmith, "The Adventures of a Strolling Player," *Collected Works,* ed. Arthur Friedman (Oxford: Clarendon, 1966), 3: 138.

27. *Thraliana* 1: 121n.

28. McIntyre, 176–77.

29. Burney *Journals* 1: 314, Oct. 14, 1773; *Life* 3: 34n.

30. *Life* 3: 35, April 11, 1776.

31. McIntyre, 3.

32. Ibid., quoting *Correspondance Littéraire,* July 1, 1765.

33. Goldsmith, *Retaliation,* lines 101–8.

34. *Portraits by Sir Joshua Reynolds,* ed. Frederick W. Hilles (New York: McGraw-Hill, 1952), 87.

35. Frances Burney, *Memoirs of Doctor Burney* (London: Moxon, 1832), 1: 354–57; the identification of Hawkins is proved by a fragmentary note by Burney himself: Roger Lonsdale, *Dr. Charles Burney: A Literary Biography* (Oxford: Clarendon, 1965), 225.

36. Arthur Conan Doyle, *A Scandal in Bohemia.*

37. *Rambler* 200; Thrale, *Anecdotes, Johnsonian Miscellanies* 1: 179.

38. T. Davies, 2: 423; Murphy, *Life of David Garrick,* 378.

39. McIntyre, 466–68, and Kendall, 152–54.

40. Christian Deelman, *The Great Shakespeare Jubilee* (London: Michael Joseph, 1964), 98–99.

41. William Roberts, *Memoirs of Mrs. Hannah More* (New York: Harper, 1834), 36.

42. Simon Schama, *The Face of Britain: The Nation through Its Portraits* (London: Penguin Random House, 2015), 290.

43. *London Journal,* 69.

44. *Life* 4: 5 and note (1780); 2: 14, spring 1766.

45. *Hebrides,* 207; *Life* 1: 480, spring 1764. Johnson's comment about Garrick "mouthing Shakespeare" was much softened in the version of the Hebrides journal that Boswell published: *Life* 5: 244–45.

46. *Life* 1: 201 (1750); *Journal of My Jaunt, Harvest 1762, Private Papers of James Boswell from Malahide Castle* (New York: William Rudge, 1928–34), 1: 128.

47. *Dr. Campbell's Diary of a Visit to England in 1775,* ed. James L. Clifford (Cambridge: Cambridge University Press, 1947), 58.

48. *Life* 3: 263–64, April 10, 1778.

49. *Life* 2: 326, March 27, 1775.

50. *Johnsonian Miscellanies* 2: 195.

51. Burney, *Memoirs* 1: 351.

52. *Life* 2: 82–83, Oct. 16, 1769.

53. "Anecdotes by the Rev. Percival Stockdale," *Johnsonian Miscellanies* 2: 333.

54. McIntyre, *Garrick,* 562.

55. Murphy, *Life of David Garrick,* 342; Kendall, 176.

56. McIntyre, 316, 606; Schama, 274.

57. *Laird of Auchinleck,* 328; Burney, *Memoirs* 2: 203.

58. Quoted by Mary Alden Hopkins, *Hannah More and Her Circle* (New York: Longman's, Green, 1947), 89–90.

59. Richard Cumberland, *Memoirs* (London: Lackington, 1806), 463.

CHAPTER 11. THE SPIRIT OF MIRTH

1. Allardyce Nicoll, *The Garrick Stage: Theaters and Audience in the Eighteenth Century* (Manchester: Manchester University Press, 1980), 36, 44.

2. Details from Nicoll, *The Garrick Stage,* and Mark S. Auburn, "Theatre in the Age of Garrick and Sheridan," *Sheridan Studies,* ed. James Morwood and David Crane (Cambridge: Cambridge University Press, 1995), 7–46.

3. *A Comparison between Laughing and Sentimental Comedy, Collected Works,* ed. Arthur Friedman (Oxford: Clarendon, 1966), 3: 212.

4. Ian McIntyre, *Garrick* (London: Penguin, 2000), 447. The playwright was Hugh Kelly.

5. Richard Cumberland, *Memoirs* (1806), in *Goldsmith: Interviews and Recollections,* ed. E. H. Mikhail (London: St. Martin's Press, 1993), 59.

6. *Retaliation,* lines 63–66; Hester Thrale is quoted in *Memoirs of the Life of John Philip Kemble,* ed. James Boaden (London: Longman, 1825), 1: 438.

7. *She Stoops to Conquer,* Act 3, *Collected Works* 5: 169.

8. Ibid., Act 4, p. 178.

9. *Boswell for the Defence,* 152, 167, 179–80; *Life* 2: 233, April 29, 1773.

10. Fintan O'Toole, *A Traitor's Kiss: The Life of Richard Brinsley Sheridan* (New York: Farrar, Straus and Giroux, 1998), 24.

11. Alan Chedzoy, *Sheridan's Nightingale: The Story of Elizabeth Linley* (London: Allison and Busby, 1997), 93.

12. O'Toole, ch. 8; the quotation is from p. 67.

13. Joseph Roach (quoting William Jackson, organist of Exeter Cathedral), "Mistaking Earth for Heaven: Eliza Linley's Voice," *Bluestockings Displayed: Portraiture, Performance and Patronage, 1730–1830,* ed. Elizabeth Eger (Cambridge: Cambridge University Press, 2013), 127.

14. Burney *Journals* 1: 249–50, Feb. 25, 1773.

15. My account is deeply indebted to Roach's essay. Elizabeth's letter is quoted on 130–31.

16. *Life* 2: 369, April 18, 1775; O'Toole, 86.

17. Ibid., 78; *Rasselas,* ch. 49; *Thraliana* 1: 502n.

18. *The Rivals* IV.ii, in *The School for Scandal and Other Plays,* ed. Michael Cordner (Oxford: Oxford University Press, 1998), 62.

19. *The Rivals* III.iii, pp. 49 and 45; I.ii, p. 19. Oscar Wilde, *The Importance of Being Earnest.*

20. *School for Scandal* I.i, p. 210.

21. Charles Lamb, "On the Artificial Comedy," *Works* (London: Methuen, 1912), 2: 165; on Palmer's Shakespearean roles, Auburn, 30.

22. Christian Deelman, "The Original Cast of *The School for Scandal,*" *Review of English Studies* 13 (1962), 258.

23. Lamb, 2: 155; Auburn, 27.

24. O'Toole, 123 (quoting Frederic Reynolds).

25. Marlies K. Danziger, *Oliver Goldsmith and Richard Brinsley Sheridan* (New York: Ungar, 1978), 134.

26. Quoted in Richard Brinsley Sheridan, *Dramatic Works,* ed. Cecil Price (Oxford: Clarendon, 1973), 470–71.

CHAPTER 12. A NEW LIFE AT STREATHAM

1. Johnson to Hester Thrale, July 8, 1784, *Letters* 4: 343.

2. Hester Thrale, *Anecdotes, Johnsonian Miscellanies* 1: 313; *Life* 3: 284–85, April 15, 1778; John Wain, *Samuel Johnson* (New York: Viking, 1975), 221.

3. Thomas Tyers, *A Biographical Sketch of Dr. Samuel Johnson, Early Biographies,* 66.

4. Quoted by James L. Clifford, *Hester Lynch Piozzi,* 2nd ed. with introduction by Margaret Anne Doody (Oxford: Clarendon, 1987), xxiii–xxiv.

5. *Life,* 1: 494 (1765); *Thraliana* 1: 52–53; Yale *Works* 19: 519–20.

6. Quoted from an 1819 manuscript by William McCarthy, *Hester Thrale Piozzi: Portrait of a Literary Woman* (Chapel Hill: University of North Carolina Press, 1985), 26.

7. Mary Hyde, *The Thrales of Streatham Park* (Cambridge: Harvard University Press, 1977), 81–82.

8. Clifford, 133.

9. Hyde, 153–54.

10. *Life* 2: 468–69, March 25, 1776.

11. Giuseppe Baretti, quoted (in translation from the Italian) by Clifford, 136–37.

12. Hyde, 162; *Thraliana* 1: 272.

13. "Dr. Burney's Evening Party," *The Common Reader, Second Series* (New York: Harcourt Brace, 1948), 123.

14. The Burney family's friend Samuel Crisp, quoted by Betty Rizzo, "Burney and Society," *The Cambridge Companion to Frances Burney,* ed. Peter Sabor (Cambridge: Cambridge University Press, 2007), 139.

15. See Roy Porter, *English Society in the Eighteenth Century,* revised edition (London: Penguin, 1991), 85–87; J. Jean Hecht, *The Domestic Servant Class in Eighteenth-Century England* (London: Routledge and Kegan Paul, 1956), 8.

16. David Piper, *The English Face,* ed. Malcolm Rogers (London: National Portrait Gallery, 1992), 138.

17. Frances Burney, *Memoirs of Doctor Burney* (London: Moxon, 1832), 2: 104–5.

18. "Anecdotes by William Seward," *Johnsonian Miscellanies* 2: 308.

19. *Thraliana* 1: 471.

20. *Life* 4: 82, April 1, 1781.

21. "Anecdotes by Hannah More," *Johnsonian Miscellanies* 2: 182, 185–86; *Life* 2: 378, May 17, 1775.

22. *Life* 2: 231, April 27, 1773.

23. *Thraliana* 2: 699.

24. *Journals* 3: 152, Sept. 16–21, 1778; *Life* 4: 275, May 15, 1784; *Thraliana* 1: 153.

25. *Journals* 3: 150–51, Sept. 16–21, 1778.

26. *Life* 4: 73, March 1781.

27. Quoted by Kate Chisholm, "The Burney Family," *The Cambridge Companion to Frances Burney,* ed. Peter Sabor (Cambridge: Cambridge University Press, 2007), 19–20.

28. Fanny to Hester Thrale, Aug. 17, 1782; to Susanna Burney, Aug. 24 and 31, Sept. 14; *Journals* 5: 101, 104, 109, 117.

29. Piper, 141.

30. *Journals* 2: 119–20, 147, May 1775.

31. Johnson to Hester Thrale, April 15, 1780, *Letters* 3: 238; *Thraliana* 1: 368.

32. Fanny to Charles Burney, *Journals* 3: 345–47, Aug. 13, 1779.

33. *Journals* 4: 168, June 1780; Oct. 29 and Nov. 1782, ibid., 5: 132, 152.

34. *Journals* 3: 35, 66, July–August 1778.

35. *Thraliana* 1: 368.

36. Fanny Burney to Mrs. Waddington, uncertain date, quoted by Clifford, 160n.

37. *Thraliana* 1: 413; Fanny to Hester, Feb. 8, 1781, *Journals* 4: 291.

38. *Life* 2: 257, May 7, 1773; *Extremes,* 322.

39. *Memoirs of Doctor Burney* 2: 191, 194–95.

40. Johnson to Boswell, Feb. 24, 1773, *Letters* 2: 10; 18n; Mary Hyde, *The Impossible Friendship: Boswell and Mrs. Thrale* (Cambridge: Harvard University Press, 1972), 18n.

41. *Life* 4: 324 (1784).

42. Ian McIntyre, *Joshua Reynolds: The Life and Times of the First President of the Royal Academy* (London: Allen Lane, 2003), 204–5.

43. Katharine C. Balderston, "Johnson's Vile Melancholy," *The Age of Johnson: Essays Presented to Chauncey Brewster Tinker,* ed. Frederick W. Hilles (New Haven: Yale University Press, 1949), 3–14.

44. *Thraliana* 1: 415n; Yale *Works,* 1: 140.

45. Johnson to Hester Thrale, June 1773, *Letters* 2: 38–39.

46. Hester's reply is given in an earlier edition of Johnson's *Letters,* ed. R. W. Chapman (Oxford: Clarendon, 1952), 1: 331–32. See John Wiltshire, *Samuel Johnson in the Medical World: The Doctor and the Patient* (Cambridge: Cambridge University Press,

1991), 47–48, and James Gray, "*Arras/Hélas!* A Fresh Look at Samuel Johnson's French," *Johnson after Two Hundred Years,* ed. Paul J. Korshin (Philadelphia: University of Pennsylvania Press, 1986), 84–86.

47. Hyde, *The Thrales of Streatham Park,* 80.

48. *Life* 2: 407 (1775).

49. "Posture Molls" and other examples of street lingo are given in Ned Ward, *The London Spy,* ed. Paul Hyland (East Lansing, Mich,: Colleagues Press, 1939), 336–58. The French police report is cited by Patrick Wald Lasowski, "La Fessée ou l'Ultime Faveur," in a special Rousseau number of the *Magazine Littéraire,* Sept. 1997, p. 30.

50. Jean-Jacques Rousseau, *Confessions, Oeuvres Complètes,* ed. Marcel Raymond et al. (Paris: Gallimard, Bibliothèque de la Pléiade, 1959–95), 1: 17, my translation; Philippe Lejeune, *Le Pacte Autobiographique* (Paris: Seuil, 1975), 70–75; Cocteau quoted by Georges May, *Rousseau* (Paris: Seuil, 1985), 8.

51. *Thraliana* 1: 159.

52. Ibid., 1: 219.

53. Ibid., 1: 384–86.

54. Balderston, 13; *Thraliana* 1: 415.

55. *Anecdotes, Johnsonian Miscellanies* 1: 263.

56. Hawkins, 275–76.

57. Hawkins, 275; *Johnsonian Miscellanies* 1: 288.

58. *Johnsonian Miscellanies* 1: 150.

59. Hester Thrale to Johnson, Oct. 2, 1777, quoted by Clifford, 155; Johnson to Hester Thrale, Oct. 6, 1777, *Letters* 3: 81.

60. Yale *Works* 1: 225, 264.

61. Ibid., 1: 133.

CHAPTER 13. BOSWELL IN SCOTLAND—AND STRATFORD

1. Lawrence Stone, *The Family, Sex and Marriage in England 1500–1800* (New York: Harper and Row, 1977), 88.

2. Brady, 43.

3. *Applause of the Jury,* 42; *Boswell for the Defence,* 349.

4. *Life* 1: 44 (1717–19).

5. *Life* 2: 157, March 28, 1772.

6. *In Search of a Wife,* 24n.

7. Pottle, 404.

8. Ibid., 407.

9. Boswell to Temple, May 3, 1769, *In Search of a Wife,* 201.

10. Girolama Nini Piccolomini to Boswell (writing in Italian), Nov. 16, 1767, *The General Correspondence of James Boswell, 1766–1769,* ed. Richard C. Cole (New Haven: Yale University Press, 1993–97), 1: 256.

11. Stone, 487.

12. *Ominous Years,* 72.

13. Ibid., 92.

14. *Life* 2: 442, March 20, 1776.

15. *In Search of a Wife,* 156; *Life* 2: 56, spring 1768.

16. *Applause of the Jury,* 280.

17. *Laird of Auchinleck,* 150.

18. Ibid., 164.

19. Ibid., 203.

20. *Wealth of Nations* III.ii, *Glasgow Edition of the Works and Correspondence of Adam Smith* (Oxford: Clarendon, 1976–83), 2: 383–84.

21. *Ominous Years,* 231.

22. *Extremes,* 106–7, 112, 192, 194, 198.

23. Ibid., 206.

24. *Life* 2: 82, Oct. 16, 1769.

25. *Laird of Auchinleck,* 283, 297.

26. Moray McLaren, *The Highland Jaunt: A Study of James Boswell and Samuel Johnson upon Their Highland and Hebridean Tour* (London: Jarrolds, 1954), 25.

27. *Ominous Years,* 34.

28. Ibid., 157, 178.

29. Boswell to Johnson, March 3, 1772; Johnson replied on March 15, 1772, *Letters* 1: 388.

30. *Life* 3: 198, Sept. 23, 1777.

31. Johnson to Boswell, Aug. 21, 1766, *Life* 2: 22.

32. See Murray Pittock, *James Boswell* (Aberdeen: AHRC Centre for Irish and Scottish Studies, 2007), 53.

33. George Otto Trevelyan, *The Early History of Charles James Fox* (London: Longman's, Green, 1880), 153, 154n.

34. *In Search of a Wife,* 59–60. Many of Boswell's anonymous pieces have been collected in *Selections from the Journalism of James Boswell,* ed. Paul Tankard (New Haven: Yale University Press, 2014).

35. James Boswell, *An Account of Corsica,* ed. James T. Boulton and T. O. McLoughlin (Oxford: Oxford University Press, 2006), 14.

36. Ibid., 21, 25.

37. *Life* 2: 80, Oct. 10, 1769.

38. Fanny Burney, letter to Samuel Crisp, Oct. 15, 1782, Burney *Journals* 5: 125.

39. Christian Deelman, *The Great Shakespeare Jubilee* (London: Michael Joseph, 1964), 7.

40. *Retaliation,* lines 109–12.

41. Ian McIntyre, *Garrick* (London: Penguin, 2000), 97.

42. Deelman, 71.

43. *In Search of a Wife,* 278.

44. *London Magazine* 38 (Sept. 1769), *Selections from the Journalism of James Boswell,* ed. Tankard, 30.

45. McIntyre, 437; Deelman, 286–87.

CHAPTER 14. AMONG THE FARTHEST HEBRIDES

1. William Wordsworth, *The Solitary Reaper,* lines 15–16; *Journey,* 88.

2. Linda Colley, *Britons: Forging the Nation 1707–1837* (New Haven: Yale University Press, 1992), 15; Roy Porter, *English Society in the Eighteenth Century,* revised edition (London: Penguin, 1991), 35.

3. *Life* 5: 140, Sept. 1, 1773.

4. *Life* 5: 13.

5. *Life* 5: 14.

6. See Pat Rogers, *Johnson and Boswell: The Transit of Caledonia* (Oxford: Clarendon, 1995), ch. 1; Adam Smith to John Douglas, March 1787, *The Glasgow Edition of the Works and Correspondence of Adam Smith* (Oxford: Clarendon, 1976–83), 6: 301.

7. *Anecdotes, Johnsonian Miscellanies* 1: 263; *Life* 2: 453, March 21, 1776.

8. Thomas Creevey, quoted by T. H. White, *The Age of Scandal* (London: Penguin, 1962), 22.

9. *Life* 3: 162, Sept. 19, 1777.

10. *Extremes,* 47.

11. *Life* 5: 23.

12. Ibid., 55.

13. Ibid., 18.

14. Ibid., 347, 382; see Rogers, ch. 3.

15. *Life* 5: 53.

16. Ibid., 47, 61.

17. Ibid., 341.

18. Ibid., 18–19.

19. *Life* 3: 410, Oct. 12, 1779.

20. *Journey,* 40.

21. Ibid.

22. Ibid., 19; *Hebrides,* 71–75.

23. *Journey,* 19–20.

24. Ibid., 25; *Life* 5: 115–16.

25. *Journey,* 29.

26. Ibid., 33.

27. *Life* 5: 132–33 (slightly altered from *Hebrides,* 100).

28. *Hebrides,* 353, *Life* 5: 355.

29. *Hebrides,* 98n.

30. *Journey,* 51.

31. Two hundred pages in the periodical *The Age of Johnson* 7, ed. Paul J. Korshin (New York: AMS Press, 1996), are devoted to the controversy. See especially the arguments and detailed scholarship of Donald Greene, Thomas M. Curley, and Howard D. Weinbrot; and also a further article by Weinbrot, "Review Essay: Johnson and Jacobite Wars XLV," *Age of Johnson* 14 (2003), 307–40.

32. *Life* 1: 430, July 14, 1763.

33. See Rogers, ch. 6.

34. *Journey,* 67.

35. *Life* 5: 186.

36. Bernard Bailyn, *Voyagers to the West: A Passage in the Peopling of America on the Eve of the Revolution* (New York: Knopf, 1986), 26; *Hebrides,* 243.

37. *Journey*, 38.
38. Ibid., 97.
39. *The Deserted Village*, lines 397–403.
40. *Journey*, 103, 130.
41. Ibid., 49.
42. *Hebrides*, 226 and note; *Life* 5: 261.
43. *Life* 5: 216–17.
44. *Hebrides*, 176–77.
45. Ibid., 188, 241.
46. Ibid., 243; *Life* 5: 278 (slightly revised).
47. *Hebrides*, 305; *Life* 5: 314–15; *Journey*, 103.
48. *Hebrides*, 121, 192.
49. *Oda*, Yale *Works* 6: 280–81.
50. *Life* 5: 282.
51. *Journey*, 145.
52. *Hebrides*, 332.
53. *Journey*, 148.
54. *Hebrides*, 336, 338.
55. *Life* 5: 360; 2: 148.
56. Ibid., 5: 346–47.
57. *Journey*, 56.
58. *Hebrides*, 149.
59. John Gibson Lockhart, *Memoirs of the Life of Sir Walter Scott* (Boston: Houghton Mifflin, 1901), 2: 195.
60. *Life* 5: 382.
61. Ibid., 2: 269n, Nov. 27, 1773.
62. Brian Finney, "Boswell's Hebridean Journal and the Ordeal of Doctor Johnson," *Biography* 5 (1982), 323.
63. *Life* 4: 199, April 10 1783.
64. Ibid., 3: 36, April 11, 1776; Rogers, ch. 2.
65. *Life* 1: 396, May 24, 1763.
66. *Journey*, 118–19.
67. James McIntyre, in *Samuel Johnson: The Critical Heritage* (London: Routledge, 1971), 240–41.
68. *Life* 2: 298, Feb. 7, 1775; Johnson to James Macpherson, Jan. 20, 1775, *Letters* 2: 168–69.

CHAPTER 15. THE WIDENING RIVER

1. Brady, 167.
2. *Preface to Shakespeare*, Yale *Works* 7: 66.
3. Garrick to Voltaire, 1764, quoted by Ian McIntyre, *Garrick* (London: Penguin, 2000), 347; *Preface*, 80.
4. *Life* 2: 15, spring 1766.

5. J. D. Fleeman, "The Revenue of a Writer: Samuel Johnson's Literary Earnings," *Studies in the Book Trade in Honour of Graham Pollard* (Oxford: Oxford Bibliographical Society, 1975), 211–30.

6. Quoted by Ian McIntyre, *Joshua Reynolds: The Life and Times of the First President of the Royal Academy* (London: Allen Lane, 2003), 255.

7. *Ominous Years*, 94.

8. Lewis P. Curtis and Herman W. Liebert, *Esto Perpetua: The Club of Dr. Johnson and His Friends* (Hamden, CT: Archon Books, 1963), 73–74.

9. Johnson to Boswell, March 11, 1777, *Letters* 3: 12. See the records of attendance given by Pat Rogers in his excellent account, "Gibbon and the Decline and Growth of the Club," *Edward Gibbon: Bicentenary Essays*, ed. David Womersley (Oxford: Voltaire Foundation, 1997), 106.

10. *Life* 2: 238, April 30, 1773.

11. *Thraliana* 1: 531–32.

12. Ibid., 1: 184.

13. Hawkins, 327.

14. *Life* 1: 421, July 5, 1763.

15. Johnson to Elizabeth Montagu, Sept. 22, 1783, and to Lucy Porter, Nov. 10, 1783, *Letters* 4: 203, 236.

16. Yale *Works* 6: 271–74.

17. *Recollections of Dr. Johnson by Miss Reynolds, Johnsonian Miscellanies* 2: 274; Herman W. Liebert, *Lifetime Likenesses of Samuel Johnson* (Los Angeles: Clark Memorial Library, 1974), 53–55.

18. *Life* 2: 33, 40, Feb. 1767. This episode is interestingly discussed by Alvin Kernan, *Printing Technology, Letters and Samuel Johnson* (Princeton: Princeton University Press, 1987), ch. 1.

19. *Life* 2: 40.

20. *Boswell for the Defence*, 104.

21. Brady, 31.

22. *Hebrides*, 231; *Life* 5: 264–65.

23. *Extremes*, 264; *Life* 3: 268, April 10, 1778.

24. *Life of Samuel Johnson with Marginal Comments . . . by Hester Lynch Thrale Piozzi*, ed. Edward G. Fletcher (London: Curwen Press, 1938), 2: 472.

25. *Thraliana* 1: 62.

26. *Life* 3: 178, Sept. 20, 1777, and 3: 167, Sept. 19, 1777.

27. *Memoirs of Richard Cumberland, Written by Himself* (London: Lackington, 1806), 251–52.

28. *Life* 2: 261–62, May 10, 1773.

29. *Boswell for the Defence*, 188–89.

30. *Hebrides*, 211–12, Sept. 23, 1773. For some reason Garrick's comment is given in the published version, *Life* 5: 250, as "*very* jocose, to be sure."

31. W. B. C. Watkins, *Perilous Balance: The Tragic Genius of Swift, Johnson, and Sterne* (Princeton: Princeton University Press, 1939); Robert Burton, *The Anatomy of Melancholy* (Oxford: Clarendon, 1989), 1: 239 (Part I, section 3, memb. 1, subsec. 2).

32. *Hebrides,* 13n.

33. *Thraliana* 1: 106.

34. *The Patriot,* Yale *Works* 10: 394.

35. Arthur H. Cash, *John Wilkes: The Scandalous Father of Civil Liberty* (New Haven: Yale University Press, 2006), 124; *Life* 5: 186.

36. *Boswelliana: The Commonplace Book of James Boswell* (London: Grampian Club, 1874), 1: 274.

37. *Life* 3: 66, May 15, 1776.

38. See Bruce Redford, *Designing the Life of Johnson* (Oxford: Oxford University Press, 2002), 104–5.

39. *Life* 3: 77, 79, May 15, 1776.

40. *Life* 4: 107, May 8, 1781.

41. *Life* 3: 302–7, April 17, 1778. See a perceptive analysis by Jo Allen Bradham, "Boswell's Narrative of Oliver Edwards," *Journal of Narrative Technique* 8 (1978), 176–84.

42. *Life* 3: 248, April 8, 1778.

43. Max Beerbohm, "A Clergyman," *The Bodley Head Max Beerbohm,* ed. David Cecil (London: The Bodley Head, 1970), 279–80.

44. Herman W. Liebert, "A Clergyman II," *Johnson, Boswell and Their Circle: Essays Presented to Lawrence Fitzroy Powell* (Oxford: Clarendon, 1965), 46.

45. *Life* 4: 276–77, May 16, 1784.

CHAPTER 16. EMPIRE

1. George Macaulay Trevelyan, *A Shortened History of England* (London: Longman's, Green, 1942), 363.

2. *Life of Savage,* ed. Clarence Tracy (Oxford: Clarendon, 1971), 93; *Idler* 81.

3. *Samuel Johnson's Prefaces and Dedications,* ed. Allen T. Hazen (New Haven: Yale University Press, 1937), 227–28.

4. *Wealth of Nations* IV.vii, *The Glasgow Edition of the Works and Correspondence of Adam Smith* (Oxford: Clarendon, 1976–83), 2: 588.

5. *Thoughts on the Late Transactions Respecting Falkland's Islands,* Yale *Works* 10: 370–71; on mortality among soldiers, see Richard B. Schwartz, *Daily Life in Johnson's London* (Madison: University of Wisconsin Press, 1983), 144.

6. Joseph Addison, *The Campaign* (1705), lines 313–14, 229–30.

7. *Theory of Moral Sentiments* VI.iii, *Glasgow Edition* 1: 239.

8. See Linda Colley, *Britons: Forging the Nation 1707–1837* (New Haven: Yale University Press, 2005).

9. See J. H. Plumb, *England in the Eighteenth Century* (London: Penguin, 1950), 127. Plumb and others have claimed that "no taxation without representation" actually originated in Ireland, but the evidence for that is sketchy.

10. Jonathan Swift, *Causes of the Wretched Condition of Ireland, The Prose Works of Jonathan Swift,* ed. Herbert Davis (Oxford: Blackwell, 1939–68), 9: 200, 205; Joshua 9: 23.

11. *Letter to Sir Hercules Langrishe, The Works of the Right Honourable Edmund Burke* (London: Bohn, 1854–89), 3: 343.

12. Thomas Campbell, *Dr. Campbell's Diary of a Visit to England in 1775,* ed. James L. Clifford (Cambridge: Cambridge University Press, 1947), 95–96. The title is misleading, since this edition includes a second visit in 1781.

13. *Second Speech on Conciliation, The Writings and Speeches of Edmund Burke,* ed. Paul Langford et al. (Oxford: Clarendon, 1991), 3: 215.

14. Johnson to William Samuel Johnson, March 4, 1773, *Letters* 2: 16.

15. *In Search of a Wife,* 292.

16. *Life* 2: 312 (1775), 5: 78, Aug. 21, 1773; *Life of Waller, Lives* 1: 277.

17. *Taxation No Tyranny,* Yale *Works* 10: 430. On this subject see Thomas M. Curley, "Johnson and America," *The Age of Johnson,* vol. 6, ed. Paul J. Korshin (New York: AMS Press, 1984), 31–73.

18. *Life* 2: 313 (1775).

19. Quoted by John Cannon, *Samuel Johnson and the Politics of Hanoverian England* (Oxford: Clarendon, 1994), 113n.

20. See the introduction to *Extremes,* xx; Boswell to Paoli, Jan. 8, 1782, an unpublished letter now at Yale, quoted by Murray Pittock, *James Boswell* (Aberdeen: AHRC Centre for Irish and Scottish Studies, 2007), 62.

21. *Extremes,* 300–301; *Life* 3: 315–16, April 19, 1778.

22. *Writings and Speeches of Edmund Burke,* 2: 458–59.

23. Ibid., 2: 450–51.

24. Ibid., 3: 165.

25. Alexis de Tocqueville, *Democracy in America,* trans. Arthur Goldhammer (New York: Library of America, 2004), 331; Tocqueville, *Voyage en Amérique,* in *Oeuvres,* ed. André Jardin et al. (Paris: Pléiade, 1991–2004), 1: 43 (my translation).

26. Richard Burke to Richard Champion, March 22, 1775, *The Correspondence of Edmund Burke,* ed. Thomas Copeland et al. (Cambridge: Cambridge University Press, 1958–78), 3: 139.

27. Wentworth Woodhouse manuscripts, quoted by Paul Langford, "Edmund Burke," *Oxford Dictionary of National Biography,* online edition, page 23.

28. *Life* 3: 233–35, April 3, 1778.

29. David Bromwich, *The Intellectual Life of Edmund Burke: From the Sublime and Beautiful to American Independence* (Cambridge: Harvard University Press, 2014), 319–20.

30. "Edmund Burke: The Man and His Times," *Woodrow Wilson: Essential Writings and Speeches of the Scholar-President,* ed. M. DiNunzio (New York: NYU Press, 2006), 92.

31. *Wealth of Nations* II.vii, *Glasgow Edition* 2: 570; Colley, *Britons,* 104.

32. Martin Postle et al., *Joshua Reynolds: The Creation of Celebrity* (London: Tate Publishing, 2005), 160.

33. Bromwich, 312–13.

34. Thomas Babington Macaulay, "Warren Hastings," *Critical and Historical Essays* (London: Methuen, 1903), 3: 148–49.

35. *Writings and Speeches* 5: 389.

36. Ibid., 4: 402.

37. Macaulay, "Warren Hastings," 162.

38. *Writings and Speeches* 6: 459.

39. *The Speeches of the Late Right Honourable Richard Brinsley Sheridan* (London: Martin, 1816), 1: 296; Gibbon to Lord Sheffield, *The Letters of Edward Gibbon,* ed. J. E. Norton (New York: Macmillan, 1956), 3: 109.

40. Lucy S. Sutherland, *The East India Company in Eighteenth-Century Politics* (Oxford: Clarendon, 1952), 367.

41. *Life* 3: 212–13, Nov. 29, 1777, and 202–3, Sept. 23, 1777.

42. Ibid., 3: 204.

43. Ibid., 3: 200–201, Sept. 23, 1777.

44. Brady, 421.

45. *No Abolition of Slavery, or the Universal Empire of Love, a Poem* (1791), lines 167, 242–50, 297–98.

46. *Narrative of the Life of Frederick Douglass, an American Slave, Written by Himself* (1845), ch. 7.

CHAPTER 17. ADAM SMITH

1. *Ominous Years,* 115.

2. Nicholas Phillipson, *Adam Smith: An Enlightened Life* (New Haven: Yale University Press, 2010), 10.

3. Phillipson, 84–96.

4. Lady Mary Coke, *The Letters and Journals of Lady Mary Coke* (Bath: Kingsmead, 1970), 1: 141.

5. Adam Smith to William Strahan, winter 1766, *Correspondence of Adam Smith,* ed. Ernest Campbell Mossner and Ian Simpson Ross (Indianapolis: Liberty Fund, 1987), 122.

6. Donald W. Livingston, *Hume's Philosophy of Common Life* (Chicago: University of Chicago Press, 1984), 1; Hume, "My Own Life," in *Essays Moral, Political, and Literary,* ed. Eugene F. Miller (Indianapolis: Liberty Classics, 1987), xxxvi.

7. Dugald Stewart, "Account of the Life and Writings of Adam Smith," *Essays on Philosophical Subjects,* ed. W. P. D. Wightman et al. (Oxford: Clarendon, 1980), 271; Boswell's letter to Temple is quoted in the *Life,* 2: 430n.

8. *Ominous Years,* 337, 264; *Laird of Auchinleck,* 385n.

9. *Theory of Moral Sentiments* VI.i, 1: 214.

10. *The Bee, or Literary Weekly Intelligencer* (Edinburgh, 1791), 3: 2–3, May 11, 1791.

11. *Life* 1: 397, May 24, 1763.

12. Ibid.; Christopher Smart, *Jubilate Agno,* Fragment D.

13. Adam Smith to Andreas Holt, Oct. 26, 1780, *Correspondence of Adam Smith,* ed. Ernest Campbell Mossner and Ian Simpson Ross (Indianapolis: Liberty Fund, 1987), 251.

14. Matthew 26: 11.

15. *Wealth of Nations* I.i, *The Glasgow Edition of the Works and Correspondence of Adam Smith* (Oxford: Clarendon, 1976–83), 2: 15.

16. See Douglas Hay and Nicholas Rogers, *Eighteenth-Century English Society: Shuttles and Swords* (Oxford: Oxford University Press, 1997), 3, 130.

17. *Ominous Years,* 289; *Life* 2: 458, March 22, 1776; Yale *Works* 1: 220.

18. *Wealth of Nations* IV.ii, *Glasgow Edition* 2: 456.

19. Ibid., I.ii, 2: 27.

20. Ibid., V.i, 2: 715.

21. Ibid., IV.ii, 2: 493, 267. On government intervention, see Andrew Skinner's introduction to his edition of *The Wealth of Nations* (London: Penguin, 1999), l–li.

22. Hans Vaihinger, *The Philosophy of "As If": A System of the Theoretical, Practical and Religious Fictions of Mankind,* trans. C. K. Ogden (New York: Harcourt, Brace, 1924).

23. Duncan K. Foley, *Adam's Fallacy: A Guide to Economic Theology* (Cambridge: Harvard University Press, 2006), 2–3.

CHAPTER 18. EDWARD GIBBON

1. Thomas Barnard to Boswell, March 25, 1794, *The Correspondence and Other Papers of James Boswell Relating to the Making of the Life of Johnson,* 2nd ed., ed. Marshall Waingrow (New Haven: Yale University Press, 2001), 399–400.

2. *Life* 2: 366, April 18, 1775.

3. D. M. Low, *Edward Gibbon* (New York: Random House, 1937), 225.

4. Edward Gibbon, *Memoirs of My Life,* ed. Georges A. Bonnard (London: Nelson, 1966), 29.

5. Gibbon, *Memoirs,* 42–43; Low, 35.

6. Gibbon, *Memoirs,* 56–61.

7. Ibid., 85n.

8. Ibid., 117.

9. Sir William Temple, *An Essay upon the Ancient and Modern Learning* (1690), final sentence.

10. Gibbon, *The History of the Decline and Fall of the Roman Empire,* ed. David Womersley (London: Penguin, 1994), ch. 9, 1: 237.

11. Gibbon, *Memoirs,* 305.

12. Ibid., 155.

13. Patricia Craddock, *Edward Gibbon, Luminous Historian, 1772–1794* (Baltimore: Johns Hopkins University Press, 1989), 338.

14. Gibbon to John Holroyd (later Lord Sheffield), Jan. 31 and April 8, 1775, *Letters,* ed. J. E. Norton (London: Cassell, 1956), 2: 64.

15. J. G. A. Pocock, *Barbarism and Religion,* vol. 2, *Narratives of Civil Government* (Cambridge: Cambridge University Press, 1999), 387; Gibbon, *Memoirs,* 156.

16. *The Memoirs of the Life of Edward Gibbon with Various Observations and Excursions by Himself,* ed. George Birkbeck Hill (London: Methuen, 1900), 331.

17. *Life* 2: 443, March 20, 1776.

18. George Colman, *Random Records* (London: Colburn and Bentley, 1830), 1: 122.

19. *Decline and Fall,* ch. 49, 3: 142.

20. Journal for August 28, 1762, *Gibbon's Journal to January 28th, 1763,* ed. D. M. Low (New York: Norton, 1929), 129.

21. *Decline and Fall,* ch. 10, 1: 253.

22. David Hume, "Of the Study of History," in *Essays Moral, Political, and Literary*, ed. Eugene F. Miller (Indianapolis: Liberty Classics, 1987), 566.

23. Winston S. Churchill, *A Roving Commission: The Story of My Early Life* (New York: Scribner, 1942), III.

24. *Decline and Fall*, ch. 9, 1: 195, referring to the younger Gordian.

25. *Memoirs*, 188; Fielding, *Tom Jones*, XIII.i.

26. Horace Walpole to Gibbon, Feb. 14, 1776, *Horace Walpole's Correspondence*, ed. W. S. Lewis (New Haven: Yale University Press, 1955), 41: 334–35.

27. Duncan Forbes, introduction to David Hume, *The History of Great Britain: The Reigns of James I and Charles I* (London: Penguin, 1970), 10; Gibbon, *Memoirs*, ed. Bonnard, 159.

28. Lytton Strachey, *Portraits in Miniature* (New York: Harcourt Brace, 1931), 161; G. M. Young, *Gibbon* (London: Rupert Hart-Davis, 1948), 93.

29. *Decline and Fall*, ch. 52, 3: 336; J. W. Burrow, *Gibbon* (Oxford: Oxford University Press, 1985), 71. Gibbon's increasing skepticism about causal claims is demonstrated by David Womersley, *The Transformation of the Decline and Fall of the Roman Empire* (Cambridge: Cambridge University Press, 1988).

30. Leslie Stephen, *Studies of a Biographer* (New York: Putnam, 1907), 139.

31. *Life* 2: 125 (1770), quoting William Maxwell; *Decline and Fall*, ch. 52, 3: 346.

32. *Memoirs,* ed. Bonnard, 181, 330n.

33. Ibid., 180.

CHAPTER 19. INFIDELS AND BELIEVERS

1. Johnson is quoting from Locke's *Essay Concerning Human Understanding* (1690), IV.xix.6.

2. Locke, *Essay Concerning Human Understanding*, IV.15.

3. David Hume, *Enquiry Concerning Human Understanding*, II.x.2.

4. *Life* 1: 398, May 24, 1763.

5. Ibid., 1: 428, July 14, 1763.

6. Edward Gibbon, *The History of the Decline and Fall of the Roman Empire*, ed. David Womersley (London: Penguin, 1994), ch. 16, 1: 520.

7. Ibid., ch. 15, 1: 465.

8. Ibid., 512.

9. Ibid., ch. 16, 540.

10. Ibid., ch. 65, 2: 852.

11. Ibid., 874; Matthew 4: 19 (addressing Peter's brother Andrew at the same time: "I will make you fishers of men").

12. Ibid., ch. 58, 600.

13. *Life* 2: 447–48, March 20, 1776.

14. *London Journal*, 278.

15. *Anecdotes, Johnsonian Miscellanies* 1: 241; *Life* 3: 229, March 31, 1778.

16. Fielding, *Tom Jones*, III.iii.

17. *Life* 4: 216, April 30, 1773.

18. *English Experiment*, 238; *Ominous Years*, 143.

19. *Life* 2: 244, May 1, 1773.
20. Hume, *The Natural History of Religion,* ed. J. C. A. Gaskin (Oxford: Oxford University Press, 1998), 184.
21. *Laird of Auchinleck,* 470; *Life* 3: 339, May 8, 1778; W. B. Carnochan, *Gibbon's Solitude: The Inward World of the Historian* (Stanford: Stanford University Press, 1987), 164.
22. *Life* 4: 299, June 12, 1784.
23. *Decline and Fall,* ch. 58, 3: 591.
24. *Ominous Years,* 201.
25. Hume, *A Treatise of Human Nature,* II.ii.4.
26. Hume to Hugh Blair, April 6, 1765, to Allan Ramsay, June 1755, *The Letters of David Hume,* ed. J. Y. T. Greig (Oxford: Clarendon, 1932), 1: 498, 224.
27. William Mure, *Selections from the Family Papers Preserved at Caldwell* (Glasgow: Maitland Club, 1854), 2: 177–78.
28. *Life* 1: 444 (expanded from the version in the *London Journal,* 317).
29. "An account of my last interview with David Hume, Esq.," *Extremes,* 11–13.
30. *Extremes* 155, Sept. 16, 1777.
31. *Applause of the Jury,* 176–77.
32. Letter from Adam Smith to William Strahan, David Hume, *Essays Moral, Political, and Literary,* ed. Eugene F. Miller (Indianapolis: Liberty Classics, 1987), xlix; *Phaedo, The Collective Dialogues of Plato,* ed. Edith Hamilton and Huntington Cairns (Princeton: Princeton University Press, 1961), 98.
33. *Life* 3: 119, June 9, 1777; *Life* 5: 31–32, quoting Psalm 99.
34. Smith to Andreas Holt, Oct. 25, 1780, *The Glasgow Edition of the Works and Correspondence of Adam Smith* (Oxford: Clarendon, 1976–83), 6: 251.

CHAPTER 20. JOHNSON NEARING THE END

1. *Johnsonian Miscellanies* 2: 391, 1: 288.
2. Johnson to Hester Thrale, Sept. 18, 1777, *Letters* 3: 68.
3. Johnson to Boswell, Aug. 24, 1782, *Letters* 4: 70; also quoted in the *Life* 4: 153.
4. *Diaries,* Yale *Works* 1: 300; review in the *Monthly Review* of an account of Heberden's contribution, quoted by Susie I. Tucker, *Protean Shape: A Study in Eighteenth-Century Vocabulary and Usage* (London: Athlone, 1967), 20. See also T. Jock Murray, "Samuel Johnson: His Ills, His Pills and His Physician Friends," *Clinical Medicine* 3 (2003), 371.
5. Johnson to Henry Thrale, June 3, 1776, *Letters* 2: 339.
6. Burney to Johnson, Nov. 11, 1782, *Letters of Dr. Charles Burney,* ed. Alvaro Ribeiro (Oxford: Clarendon, 1991), 1: 353.
7. Johnson to Hester Thrale, June 19, 1783, *Letters* 4: 151–53.
8. Hawkins, 193, 273.
9. The quotation is credited to "Hill"—that is, John Hill's *History of the Materia Medica* (1751).
10. Johnson to John Ryland, Sept. 2, 1784, *Letters* 4: 389; Tim Aurthur and Steven Calt, "Opium and Samuel Johnson," *Age of Johnson* 17 (2006), 86.

439

11. "Anecdotes by Hannah More," *Johnsonian Miscellanies* 2: 201; *Life* 4: 239, Sept. 1783, quoting William Bowles.
12. *Life* 4: 99, April 20, 1781.
13. See John Wiltshire, *Samuel Johnson in the Medical World: The Doctor and the Patient* (Cambridge: Cambridge University Press, 1991), ch. 6.
14. Johnson to Dr. Thomas Lawrence, Jan. 17, 1782, *Letters* 4: 6; *On the Death of Doctor Robert Levet, Poems* 314–15; *Life* 4: 427, alluding to Luke 12: 48.
15. Quoted by Ruby Cohn, *Just Play: Beckett's Theater* (Princeton: Princeton University Press, 1980), 299–300.
16. *Thraliana* 1: 145.
17. On Thrale's responsibility for the bond, see Mary Hyde, *The Thrales of Streatham Park* (Cambridge: Harvard University Press, 1977), 219–20.
18. Hester Thrale to Mrs. Lambart, quoted by James L. Clifford, *Hester Lynch Piozzi* (Oxford: Clarendon, 1987), 190.
19. *Thraliana* 1: 489–90.
20. Hester Thrale to Johnson, April 28, 1780, *Life* 3: 422–23; *Diaries,* Yale *Works* 304; Burney *Journals* 4: 386, June 29, 1781.
21. The epitaph is printed by Hawkins, 332–338; I follow the translation provided by the editor, 442.
22. John Wain, *Samuel Johnson* (New York: Viking, 1974), 355; Mary Hyde, *The Impossible Friendship: Boswell and Mrs. Thrale* (Cambridge: Harvard University Press, 1972), 66, 131–34.
23. *Thraliana* 2: 824.
24. Johnson to Hester Thrale, April 16, 1781, *Letters* 3: 340; *Thraliana* 1: 492.
25. *Thraliana* 1: 495, 498; Hyde, *The Thrales of Streatham Park,* 232n.
26. Yale *Works* 1: 337–38.
27. Johnson to Boswell, May 3, 1777, *Letters* 3: 20; *Life* 1: 425, July 6, 1763; *Lives* 1: xxvi; *Diaries,* 303–4.
28. *Lives* 1: 311, 2: 175.
29. *Lives* 3: 420; *Life* 2: 164, March 28, 1772.
30. *Lives* 3: 456; Horace Walpole to William Mason, Jan. 27, 1781, *The Yale Edition of Horace Walpole's Correspondence,* ed. W. S. Lewis (New Haven: Yale University Press, 1954–1983), 29: 97.
31. *Life of Gray, Lives* 3: 441.
32. *Life of Cowley, Lives* 1: 42.
33. *Life of Dryden, Lives* 1: 454.
34. *Life of Milton, Lives* 1: 194, 183–84.
35. *Life of Pope, Lives* 3: 188.
36. Ibid., 3: 217.
37. Lytton Strachey, *Books and Characters* (New York: Harcourt Brace, 1922), 74–79; Walter Raleigh, *Six Essays on Johnson* (Oxford: Clarendon, 1910), 26.
38. Johnson to Hester Thrale, Nov. 13, 1783, *Letters* 4: 238–40.
39. Frances Burney, *Memoirs of Doctor Burney* (London: Moxon, 1832), 2: 110–11.
40. *Thraliana* 1: 452.

41. Ibid., 1: 559.
42. Ibid., 1: 559–61.
43. Burney *Journals* 5: 393–94, Sept. 1783.
44. Leslie Stephen, *Studies of a Biographer* (New York: Putnam, 1907), 114.
45. *Memoirs of Doctor Burney* 2: 246–47.
46. Fanny Burney to Hester Thrale, June 1784, *Journals and Letters,* selected by Peter Sabor and Lars E. Troide (London: Penguin, 2001), 203–4.
47. Elizabeth Montagu to Elizabeth Vesey, July 15, 1784, quoted by Clifford, *Hester Lynch Piozzi,* 229.
48. Hester Chapone to William Weller Pepys, Aug. 24, 1784, ibid., 231; *Hamlet* iv.iii.
49. Johnson to Hester Thrale, July 2, 1784, *Letters* 4: 338.
50. *The Piozzi Letters,* ed. Edward A. Bloom and Lillian D. Bloom (Newark: University of Delaware Press, 1989–2002), 1: 81–82.
51. Virgil, *Aeneid* VI. 425; Johnson to Hester Thrale, July 8, 1784, *Letters* 4: 343–44.
52. Fanny to Susanna, Nov. 28, 1784, *Journals and Letters,* selected by Peter Sabor and Lars E. Troide (London: Penguin, 2001), 205.
53. Katharine C. Balderston, "Johnson's Vile Melancholy," *The Age of Johnson,* ed. Frederick W. Hilles (New Haven: Yale University Press, 1949), 14.
54. *Life* 4: 326 and 339, June 22 and July 1, 1784.
55. Ibid., 4: 406–7, Dec. 1784.
56. Ibid., 4: 411, 413.
57. Ibid., 4: 400–401; *Macbeth* V.iii.
58. Hawkins, 356.
59. *Life* 4: 374; Hawkins, 357.
60. *Life* 4: 417–18.
61. Ibid., 420–21.
62. *Rambler* 6.
63. *Applause of the Jury,* 271.
64. Thomas Tyers, *A Biographical Sketch of Dr. Samuel Johnson, Early Biographies,* 87.

CHAPTER 21. BOSWELL ON THE DOWNHILL SLOPE

1. Undated entry in *Boswelliana: The Commonplace Book of James Boswell,* ed. Charles Rogers (London: Grampian Club, 1874), 225.
2. *Laird of Auchinleck,* 467.
3. *Ominous Years,* 78.
4. Ibid., 477.
5. *Life* 1: 409, June 25, 1763.
6. *Life* 3: 176–78, Sept. 20, 1777. On the Auchinleck estate see John Strawhorn, "Master of Ulubrae: Boswell as Enlightened Laird," *Boswell: Citizen of the World, Man of Letters,* ed. Irma S. Lustig (Lexington: University Press of Kentucky, 1995), 117–34.
7. Boswell to Edmond Malone, Jan. 29, 1791, *Johnsonian Miscellanies* 2: 28.
8. *Applause of the Jury,* 11.
9. *Laird of Auchinleck,* 10.
10. Ibid., 412.

11. *Holland,* 55.

12. *Hebrides,* 375.

13. Robert Burns, *Tam O'Shanter,* lines 5–6; *The Author's Earnest Cry and Prayer, to the Right Honorable the Scotch Representatives in the House of Commons,* lines 55–58. On the meeting that never happened, see David W. Purdie, "'Never Met—and Never Parted': The Curious Case of Burns and Boswell," *Studies in Scottish Literature* 33 (2004), 169–76.

14. *Laird of Auchinleck,* 198; the missing eighteen pages came at the end of 1780.

15. Ibid., 429, 431.

16. *Applause of the Jury,* 320, 330.

17. *Life* 3: 167, Sept. 19, 1777.

18. *Ominous Years,* 358.

19. *Life* 2: 450; *Ominous Years,* 351–52. On this highly revealing relationship, see Gordon Turnbull, "Criminal Biographer: Boswell and Margaret Caroline Rudd," *Studies in English Literature* 26 (1986), 511–35.

20. *English Experiment,* 45; Brady, 320, 382, 319.

21. *English Experiment,* 10, 34–37.

22. Ibid., 56.

23. *Joshua Reynolds: The Creation of Celebrity,* ed. Martin Postle (London: Tate Publishing, 2005), 154.

24. Brady, 293.

25. Adam Sisman, *Boswell's Presumptuous Task: The Making of the Life of Dr. Johnson* (New York: Farrar, Straus and Giroux, 2001), 291.

26. *English Experiment,* 189.

27. Ibid., 191.

28. Ibid., 31.

29. Ibid., 78–79, 83.

30. *Laird of Auchinleck,* 418.

31. *Letters* 4: 4, Jan. 5, 1782; *Life* 4: 136.

32. *English Experiment,* 201.

33. Ibid., 204.

34. Ibid., 280–81, 285–86.

35. *Great Biographer,* 9.

36. *English Experiment,* 110.

37. *Great Biographer,* 68–69, 73, 86.

38. *Anecdotes, Johnsonian Miscellanies* 1: 309.

39. *Great Biographer,* 19; *Life* 1: 7.

40. *Great Biographer,* 196.

41. *Great Biographer,* 34, 207–8.

42. Thomas Babington Macaulay, "Samuel Johnson," *Critical and Historical Essays* (London: Methuen, 1903), 1: 368.

43. Boswell to Anna Seward, April 30, 1785; *The Correspondence and Other Papers of James Boswell Relating to the Making of the Life of Johnson,* 2nd ed., ed. Marshall Waingrow (New Haven: Yale University Press, 2001), 79; *Life* 1: 25; Ralph Rader, "Literary Form

in Factual Narrative: The Example of Boswell's Johnson," *Essays in Eighteenth-Century Biography,* ed. Philip B. Daghlian (Bloomington: Indiana University Press, 1968), 8.

44. *Great Biographer,* 146.
45. *Critical Review,* second series 2 (1791), 334.
46. *Professor Borges: A Course on English Literature,* ed. Martín Arias and Martín Hadius, trans. Katherine Silver (New York: New Directions, 2013), 96.
47. Horace Walpole to the Countess of Upper Ossory, Jan. 16, 1786, *The Yale Edition of Horace Walpole's Correspondence,* ed. W. S. Lewis (New Haven: Yale University Press, 1954–1983), 33: 509 and note.
48. *Great Biographer,* 201; Brady, 577.
49. *Great Biographer,* 79.
50. Ibid., 211, 57.
51. Ibid., 258–59.
52. Ibid., 221.
53. Ibid., 64n.
54. Ibid., 125.
55. See Brady, 402, and *Great Biographer,* 302n.
56. *Great Biographer,* 242, 245; *London Journal,* 98.
57. Ian McIntyre, *Joshua Reynolds: The Life and Times of the First President of the Royal Academy* (London: Allen Lane, 2003), 446–47, 489, 527.
58. *Great Biographer,* 305.
59. Frances Burney, *Memoirs of Doctor Burney* (London: Moxon, 1832), 2: 191.
60. "Boswell's *Life of Johnson,*" *Thomas Carlyle's Collected Works* (London: Chapman and Hall, 1869), 33–34.
61. Quoted by Sisman, *Boswell's Presumptuous Task,* 284.
62. Joseph Farington, *Diary,* ed. James Grieg (London: Hutchinson, 1922), 1: 95; William B. Ober, M.D., *Boswell's Clap and Other Essays: Medical Analyses of Literary Men's Afflictions* (Carbondale: Southern Illinois University Press, 1979), 26–29.
63. Brady, 489.

EPILOGUE

1. Sheridan, *The Rivals* 4: 2.
2. *Thraliana* 2: 744; Felicity A. Nussbaum, "Hester Thrale: 'What Trace of the Wit?'" *Bluestockings Displayed: Portraiture, Performance and Patronage, 1730–1830,* ed. Elizabeth Eger (Cambridge: Cambridge University Press, 2013), 203.
3. *Thraliana* 2: 768.
4. James L. Clifford, *Hester Lynch Piozzi,* 2nd ed. (Oxford: Clarendon, 1987), 407–8.
5. *Thraliana* 2: 1099.
6. Clifford, 455–56.
7. *Letter to a Noble Lord, The Writings and Speeches of Edmund Burke,* ed. Paul Langford and William B. Todd (Oxford: Oxford University Press, 1981), 9: 162.
8. Ibid., 164; Milton, *Paradise Lost* I. 196.
9. *Letter to a Noble Lord,* 171.

10. See Fintan O'Toole, *A Traitor's Kiss: The Life of Richard Brinsley Sheridan* (New York: Farrar, Straus and Giroux, 1998), 141–42.

11. T. H. Sadlier, ed., *The Political Career of Richard Brinsley Sheridan* (Oxford, 1912), appendix, 85.

12. Thomas Medwin, *Conversations of Lord Byron* (London: Colburn, 1824), 235.

13. O'Toole, 459.

14. Christopher Clayton, "The Political Career of Richard Brinsley Sheridan," *Sheridan Studies,* ed. James Morwood and David Crane (Cambridge: Cambridge University Press, 1995), 147.

15. Edward Gibbon, *Memoirs of My Life,* ed. Georges A. Bonnard (London: Nelson, 1966), 189.

16. John Thomas Smith, *Nollekens and His Times* (London: Colburn, 1829), 1: 49–50.

17. *Life* 2: 262, May 10, 1773.

18. *Edinburgh Review* 76 (1843), 545.

19. Fanny to Susanna Burney, Feb. 1789, *Journals and Letters,* selected by Peter Sabor and Lars E. Troide (London: Penguin, 2001), 280–82.

20. Fanny to Susanna and Frederica Locke, Nov. 1787, ibid., 253.

21. See Margaret Anne Doody, "Burney and Politics," and George Justice, "Burney and the Literary Marketplace," *The Cambridge Companion to Frances Burney,* ed. Peter Sabor (Cambridge: Cambridge University Press, 2007), 101, 156.

22. Fanny Burney to Susanna Burney, April 1793; see Margaret Anne Doody, "Burney and Politics," and Betty Rizzo, "Burney and Society," *Cambridge Companion to Frances Burney,* 101–2.

23. Rizzo, 145.

24. Thomas Babington Macaulay, "Madame D'Arblay," *Critical and Historical Essays* (London: Methuen, 1903), 3: 257–58.

25. David Cannadine et al., *New Annals of the Club* (London: Henry Sotheran, 2014), 124–33.

Illustration Credits

12. Thomas Rowlandson after Samuel Collings, *Imitations at Drury Lane Theatre, Picturesque Beauties of Boswell.* Metropolitan Museum of Art, New York.

13. Thomas Rowlandson, *The Canterbury-Dover Coach Passing Vanbrugh Castle.* Yale Center for British Art.

14. Thomas Sheridan as Brutus, engraving by Charles White after James Roberts. Extra-illustrated *Life of Johnson,* Houghton Library, Harvard University, MS Hyde 76.

15. Boswell's London.

16. The Waxwork. John Thomas Smith, *Antiquities of London and Its Environs* (London, 1791–1800). Houghton Library, Harvard University, fHEW 9.13.14.

17. William Hogarth, *The Four Times of Day: Morning.* Metropolitan Museum of Art, New York.

18. Paul Sandby, *The Muffin Man. Twelve London Cries Done from the Life.* Yale Center for British Art.

19. William Hogarth, final print in *The Idle Prentice* series. Metropolitan Museum of Art, New York.

20. Paul Sandby, *Last Dying Speech and Confession. Twelve London Cries.* Yale Center for British Art.

21. Davies's shop. *Life of Johnson,* ed. Ingpen.

22. Frontispiece, *Life of Johnson,* ed. Ingpen.

23. Inner Temple Lane. *Life of Johnson,* ed. Ingpen.

24. The Mitre Tavern, wood engraving. Extra-illustrated *Life of Johnson,* Houghton Library, Harvard University.

25. Edward Rooker, *Covent Garden Piazza.* Yale Center for British Art.

26. Louis Philippe Boitard, *The Imports of Great Britain from France.* Yale Center for British Art.

27. Rousseau's Balcony at Môtiers. Photograph by Leo Damrosch.

28. *Pascalis de Paoli. Dux Corsorum pro Libertate Pugnantium,* stipple engraving by Johann Esaias Nilson, after L. de Montagna. Extra-illustrated *Life of Johnson,* Houghton Library, Harvard University.

29. Sir John Hawkins. *Life of Johnson,* ed. Ingpen.

30. Facsimile signatures of the Club. *Illustrations of the Life and Times of Samuel Johnson* (London: John Murray, 1837).

31. William Hogarth, *Beer Street.* Yale Center for British Art.

32. Charles Addams, "Dr. Johnson gets off a good one." *New Yorker* 58 (Oct. 18, 1982). ©1982 Charles Addams. With permission of the Tee and Charles Addams Foundation.

33. Topham Beauclerk. *Life of Johnson,* ed. Ingpen.

34. William Daniell after George Dance, *Bennet Langton.* Yale Center for British Art.

35. Samuel William Reynolds, mezzotint after Joshua Reynolds, self-portrait 1747–48. Yale Center for British Art.

36. *Oliver Goldsmith,* engraving by John Taylor Wedgwood after Reynolds. Extra-illustrated *Life of Johnson,* Houghton Library, Harvard University.

37. *Oliver Goldsmith,* J. Bretherton after Henry William Bunbury. Hyde Collection, Houghton Library, Harvard University, Hyde MS 100.

38. William Makepeace Thackeray, *Johnson and Goldsmith. Life of Johnson,* ed. Ingpen.

39. 40 Leicester Square. *Life of Johnson,* ed. Ingpen.

40. Pietro Antonio Martini after Johann Heinrich Ramberg, *The Exhibition of the Royal Academy, 1787.* Yale Center for British Art.

41. Valentine Green, mezzotint after Joshua Reynolds, self-portrait, 1780. Yale Center for British Art.

42. Joshua Reynolds, self-portrait, 1788. *Life of Johnson,* ed. Ingpen.

43. William Ridley, stipple engraving after W. H. Brown, *Edmund Burke.* Extra-illustrated *Life of Johnson,* Houghton Library, Harvard University.

44. James Gilray, *Burke as a Jesuit.* Peter Burke, *The Public and Domestic Life of Edmund Burke* (London: Ingram Cooke, 1853).

45. Burke as orator. *Life of Johnson,* ed. Ingpen.

46. Charles James Fox. Yale Center for British Art.

47. Charles Spooner after Benjamin Wilson, mezzotint, *Garrick in the Character of King Lear.* Yale Center for British Art.

48. Edward Fisher after Joshua Reynolds, *Garrick between Tragedy and Comedy,* mezzotint. Yale Center for British Art.

49. Samuel William Reynolds after Johann Zoffany, *Garrick in the Character of Abel Drugger,* mezzotint. Yale Center for British Art.

50. W. B. Cooke after P. Dent, *The Garricks' House at Hampton.* Hyde Collection, Houghton Library, Harvard University, Hyde MS 100.

51. Thomas Rowlandson, *The Actresses' Dressing Room at Drury Lane,* watercolor with pen and ink. Yale Center for British Art, Paul Mellon Collection.

52. Richard Sawyer after Philippe Jacques de Loutherbourg, *David Garrick.* Mrs. Clement Parsons, *Garrick and His Circle* (New York: Putnam, 1906).

53. Robert Edge Pine, mezzotint, *Garrick* (1779). Yale Center for British Art.

54. Thomas Rowlandson, etching, *Covent Garden.* Metropolitan Museum of Art, New York.

55. Thomas Rowlandson, *An Audience at Drury Lane Theatre,* watercolor with pen and ink. Yale Center for British Art.

56. Thomas Rowlandson, *An Audience Watching a Play at Drury Lane Theatre,* watercolor with pen and ink. Yale Center for British Art.

57. William Dickinson after Joshua Reynolds, mezzotint, *Mrs. Sheridan as Saint Cecilia.* Yale Center for British Art.

58. The summer house at Streatham. *Johnsoniana: Anecdotes of the Late Samuel Johnson,* ed. Robina Napier (London: George Bell, 1884).

59. Streatham Place. *Life of Johnson,* ed. Ingpen.

60. Samuel Johnson. Hyde Collection, Houghton Library Harvard University, Hyde MS 100.

61. Giuseppe Marchi after Johann Zoffany, *Hester Maria Thrale, aged 20 Months.* Yale Center for British Art.

62. Edward Finden, stipple engraving after Joshua Reynolds, *Hester Thrale.* Yale Center for British Art.

63. E. Scriven after Joshua Reynolds, *Henry Thrale. Life of Johnson,* ed. Ingpen.

64. Hannah More. *Life of Johnson,* ed. Ingpen.

65. Francesco Barolozzi after Joshua Reynolds, *Mrs. Montagu.* Yale Center for British Art.

66. Charles Burney, after Reynolds. Hyde Collection, Houghton Library, Harvard University, MS Hyde 76.

67. James Hardy after Joshua Reynolds, *Giuseppe Baretti*. Stipple engraving and etching, Yale Center for British Art.

68. Letter from Boswell to Johnson. Hyde Collection, Houghton Library, Harvard University.

69. Daniell after George Dance, *General Paoli*. *Life of Johnson*, ed. Ingpen.

70. J. S. Miller after Samuel Wale, *James Boswell Esq. in the Dress of an Armed Corsican Chief*. Hyde Collection, Houghton Library, Harvard University, MS Hyde 76.

71. Driving rapidly in a post-chaise. Ernest H. Shepard, in *Everybody's Boswell*, ed. and abridged F. V. Morley (New York: Harcourt, Brace, 1930).

72. Thomas Rowlandson after Samuel Collings, *Walking up the High Street, Picturesque Beauties of Boswell*. Hyde Collection, Houghton Library, Harvard University, MS Hyde 76.

73. Rowlandson after Collings, *Scottifying the Palate*. Hyde Collection, Houghton Library, Harvard University, MS Hyde 76.

74. Charles John Smith after Thomas Trotter, *Johnson on the Isle of Mull*. *Life of Johnson*, ed. Ingpen.

75. Robert Brandard after William Henry Bartlett, *Slaines Castle, near Peterhead*. Extra-illustrated *Life of Johnson*. Hyde Collection, Houghton Library, Harvard University, MS Hyde 76.

76. Brandard after Bartlett, *The Buller of Buchan, near Peterhead*. Extra-illustrated *Life of Johnson*. Hyde Collection, Houghton Library, Harvard University, MS Hyde 76.

77. Boswell and the maids. Shepard, *Everybody's Boswell*.

78. J. Storer after E. Dayes, *Temple Bar from Butcher Row*. *Life of Johnson*, ed. Ingpen.

79. Bolt Court. *Life of Johnson*, ed. Ingpen.

80. Anna Williams. Hyde Collection, Houghton Library, Harvard University, MS Hyde 76.

81. Joshua Reynolds, Samuel Johnson. *Life of Johnson*, ed. Ingpen.

82. William Hogarth, *John Wilkes*. Chauncey Brewster Tinker, *Young Boswell* (Boston: Atlantic Monthly Press, 1922).

83. Edward Dayes, *Butcher Row*. Extra-illustrated *Life of Johnson*. Hyde Collection, Houghton Library, Harvard University, MS Hyde 76.

84. John Kay, *The Author of The Wealth of Nations*. Extra-illustrated *Life of Johnson*. Hyde Collection, Houghton Library, Harvard University, MS Hyde 76.

85. Edward Gibbon, after Reynolds. Extra-illustrated *Life of Johnson*. Hyde Collection, Houghton Library, Harvard University, MS Hyde 76.

86. Gibbon at Lausanne, lithograph by C. Constans after Brandoin, "after the original in the possession of Mons. le Professeur Lovade de Lausanne." Hyde Collection, Houghton Library, Harvard University, MS Hyde 100.

87. William Holl after Allan Ramsay, *David Hume*. Extra-illustrated *Life of Johnson*. Hyde Collection, Houghton Library, Harvard University, MS MS Hyde 76.

88. Johnson to Hester Thrale. Hyde Collection, Houghton Library, Harvard University, MS Hyde 76 II.i seq. 98.

89. Edmond Malone. *Life of Johnson,* ed. Ingpen.
90. E. Finden after George Langton, Boswell. *Life of Johnson,* ed. Ingpen.
91. Boswell by Thomas Lawrence. *Life of Johnson,* ed. Ingpen.
92. George Dance, *Hester Piozzi. Life of Johnson,* ed. Ingpen.
93. Plaster cast of bust by Joseph Nollekens, *Samuel Johnson.* Yale Center for British Art.

COLOR PLATES

1. Canaletto, *The Thames and the City of London from Richmond House,* 1747. By permission of the Trustees of the Goodwood Collection.
2. Thomas Rowlandson, *Charing Cross.* W. H. Pyne and William Combe, *The Microcosm of London, or, London in Miniature* (London: Ackermann, 1808–10). Houghton Library, Harvard University.
3. John Collet, *London Street Scene* (also known as *The Bath Fly*), 1770. Yale Center for British Art.
4. Maria Verelst, *Elizabeth Johnson.* Hyde Collection, Houghton Library, Harvard University.
5. Allan Ramsay, *Lord Auchinleck.* Yale Center for British Art, Paul Mellon Collection.
6. Auchinleck House, photograph by Angus Bremner, courtesy of the Landmark Trust.
7. *The Parade,* aquatint by J. Bluck after Augustus Pugin and Thomas Rowlandson after Samuel Collings. Extra-illustrated *Life of Johnson,* Houghton Library, Harvard University.
8. Balthasar Nebot (c. 1700–c. 1770), *View of Covent Garden with Saint Paul's Church* (1750). © Tate, London 2017.
9. Thomas Rowlandson, *Covent Garden.* Pyne and Combe, *The Microcosm of London.* Houghton Library, Harvard University.
10. John Boydell, *Old London Bridge.* Yale Center for British Art.
11. Billingsgate. Thomas Pennant, *Some Account of London* (1805), extra-illustrated copy. Houghton Library, Harvard University.
12. George Willison, *James Boswell.* By permission of Scottish National Portrait Gallery.
13. The Turk's Head Tavern. *Illustrations of the Life and Times of Samuel Johnson* (London: John Murray, 1837). Houghton Library, Harvard University.
14. Frances Reynolds, *Samuel Johnson.* By permission of Quaker and Special Collections, Haverford College.
15. Thomas Rowlandson, *The Exhibition Stare-Case, Somerset House,* watercolor and pen and ink. Yale Center for British Art.
16. William Hogarth, *Garrick as Richard III.* By permission of the Walker Art Gallery, Liverpool. Purchased by the Walker Art Gallery with the assistance of the Art Fund in 1956.
17. *A View of London from the Thames, Taken Opposite the Adelphi.* Pyne and Combe, *The Microcosm of London.* Houghton Library, Harvard University.
18. Johann Zoffany, *The Garricks' Villa at Hampton.* Courtesy of the Garrick Club, London.
19. Joshua Reynolds, *Frances Abington.* Yale Center for British Art.
20. Streatham Place. Hyde Collection, Houghton Library, Harvard University, Hyde MS 74.
21. William Hogarth (1697–1764), *Six of Hogarth's Servants.* © Tate, London 2017.

22. Edward Francesco Burney, *Frances d'Arblay* [Fanny Burney]. © National Portrait Gallery, London.

23. Richard Samuel, *Portraits in the Characters of the Muses in the Temple of Apollo.* © National Portrait Gallery, London.

24. *Margaret Montgomerie Boswell,* artist not known. 2003JM-16, Houghton Library, Harvard University.

25. Henry Singleton, *James Boswell and His Family.* By permission of Scottish National Portrait Gallery.

26. *The King's Library.* W. H. Pyne, *The History of the Royal Residences* (London: A. Dry, 1829). Houghton Library, Harvard University (Hou f *97-C-49).

27. Max Beerbohm, *In the Shades.* Courtesy of Dr. Johnson's House Trust Ltd.

28. James Gillray, *Richard Brinsley Sheridan.* Hyde Collection, Houghton Library, Harvard University, MS Hyde 76.

29. James Barry, *Samuel Johnson.* © National Portrait Gallery, London.

30. Joshua Reynolds, *James Boswell.* © National Portrait Gallery, London.

31. Attributed to Johann Zoffany, *Bennet Langton Contemplating the Bust of Johnson.* With permission of the Samuel Johnson Birthplace Museum, Lichfield.

Index

Page numbers in italics indicate illustrations.